'N'

10.30AM

D1391112

THE RISE

OF EVANGELICALISM

A HISTORY
OF EVANGELICALISM

THE RISE
OF EVANGELICALISM

THE AGE OF EDWARDS, WHITEFIELD
AND THE WESLEYS

MARK A. NOLL

ivp

APOLLOS (an imprint of Inter-Varsity Press),
38 De Montfort Street, Leicester LEI 7GP, England
Email: ivp@uccf.org.uk
Website: www.ivpbooks.com

First published 2004

British Library Cataloguing in Publication Data
A catalogue record for this book is available from the British Library.

ISBN 1–84474–001–3

Set in Monotype Garamond 11/13pt
Typeset in Great Britain by Servis Filmsetting Ltd, Manchester
Printed and bound in Great Britain by Creative Print and Design (Wales), Ebbw Vale

Inter-Varsity Press is the publishing division of the Universities and Colleges Christian Fellowship (formerly the Inter-Varsity Fellowship), a student movement linking Christian Unions in universities and colleges throughout Great Britain, and a member movement of the International Fellowship of Evangelical Students. For more information about local and national activities write to UCCF, 38 De Montfort Street, Leicester LEI 7GP, email us at email@uccf.org.uk, or visit the UCCF website at www.uccf.org.uk.

CONTENTS

To

W. R. Ward
John Walsh
David Hempton
Bruce Hindmarsh

ACKNOWLEDGMENTS

I would like to thank audiences at several institutions for the privilege of trying out different parts of this book as lectures and for the stimulating exchanges that resulted: Bethel College, Kansas (with Keith Sprunger and Jim Juhnke); the Newberry Library, Chicago; Regent College, Vancouver (with Thena Ayres and Marilyn Hoeppner); Tyndale College and Seminary, Toronto (with Jeff Greenham and Brian Stiller); and the Wheaton College faculty (with Mark Husbands and Tim Larsen). Students in seminars at the Harvard Divinity School, the Divinity School of the University of Chicago, and Wheaton College likewise listened patiently, researched eagerly and conversed intelligently on the themes of this book.

By introducing me to the serious study of evangelicalism in Canada and by assiduously building bridges among historians from throughout the world, my late friend George Rawlyk has been a constant inspiration in work on this project. One of George's younger friends, Mark Hutchinson of Sydney, Australia, was especially helpful with encouragement and books. Another friend, David Hempton, kindly provided a reading of Chapter 5. For unusually helpful work as a graduate assistant, I am pleased to thank Luke Harlow. The network of historians connected by Wheaton College's Institute for the Study of American Evangelicals has continued to offer friendship, encouragement and instruction in nearly equal measure. In different forms, the same is true of my family.

David Bebbington and Bruce Hindmarsh not only read complete drafts of the manuscript with sympathy, but also added perspective, shared bibliography and challenged interpretations in the most helpful way imaginable.

Finally, I am pleased to acknowledge singular historical inspiration by dedicating this book to four scholars whose innovative research, precise prose and judicious judgments have undergirded its writing from first to last. Mistakes remain all mine; insights come mostly from them.

ABBREVIATIONS AND SHORT TITLES

BDEB	*The Blackwell Dictionary of Evangelical Biography, 1730–1860*, 2 vols. Donald M. Lewis (ed.) (Oxford: Blackwell, 1995).
Bebbington, *Evangelicalism*	D. W. Bebbington, *Evangelicalism in Modern Britain: A History from the 1730s to the 1980s* (London: Unwin Hyman, 1989).
Ch. Wesley, *Reader*	*Charles Wesley: A Reader*, John R. Tyson (ed.) (New York: Oxford University Press, 1989).
Dallimore, *Whitefield*	Dallimore, Arnold A., *George Whitefield: The Life and Times of the Great Evangelist of the Eighteenth-Century Revival*, 2 vols (Westchester: Cornerstone, 1970, 1979).
DSCHT	*Dictionary of Scottish Church History and Theology*, Nigel M. de S. Cameron et al. (eds.) (Edinburgh: T. & T. Clark; Downers Grove: InterVarsity, 1993).
Edwards, *Works*	*The Works of Jonathan Edwards*, Perry Miller, John E. Smith and Harry S. Stout (eds.) (New Haven: Yale University Press, 1957–).
Evangelicalism	*Evangelicalism: Comparative Studies of Popular Protestantism in North America, the British Isles, and Beyond, 1700–1990*, Mark A. Noll, David W. Bebbington and George A. Rawlyk (eds.) (New York: Oxford University Press, 1994).
Heitzenrater, *Wesley*	Heitzenrater, Richard P., *Wesley and the People Called Methodists* (Nashville: Abingdon, 1995).
Rack, *Wesley*	Rack, Henry D., *Reasonable Enthusiast: John Wesley and the Rise of Methodism* (Philadelphia: Trinity, 1989).

Tyerman, *Wesley* Tyerman, Luke, *The Life and Times of the Rev. John Wesley*, 3 vols, 3rd ed. (London: Hodder & Stoughton, 1876).

Tyerman, *Whitefield* Tyerman, Luke, *The Life of the Rev. George Whitefield*, 2 vols (London: Hodder & Stoughton, 1876).

Ward, *Awakening* Ward, W. R., *The Protestant Evangelical Awakening* (New York: Cambridge University Press, 1992).

Watts, *Dissenters* Watts, Michael, *The Dissenters*, vol. 1: *From the Reformation to the French Revolution*; vol. 2: *The Expansion of Evangelical Nonconformity, 1791–1859* (Oxford: Clarendon, 1978, 1995).

Wesley, *Journal* *The Journal of the Rev. John Wesley*, 8 vols, Nehemiah Curnock (ed.) (London: Epworth, 1938 [orig. 1911–1912]).

Wesley, *Letters* *The Letters of the Rev. John Wesley*, 8 vols, John Telford (ed.) (London: Epworth, 1938).

Wesley, *Works* (new) *The Works of John Wesley*, Bicentennial Edition, Richard P. Heitzenrater and Frank Baker (eds.) (Oxford: Oxford University Press, and Nashville: Abingdon, 1975–).

Wesley, *Works* (1872) *The Works of John Wesley*, 14 vols, Thomas Jackson (ed.) (London: Wesleyan Conference Office, 1872).

Whitefield, *Journals* *George Whitefield's Journals* (London: Banner of Truth, 1960).

INTRODUCTION

On Friday 19 September 1740, George Whitefield sat down for a theological conversation with the Anglican clergy of Boston, Massachusetts. Whitefield was just at the start of one of the most extraordinary preaching tours of that or any era. Before the tour came to an end in late November, he would preach in seven of the American colonies, often two or three times a day, and to crowds regularly into the thousands. It is likely that the total number of his hearers in these ten weeks (with, of course, some attending several times) equalled at least half the total population of these seven colonies. This charismatic personality, himself an Anglican minister not yet twenty-five years old, had already been preaching to large crowds in England for more than four years. From early in 1739 he had taken the radical step of preaching out of doors, and with fantastic results. While thousands thronged to hear his affecting message of the New Birth in Jesus Christ, nervous leaders of the Church of England and some anxious members of the upper classes worried about the threat to public order. Whitefield had made one earlier trip to North America in order to preach and organize an orphanage in the new colony of Georgia. Now he was back.

After a brief stop-over in Georgia, Whitefield turned north. He arrived at Newport, Rhode Island, on 14 September. On Tuesday 16 September he preached twice in that small port city to audiences of a least a thousand. During his short stay in Newport – an active trading centre with its prosperity as dependent on the slave-trade as on the ability to smuggle goods past British inspectors – Whitefield had startled his audience at one point by asking, 'What will become of you, who cheat the King of his taxes?' But mostly he concentrated on telling his rapt listeners how important it was 'not to rest till they found rest in Jesus Christ'.[1]

---

[1] Whitefield, *Journals*, 456, 455. (For the short titles and abbreviations used in notes, see list on pp. 9–10 above.)

Two days after leaving Newport, Whitefield arrived in an expectant Boston. Local printers had been stoking interest by pumping out new editions of his printed sermons, earlier numbers of his journal and also pamphlets attacking his ministry. The city's four newspapers had been filled for months with sensational reports of Whitefield's triumphs in the colonies and the mother country. Whitefield and his publicist, William Seward, had been writing regularly to ministers in the Boston area as well as to the newspapers in order to heighten anticipation. The ground was well prepared for what turned out to be a rich spiritual harvest.

But first there was resistance to overcome. On the morning of 19 September, Whitefield was taken to meet the governor, and then attended prayers at Boston's Old North Anglican Church. After the service, he was escorted to the home of Dr Timothy Cutler, the Church of England's Commissary and senior minister in New England. It was time to face some music.

Whitefield later reported in his published journal that the five Anglican clergymen whom he visited treated him cordially, but also that they wasted no time before bombarding him with accusatory questions:

- We hear that you called Gilbert Tennent, the Presbyterian revivalist in New Jersey, a '*faithful* minister of Jesus Christ', but surely someone ordained as a Presbyterian could not be a real minister? Whitefield averred that he did indeed think Tennent was a faithful minister.
- How come your supposed friend and colleague, Charles Wesley, supports the Church of England so vigorously but you do not? Whitefield replied that he believed God had changed Wesley's mind on this subject and that now Wesley was as willing to work with non-Anglicans as Whitefield himself was.
- We have heard that when you were in Savannah, you allowed a Baptist minister to take part in a communion service that you led. Could this really be true? Whitefield replied that not only was this rumour true, but that he was actually prepared himself as a properly ordained minister of the Church of England to receive communion from the hand of a Baptist!

At this point, Whitefield then went on to make a most important general statement: 'It was best to preach the new birth, and the power of godliness, and not to insist so much on the form: for people would never be brought to one mind as to that; nor did Jesus Christ ever intend it.'[2]

Whitefield's fellow-Anglicans could not be convinced, but they had heard him articulate a defining principle of Protestant evangelicalism. In the evan-

---

[2] Ibid., 458.

gelical movement that began with revivalists like Whitefield, Charles Wesley, his brother John, Gilbert Tennent and many others, and that would spread over the course of the centuries to touch every continent of the globe, the foundation was unswerving belief in the need for conversion (the New Birth) and the necessity of a life of active holiness (the power of godliness).

As the discussion in Boston on 19 September 1740 went on, Whitefield made a further statement to his sceptical interrogators that was equally definitive for the later history of evangelical Christianity. When one of the Boston Anglicans insisted that the Church of England was the only true church, because it followed exactly the ecclesiastical pattern provided by Jesus himself, Whitefield could not agree. To him there was much greater flexibility in the gospel: 'I saw regenerate souls among the Baptists, among the Presbyterians, among the Independents, and among the Church [i.e., Anglican] folks – all children of God, and yet all born again in a different way of worship: and who can tell which is the most evangelical?'[3]

The concentration on conversion and holy living that marked Whitefield's activity, as well as his flexibility with respect to church forms and inherited religious traditions, have always been important characteristics of evangelical movements. Such movements are the concern of this book and the other four volumes in the series, which seeks to offer a general history of evangelicalism in the English-speaking world since the eighteenth century, as also in other world regions touched by the activities of such evangelicals. But because 'evangelical' and 'evangelicalism' are words describing complex realities, it is wise to pause at the outset to define how these terms will be put to use in this five-volume series.

The word 'evangelical' has carried several different senses throughout history, but almost all are related to its etymological meaning of 'good news'. The English word 'evangelical' comes from a transliteration of the Greek noun *euangelion*, which was regularly employed by the authors of the New Testament to signify the glad tidings – the good news, the gospel – of Jesus who appeared on earth as the Son of God to accomplish God's plan of salvation for needy humans. Translators of the New Testament usually used the word 'gospel' for *euangelion*, as in passages like Romans 1:16: 'For I am not ashamed of the gospel (*euangelion*) of Christ: for it is the power of God unto salvation to every one that believeth: to the Jew first, and also to the Greek' (King James Version). Thus, 'evangelical' religion has always been 'gospel' religion, or religion focusing on the 'good news' of salvation brought to sinners by Jesus Christ.

---

[3] Ibid.

Already in the English Middle Ages the adjective 'evangelical' was being used in various ways: for example, to describe the message about salvation in Jesus, to designate the New Testament that contained this message and to single out specifically the four Gospels (Matthew, Mark, Luke and John) in which the life, death and resurrection of Jesus are portrayed.[4] Along with these usages, medieval students of the Bible regularly referred to the Old Testament book of Isaiah as 'the evangelical prophet', because Christian interpreters held it to be a forecast of the life and work of Christ.

During the sixteenth century the word 'evangelical' began to take on a meaning associated specifically with the Protestant Reformation. Martin Luther, the first great Protestant leader, proclaimed an 'evangelical' account of salvation in Christ over against what he considered the corrupt teachings of the Roman Catholic Church. Used this way, 'evangelical' rapidly assumed a critical cast, since it was posing a contrast between faithful adherence to the gospel message of the New Testament and Catholic perversions of that message. In the heat of conflict, the positive and negative connotations of 'evangelical' multiplied rapidly:

- it stood for justification by faith instead of trust in human works as the path to salvation;
- it defended the sole sufficiency of Christ for salvation instead of the human (and often corrupted) mediations of the church;
- it looked to the once-for-all triumph of Christ's death on the cross instead of the repetition of Christ's sacrifice in the Catholic mass;
- it found final authority in the Bible as read by believers in general instead of what the Catholic Church said the Bible had to mean; and
- it embraced the priesthood of all Christian believers instead of inappropriate reliance upon a class of priests ordained by the church.

The centuries since the sixteenth-century Reformation have worn away these sharp contrasts to the extent that volumes in this series treating the twentieth and early-twenty-first centuries will include some consideration of groups that today can be called both evangelical and Roman Catholic.

In the sixteenth century, however, differences were so strong that 'evangelical' became a virtual synonym for 'Protestant'. This equation of evangelical and Protestant has remained strong on the European continent. When in 1817, for example, the Lutheran and Calvinist (or Reformed) churches of Prussia

---

[4] On the range of meanings, see *The Oxford English Dictionary*, 2nd ed. (Oxford: Clarendon, 1989), 5:447–450.

were amalgamated into a single denominational Union, the resulting body was called the Evangelical Church. In many places around the world to this day, Lutheran churches retain this older sense of the term (for example, the Evangelical Lutheran Church of Papua New Guinea, the Evangelical Lutheran Church in America, or [in India] the Tamil Evangelical Lutheran Church).[5]

The specific sense of the term 'evangelical' as used in this book and this series comes not out of continental Europe but from eighteenth-century Britain. It is a usage designating a set of convictions, practices, habits and oppositions that resemble what Europeans describe as 'pietism'. Pietist movements of spiritual renewal arose during the second half of the seventeenth century within the Lutheran and Reformed state-churches of Germany, Holland, Switzerland and other parts of Central Europe. The movements were diverse. But the most visible figure of these pietist movements eventually became Philip Jakob Spener, a Lutheran minister in Frankfurt, who in 1675 published a manifesto entitled *Pia Desideria* ('The Piety We Desire'). It called for a renewal of inward spiritual life, more active lay-participation in day-to-day Christianity, less fixation on church order, and broader use of the Bible by everyone in the church. As we see later in this book, the European pietist movements played a significant role in the beginning of evangelical movements in Britain, and the main themes of pietism anticipated the main themes of evangelicalism.

During the middle third of the eighteenth century, a similar series of interconnected renewal movements arose in England, Wales, Scotland, Ireland and Britain's North American colonies. These movements were the beginnings of the evangelicalism charted in this series. They grew out of the Protestant Reformation as it had been experienced in the British Isles, but more was going on than a mere repetition of Reformation beliefs and practices. A series of revivals – or intense periods of unusual response to gospel preaching linked with unusual efforts at godly living – marked the origin of a distinctly evangelical history. In Britain these precipitating events were known as the 'Evangelical Revival', while in the American colonies they were called the 'Great Awakening'.

Two complementary perspectives are useful for defining the evangelical history that began with these revivals. On the one hand, evangelicalism was constituted by the individuals, associations, books, practices, perceptions and networks of influence shared by the promoters of the eighteenth-century

---

[5] In modern Germany, a new coinage, *evangelikal*, has been used recently as an equivalent for the more generic sense of 'evangelical' in English. The historic term *evangelisch* continues as the term for the Lutheran churches.

revivals and their descendants. Thus, the Evangelical party in the Church of England has been the group within that denomination that grew out of the revival and has continued to promote its major emphases.[6] In the same historical perspective, modern-day pentecostals must be considered parts of the broader evangelical family since they are descended from nineteenth-century leaders who emphasized Holiness and the work of the Holy Spirit, and who were themselves decisively shaped by the teaching of several important leaders of the eighteenth-century revivals, especially John and Charles Wesley. Similarly, many of the newer churches that have grown so rapidly in the Two-Thirds World over the last seventy-five years may also be viewed as related to evangelicalism since most of them have enjoyed some significant contact at some stage of their development with evangelical (or pietist) missionaries from North America, Britain or the Continent. Regarded from this angle, a history of evangelicalism is an effort to trace out an ever-expanding, ever-diversifying family tree with roots in the eighteenth-century revivals.

Yet evangelicalism was always also constituted by the convictions that emerged in those revivals and that drove its adherents in their lives as Christians. In this sense, evangelicalism designates a consistent pattern of convictions and attitudes that have been maintained over the centuries since the 1730s. Many efforts have been made to summarize those convictions and attitudes. One of the most effective is offered by David Bebbington, who has identified four key ingredients of evangelicalism:

- conversion, or 'the belief that lives need to be changed';
- the Bible, or 'the belief that all spiritual truth is to be found in its pages';
- activism, or the dedication of all believers, including laypeople, to lives of service for God, especially as manifest in evangelism (spreading the good news) and mission (taking the gospel to other societies);
- crucicentrism, or the conviction that Christ's death was the crucial matter in providing atonement for sin (that is, providing reconciliation between a holy God and sinful humans).[7]

These core evangelical commitments have never by themselves yielded cohesive, institutionally compact or clearly demarcated groups of Christians. But they do serve to identify a large kin-network of churches, voluntary societies, books and periodicals, personal networks and emphases of belief and practice.

---

[6] 'Evangelical' appears here capitalized when reference is to this party in the Church of England; for more generic uses, 'evangelical' appears in lower case.

[7] Bebbington, *Evangelicalism*, 1–17, with quotations on 3, 12.

By identifying the evangelicals of this book and this five-volume series with reference to genealogical connections and principled convictions, we are able to maintain both focus and flexibility. Emphasis throughout will be on people and movements descended from the eighteenth-century British and North American revivals, but also on the Christian movements in the English-speaking world that, whatever their connection to those revivals, have embraced the historic evangelical principles. Thus, although many Independents or Congregationalists participated in the eighteenth-century revivals, some of their descendants drifted towards a Unitarianism that set aside traditional evangelical convictions about a Christ-centred atonement, and so those descendants are not part of the story here.[8] By contrast, other religious groups, like some Mennonites and Quakers, which had little to do with the eighteenth-century revivals, have moved in their convictions towards the historic evangelical principles and so will become part of the evangelical history told in these volumes, especially for those periods when they began to share activities with other recognizably evangelical groups.

Evangelicalism is too loose a designation ever to have produced a tidy historical record. To be sure, some thoroughly evangelical denominations possess well-organized and conveniently available archives. But many evangelicals have been active in mixed denominations where evangelical emphases exist alongside other convictions. Evangelicals have also established many stand-alone churches of the sort that are always difficult to document. And still more evangelicals have devoted much of their energy to multi-denominational voluntary societies. Difficulties in controlling the subject notwithstanding, it is still possible to present a coherent history of evangelicalism as defined by genealogy and by principle.

By the same token, however, it is important to realize that the emphases of evangelicalism have shifted as they came to expression in different times and places. The late Canadian historian, George Rawlyk, who did so much to promote study of evangelical churches and movements in his native land, shrewdly observed on several occasions that evangelicalism has constituted a fluid subject.[9] The four main principles identified by David Bebbington do not exist in the same proportions or exert the same effects in all times and

---

[8] For this denomination, the usual term in Britain during the eighteenth and early nineteenth centuries was 'Independent', but in North America 'Congregationalist'.

[9] For example, G. A. Rawlyk, 'Introduction', in Rawlyk (ed.), *Aspects of the Canadian Evangelical Experience* (Kingston and Montreal: McGill-Queen's University Press, 1997), xiv–xvii. On the importance of internal changes over time, see also Bebbington, *Evangelicalism*, 3–4.

places. Sometimes the experience of conversion takes precedence, at others the concentration on Scripture as ultimate religious authority, and still others the importance of missionary or social action. The evangelical traditions consistently maintain the major evangelical traits, but they have done so with a tremendously diverse array of emphases, relationships and special concerns.

Similarly, the flexibility of evangelicalism means that evangelical groups appear in different shapes depending upon where they are found. In this book we examine what it meant for evangelical convictions to take shape in England, Wales, Scotland, Ireland, New England, the middle American colonies, the southern colonies, two regions of Canada, the West Indies and (by the end of the book) Australia, India and South Africa as well. Because conditions in these different regions were never the same – for church affairs as well as for political, economic, cultural and social life – evangelical Christianity assumed noticeably different forms as evangelicals adapted themselves to the circumstances of their own locales. In the same way, evangelical emphases played out differently in the state-supported established churches of the eighteenth century than they did among Baptists, Independents (outside of New England), Presbyterians (outside of Scotland) and other Dissenters who opposed the established churches. The Methodists, who began as a voluntary movement within the established Church of England and Wales but then founded independent denominations at the end of the eighteenth century, gave expression to evangelical convictions in still other circumstances. Later volumes in this series will chart even more variations as they trace the movement of even more varieties of evangelicals in even more ecclesiastical and geographical settings.

The subject matter of this and succeeding books, in other words, should never be looked upon as a hard-edged, narrowly defined denomination. Rather, evangelicalism was and is a set of defining beliefs and practices easier to see as an adjective (for example, Evangelical Anglicans, evangelical missionary efforts, evangelical doctrine) than as a simple noun. Yet cohesion has always been present, both from the common original commitment to revival and from the strength of shared convictions. The books of this series will chart that cohesion, though never to the neglect of the great range of intra-evangelical differences.

The series

The five volumes in this *History of Evangelicalism* will differ somewhat because their authors differ in education, perspective, denominational affiliation, details of theological commitment and geographical location. But the books will be joined in their use of a general definition of evangelicalism as outlined above, and they will also be united by common intentions for the series. We hope the books will be accessible to a wide range of readers, that they will provide interesting interpretations more than just factual details and that they will provide enough scholarly references so that interested readers can pursue their own further research. The volumes rely on primary sources whenever possible, but their nature as synthetic interpretations requires also a broad use of the most reliable secondary literature as well.

Each of the volumes will focus on a specific 'age' of evangelical history, designated by a major figure or figures of that era. Yet the authors also realize that periodization is always artificial and so they do not hesitate to move backwards and forwards with reference to other times and places as it best suits their interests. There will also be modest chronological overlap between the volumes, since important points of emphasis and patterns of development do not always conform neatly to the chronological parameters assigned for the volumes. Yet this overlap will be minimal and will not compromise the presentation of a continuous narrative for the nearly three centuries of evangelical development treated in the five books.

The series also works hard at presenting a genuinely international story. By trying to keep many places in view at the same time, authors may tempt confusion as they expand upon trans-national evangelical connections, where historical literature is sometimes in short supply, at the expense of full-scale treatment of individual national histories, where there is often a great volume of expert secondary material. There are, however, two important reasons for maintaining an international perspective. First, it recognizes the sometimes neglected historical reality that the significant evangelical movements in any one place have almost always been linked to evangelical movements in other places. But, second, the books also intend to be useful in the contemporary world, where evangelical Christian movements have multiplied far, far beyond the narrow geographical confines of Britain and North America. The 2001 edition of David Barrett's *World Christian Encyclopedia* testifies eloquently to the current situation. With a definition quite similar to the one provided above, Barrett finds over twice as many evangelicals in each of Nigeria (22.3 million) and Brazil (27.7 million) as in Britain (11.6 million), and more in Nigeria and Brazil together (50.0 million) than in the United States (40.6 million). In addition, he counts at least five million evangelicals in each of India, South Korea, South Africa, Kenya and Ethiopia; and at least one million more in eight other African countries, five Asian or Pacific, five Latin American, three European and one North American. And of this worldwide distribution of evangelicals today, considerably more than half speak English as their first or second language.[10] To the extent possible, the books in this series will therefore try to show how the convictions and activities of earlier evangelicals led to the contemporary reality of worldwide evangelicalism.

This book

For this first book in the series, Britain and North America will absorb most of our attention. Yet it should also soon become apparent why the dynamic evangelical religion that emerged in London, Bristol, Cambuslang (Scotland), Dublin, Northampton (Massachusetts, but also Northampton, England), Philadelphia and Falmouth (Nova Scotia) pushed rapidly to the corners of Britain, the North American British empire and soon to points much further afield.

About that dynamic religion, it is important to note that I attempt to treat it from both 'inside' and 'outside'. As myself an evangelical Christian, I am convinced that the copious flow of religious language on which the early evangelical movements were borne corresponded, at least in considerable measure, to spiritual realities. In my view, the invitation of the 1759 hymn by Joseph Hart, a Calvinist Independent from London whose hymns were widely reprinted by the Methodists, spoke of literal reality as well as psychological relief:

> Come, ye sinners, poor and needy,
>   Weak and wounded, sick and sore;
> Jesus ready stands to save you,
>   Full of pity, love, and power:
>   He is able,
> He is willing: doubt no more.

Evangelical religion, as understood by the evangelicals themselves, will thus make up a prominent part in what follows.

At the same time, it is as necessary as it is responsible to treat the early decades of evangelicalism as fully enfleshed in the social, communal, political and intellectual history of that era. Since Christianity is a religion of the Incarnate Christ, Christian historians have full licence to treat the stories of Christian communities as incarnated in their own situations, just so long as they do not reduce those stories to only those situations. As the theologian

---

[10] These figures are from David B. Barrett et al., *World Christian Encyclopedia* (2nd ed., New York: Oxford University Press, 2001).

David Wells has put it for his own interests in theology, so the historian may affirm as well for historical narratives: 'Theology is about ideas but there can be no ideas without people, no Christian people without churches, no churches without contexts that are political, social, and cultural in nature.'[11] If attention to the contexts (the outside story) of early evangelicalism predominates in this book, it is not because there was no inner spiritual story, but because historical research is usually better equipped to deal with the contexts in which spiritual realities occur than with the realities themselves.

The major effort of this book is to provide a coherent, multi-national narrative of the origin, development and rapid diffusion of evangelical movements in their first two generations. It deals quite briefly with interesting and vitally important aspects of early evangelicalism, like theology, hymnody, gender, warfare, politics and science, which have each been the subject of full-scale, sometimes controversial scrutiny in their own right. It is my hope that the narratives here will stimulate more and even richer studies of the same sort. But as an introductory work, the focus here is on the story, especially as illustrated by recent historical research on a number of sometimes neglected topics like interconnections across the Atlantic and between the European continent and Britain, as well as the importance of Africans, women and laypeople in fuelling early evangelicalism. At the same time, much of the book is devoted to the landmark individuals, landmark events and landmark organizations that have been featured in most other treatments of the movement. The book's title suggests how central such landmarks remain.

The book ends with developments in the mid-1790s, by which time the great early Methodists, like George Whitefield, Howell Harris, the Wesleys and the Countess of Huntingdon, have passed from the scene, and full-scale British mobilization against revolutionary France has begun. The story is carried a little further for Canada and some missionary regions, in order to trace the impact of events begun earlier. But 1795 is usually the date in view for bringing these narratives to a close.

The book contains many biographical sketches, with the longest of these portraying the era's best-known leaders: Jonathan Edwards, John Wesley, George Whitefield, Charles Wesley, Selina, Countess of Huntingdon, John Newton, William Wilberforce, Hannah More – but with many other lesser-known figures appearing as well. In gathering this biographical material, it has been immensely helpful to be able to consult the *Blackwell Dictionary of Evangelical Biography* (1995), which, under the editorship of Donald Lewis, has

---

[11] David F. Wells, 'The Debate over the Atonement in Nineteenth-Century America',
     Bibliotheca Sacra 144 (October – December 1987): 372.

opened up the personal interconnections within the movement as never before.

The overarching goal in the use of biographical material, as well with all other sources, has been to clarify the significance of what happened when hundreds, then thousands, then tens of thousands, came to agree with George Whitefield that 'it was best to preach the new birth, and the power of godliness, and not to insist so much on the form'. In pursuing that goal, the book also intends to suggest that Whitefield was posing a most important question when, after observing to the Anglicans of Boston that he had seen different ones 'born again in a different way of worship', he went on to ask, 'who can tell which is the most evangelical?'

1. LANDSCAPES: POLITICAL, ECCLESIASTICAL, SPIRITUAL

The geography of the English-speaking world changed significantly over the course of the eighteenth century because of both political events in the British Isles and the expansion of Britain's first overseas empire.[1] These and related developments – as much in ecclesiastical and spiritual geography as in physical and political geography – exerted compelling influence on the emergence of evangelical Christianity.

Politics, populations and spaces

The extent of political change can be suggested by alterations in colonial holdings and the naming of nations between 1660, when Charles II was restored to the English throne, and 1815, when the final victory over Napoleon at the Battle of Waterloo ended what some historians have called the 'Second Hundred Years War' between the French and the British. In 1660, the monarch ruled over a united kingdom embracing England and Wales. England's king was also the monarch of Scotland, but the Scots, with their own parliament, their

---

[1] I have been guided in the general comments of this chapter especially by *The Oxford History of the British Empire*, vol. 1: *The Origins of Empire*, ed. Nicholas Canny; vol. 2: *The Eighteenth Century*, ed. P. J. Marshall (Oxford and New York: Oxford University Press, 1998).

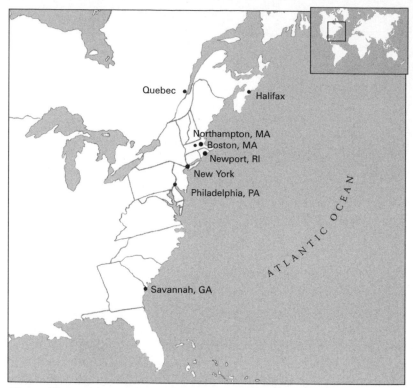

MAP OF NORTH AMERICA

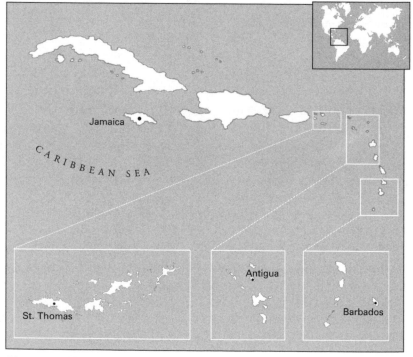

MAP OF THE WEST INDIES

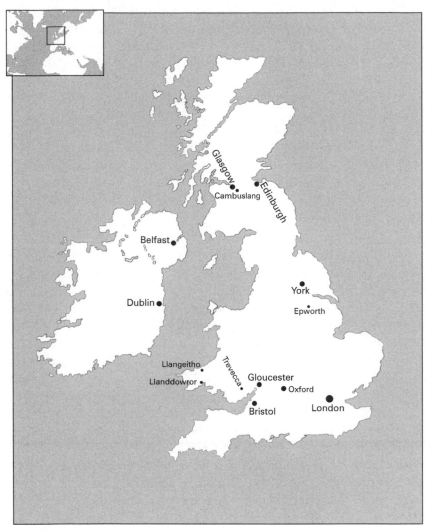

MAP OF GREAT BRITAIN

own legal code and their own Presbyterian church, were very conscious that they constituted a separate nation. Similarly, Ireland also remained a sister kingdom, with England's monarch as its ruler. Much more than Scotland, however, Ireland and its heavily Catholic population was a source of constant frustration to English rulers as they tried to work their will on the island, including two invasions of reconquest in the years 1649–1652 and 1689–1691.

By 1815, Scotland and Ireland had lost whatever independent status they once enjoyed, and both were joined with England and Wales into the United Kingdom of Great Britain and Ireland.[2] Union with Scotland was implemented in 1707; it represented a trade-off in which the Scots lost their political independence and their own parliament in exchange for the liberty to trade and move freely in the rapidly expanding British empire. The latter provision proved especially important for evangelical history when energetic religious figures from Scotland and the North of Ireland became important leaders in new-world evangelical movements. Union with Ireland in 1801 represented the culmination of a more tragic history. In 1798, Britain had violently put down an uprising of 'United Irishmen' that was led by both Protestants and Catholics who were inspired by the examples of the American and French Revolutions. The full political incorporation of Ireland shortly thereafter was intended by the British Parliament to secure Ireland against such disorder in the future. The promise held out to Ireland's majority Catholic population – that Union would lead to much fuller civil rights – was not, however, entirely fulfilled. As with the earlier Scottish Union, so too did Ireland's incorporation into 'Great Britain' play a significant role in later religious developments, since Irish versions of evangelicalism tended to be more assertive, more eschatological and more missionary-minded than their English counterparts. These distinctives would re-echo around the world when, in the decades that followed, great tides of emigration rolled out of Ireland.

Change was also evident in developments outside the British Isles. In 1660, England was casually overseeing a small collection of colonies in North America (Newfoundland, New England, the Chesapeake Bay) and the West Indies. Settlers in these colonies sometimes held out great hopes for their growth into strong centres of commerce and civilization, but England's rulers were more concerned about the colonies' value for new-world competition against the French, who were colonizing in Acadia (later Nova Scotia) and to the north of the St Lawrence River; the Dutch, who maintained a colony

---

[2] This political entity remained intact until 1922, when the Irish Free State broke from the United Kingdom. The six northern Irish counties that remained loyal were incorporated into the United Kingdom of Great Britain and Northern Ireland.

stretching up the Hudson River from New Amsterdam (later New York City); and the Spanish, who had already established extensive holdings in Florida and the Caribbean islands as well as in Central and South America. In 1660 there were more English colonists in the West Indies, with Barbados and Jamaica as the largest settlements, than in either New England or the Chesapeake (Virginia and Maryland).

By 1815 colonial relationships had been doubly transformed. The first transformation occurred in the thirteen colonies that stretched from Massachusetts to Georgia on the North American mainland, since from 1776 these settlements were no longer possessions of Great Britain but the constituent parts of a new United States of America, which had successfully fought Great Britain for its independence. The second transformation was a by-product of the century's intermittent wars with France and served as partial compensation for losing the thirteen colonies. It involved the strengthening by both settlement and conquest of British rule in Canada and the West Indies and its extension into a hodge-podge of new territory: coastal regions of Central and South America, the west coast of Africa, the Cape Colony on the far southern tip of Africa, the island of Mauritius in the Indian Ocean, the southern and eastern coastlands of the Indian sub-continent and the southeastern corner of Australia. By the end of the Napoleonic wars, the English-speaking world included two separate nations (the United Kingdom and the United States) as well as a number of British colonies sprinkled throughout the rest of the globe. Significantly, wherever the British and the Americans traded, colonized or explored, evangelical religion was there as well.

As dramatic as were the changes in political boundaries, so also was the sharp rise in population (see Table 1 on p. 28). Population growth was most rapid in the outlying regions with, for example, the number of people in the thirteen colonies that became the United States multiplying by more than twenty times over the course of the eighteenth century alone. Still, it is as important to remember for religious history as for political or economic history that in this century the centre of the English-speaking world remained England. As an indication of comparative size (as also of wealth, influence and visibility), the population of Wales was greater than the population of the mainland North American colonies until some time early in the century. The city of London alone, which already by 1700 stretched over four densely packed miles from east to west, had more people than all of the British colonies in 1700, more people than the thirteen mainland colonies until roughly 1725, and about as many people as all New England as late as 1800. Even with the loss of the American colonies, the population of Britain and her empire nearly doubled in this hundred-year period, with the most rapid growth in the second half-century. What this unprecedented population expansion meant for evangelical religion was a constantly rising reservoir of recruits as well as a social landscape stressed, strained and, in some urban locations, overburdened by a burgeoning supply of people.

Table 1: Population estimates[3]

(all figures in thousands; Native Americans not included)

	1700	1750	1800
England and Wales[4]	5,300	6,300	9,061
– London	520	675	1,050
Scotland	1,050	1,265	1,625
Ireland[5]	2,500	3,191	5,216
US – New England	92	360	1,233
US – mid-Atlantic	51	268	1,454
US – southern	107	542	2,621
West Indies	147	330	760
Canada[6]	17	71	362
Total	9,264	12,327	22,332
France	19,669	21,000	27,349

Percentage population growth
1700 to 1750:   33%
1750 to 1800:   81%

All 'US' figures are for colonial Britain until 1776.

---

[3] Sources: B. R. Mitchell, *Abstract of British Historical Statistics* (Cambridge: Cambridge University Press, 1962); B. R. Mitchell, *International Historical Statistics: Europe, 1750–1988* (3rd edn., New York: Stockton, 1992); B. R. Mitchell, *International Historical Statistics: The Americas, 1750–1988* (2nd ed., New York: Stockton, 1993), 7 (for Canada in 1800); *Historical Statistics of the United States: Colonial Times to 1957* (Washington: US Bureau of the Census, 1960); *The Oxford History of the British Empire*, vol. 2: *The Eighteenth Century*, ed. P. J. Marshall (New York: Oxford University Press, 1998), 100, 433 (for West Indies); and Stephen Inwood, *A History of London* (New York: Carroll & Graf, 1998), 411.

[4] About one-sixteenth of the population (1800) in Wales.

[5] About one-fifth of the population (1800) in the six counties that later became Northern Ireland.

[6] Combining French and British settlements.

As fast as British (and American) populations were growing, it is important to remember that throughout this entire period France remained far and away the largest nation of western Europe. This fact helps explain why Protestant fear of France – and its Roman Catholic religion – remained so important for all regions of the British empire.

For a history of evangelicalism it is also pertinent to note the ethnic and linguistic make-up of the 'English-speaking' world. Naturally the majority of individuals in the British Isles and in British settlements overseas spoke some variety of English. But various Celtic languages – Cornish in the far southwest of England, different kinds of Gaelic in the Scottish Highlands and Ireland, and Welsh in Wales – remained in use as well. There was also a very significant population of native-born speakers of West African languages or their children and grandchildren. In 1800 about 10% of the approximately 22 million people in Britain, her colonies and the United States were of African descent, with slightly more than half of these in the United States and the remainder heavily concentrated in the British West Indies. A wide variety of Native Americans also constituted a significant population in North America. At the same time, there were also in the American colonies-become-states thousands who spoke Dutch as their mother tongue and tens of thousands who spoke German. In Canada (better known then as British North America) there lived about 200,000 French speakers. With the exception of the French Canadians, who remained overwhelmingly Roman Catholic, each of these minority linguistic populations would at some point in the second half of the eighteenth century show a greater openness to evangelical preaching, conversion and practice than the general population of the 'English-speaking' world.

Ecclesiastical geography

For a history of evangelicalism, ecclesiastical geography is just as important as the physical geography of the nine separate English-speaking areas (England, Wales, Scotland, Ireland, New England, the mid-Atlantic, the American South, the West Indies and Canada). In the early eighteenth century, it was at once a very simple and a very complex picture. The simplicity lay in the nearly universal deference to the principle of tax-supported, church–state religious establishment. The complexity lay in the undertow of dissenting movements that resisted these establishments and in the fact that different establishments existed in different parts of the British empire.

Evangelicals would emerge among both establishmentarians and those who dissented from the establishments. In fact, almost as soon as distinctly evangelical emphases appeared, they functioned as bridges for fellowship and cooperative action between Dissenters and establishmentarians. None the less, the shape of the eighteenth-century ecclesiastical landscape was vitally significant for the development of evangelicalism. Precisely because the stress on personal religious experience, warm-hearted Christian fellowship and individual interpretation of the Bible was so powerful among all evangelicals, the evangelical movement by its very existence acted as a solvent for hard-edged definitions of the church. As it emerged successfully in an ecclesiastical landscape divided between state churches and Dissenting churches, evangelicalism had the effect of relativizing all questions concerning the nature, role and spiritual status of the church itself.

For this entire period the Church of England was the legally constituted and tax-supported established church in England and Wales, Ireland and the West Indies. Until the American War for Independence, it was also the established church in the southern colonies of the North American mainland. Throughout the eighteenth century it enjoyed a quasi-established position in the Maritime colonies of eastern Canada. The status of non-Anglicans varied considerably in these different regions. In the early eighteenth century about 6% of England's population adhered to Dissenting churches descended from the Puritans or other protest movements from the reigns of Elizabeth I (1558–1603) and James I (1603–1625).[7] The Presbyterians made up slightly more than half of English and Welsh Dissenters, but there were also substantial numbers of Independents (or Congregationalists), Baptists, Quakers and a tiny, closely monitored Roman Catholic population. Toleration of Protestant Dissenters had been won officially with the Glorious Revolution in 1689 and was confirmed, after some uncertainty, in the last years of Queen Anne's reign (1702–1714). So long as Roman Catholic descendants of the ousted James II enjoyed French support for their efforts to recapture the British throne, England's Roman Catholics encountered much more official opposition than Protestant Dissenters.

Denominational proportions were reversed in Ireland where the Anglican Church of Ireland, though relatively wealthy, enjoyed the support of only a small fraction of the island's population. The great majority of the Irish remained Roman Catholic, even though the United Kingdom legislated (and occasionally enforced) a series of harsh penal measures in the effort to restrain the Catholic presence. By contrast, the regime treated the substantial number of Irish Presbyterians, who were descended from Scottish and

---

[7] The figures are from Watts, *Dissenters*, 1:270, with helpful maps of Nonconformist distribution on the following pages.

English settlers in the seventeenth century and who were increasingly concentrated in the northern province of Ulster, with a great deal of leniency. From 1672, the Irish Presbyterians even received an intermittent *regium donum*, or royal gift, from the English monarch. This gift became larger and more regular after the Ulster Presbyterians supported first William III in his successful conflict (1688–89) with the ousted James II and then the new line of Hanoverian monarchs who in 1714 succeeded to the British throne. Throughout the eighteenth century, approximately 75–80% of the Irish population remained Catholic. The remainder was divided almost entirely between Church of Ireland Anglicans, who probably made up a slight majority of Protestant Ireland, and Presbyterians, who predominated in the north.[8]

Other variations of Anglican establishment were present in the colonies. In Virginia, Maryland, North Carolina, South Carolina and Georgia, Anglicans defended their rights as the established church more fiercely than in the mother country.[9] In these states, non-Anglicans were treated with great harshness as late as the 1770s. In Virginia, Samuel Davies succeeded in founding a network of evangelical Presbyterian congregations in the late 1740s and early 1750s, but only after the most careful preparatory negotiations with the colony's government and only after he had distinguished himself by vigorous support of the colony during the French and Indian War.[10] In the West Indies, Anglicanism was not only the established church, but virtually the only church until the middle of the eighteenth century. (There were eleven parishes in Barbados by 1700 and fifteen in Jamaica, although the construction of church buildings and the placement of rectors always lagged behind the formal designation of parishes.)[11] In Nova Scotia, early provision was made to favour the Anglican Church, but, by contrast to the West Indies, Congregationalists, Baptists, Lutherans, other Protestants and a sprinkling of Roman Catholics

---

[8] See R. F. Foster, *Modern Ireland, 1600–1972* (London: Penguin, 1989), 200; and S. J. Connolly, *Religion, Law, and Power: The Making of Protestant Ireland, 1600–1760* (Oxford: Clarendon, 1992), 144–197.

[9] Maryland had been founded in the early 1630s as a new-world enclave for British Roman Catholics; but after Maryland Protestants participated in the Glorious Revolution of 1688 with their own rebellion against existing government, the Anglican Church became the established religion in this colony too.

[10] George William Pilcher, *Samuel Davies: Apostle of Dissent in Colonial Virginia* (Knoxville: University of Tennessee Press, 1971).

[11] Boyd Stanley Schlenther, 'Religious Faith and Commercial Empire', in *Oxford History of the British Empire*, 2:129–139.

competed with the Church of England right from the beginning of settlement. The result was a limbo where Anglicans, and sometimes the Nova
Scotia government, acted as if the Church of England was established, but
non-Anglicans did not.[12]

It is important to recognize, however, that the Church of England was only
one of the established churches in the first British empire. Since the
Reformation, Scotland had maintained a Presbyterian state church, though
with frequent periods during which this establishment was challenged by the
Crown in league with local Scottish Episcopalians. But when the northern
nation declared its support for the new monarchs, William and Mary, during
the Glorious Revolution of 1688–1689, and when it joined Great Britain
through the Act of Union in 1707, Presbyterianism won unequivocal recognition as Scotland's established church. North of the River Tweed, in other
words, Episcopalians became dissenters. By the 1730s small dissident movements began to break away from the established Presbyterian Kirk, but these
groups were themselves Presbyterian whose leaders held that the Kirk was not
living up to true Presbyterian ideals. The Highlands offered a different kind of
dissent, for its poor, isolated and Gaelic-speaking population was mostly
Catholic, Episcopal or functionally pagan.

In New England, the Puritan settlers had established a Congregational
state church that throughout the seventeenth century probably enjoyed the
loyalty of a larger proportion of the local population than any other established church in the empire. By the early eighteenth century a few Baptists and
Quakers had established a foothold and from the 1720s there also existed a
handful of Anglican churches. But the Puritan colonies of Massachusetts,
Connecticut and New Hampshire treasured their 'New England Way' and
only reluctantly relaxed commitment to the principle of establishment. (Ves-
tiges of state support for the Congregational churches lingered in Connecticut until 1818 and in Massachusetts until 1833.)

Another form of *de facto* establishment was added to the empire when in
1763 at the end of the French and Indian War (or Seven Years' War as it was
called in Europe), France ceded Quebec to Britain. Official British policy was
aimed at turning the very French and very Catholic Quebecois into good
British Protestants, but that policy never had a chance. Britain periodically
acknowledged this reality. The Quebec Act of 1774, for instance, strengthened the tax-supported, state-sponsored centrality of Quebec's Roman

---

[12] Ann Gormon Condon, '1783–1800: Loyalist Arrival, Acadian Return, Imperial Reform',
in Phillip A. Buckner and John G. Reid (eds.), *The Atlantic Region to Confederation: A
History* (Toronto: University of Toronto Press, 1994), 195–198.

Catholic Church; in exchange, the Catholic bishops kept their people out of the rebellion of the thirteen colonies to the south of Quebec.

Finally, as yet another variation on church–state patterns, the mid-Atlantic colonies on the North American mainland somehow managed to get along without any established churches at all. Rhode Island in New England also survived without a state church but, from its earliest days under Roger Williams, this tiny colony was widely perceived as an eccentric deviant into which all sorts of nonconforming dregs could be safely flushed from the more respectable colonies. New York, New Jersey and Pennsylvania were different – rapidly growing, economically prosperous and well supplied with churches – but with churches of different kinds. By the early eighteenth century, the possibility of establishing one state church in these colonies was ruled out by the simple sweep of events that brought into this region Anglicans, Quakers, Roman Catholics, Jews, Presbyterians, Congregationalists, Dutch Reformed Mennonites, Moravians, German Reformed and smaller numbers of several other religious bodies.[13]

Evangelicalism would eventually flourish best in the kind of deregulated religious environment witnessed in the American middle colonies. In the eighteenth century, however, evangelical impulses were strongest in the established churches of England, Scotland and New England, though with a different flavour depending on whether the establishment was Anglican, Presbyterian, or Congregational. It would mark an important transition in evangelical history, as well as in the history of the United States, when the new American Constitution of 1789 prohibited the national government from favouring any particular denomination as an established church (this provision left the individual states free to act as they pleased). Where, in the eighteenth century, evangelical history was dominated by members of established churches, and Dissenters played only a secondary role, that situation would be reversed in later centuries when non-establishmentarian evangelicals moved into prominence and evangelicals from established churches became less important.

Spiritual geography

The spiritual health of the English-speaking world on the eve of the evangelical revivals has always been a subject for controversy. Debates over where

---

[13] See especially Richard W. Pointer, *Protestant Pluralism and the New York Experience: A Study of Eighteenth-Century Religious Diversity* (Bloomington: Indiana University Press, 1988).

spiritual life was decaying, where it was ripe for renewal or where it was ticking along smoothly have never stopped since the first organized revivals of the 1730s. Once self-conscious evangelical groups emerged, it was only to be expected that they would paint a dark picture of spiritual conditions before evangelical awakeners arrived on the scene. It came naturally to Jonathan Edwards, for instance, to describe the residents of Northampton, Massachusetts, before its remarkable revival of 1734–1735, as being 'very insensible of the things of religion' and of experiencing 'a time of extraordinary dullness in religion'.[14] Similarly, evangelicals would later quote with approval the judgment offered in 1736 by the Irish bishop and philosopher, George Berkeley, that the realm was threatened by the impiety of its magistrates, which in turn was being communicated rapidly to the masses of its people: 'Our prospect is very terrible and the symptoms grow stronger every day ... The youth born and brought up in wicked times, without any bias to good from early principle or instilled opinion, when they grow ripe must be monsters indeed. And it is to be feared, that age of monsters is not far off.'[15] The claim that spiritual life was flagging during the eighteenth century would be made in even stronger terms by proponents of the High Church Oxford Movement in the 1830s. But partisan judgments must not be allowed to frame the whole discussion. More impartial judges have concluded that the actual state of religion was not as decrepit as later evangelicals and Anglo-Catholics perceived it. Still, even objective evaluators have recognized that confident religious life, persuasive preaching of the gospel and effective Christian pastoring were in relatively short supply during the first decades of the eighteenth century.[16]

---

[14] Edwards, *A Faithful Narrative of the Surprising Work of God* (1737), in Edwards, *Works*, vol. 4: *The Great Awakening*, ed. C. C. Goen (1972), 146.

[15] George Berkeley, *A Discourse Addressed to Magistrates and Men in Authority. Occasioned by the Enormous Licence, and Irreligion of the Times* (Dublin, 1736), in *The Works of George Berkeley*, 3 vols., ed. George Sampson (London: George Bell & Sons, 1898), 3:195.

[16] The key work asserting that eighteenth-century Anglicanism was not as decrepit as its Anglo-Catholic, evangelical and secular critics later contended was Norman Sykes, *Church and State in England in the Eighteenth Century* (Cambridge: Cambridge University Press, 1934). For judicious assessment of interpretations of the eighteenth-century situation in general, see John Walsh, Colin Haydon and Stephen Taylor (eds.), *The Church of England, c.1689–c.1833* (Cambridge: Cambridge University Press, 1993), especially Walsh and Taylor, 'Introduction: The Church and Anglicanism in the "Long" Eighteenth Century', 1–64.

The Church of England

Conditions in the Church of England were of special importance for the whole English-speaking world since this church was tied so closely to Parliament, the British Crown and the empire. Not only was Anglicanism the official religion for well over half of the English-speaking population, but it was also the dominant reference for Dissenters in England, Wales and Ireland, as well as for the empire's other established churches.

Because of its size and centrality, it was significant for later evangelical developments that the Church of England was labouring under serious difficulties in the early eighteenth century.[17] Although its bishops and parish clergy were usually not simply time-serving hacks consumed by a desire for status (as they were once routinely depicted), the widespread practices of pluralism and non-residence did undercut Anglican effectiveness. When a local church's formally installed rector did not live in that parish (non-residence), a curate might be supplied, but not always. Non-residence was linked to pluralism, because when a minister secured the rights to another parish, or a post in a cathedral or university, as a holder of plural benefices he could not be in more than one place at a time. A different kind of non-residence hampered the twenty-seven Anglican bishops of England and Wales, for they held seats in the House of Lords and were expected to attend the annual meetings of Parliament. Some of the weaknesses of the Anglican parish system can be excused as a result of inadequate funding or simple structural defects, but whether the problem was greed or something more benign, the result was the same – Anglican attention to the care of souls was not keeping pace with the growth of population or the spiritual needs of English, Welsh and Irish parishioners.

The Church of England had also been seriously disturbed by political turmoils in the early decades of the century. Especially dramatic was a furore over charges made in 1709 by Henry Sacheverell, a High Church Tory, that Dissenters, Whigs and Low Church Anglicans were a pernicious threat to the realm.[18] Then in 1715 a similar uproar occurred when Whigs and Low Church

---

[17] These difficulties are well canvassed in Walsh, Haydon and Taylor, *Church of England*.

[18] The term 'Whig' originated as a designation for Scottish opponents of English ecclesiastical imperialism but was taken over into England as a term of reproach for those who did not want the Catholic Duke of York to become king as James II; it later became used more broadly for those who approved the settlement of William and Mary in 1689 and who favoured the Hanover succession in 1714. The term 'Tory' began as an Irish epithet but was likewise taken into England's vocabulary as a term for those who leaned against the new regime of William and Mary and the settlement of the Hanovers. See DSCHT, 865–866 (John WolVe, 'Whigs').

Anglicans accused Tories and their High Church allies of assisting the French-backed army that invaded Scotland with the aim of restoring the monarchy to the Roman Catholic son of the ousted James II. In 1717 there was another great kerfuffle when Benjamin Hoadly, the Bishop of Bangor, and a Low Church Whig, blasted away at Tory and High Church principles for promoting ecclesiastical and civil tyranny. Public agitation in London and elsewhere reached extraordinary heights during these controversies; the net effect was to sacrifice interest in day-to-day religious belief and practice to the convulsions of political controversy.

The Church of England seemed also to be fertile ground for latitudinarian ideas that troubled serious believers of whatever sort, including the early evangelicals.[19] In reaction to what they regarded as the over-zealous enthusiasm of Puritanism and the coercive tyranny of Roman Catholicism, a considerable number of Anglican intellectuals were proposing a calmer, more self-controlled, more reasonable religion. The sermons of Archbishop Tillotson, which were read widely in Britain and the colonies for more than a generation after his death in 1694, stressed duty, human effort and common morality much more than original sin, a substitutionary atonement and the work of the Holy Spirit. The impressive weight of John Locke's writing – especially his *Letters Concerning Toleration* (1689–1692), *Essay on Human Understanding* (1690) and *The Reasonableness of Christianity* (1695) – amounted to an influential commendation of human reason over any traditional religious authority. When in 1712 the clergyman Samuel Clarke published his *Scripture-doctrine of the Trinity*, which leaned towards a Unitarian interpretation of the Bible, he was roundly attacked, but the church did not force a retraction. To alarmed defenders of traditional Christian orthodoxy, like Samuel Wesley, the father of John and Charles, the latitudinarian drift in Anglicanism seemed headed straight towards deism. Deism was never a formally organized movement, but rather a catchword for the ideas of several well-placed individuals who wanted to replace traditional Christianity with a religion of mere morality and a very distant god. Concern about deism rose steadily in response to manifest public disdain for the supernatural (John Toland, *Christianity Not Mysterious*, 1696), disrespect for the Christian ministry (Anthony Collins, *A Discourse of Free Thinking*, 1713), denial of the miraculous (Thomas Woolston,

---

[19] Expert discussion is provided by Isabel Rivers, *Reason, Grace, and Sentiment: A Study of the Language of Religion and Ethics in England, 1660–1780*, 2 vols (New York: Cambridge University Press, 1991, 2000); and David A. Pailin, 'Rational Religion in England from Herbert of Cherbury to William Paley', in Sheridan Gilley and W. J. Shiels (eds.), *A History of Religion in Britain* (Oxford: Blackwell, 1994), 211–233.

Six Discourses on Miracles, 1727–1730) and denigration of Christianity's unique status (Matthew Tindal, *Christianity as Old as the Creation*, 1730). Orthodox apologists like Bishop Joseph Butler (*The Analogy of Religion, Natural and Revealed, to the Constitution and Course of Nature*, 1736) and Bishop William Warburton (*The Divine Legislation of Moses*, 1737–1741) did a credible job of defending Christian teaching against such deist works.[20] Yet by the 1730s, lingering doubts raised by deist contentions and the concentration of orthodox responses on rational arguments were prime factors, in both England and far-flung outposts of empire, that prepared the way for new efforts at promoting a more emotionally satisfying Christianity.

To many under the care of the Church of England, however, its greatest problem was not so much failure at responding to specific intellectual challenges as its general torpor – slow to reform itself, slow to find a healing voice in the tangled politics of the era, slow to provide churches for the new urban populations, slow to evangelize the unreached at home and the non-Christian masses in new foreign possessions like India. To be sure, defenders of active Christianity were never lacking in the church. William Law, for example, ably defended Christian traditions in his *Three Letters to the Bishop of Bangor* (1717), refuted Matthew Tindal's deism in his *The Case of Reason* (1732), and inspired many with his *A Serious Call to a Devout and Holy Life* (1728). But such influences were comparatively rare and the revival of Anglicanism they sought seemed remote.

Dissent in England

English Dissent looked even less promising as a source of religious renewal.[21] The Dissenters could boast outstanding academies where local ministers offered training in the classics, theology and modern science to Nonconformists excluded from Oxford and Cambridge by the requirement that undergraduates subscribe to the Thirty-Nine Articles and participate in Anglican worship. The most notable of these academies was conducted by Philip Doddridge (1702–1751) at Northampton in the centre of England as a school

---

[20] On the success in his own time of Warburton's apologetics, as well as the orthodox Anglican antipathy to Methodist 'enthusiasm', see B. W. Young, *Religion and Enlightenment in Eighteenth-Century England: Theological Debate from Locke to Burke* (Oxford: Clarendon, 1998), 151–157, 167–212.

[21] For a survey, see Watts, *Dissenters*, 1:263–393. But for an account stressing a stronger contribution by Dissent to the mid-century revival, see Geoffrey G. Nuttall, 'Methodism and the Older Dissent: Some Perspectives', *United Reformed Church Historical Society Journal* 2 (1981): 259–274.

serving Dissenters of all varieties from England as well as some students from
Scotland and Ireland. Doddridge's warm personal piety, his eager promotion
of Bible distribution and missionary societies, his theology of 'mere
Christianity' that followed the ecumenical ideals of Richard Baxter from the
seventeenth century, and friendly contacts with the Wesleys and George
Whitefield marked him as one of the most important forerunners of the later
evangelical movement. Not the least of his contributions were his hymns, like
'Hark the glad sound! the Saviour comes' and 'O happy day, that fixed my
choice/On thee, my Saviour and my God!' In his efforts, Doddridge joined
the other great leader of early eighteenth-century English Dissent, Isaac Watts
(1674–1748). As one of the Christian church's greatest hymnwriters, Watts
provided much for later evangelicals to sing in countless venues and with stu-
pendous effect: for example, 'Come, ye that love the Lord', 'Join all the glorious names', 'When I can read my title clear', 'Jesus shall reign where'er the
sun', and 'When I survey the wondrous cross'.

Yet despite the signal contributions of Doddridge, Watts and a few other
Dissenters like the Welsh Baptist preacher Enoch Frances, Nonconformity
was declining as a movement and weakening as a theological force.[22]
Estimates of the magnitude of the decline vary, but most observers have
agreed that the Dissenters were not even maintaining their former numbers
despite a rising general population. Worried leaders eventually published substantial books appealing for a turn-around, like Doddridge's *Free Thoughts on the
Most Probable Means of Reviving the Dissenting Interest* (1730) and Watts's *An
Humble Attempt towards the Revival of Practical Religion among Christians* (1731).

The most worrying development among Dissenters in the early eighteenth
century concerned doctrine, in particular the creeping advance of Arian views.
In February 1719 a substantial gathering of over one hundred leading
Presbyterian, Congregational and Baptist ministers deliberated at length in
London's Salters' Hall over a momentous question.[23] The body had received a
formal appeal for advice from Dissenting ministers in Devon and Cornwall
who were at their wits' end dealing with local ministers who, after reading
Samuel Clarke and other advanced thinkers, refused to subscribe to the traditional Trinitarian confessions of their churches. The technical issue was
whether it was enough for ministers to promise to follow only the Scriptures.
The real issue was whether these traditionally Trinitarian denominations had
room for Arians, who regarded Christ as more than man but also as distinctly

---

[22] On Frances, see Eifion Evans, *Daniel Rowland and the Great Evangelical Awakening in Wales*
(Edinburgh: Banner of Truth, 1985), 15.

[23] The account here follows Watts, *Dissenters*, 1:374–377.

less than fully God. The vote at Salters' Hall was close (57–53), but went against the confessional Trinitarians. From that time Arian views advanced rapidly among the English Presbyterians and General (or Arminian) Baptists. They also grew in strength among Presbyterians in Ireland and, somewhat less rapidly, in the Scottish Kirk. Even Isaac Watts in his last years began to doubt the adequacy of traditional Trinitarian formulas. This doctrinal indecisiveness, when combined with the Dissenters' slippage in many English and Welsh localities, offered anything but a welcoming climate for robust evangelical religion.

Wales, Ireland, Scotland

The uncertainties of Christianity in England at the centre of the empire were reflected to one degree or another at the empire's margins. In Wales, Ireland and the Scottish Highlands tensions remained high between the speakers of English who exercised power and majority populations who spoke the Celtic languages. Resentment against the established churches did nothing to prepare the way for spiritual renewal in the Celtic regions. The Anglican Church of Ireland, which was forced to exert its place as a tax-gathering established church against a much larger Catholic population and a rapidly growing Presbyterian presence, was just as unpropitiously situated for renewal because of its preoccupations with maintaining power.

The groundwork for revival was more securely in place among Presbyterians in Scotland and the north of Ireland, where stronger currents of historic Calvinism survived. To these currents was also sometimes added the fervent piety of the 'communion season' – celebrations of the Lord's Supper that involved several Sundays of preparatory sermons followed by an intense weekend of concentrated preaching and then communion.[24] These seasons had sparked notable local revivals as far back as the 1620s. Both the flow of immigration – from Scotland to Ireland, and then from Ulster to the colonies – as well as ongoing communication with other Calvinist churches in England, the Continent and New England kept Scottish and Ulster Presbyterians alert to the ebb and flow of renewal among international Calvinists. The published sermons of the English Puritans circulated widely in those networks and so did concern for conversion, concentration on divine grace and convictions about the need for daily holiness.

---

[24] See especially Leigh Eric Schmidt, *Holy Fairs: Scottish Communions and American Revivals in the Early Modern Period* (Princeton: Princeton University Press, 1989), 21–31, 41–49; Marilyn J. Westerkamp, *Triumph of the Laity: Scots–Irish Piety and the Great Awakening, 1625–1760* (New York: Oxford University Press, 1988), 15–42; and *DSCHT*, 200 (D. E. Meek, 'Communion Seasons').

More obvious in both the Kirk of Scotland and Irish Presbyterianism, however, were trends moving at cross purposes with evangelical piety. In Scotland, an Act of Parliament in 1712 defined the terms of the Treaty of Union (1707) by restoring the rights of patrons to appoint (or sometimes merely nominate) ministers for the local churches. Dissatisfaction with this system would simmer continuously for the next two centuries; occasionally it boiled over into scalding controversy and schism. Whatever the merits of arguments for and against patronage, the Scots' enduring fixation on the legal and property rights of patrons, ministers and congregations had the effect of distracting the whole nation from innovative steps aimed at spiritual renewal.

Irish Presbyterians, who were Dissenters over against the Church of Ireland but who functioned as a quasi-establishment in Ulster, mostly avoided the Scottish imbroglios over patronage. Yet with their Scottish colleagues they were influenced by the spread of Enlightenment opinions that undercut the force of traditional Calvinism. In the early eighteenth century, the Scottish church twice put on trial their main theological teacher at the University of Glasgow, John Simson (1667–1740).[25] The charge was that Simson diluted the Westminster Confession by incorporating too much of Isaac Newton's mechanistic science, relying too much on rational argumentation in the struggle against deism and inching much too close to Arianism. The trials produced an inconclusive result: Simson was eventually suspended from his teaching duties, but kept his status on the faculty of divinity. Those who worried about the fate of Presbyterian orthodoxy were not reassured when a growing number of Irish ministers objected to subscribing to the Westminster Confession on the grounds that such an action required inappropriate deference to a merely man-made formula. By the 1720s, these Irish 'new lights' included some who seemed to be following the well-worn path towards Arianism.

The influential teaching and writing of Francis Hutcheson (1694–1746) also seemed to be moving Presbyterians on both sides of the Irish Sea away from the evangelical aspects of their Calvinistic inheritance.[26] Hutcheson was born in Ireland and served there after training at Glasgow under Professor

---

[25] See especially Anne Skoczylas, *Mr. Simson's Knotty Case: Divinity, Politics, and Due Process in Early 18th-Century Scotland* (Kingston and Montreal: McGill-Queen's University Press, 2001).

[26] For introductions, see Mark Valeri, 'Francis Hutcheson', in Emory Elliott (ed.), *American Colonial Writers, 1735–1781* (Detroit: Gale, 1984); and Mark A. Noll, *America's God, from Jonathan Edwards to Abraham Lincoln* (New York: Oxford University Press, 2002), 97–101.

Simson, but his real influence came as professor of moral philosophy at Glasgow, where he served from 1730 until his death. Against the traditional Calvinist doctrine of original sin, Hutcheson posited a natural moral sense, universally existing in all humans, that pointed the way to proper ethical behaviour. His political values also linked him with radicals who treated traditional religion as well as the constraints of church–state public order as barriers to human happiness. Hutcheson did not specifically attack traditional Calvinist doctrines, but he clearly was pushing ideas of both human nature and the good life towards an aesthetic, refined ideal instead of towards traditional piety.

By the 1730s, Presbyterianism in Scotland and Ulster occupied a position analogous to that of Anglicanism in England and Wales. Much confessional Christianity survived from earlier years, and space existed for fresh evangelical concerns. But liberalizing theology, along with widespread concerns for property and propriety, seemed more powerful in the churches as a whole. These were the conditions that spurred at least a few ministers to suggest that only a special effusion of divine grace poured out for the conversion of sinners could rescue the gospel cause. John Maclaurin of Glasgow went public with such thoughts in 1723 ('The Necessity of Divine Grace to Make the Word Effectual'), but for many years his was a lonely voice.[27]

American colonies

The American colonies, which were much more sparsely populated than the British Isles, none the less shared at least some of the religious trends at work in the mother country. The growth of cities, the increase of commerce and the dispersion of population into frontier regions created a degree of social uncertainty similar to that which the industrialization of society was starting to bring to Britain. If few ties of religion, ethnicity or even trade connected the colonies to each other, they were all being drawn towards their British centre in a common process of Anglicization whereby each of the far-flung colonial regions was linked more closely to the fashionable clothing, politics, speech and also religion of the mother country.[28] Evangelical leaders would criticize the growing fixation upon metropolitan fashion and London luxury, but they would also be among the prime beneficiaries when news of awakenings in London and throughout Britain was communicated to the colonies. Beyond

---

[27] For expert discussion, see Michael J. Crawford, *Seasons of Grace: Colonial New England's Revival Tradition in its British Context* (New York: Oxford University Press, 1991), 41.

[28] See especially T. H. Breen, 'An Empire of Goods: The Anglicization of Colonial America, 1690–1776', *Journal of British Studies* 25 (1986): 487–499.

the influence of British fashion, which was growing everywhere in North America, however, the colonial regions still pursued separate religious paths.

New England's Puritan tradition was weakening but remained the most vigorous religious system in the colonies, and maybe in the entire British empire. Signs of weakness included the very fast days called by local officials that allowed ministers to bemoan the passing of true godliness. An upstart worldling like Benjamin Franklin could satirize treasured Puritan traditions, which he did as a sixteen-year-old in 1722 for his brother's Boston newspaper. Ministers outside of Boston were worrying about the construction of elegant church buildings and the general lust for luxury in that metropolis, while in his pastorate along the Connecticut River Valley Jonathan Edwards was concerned that Arminian ideas were beginning to influence the biblical expositions of his fellow pastors. Yet the Puritan sense of duty as well as the Puritan sense of living under the direct inspection of God left New England a religiously tender place. Ministers might be issuing imprecations aimed at inducing guilt rather than comfortable words promising grace. Yet even more than in Scotland (the region that New England most closely resembled as a local Calvinist establishment with a vigorous clerical corps within an Anglican British empire), the same resources of faithful preaching, a living theological inheritance and earnest religious sensibility lay close at hand for the purposes of religious revitalization.[29]

The situation was quite different in the mid-Atlantic colonies of New York, New Jersey and Pennsylvania, where churches struggled to meet the needs of populations extending westward into the raw wilderness and where in settled regions numerous denominations competed against each other. Gospel emphases were always present among Presbyterians and Baptists, as well as some Quaker, Dutch Reformed, German Reformed and German sectarian bodies. In particular, middle-colony Presbyterians sustained active connections with fellow-Calvinists in Scotland, the north of Ireland, New England and even the Continent. These connections primed Presbyterian leaders like Gilbert Tennent of New Brunswick, New Jersey, for news of revival. But the variety of peoples, backgrounds and churches – at the time, unprecedented in the whole world – meant that ministers and the laity were making things up as they went along. Outside the emerging metropolises of New York and Philadelphia the struggle to provide education, civic guidance and regular pastoral ministry to a thinly inhabited terrain absorbed most of the churches' energies. In retrospect, the

---

[29] The great staying power of that heritage is a main theme of Harry S. Stout, *The New England Soul: Preaching and Religious Culture in Colonial New England* (New York: Oxford University Press, 1986).

middle colonies, like New England, also seemed prepared for revival, but in their case it was because of unrealized religious longing created by an avalanche of new experiences rather than because of a unified religious tradition with strong evangelical elements.

Frontier regions of all colonies south of New England resembled the situation in Canada, the Scottish Highlands and the West Indies. Churches in these areas were for the most part so preoccupied with basic problems of survival, or so caught up in this-worldly pursuit of gain, that there was not much response to the early stages of evangelical outreach.

The southern regions of North America offered particular challenges to formal religion of any variety. Population was rising rapidly in the original Chesapeake colonies of Virginia and Maryland, and serious settlement was also taking place in the newer colonies of North Carolina (chartered 1663), South Carolina (divided from North Carolina in 1712) and Georgia (1732). But dictated by the requirements of a producer economy featuring the growing of tobacco, settlement tended to be dispersed along rivers or scattered in small coastal communities and in backcountry homesteads. Anglican ministers were harder working and more faithful to Christian traditions than their opponents portrayed them, but their tasks were immense. The physical scope of ministerial responsibilities was beyond British imagining – many southern clergy were responsible for more territory than many English bishops. The absence of a bishop on the American side of the Atlantic meant that candidates for ordination had to make the long, dangerous voyage to England and return. The system of African-American slavery, which was firmly in place by the 1690s, added further strain. Slave society encouraged a culture of violence that brutalized blacks and whites, a division of moral responsibilities that left religion to be looked after by women in the home, and a fixation by white males on questions of personal honour. Southern blacks as well as whites would eventually respond with real fervour to evangelical preaching, but southern society as a whole contained more elements inimical to evangelicalism than any other colonial region.

Spiritual and political realities
Finally, the spiritual geography of the entire British empire was marked by two features that worked in different ways to ease the way for the spread of the evangelical message. First, with increasing ardour throughout the eighteenth century, loyal Britons experienced a sharpening sense of antagonism to the Roman Catholic Church. In the minds of many there was a natural affinity between freedom, prosperity, the King James Version of the Bible and faithful loyalty to the British Crown, as opposed to a corresponding affinity between oppression, poverty, the Latin mass and craven loyalty to

France. What historian Linda Colley has called 'a vast superstructure of prejudice' against 'Catholics and Catholic states' was a legacy of the past that grew even stronger over the course of the eighteenth century.[30]

A second historical legacy was the common assumption that Britain constituted a confessional Christian state, not in vague or abstract terms but with specific reference to the Trinity of classical Christian theology.[31] Throughout the eighteenth century, many challenges would arise to the belief that state churches were institutions ordained by God and that the basis of state-church religion should be the historic Christian faith. But both of those notions remained very strong throughout the whole extent of British rule. Neither active personal piety nor conscientious holy living was necessarily the consequence of holding these assumptions, but as assumptions they did not begin to give way for a long time. The result, as with Britain's residual anti-Catholicism, was to maintain an acknowledged public framework for Protestant religion. Evangelical preachers might face the daunting task of breathing life into the corpse of Christendom but, at least from some perspectives, that task was less comprehensive than labouring for the creation of Christianity *tout court* and *de novo*.

---

[30] Linda Colley, *Britons: Forging the Nation, 1707–1837* (New Haven: Yale University Press, 1992), 36.

[31] I am following here J. C. D. Clark, *English Society, 1660–1832*, 2nd ed. (Cambridge: Cambridge University Press, 2000), 26–34.

2. ANTECEDENTS, STIRRINGS

The public upsurge of piety that became known as the Evangelical Revival in Britain and the Great Awakening in America did not arise out of thin air. When revival came, it took shape under the direct influence of three earlier Christian movements: an international Calvinist network in which English Puritanism occupied a central position, the pietist revival from the European continent and a High Church Anglican tradition of rigorous spirituality and innovative organization.[1] In turn, these specific movements were themselves indications of the great religious changes that began with the Reformation.

Broader European background

In the 150 years after the Protestant Reformation of the 1520s, Europe was transformed by religion. Some of that transformation was direct, as fervent cadres of Lutherans, Calvinists, Anglicans and Anabaptists joined equally ardent legions of Catholics – including Jesuits, Ursulines and Theatines – in setting out to reform both church life and private Christian practice. But a

---

[1] For Anglican and Puritan roots, the best short statement is John Walsh, 'Origins of the Evangelical Revival', in G. V. Bennett and Walsh (eds.), *Essays in Modern Church History in Memory of Norman Sykes* (New York: Oxford University Press, 1966), 132–162; similarly for pietist influences, the key is Ward, *Awakening*, 296–352.

great deal of the transformation was also indirect. The splintering of European Christendom caused by competing attempts at comprehensive church reform opened intellectual and political space for centres of power and concentrations of interest that escaped the oversight of the churches. So it was that expanding commerce, absolutist monarchs, rising nation states and increasing confidence in scientific procedure all arose as alternatives to the once-dominant ideal of a Europe unified around the sacred guidance of an authoritative church. Horrific bloodshed in the mid-seventeenth century – on the Continent during the Thirty Years War of 1618 to 1648, and in England, Scotland and Ireland with the battles of the Puritan Revolution from 1640 to 1660 – left the older ideal of a common, unified, all-encompassing European *corpus christianorum* fatally wounded. Soon, because of changes precipitated by both religious and non-religious causes, the practices of religious life as well as religion's place in European societies began to be transformed.[2]

The transformations of European religion, however, were never uniform. In some regions the traditional Christian churches became tools of statecraft devoted to the sovereign rule of absolute monarchs. This path was the course pursued with Roman Catholicism in the France of Louis XIV (reigned 1643–1715), with Orthodoxy by Peter the Great in Russia (1689–1725) and with Protestantism by successive rulers of an expanding Brandenburg-Prussia (Frederick William, the Great Elector, 1640–1688; Frederick I, 1688–1713; and Frederick William I, 1713–1740). For some elite intellectuals the transformation was to replace religious authorities with a self-confident new regime of reason and science. This path was followed by those who promoted the rationalism of René Descartes (1596–1650), the natural mechanics of Sir Isaac Newton (1642–1727), the empirical philosophy of John Locke (1632–1704) and above all the worldliness of the eighteenth-century French *philosophes*. Before the mid-seventeenth century, there had been no room in Europe for intellectuals who did not defer to divine revelation and its authoritative ecclesiastical interpreters, whether Catholic or Protestant. But from that time the

---

2   For broad and helpful overviews, see Paul Hazard, *The European Mind, 1680–1715* (ET, London: Hollis & Carter, 1953); Jaroslav Pelikan, *The Christian Tradition*, vol. 4: *Reformation of Church and Dogma (1300–1700)* (Chicago: University of Chicago Press, 1984), 332–385; Charles Taylor, *Sources of the Self: The Making of the Modern Identity* (Cambridge, MA: Harvard University Press, 1989); J. B. Schneewind, *The Invention of Autonomy: A History of Modern Moral Philosophy* (New York: Cambridge University Press, 1998); and W. R. Ward, *Christianity Under the Ancient Régime, 1648–1789* (New York: Cambridge University Press, 1999).

number of such thinkers proliferated, including Benedict Spinoza (1632–1677), Pierre Bayle (1647–1706), Richard Simon (1638–1712), Voltaire (1694–1778), Rousseau (1712–1778) and the authors of the *Encyclopédie* (published 1751–1780).[3] Among traditional Roman Catholics, both political and intellectual circumstances made it necessary for the church's leaders to concentrate on regaining lost authority rather than simply exercising it. Not until the nineteenth century and the end of Napoleon's manipulation of the church did the Catholic struggle for reinvigorated self-direction achieve even partial success.

Alongside these other changes in European religion occurred widely spread, but at first poorly organized, transformations of practical religion among individuals and in local communities. These transformations involved a series of interlocking tendencies:

- from Christian faith defined as correct doctrine towards Christian faith defined as correct living;
- from godly order as the heart of the church's concern towards godly fellowship as a principal goal;
- from authoritative interpretation of Scripture originating with ecclesiastical elites towards lay and more democratic appropriation of the Bible;
- from obedience towards expression;
- from music as performed by well-trained specialists towards music as a shared expression of ordinary people;
- from preaching as learned discourses about God towards preaching as impassioned appeals for closing with Christ.

Together, these newer emphases have been called 'the religion of the heart'. They were found among some Catholics, like the Jansenists of Port Royal in France, and among some Orthodox, like the Old Believers and other sectarian movements in Russia, and they were manifest as well in the eighteenth-century rise of Hasidic Judaism.[4] But such changes were most intense and exerted their most enduring influence among Protestants in Central Europe and in the English-speaking islands on Europe's western fringe. To be sure, examples of more personal, more experiential, less formal, less hierarchical Christian faith had always been present in Christian history. But now

---

[3] For a sensitive treatment of this process, see Michael J. Buckley, SJ, *At the Origins of Modern Atheism* (New Haven: Yale University Press, 1987).

[4] For an overview, see Ted A. Campbell, *The Religion of the Heart: A Study of European Religious Life in the Seventeenth and Eighteenth Centuries* (Columbia: University Press of South Carolina, 1991).

in early modern Europe such examples were proliferating; they led directly to evangelicalism.

Puritanism and the Calvinist Internationale

In England, the Puritan movement featured many themes that eighteenth-century evangelicals would later promote as well, especially intense preaching about the need for a saving Christ and calculated opposition to the merely formal religion that Puritans saw infecting the Church of England. In most general terms, the Puritan movement had represented a desire to finish the English Reformation, to complete the work of purifying church, society and self that began under Henry VIII (reigned 1509–1547) and Edward VI (reigned 1547–1553), was temporarily reversed under the Roman Catholic Mary I (reigned 1553–1558), but was eventually secured under Elizabeth I (reigned 1558–1603).[5] Puritans rejoiced in the general course of sixteenth-century English history, but they also believed they needed to push onwards vigorously in order to complete the good work that had begun. As the movement gathered strength in the late sixteenth and early seventeenth centuries, Puritans produced a spate of devotional writing that dealt directly with the experiential work of God among the redeemed. Examples of this literature were reprinted frequently at home and abroad, especially through German and Dutch translations. Those translations would mean a great deal for European pietists, many of whose works, in turn, would be translated into English as an inspiration for the evangelicals.

The Puritan movement was also sustained by theologians like William Perkins (1558–1602), who was renowned for carefully charting the path that repentant sinners could take to find the Saviour.[6] It included lay leaders like John Winthrop (1588–1649) of Massachusetts and Oliver Cromwell (1599–1658), England's Lord Protector, whose own conversions and serious dedication to biblical religion measurably shaped their public lives.[7] Puritanism was driven by its preachers of grace, like John Cotton (1584–1652) and Thomas Shepard (1605–1649), who began their careers in England but then became

---

[5]   See especially Patrick Collinson, *The Elizabeth Puritan Movement* (Berkeley: University of California Press, 1967).

[6]   *The Works of William Perkins*, ed. Ian Breward (Abingdon: Sutton Courtenay, 1970).

[7]   Especially helpful are Edmund S. Morgan, *The Puritan Dilemma: The Life of John Winthrop* (Boston: Little, Brown, 1958); and Robert S. Paul, *The Lord Protector: Religion and Politics in the Life of Oliver Cromwell* (London: Lutterworth, 1955).

spiritual leaders of the Puritan migration to New England.[8] In all of these expressions, Puritans anticipated the later preoccupations of many evangelicals.

Yet even as it pushed towards a more personal and more internal practice of the Christian faith, Puritanism still remained a traditional religion of traditional European Christendom. Not until the English Civil Wars (1640ff.) and the rise of Cromwell did Puritans even begin to consider the notion that reform of self could be separated from systematic reform of church and nation. And so as Puritans promoted the need for heart-felt personal faith, they also promoted coercive plans for the comprehensive reform of society. During the years 1649 to 1660 – the Interregnum between the execution of Charles I and the Restoration of the monarchy under Charles II – a growing number of Puritans came to agree with Cromwell that a limited degree of toleration was compatible with an orderly society. But precisely this cautious prospect of self-chosen religion badly frightened most of the English people; after Cromwell died in 1658, the English scurried back. Once again they sought the protection of a king, strengthened the established church, embarked on new persecution of Dissent and exalted the ideal of a society unified under God, the monarchy and the national Anglican Church.

The Puritan migration to New England began in 1620 with the separatistic colony at Plymouth, and then gathered force with the establishment from 1630 of the Massachusetts, Connecticut and New Haven colonies. (Plymouth was later joined to Massachusetts and New Haven to Connecticut.)[9] In New England, the hegemony of Puritan rule lasted longer than in England, but only because its Puritan leaders were willing to relax their early stress on conversion as a prerequisite for church membership in order to preserve the structures of a comprehensively Christian society. For the New Englanders, the Half-Way Covenant of 1662 was a compromise: it kept alive teaching about the need for God's covenant of grace as the key to salvation, and so stipulated that only those who experienced such grace were eligible for the sacrament of communion. But it also reaffirmed the comprehensiveness of society by including most children as participants in a half-way covenant – parents who had not testified to grace in their lives could none the less bring their children to be baptized. The compromise perpetuated the Puritan

---

[8] See especially *God's Plot: The Paradoxes of Piety, Being the Autobiography and Journal of Thomas Shepard*, ed. Michael McGiffert (Amherst: University of Massachusetts Press, 1972).

[9] The best study joining developments in the two regions is Stephen Foster, *The Long Argument: English Puritanism and the Shaping of New England Culture, 1570–1700* (Chapel Hill: University of North Carolina Press, 1991).

concern for individual salvation but domesticated that concern by also perpetuating the ideal of a comprehensive, unified society. Within the larger
scope of the seventeenth century, the Puritan churches of New England
seemed to be drifting in the direction of the English situation from which
they had fled – especially by emphasizing formal professions, heightened
cooperation between state and church and strong resistance to religious
dissent. Yet, however it was developing, Puritan New England was too small
and too far away to bring much evangelical influence to bear on British religious life, even if evangelical practices had flourished.

Puritans did promote the kind of grace-centred Protestantism that would
rise again in the evangelical revival. But they also compromised it. The revolt
of Parliament in the early 1640s, the bitter warfare that followed (including
great bloodshed in Ireland between Catholics and Protestants), the experience
of Cromwell's military near-dictatorship and the multiplied profusion of new
sects in the 1640s and 1650s gave many English men and women a religious
fright from which they did not recover for over a century.[10] Puritanism might
mean strong preaching for conversion, the search for personal godliness and a
devotion to lay study of Scripture, but it also seemed to entail less edifying
consequences:

- 'enthusiasm', where especially the lower orders pretended to hear the voice
  of God in their own ears;
- antinomianism, where private religious inspiration excused people from
  observing ordinary laws, morality and reasonable public duties;
- reverse intolerance, where 'the saints' persecuted their enemies as vigorously as they had been persecuted themselves.

By restoring the monarchy in 1660, the English nation as a whole indicated
that it had had its fill of what many considered the logical consequences of
Puritanism: Quakers running naked through the streets in order to disrupt regularly scheduled worship; iconoclasts trashing precious statuary and stained
glass in ancient churches; intrusive moralists shutting down theatres and
closing up taverns; and doctrinal precisionists battling each other remorselessly
over fine questions of predestination, the sacraments and proper church order.
Even as Puritan teachers, devotional works and habits of domestic worship
kept alive a more experiential religion, the excesses of Puritanism (at least as
these were widely perceived) made later evangelical movements suspect to the

---

[10] That fright is well communicated in a recent popular novel, Iain Pears, *An Instance of the
     Fingerpost* (London: Jonathan Cape, 1997).

many who associated that kind of religion with enthusiasm, antinomianism, supercilious intolerance and general social disorder.

From the 1660s to the 1730s, English nervousness about the social and intellectual consequences of aggressive heart religion made it virtually impossible for evangelical movements to gather a critical mass. Yet important figures from the Puritan era did succeed in keeping evangelical emphases alive in Britain and North America. Among the most important of those figures were two influential pastor-authors and one self-taught literary genius.

Joseph Alleine (1634–1668) was a Presbyterian pastor of Puritan convictions who was ejected from his pulpit in Taunton in 1662, when Charles II expelled all ministers who would not conform to the discipline of the national Church of England (more than 2,000 in all). Although Alleine himself was later imprisoned for his beliefs and never held a regular appointment again, later generations eagerly snatched up copies of his tract, *An Alarm to the Unconverted* (first published 1672). It spotlighted scriptural study and preaching as the instruments of conversion, which Alleine described as combining an 'internal cause ... free grace alone', and an 'external cause ... the merit and intercession of the blood of Jesus'.[11]

Similarly, Richard Baxter (1616–1691), who was also ejected in 1662, remained an active proponent of many convictions that would propel later evangelical movements. Baxter's writings, like *The Saints' Everlasting Rest* (1650), were well known among later evangelicals, but even more characteristically evangelical was the way he positioned himself in the religious life of his own time. For one thing, Baxter stood midway between the sturdy Calvinism by which most of the Puritan gospel preachers steered their way and a more Arminian conception of God's work in the world such as the Wesleys would later promote. For another, he was an early defender of what he famously called 'mere Christianity' – or the principle that cooperation among various kinds of Christians was much more important than contentions over the points that divided them from each other. 'If the name CHRISTIAN', he once wrote, 'be not enough, call me a CATHOLICK CHRISTIAN; not as that word signifieth an hereticating majority of Bishops, but as it signifieth one that hath no Religion, but that which by Christ and the Apostles was left to the Catholic Church, or the Body of Jesus Christ on Earth.'[12] In both of

---

[11] Joseph Alleine, *An Alarm to the Unconverted* (London: Banner of Truth, 1959), 27.

[12] For C. S. Lewis's reference to Baxter, see *Mere Christianity* (London: Geoffrey Bles, 1952), vi. Baxter is quoted here from N. H. Keeble, *Richard Baxter: Puritan Man of Letters* (Oxford: Clarendon, 1982), 24. On the connections, see Keeble, 'C. S. Lewis, Richard Baxter, and "Mere Christianity"', *Christianity and Literature* 30 (spring 1981): 27–44.

these stances Baxter marked out terrain that many evangelicals of later generations would also occupy.

An unlikely source of even greater evangelical influence was John Bunyan (1628–1688), the tinker of Bedford and Nonconformist lay preacher, who was imprisoned intermittently for his Puritan convictions from 1660 to 1672. Bunyan's *Pilgrim's Progress* (1678, 1684), with its moving allegory tracing the journey of 'Christian' from the City of Destruction through the loss of his burden of sin at the cross to his entrance into the Celestial City, enjoyed a vast number of readers. Bunyan's *Grace Abounding to the Chief of Sinners* (1666) was read almost as widely and did much to promote the careful self-examination, the intense struggles against inward sins and the comforting reliance on scriptural promises of grace that would be so important among later evangelicals. Themes that were kept alive in such Puritan works meant that the rise of evangelicalism in the eighteenth century signalled a revival of earlier spiritual themes, if not the revival of Puritanism as a complete social movement.[13]

In North America, even with formalism growing in the churches and even after the disastrous Salem witch trials (1692–93) highlighted the dangers of state power enforcing religious conformity, lively strands of experiential Christian faith also remained quite strong.[14] Cotton Mather (1663–1728), the prolific pastor of Boston's Old North Congregational Church, was one major figure who in dozens of works hammered away on principles that would later inspire many evangelicals. These principles included conversion defined as the gracious work of the Holy Spirit, holiness exalted as the birthright of every born-again Christian, evangelism urged among high estate and low, and voluntary associations promoted as the Spirit's means to accomplish God's work in the world. Although Mather's publications were reprinted by later evangelicals not nearly as often as those by Alleine, Baxter and Bunyan, it is noteworthy that at the height of New England's Great Awakening, friends of revival reissued a series of Mather's works that supported their cause: in 1740, *Family Religion Excited and Assisted*, which guided parents in teaching gospel themes in the home; 1741, *The Case of a Troubled Mind*, which offered assistance focused

---

[13] For a catalogue and expert assessment of seventeenth-century Puritan writings republished by leaders of the evangelical awakenings, see Charles E. Hambrick-Stowe, 'The Spirit of the Old Writers: The Great Awakening and the Persistence of Puritan Piety', in Francis J. Bremer (ed.), *Puritanism: Transatlantic Perspectives on a Seventeenth-Century Anglo-American Faith* (Boston: Massachusetts Historical Society, 1993), 277–291.

[14] This paragraph depends on Richard F. Lovelace, *The American Pietism of Cotton Mather: Origins of American Evangelicalism* (Grand Rapids: Eerdmans, 1979).

on Christ's mercy for those who laboured under the awareness of sin; and 1742, *Early Piety Exemplified*, a funeral sermon for an eight-year-old girl, which showed how holiness could be experienced even at an early age.

For reasons related to its political and ecclesiastical history, Scotland's situation must be distinguished from situations in England and the American colonies. But from Scotland also in the later seventeenth and early eighteenth centuries came leaders who, while rooted in state-church assumptions and committed to high standards of doctrinal orthodoxy, also promoted distinctly evangelical emphases. As an example, Thomas Boston (1676–1732) of Ettrick, to the south of Edinburgh, organized his influential career as preacher and author around the themes of humanity's 'fourfold state': innocence, nature (after the fall), grace and then eternal life (in glory or in damnation).[15] When Boston's collection of sermons, *Human Nature in its Fourfold State* was published in 1720, it won immediate popularity. That popularity continued (it may have been the most often reprinted book in eighteenth-century Scotland) primarily because of its strongly evangelical message. Boston's stress on the supernatural character of conversion and on conversion as the beginning of holy living made possible by the work of the Holy Spirit was read with appreciation by George Whitefield, Jonathan Edwards, John Wesley and other leaders of the evangelical movement.

Boston, it is not surprising, was also the key figure behind the reprinting in 1718 of *The Marrow of Modern Divinity*, a book by the English Puritan, Edward Fisher, that had been first published at London in 1645.[16] Its argument that the regenerate Christian believer would normally have a real assurance of saving faith had been fairly standard for mid-seventeenth-century Puritans, but now it troubled Church of Scotland officials who feared that such a stress on assurance would spin off into an antinomian disregard for the normal conventions of the law. A great pamphlet controversy resulted, as well as, in typical Scottish fashion, a tremendous flurry of petitions, counter-petitions and judgments in presbytery, synod and General Assembly. The upshot of the controversy was that the Presbyterian Kirk affirmed its leaning towards a legal interpretation of the covenant (God and humans entered into mutual obligations with each other), while 'the Marrow brethren', who sided with Boston, affirmed a gracious interpretation of the covenant (God's offer of fellowship

---

[15]   This material on Boston is from Philip Graham Ryken, *Thomas Boston as Preacher of the Fourfold State* (Edinburgh: Rutherford House, 1999), with 299–303 on the widespread circulation of Boston's main work.

[16]   For definitive treatment, see David C. Lachman, *The Marrow Controversy* (Edinburgh: Rutherford House, 1988).

with repentant humans rested solely on his mercy in Christ). Later evangelicals would look back on this incident both as a sign of theological weakness in
the Scottish state church and as a courageous defence of the gospel by Boston
and his colleagues. Along with personal and spiritual aspects of English and
American Puritanism, the deep strand of personal piety in Scottish Presbyterian Calvinism also represented an important way-station on the road to the
Evangelical Awakening.

By the late 1730s, when modern evangelicalism emerged, the traditions of
experiential Calvinism had weakened considerably throughout all parts of the
British empire, but they were being kept alive by many preachers in Massachusetts and Connecticut, by several capable ministers in Scotland and Ireland
and by somewhat lonely voices among English Nonconformists like Philip
Doddridge and Isaac Watts. Most significantly for what followed was the
network that continued to link these Calvinists to each other, for when revival
did flicker at isolated venues in the empire, this network sprang immediately
into action. News spread by Calvinists to other Calvinists became the breeze
that fanned the broader revival into life.[17]

Continental pietism

Almost as important in preparing the way for later evangelicalism were events
taking place in central Europe. As historian Reginald Ward has demonstrated persuasively, a great range of connections – literary, personal, pastoral,
hymnic – linked the spirituality of continental pietism to almost every phase
of the British and American Evangelical Awakenings.[18] The pietists, who had
themselves greatly benefited from the books of English Puritans, returned the
favour many times over by pointing English-speaking evangelicals to ideals of
true religion, models of organized philanthropy, a specific way of talking
about conversion and a new focus on the assurance of salvation.

---

[17] The suggestion that transatlantic contact was slowing in the early eighteenth century is
     advanced by Francis J. Bremer, *Congregational Communion: Clerical Friendship in the Anglo-
     American Puritan Community, 1610–1692* (Boston: Northeastern University Press, 1994),
     249–256. But that it had never faded is the conclusion of Susan Durden O'Brien, 'A
     Transatlantic Community of Saints: The Great Awakening and the First Evangelical
     Networks, 1735–1755', *American Historical Review* 91 (1986): 311–332.

[18] Alongside Ward, *Awakening*, see also Ward, *Christianity Under the Ancient Régime*, 131–146;
     and Ward, *Kirchengeschichte Großbritanniens vom 17. bis zum 20. Jahrhundert* (Leipzig:
     Evangelische Verlagsanstalt, 2000), 19–86.

Over the course of the seventeenth century, German-speaking lands especially had witnessed a growing attention to the inner life of faith.[19] Even as a
harder-edged Protestant Orthodoxy, which featured a scrupulous attention to
doctrinal correctness, emerged among Lutherans and the Reformed, and even
as the Orthodox Reformed and Lutheran churches became increasingly preoccupied with questions of social and intellectual order, other voices appealed
for active and vital personal religion. Chief among these was Johann Arndt, a
Lutheran minister from Brunswick in the north of Germany, who early in the
century brought out a multi-volume appeal entitled *On True Christianity*
(1605–1610). Not only was this work republished constantly over the decades
that followed, both in German and in many translations, but it also provided
later pietists and evangelicals with a template for analysing the spiritual state of
churches and nations: nominal, formal, heady and control-conscious religion
was one thing, but *true* Christianity that engaged heart with mind, that spurred
the faithful to action with the love of Jesus, was something entirely different. In
Arndt's own case, the way to 'true Christianity' lay in appropriating selective
aspects of medieval spirituality, as outlined, for example, in Thomas à Kempis's
On the Imitation of Christ. But even when later awakeners turned more directly to
lay appropriation of Scripture, to explicit appeals for conversion or to innovations like small groups of the laity meeting for prayer and fellowship, they followed Arndt's lead by proposing genuine Christian practice as a way of reviving
the tired, bureaucratic, official and unspiritual religion of the state churches.

The importance of Arndt's example was powerfully illustrated in the rise of
Germany's pietist movement during the last quarter of the seventeenth century.
This movement would become a crucial stimulus, in several of its varieties, for
 later evangelical awakenings in English-speaking lands. It would also produce
the vanguard of Protestant foreign missions, to which British and American
evangelicals eventually made a great contribution, though only after the cross-
cultural labours of several pietist groups had been well and thoroughly established. Significantly, pietism as a recognizable movement began in 1675 with the
publication of a lengthy preface attached to a reprinting of a book of sermons
by Johann Arndt. The author of this important work was Philip Jakob Spener,
at the time the forty-year-old pastor of the main Lutheran church in Frankfurt,
which was then, as now, a hub of commerce and communication.

Spener's preface, soon published separately as *Pia Desideria* ('Pious Wishes'
or 'The Piety We Desire'), revealed its debt to Arndt in the shape of its analysis

---

[19] For outstanding summaries, see Ward, *Awakening*, and Martin Brecht (ed.), *Geschichte des
Pietismus*, vol. 1: *Der Pietismus vom Siebzehnten bis zum frühen achtzehnten Jahrhundert*
(Göttingen: Vandenhoeck & Ruprecht, 1993).

of Germany's spiritual problem: despite much church activity, there were few in Germany who 'really understand and practice true Christianity (which consists of more than avoiding manifest vices and living an outwardly moral life)'. Practitioners of merely formal religion fooled themselves and others by holding counterfeit faith to be the genuine article: 'What they take to be faith and what is the ground of their teaching is by no means that true faith which is awakened through the Word of God, by the illumination, witness, and sealing of the Holy Spirit, but is a human fancy.'[20]

To counteract Germany's parlous religious situation, Spener proposed a series of six remedies. The gist of what he advocated would be repeated time and again by pietists and evangelicals in the centuries that followed. (1) There must be a return to the Scriptures, for only in the Bible do we find the good news of the gospel and 'the rules for good works' that please God. (2) Lay people must again take an active role in religious life. Most significantly, in his exhortation for greater lay spiritual initiative Spener outlined a plan for what he called 'the ancient and apostolic kind of church meetings' where lay people (women and men) gathered outside of regular church hours for biblical study and spiritual encouragement. Spener had in fact already instituted such meetings in Frankfurt, which came to be called *collegia pietatis*. In countless variations the presence of such small-group gatherings would become a defining feature of later evangelical life. (3) Christians must move beyond mere acknowledgment of correct beliefs to lives of active godliness: 'If we can ... awaken a fervent love among our Christians, first toward one another and then toward all men ... and put this love into practice, practically all that we desire will be accomplished.' (4) Harsh religious controversies must be stopped and then replaced with 'a practice of heart-felt love toward all unbelievers and heretics'. (5) The ministry must be reserved for men who 'are themselves true Christians' and not just place-servers eager for power or prestige. (6) Finally, students training for the ministry should be well versed in the practices of godliness and not merely trained to parrot theories of the spiritual life.[21]

Spener's tract for the times stimulated a tremendous response. Some Orthodox ministers blasted it as 'enthusiastical'; they contended that to give such free rein to the uninstructed laity was surely to undermine sound theology and stable church order. The critics were not entirely wrong, even if, in their zeal for religious stability, they overlooked the spiritual need to which Spener's appeal spoke so directly.

---

[20] Philip Jacob Spener, *Pia Desideria*, trans. Theodore G. Tappert (Philadelphia: Fortress, 1964), 45–46.

[21] Ibid., 87, 89, 96, 99.

In the event, the positive response was greater than the criticism. In later positions at Dresden (Saxony) and then Berlin (Brandenburg-Prussia), Spener attracted a loyal following, including especially the organizational genius August Hermann Francke (1663–1727), who, with a whole team of like-minded pietists, embarked on a great surge of religious construction. Their activity included founding the University of Halle in 1694, publishing a wide array of devotional and spiritual books, establishing Europe's largest orphan house, sending out the first Protestant missionaries and developing the efficient manufacture and distribution of pharmaceuticals as a way of funding these many good works.

By the start of the eighteenth century pietist impulses were spreading rapidly beyond the Halle circle. The mystical historian, Gottfried Arnold (1666–1714), who had been won to pietism by Spener, struck off in his own direction with a curious but widely read work, the *Impartial History of Churches and Heretics* (1699–1700). This argument-cum-document combined aggressive criticism of existing churches with a massive historical record of the church as an invisible, spiritual body where earnest seekers could find both Spirit and truth.[22] Soon, as well, pietist influences were at work in the Württemberg area of southwest Germany, where within a few years the biblical scholar Johannes Albrecht Bengel (1687–1752) began his magisterial studies in the textual criticism and exegesis of the New Testament. By that time pietist beliefs, practices and criticisms of formal religion were spreading rapidly into Scandinavia, the Netherlands, and Switzerland and also among the hard-pressed Protestants of Bohemia, Moravia, Salzburg and Silesia, who struggled to survive under the heavy hand of the Catholic Austrian monarchy. In 1722 a Saxon count, Nicholas Ludwig von Zinzendorf, who had been a student of Francke, provided shelter for a small group of exiles from Silesia. This small act had immense consequences for the English-speaking as well as the European world.

Zinzendorf, (1700–1760) was a winsome, eccentric and headstrong Saxon nobleman motivated by an intensely Christ-centred faith.[23] Shortly after Zinzendorf, as a young man, acquired a substantial estate in southeast Saxony, he opened its grounds to refugees driven out of Bohemia and Moravia (modern-day Czech Republic) by pressure from Catholic authorities.

---

[22] Hans Schneider, 'Der radikale Pietismus im 17. Jahrhundert', *Geschichte des Pietismus*, vol. 2: *Der Pietismus vom 17. bis zum frühen 18. Jahrhundert* (Göttingen: Vandenhoeck & Ruprecht, 1993), 410–418; and Schneider, 'Gottfried Arnold', *Geschichte des Pietismus*, vol. 2: *Der Pietismus im 18. Jahrhundert* (Göttingen: Vandenhoeck & Ruprecht, 1995), 116–119.

[23] Ward, *Awakening*, 116–159; Ward, *Christianity Under the Ancient Régime*, 112–125; and *BDEB*, 1226–1227 (Peter Lineham, 'Zinzendorf').

These were members of the Unity of Brethren, or Moravians, remnants of the pre-Reformation Hussite church who had been forced into exile by the Catholic Habsburg monarchy. At Zinzendorf's estate, 'Herrnhut' (the Lord's Protection), he oversaw a religious movement that combined pietistic Lutheranism of the sort he had learned from Francke at Halle with a revivalistic faith that the Moravians carried with them from awakenings in their native lands. Contact between representatives of the Renewed Unity of the Brethren and early English evangelicals would have the most far-reaching consequences imaginable.

Moravian influence in English-speaking regions was, however, only one instance of pietism's broader significance. News of revival in the hard-pressed Austrian lands, and then of Protestants being expelled from those Catholic territories, angered, encouraged and inspired a wide range of observers throughout the English-speaking world. Major figures of later British and American evangelicalism like Gilbert Tennent, Jonathan Edwards and John Wesley were connected personally or by correspondence with pietists who encouraged their English-speaking confrères to join them on the paths of active personal godliness. The pietist promotion of true or genuine Christianity as a remedy for the ills of merely formal churches reinforced a similar mode of analysis that had been practised by the Puritans. As an indication of the importance of the continental–British connection, when John Wesley began a 'Christian Library' for the benefit of his Methodist itinerants in 1746, the first title he abridged for the series was Arndt's *True Christianity*. Wesley's later *Notes on the New Testament* were mostly an abridgment of commentaries by J. A. Bengel.[24]

The pietist promotion of godliness – defined as an inner experience of God's work, confirmed by personal study of the Scriptures – encouraged British and colonial evangelicals to imitate pietist styles of worship, pietist preaching and pietist voluntary organization. The example of pietists mobilized for the doing of good – to orphans, to slaves, to distinct groups within the community (men, women, the young, the old), to those who had never heard the gospel – offered direct inspiration for many of the most significant practical works taken up by British and American evangelicals throughout the eighteenth century.

Continental pietists also communicated to their English-speaking counterparts an intense devotion to hymnody. The spiritual life of German churches between the time of Arndt and the era of Spener – especially during the gruesome slaughter of the Thirty Years War (1618–1648) – had been sustained in large part by hymns proclaiming the gracious mercy of Christ as the only hopeful recourse for the sorrowful realities of human existence. Many of these

---

[24] Ward, *Christianity Under the Ancient Régime*, 133; and Rack, *Wesley*, 347, 382.

hymns were later translated into English, including 'Ah, holy Jesus, how hast thou offended? ... I it was denied thee: I crucified thee', by Johann Heerman (1585–1647); 'If thou but suffer God to guide thee' from Georg Neumark (1621–1681); and, by the greatest of these hymnwriters, Paul Gerhardt (1607–1676), 'Why should cross and trial grieve me?' and the translation out of Latin of 'O sacred head, now wounded'. When formally organized pietist movements emerged through the work of Spener, Francke, Bengel and others, so too did direct, simple, but also gospel-centred hymnody revive with a great quantity of new songs speaking to, for, through and in the human spirit of eager lay singers. Through several specific hymns, but even more in the commitment to hymns as a form of spiritual nurture and experience, the continental pietists blazed a path that English-speaking evangelicals eagerly followed.

The heart-concerns of Puritanism and pietism were never exactly the same as the heart-concerns of evangelicalism. Evangelicals stood very differently towards the body politic than did earlier Puritans; English-speaking evangelicals understood gospel religion against a different social background than did European pietists. Yet even with the differences of context fully acknowledged, Puritanism, pietism and evangelicalism were joined closely as analogous religious movements. Chief among their similarities was the common conviction that God could actually, actively and almost tangibly transform repentant sinners who put their trust in him.

High Church spirituality

A third important antecedent for evangelicalism came from High Church Anglicans, despite the fact that the High Church party had suffered greatly in the two generations before 1740.[25] At the Glorious Revolution of 1688, some of its most attractive leaders, like Bishop Thomas Ken (author of 'Praise God, from whom all blessings flow'), were deposed from their offices because they felt the oaths they had sworn to the ousted monarch James II prevented them from swearing fidelity to William and Mary. The fortunes of these non-jurors (non-swearers) and their High Church colleagues fell again when they were linked to the Jacobites, who supported efforts by James II's descendants to re-take the throne. Despite such difficulties, a vigorous strand of High Church piety survived in London and many country parishes. The crucial

---

[25] See especially the early chapters in John Walsh, Colin Haydon and Stephen Taylor (eds.), *The Church of England, c.1689–c.1833* (New York: Cambridge University Press, 1993).

spiritual emphasis for this movement was its stress on 'primitive Christianity', or the faith thought to have been practised with great purity in the church's very first centuries. Works like William Cave's *Primitive Christianity: or, the Religion of the Ancient Christians in the First Ages of the Gospel* (1673) and Anthony Horneck's *The Happy Ascetick ... Concerning the Holy Lives of the Primitive Christians* (1681) defined the ideal: imitation of the faith and life of early believers, ascetic practice for the self, godly discipline for society and regular participation in the church's celebration of the Eucharist.[26]

Samuel and Susannah Wesley, the parents of John and Charles, were both diligent advocates of this High Church apostolic primitivism. Samuel may even have helped draft the defence used by the controversial High Churchman Dr Sacheverell at his much-watched trial in 1710. Both older Wesleys had converted to Anglicanism after being raised in Dissenting households. Susannah, in fact, was so sincere in her High Church principles that she once precipitated a temporary separation from her husband by refusing (in non-juring fashion) to join him in family prayers for the new monarchs. Differ as they might on details of High Church conviction, the senior Wesleys were united in seeking the High Church ideal of Christian primitivism. From this commitment came efforts to catechize their own and other children, strenuously conscientious standards of personal morality and frequent celebrations of communion. Later evangelical movements would alter the terms of emphasis, especially by turning to the book of Acts as the model for primitive Christianity, but the primitivist urge remained a very important High Church bequest to nascent evangelicalism.

Samuel Wesley was also a committed advocate of the voluntary religious societies that High Church Anglicans had been establishing from the late 1670s.[27] The societies were first set up in London and then in many other English localities, with the express intent of promoting personal piety and doing good among the people as a whole. In 1699, Josiah Woodward published an influential tract, *An Account of the Rise and Progress of the Religious Societies in the City of London*, which described the purposes of the societies in considerable detail. It was reprinted at least four times over the next quarter-century and remained popular especially for the sample rules it offered for these small

---

[26] See Eamon Duffy, 'Primitive Christianity Revived: Religious Renewal in Augustan
     England', in Derek Baker (ed.), *Renaissance and Renewal in Christian History* (Oxford:
     Blackwell, 1977), 287–300.
[27] In this paragraph I am following John Walsh, 'Religious Societies: Methodist and
     Evangelical, 1738–1800', in W. J. Shiels and Diana Wood (eds.), *Voluntary Religion*
     (Oxford: Blackwell, 1986), 279–302; and Henry D. Rack, 'Religious Societies and the
     Origins of Methodism', *Journal of Ecclesiastical History* 38 (October 1987): 582–595.

groups. One year after Woodward published this influential report, Samuel Wesley brought out his own enthusiastic pamphlet, *Letters Concerning the Religious Societies*, which pictured them as prime movers for broad-based spiritual renewal. A few Anglican bishops expressed worries that these societies, which were particularly attractive to serious-minded young men, could run off into enthusiasm. But Woodward, Samuel Wesley and other proponents ably defended the societies as a useful supplement to ordinary church functions.

The two most important Anglican special-purpose agencies of this period were extensions of the society idea. The SPCK (Society for Promoting Christian Knowledge, founded 1698) distributed Bibles and Christian literature and also built charity schools in England, Wales and the colonies. The SPG (Society for the Propagation of the Gospel in Foreign Parts, 1701) was designed to take Anglican worship overseas and to evangelize non-Christians within the monarch's domains. Both agencies represented an extension of High Church activism already well developed in the local religious societies. Both provided early evangelicals, especially John and Charles Wesley, with multiplied opportunities for Christian service.

The important debt of evangelicalism to High Church Anglican voluntarism has been often obscured, especially since so many evangelicals railed so forcefully against what they considered the pallid formalism of Anglican religion. Yet this Anglican tradition was always of telling significance, and not only in the confines of the Church of England. As in England, early evangelical leaders in Wales, Scotland and New England organized those who responded to their gospel preaching as voluntary societies within the state churches. It was instinctive to do so, not only because the pietists abroad were showing the way, but because voluntary lay organization had become so widely accepted in recent Anglican history as well.

Confluence

The significance of Puritanism, pietism and High Church Anglicanism for what would become evangelicalism is suggested by unconnected events at Oxford and Herrnhut in the late 1720s. At the former location in late 1728 or early 1729, Charles Wesley, an undergraduate at Christ Church and the youngest son of Samuel and Susannah, was becoming serious about religion at the same time as university officials were issuing official warnings about the dangers of deism.[28] To this loyal Anglican, it came naturally to seek out two

---

[28] Ch. Wesley, *Reader*, 4–6.

other students of like mind – Robert Kirkham and William Morgan – and with them to meet for prayer, spiritual reading, self-examination and good deeds for the less fortunate. The gatherings were casually organized, but also unmistakably cast in the mould of the High Church societies that had flourished over the previous half-century. When Charles's older brother John returned to Oxford the next year, the society's organization was firmed up, it expanded its membership slightly, and scoffers began to deride the group as a 'Holy Club' and its members as 'Bible-Moths', 'Enthusiasts', 'Supererogation-Men' and 'methodists'.[29] In just a few more years, John Wesley would republish Cave's *Primitive Christianity* and Horneck's *Happy Ascetick* for his Methodist itinerants, along with a multitude of works from Puritan and pietist authors.[30]

Much more dramatic were the happenings at Herrnhut in Saxony.[31] By the summer of 1727 over 200 people had accepted Count Zinzendorf's invitation to settle on his estates, some from Moravia and Bohemia, and others from throughout the German-speaking lands. Zinzendorf himself was busy promoting the books of Lutheran pietism, but he was also reading Johannes Amos Comenius (1592–1670), the great teacher of the Hussite Bohemians who had taken refuge at Herrnhut. In the last days of August, Zinzendorf's rag-tag entourage of exiles and emigrants underwent spiritual experiences of pentecostal intensity. They were sparked by the dramatic conversions of four young girls who, after struggling with personal doubt about their own salvation, had then received unusual assurance of God's grace. A first communion for two of the girls became the occasion for a particularly moving time of worship. A few days later, on the night of 29 August, girls and boys in separate meetings engaged in 'heart-rending praying and singing' from 10 pm to 1 o'clock the next morning. In the words of a contemporary Moravian chronicler, 'So powerful a spirit prevailed among the children as is beyond words to describe.'[32] From these experiences the modern Moravian movement was born. Within a matter of weeks, Zinzendorf was organizing the Moravians into small groups (or bands) for their mutual spiritual encouragement, many of the Moravians had begun to record their personal spiritual journeys in diaries and letters, and the whole body was gathering frequently to pose and discuss pressing issues of personal spirituality and corporate direction (all carefully minuted). In short, they were minting the coin of the Methodist economy.

Meanwhile, a few English Dissenters, including Isaac Watts, were exchang-

---

[29] For these names, see Heitzenrater, *Wesley*, 41; and Rack, *Wesley*, 84.

[30] Duffy, 'Primitive Christianity Revived', 299–300.

[31] This account follows Ward, *Awakening*, 126–128.

[32] Ibid., 127.

ing letters with a few New England Congregationalists like Benjamin Colman, who by the time that Cotton Mather died in 1728 had emerged as Boston's leading minister. Lines of Puritan, High Anglican and pietist spiritual influence were beginning to come together.

Stirrings

Unlike the situation on the Continent, where pietism in several varieties was a recognized force by the early eighteenth century, there was not even a semi-organized movement of English-speaking 'gospel' religion until several decades later. But what was going on in Britain and the colonies during the early years of the century was critical for the later history of organized evangelicalism: widely scattered events and circumstances were creating the conditions in which revival might take fire; many English-speaking ministers and lay people were coming to share Johann Arndt's way of reasoning about true Christianity; and a growing number of people who were in position to make a difference were undergoing the life-changing experience of conversion.

In the early decades of the eighteenth century a number of unconnected events outlined what, in retrospect, can be seen as anticipations of evangelical renewal. In 1707 strange happenings were reported from far-away Silesia, a principality nestled between Roman Catholic Poland and Lutheran Saxony, but under the anxious control of the Catholic Holy Roman Emperor, who was also the King of Austria.[33] In that year, Silesia's historic Protestant population was heartened when Sweden's King Charles XII intervened on its behalf. Yet it was difficult to take advantage of the relief won by Charles, since all Protestant churches in Silesia had earlier been closed. In this vortex of conflict, the pietist troops in Sweden's army took to worshipping out of doors in the open air, Silesian children continued such camp meetings by gathering for prayer and singing in fields and forests during the week, adults were soon moved to confess their sins and reform their lives, and a variety of pietist itinerants circulated among the small groups set up to perpetuate this time of religious refreshing. In the years that led up to the flight of the Moravians to Germany, similar events recurred in Silesia and also in neighbouring Teschen, a duchy even more firmly under the control of Catholic Austria. New ways of enacting a new form of revival were breaking upon Protestant consciousness.

At just about the same time in far-distant Wales, an energetic young Anglican minister, Griffith Jones, was embarking on a pastoral career marked

---

[33] Ibid., 70–77.

by other innovations.[34] After a local grammar-school education, Jones was installed in 1716 as the Anglican minister of the parish of Llanddowror in Carmarthenshire, southern Wales. Soon thereafter Jones began regular itinerations outside his own parish, sometimes preaching in churchyards or open fields in order to accommodate the crowds that came to listen. These sermons were rousing events, filled with imprecations against wakes, fairs and other popular dissipations, but also holding out repentance, regeneration and union with Christ to all – high-born or low – who would call upon the name of the Lord. Soon Jones was promoting the distribution of the Welsh Bible and other Christian literature in that language, and he was actively promoting education in basic Welsh literacy for children and adults alike. These latter activities were formalized in 1731 with the establishment of a circulating school movement whereby itinerant teachers moved from parish to parish and, after gaining permission from the local Anglican officials, taught locals to read the Bible, the Anglican Prayer Book and other Christian writings in Welsh. The cumulative effect of these schools was greatly to expand the literacy of the Welsh, but also to prepare the way for revival. Methodism later progressed most rapidly in Wales where the circulating schools were strongest.

In the churches of New England there were other signs of vital piety linked to the Puritan past. Direct preaching for conversion and intense longing to live for God did wax and wane throughout the course of New England's Puritan history. It is a fair judgment that in the early eighteenth century such vital concerns were on a gradually declining course as more New Englanders experienced a degree of material prosperity, more moved away from their original towns and more came to imitate the fashions of the English gentry. Yet intense experience of the gospel and its effects never faded entirely away. Not only did they mark the long ministry of Cotton Mather in Boston; they could be found in the hinterland as well. As Jonathan Edwards later reported, his grandfather and predecessor as minister in Northampton, Massachusetts, Solomon Stoddard, had witnessed several unusual 'harvests' of souls, with the last major in-gathering in 1712 and a smaller recurrence in 1718.[35] Historian Michael Crawford has found records

---

[34] Eifion Evans, *Daniel Rowland and the Great Evangelical Awakening in Wales* (Edinburgh: Banner of Truth, 1985), 31–33; Owain W. Jones, 'The Welsh Church in the Eighteenth Century', in David Walker (ed.), *A History of the Church in Wales* (Penarth: Church in Wales Publications, 1976), 107–109; and *BDEB*, 620–621 (Geraint H. Jenkins, 'Griffith Jones').

[35] Edwards, *A Faithful Narrative of the Surprising Work of God* (1737), in Edwards, *Works*, vol. 4: *The Great Awakening*, ed. C. C. Goen (1972), 146.

of at least fifteen other such New England spiritual harvests, mostly in towns along the Connecticut River, in the two decades between 1712 and 1732.[36]

Only a few years after Stoddard's last harvest, unprecedented religious excitement appeared also among Dutch and English settlers in the lightly populated Raritan River Valley of central New Jersey. From his arrival in this colony in early 1720 as the minister for six tiny Dutch settlements, Theodore Frelinghuysen (1691–c.1747) was preaching a message of conversion, organizing his congregation into small groups for study and prayer, urging them to pray publicly and extemporaneously, reserving communion for those who could make a convincing profession of saving faith, and warning about the danger that politics might divert the church from its proper spiritual tasks.[37] To America, Frelinghuysen was bringing the fruits of East Frisian pietism, which represented a blend of emphases from several renewal movements in western and northern Germany as well as the Netherlands. Not only did Frelinghuysen's labours quicken many among the Dutch Reformed to whom he preached; they also began to inspire a few English-speaking ministers. When in 1727 Gilbert Tennent took up his charge as minister of the Presbyterian Church in New Brunswick, Tennent quickly became convinced that he should model his ministry on what Frelinghuysen was attempting in his churches. Before long Tennent had convinced several other young Presbyterians that Frelinghuysen's kind of piety was exactly what their church also needed.

Far removed from the new world in space but surprisingly close in spirit were the results of another occurrence of long-lasting evangelical significance. The mass expulsion of Protestants from the city and territory of Salzburg, an area long under firm Catholic control, but where Protestants had been tolerated because of their ability to contribute financially to principality and archdiocese, was a sensational event of tremendous international interest.[38] The area's fragile peace was broken in the late 1720s when active pietists itinerated in town and countryside and when lay Protestants organized night meetings for the singing of hymns and exhortations from fervent lay people (including women). In early 1731 the district's miners, with a long Protestant tradition, began actively to evangelize among their nominally Protestant and Catholic neighbours. The result was a sudden crackdown by the local archbishop, who, in November

---

[36] Michael J. Crawford, *Seasons of Grace: Colonial New England's Revival Tradition in its British Context* (New York: Oxford University Press, 1991), 108.

[37] Milton J. Coalter, Jr, *Gilbert Tennent, Son of Thunder: A Case Study of Continental Pietism's Impact on the First Great Awakening in the Middle Colonies* (Westport: Greenwood, 1986), 12–16; and Ward, *Awakening*, 229–230, 244–246.

[38] Ward, *Awakening*, 93–107.

1731, gave the Protestants of his region a mere eight days to pack up and clear out. Over the next weeks, perhaps 25,000 Protestants marched away, with many invited to Prussian lands far to the north, but with some taken in by Holland, England (as a way-station to the new colony of Georgia) and other Protestant countries. The plight of the Salzburgers became an immediate sensation in the popular press of northern Europe. More important for the future of Protestant Christianity in Europe, the refugees and their supporters found tremendous comfort in specifically pietist teachings. Their story seemed to say that although buildings, possessions, security and historic communities might be gone, the transforming effects of personal forgiveness and personal union with Christ could never be taken away. John Wesley, George Whitefield and Jonathan Edwards were only some of the evangelicals to meet and be influenced by refugees from Salzburg. In short, long before organized evangelical movements existed, significant groups in Britain, the colonies and continental Europe were already beginning to practise distinctly evangelical forms of Christian faith.

Also in the early decades of the eighteenth century, the contrast between genuine Christianity and its artificial imitators was becoming an ever more persistent theme in literature read by earnest seekers after righteousness. In 1732 or 1733, George Whitefield, as a young Oxford student who was ardently engaged in a personal search for God, met Charles Wesley. Wesley immediately began to feed books to his new friend. They included a work of the pietist leader, August Hermann Francke, and also Henry Scougal's *The Life of God in the Soul of Man*, the latter a book by a short-lived Scottish Episcopalian (1650–1678), which, despite its author's ecclesiastical allegiance, was much admired by both English Puritans and Scottish Presbyterians. In its pages, Whitefield read that although many people thought of Christianity as 'Orthodox Notions and Opinions' or 'external Duties' or 'rapturous Heats and extatic Devotion', these impressions were all mistaken. Rather, 'True Religion is an Union of the Soul with God, a real Participation of the Divine Nature, the very Image of God drawn upon the Soul, or in the Apostle's Phrase, *It is Christ formed within us*.'[39] Whitefield's comment was that 'though I had fasted, watched and prayed, and received the Sacrament long, yet I never knew what true religion was, till God sent me that excellent treatise by the hands of my never-to-be-forgotten friend'.[40]

A similar critique was found in William Law's *A Serious Call to a Devout and Holy Life* (1728), a work of special importance to John Wesley and several

---

[39]   Henry Scougal, *The Life of God in the Soul of Man* (Boston: G. Rogers & D. Fowle, 1741), 4–6.

[40]   Whitefield, *Journals*, 46–47; and Dallimore, *Whitefield*, 1:72–73.

other leading evangelicals. Law drove home relentlessly the contrast between lives satisfied with 'riches, prosperity, pleasures, indulgences, social position and honor', even when associated with the church, and those who seek 'that religion or devotion which is to govern the ordinary actions of our life'.[41] The same contrast was underscored by Isaac Watts, whose didactic tracts were almost as widely distributed as his hymns. In one of them he wrote, 'True Christianity, where it reigns in the heart, will make itself appear in the purity of life ... The fruits of the Spirit are found in the life and the heart together ... Let us never content ourselves with any exercise of lively devotions unless we feel our corrupt affections in some measure subdued thereby.'[42] Criticism of a merely nominal faith was not overwhelming in pre-revival Britain, but by the early 1730s it was gaining in strength and significance.

Also growing in number were instances of life-changing conversion. At the heart of the more formal evangelical movements that emerged in the 1740s was the experience of conversion, but also anguished turmoil over how to be sure that one was converted as well as intense theological controversy over the respective roles of God and humans in the process. Well before that time, however, many lives had been turned around by the indisputable reality of personal conversions. Although mostly unknown to each other, the converts were undergoing experiences that became paradigmatic for later evangelical-ism – both for what they expected to happen and for how they then preached the grace they themselves had experienced.

In south Wales at, or shortly after, the start of the new century, the teen-aged Griffith Jones was tending sheep when in a dream an angel displayed to him the joys of heaven and the terrors of hell, and then told him of God's commission to rescue souls through his preaching.[43] Not too many years later, in 1717, Gilbert Tennent, still a young man in Ulster at about the same stage of life as Jones when he experienced his dreams, began to undergo what he called 'law work', an increasingly strong sense of condemnation because of moral failings measured against the standard of God's law. For Tennent, this

---

[41] William Law, *A Serious Call to a Devout and Holy Life* (1728), quoted here from David Lyle Jeffrey (ed.), *A Burning and a Shining Light: English Spirituality in the Age of Wesley* (Grand Rapids: Eerdmans, 1987), 146, 143. For the effect of Law on Wesley, see Heitzenrater, *Wesley*, 43.

[42] Isaac Watts, *Abuses of the Emotions in Spiritual Life* (1746), quoted here from Jeffrey, *Burning and Shining Light*, 76.

[43] For this account but also questions about its authenticity, see A. Skevington Wood, *The Inextinguishable Blaze: Spiritual Renewal and Advance in the 18th Century* (Grand Rapids: Eerdmans, 1960), 41; and *BDEB*, 620.

crisis of conscience lasted for a number of years, until in 1723 a breakthrough occurred and he was given a sense of God's graciousness to him in Jesus Christ. By this time, Tennent had migrated with his family to America and had been the beneficiary of counsel from his father William, a Church of Ireland minister in the old world who became a Presbyterian when he arrived in the new and soon began to conduct a classical grammar school alongside his church.[44] This personal experience of conversion was the background for the younger Tennent's earnest interest in the work of the pietist Frelinghuysen.

It was during the extended period of Gilbert Tennent's conversion in 1721 that a young New Englander, again about the same age, found himself undergoing an equally momentous change of heart. Jonathan Edwards, who had already been studying theology but who was greatly troubled by the doctrine of God's complete sovereignty, experienced 'that sort of inward, sweet delight in God and divine things that I have lived much in since'. The occasion for this experience was Edwards' reading of 1 Timothy 1:17 ('Now unto the King eternal, immortal, invisible, the only wise God, be honour and glory for ever and ever. Amen'). Thereafter, Edwards 'began to have a new kind of apprehensions and ideas of Christ, and the work of redemption, and the glorious way of salvation by him'.[45]

The number of individuals undergoing such spiritual transformations continued to increase. In 1733 at St Gennys, Cornwall, the thirty-five-year-old Anglican rector, George Thomson, was converted through a dream of his own death and judgment and by reading Paul's message in Romans 3:24 of 'being justified freely by his grace through the redemption that is in Christ Jesus'.[46] Shortly thereafter in Lincolnshire, Thomas Adam (1701–1784) was jolted from formal faith towards evangelical convictions by reading William Law's mystical works.[47]

The pattern was becoming widespread. Clearly something was going on. More and more individuals were being deeply affected by the gospel. Soon more and more connections were linking such people with each other. Soon more and more instances occurred where large numbers of people became serious about their need for God. Next came revival.

---

[44] Coalter, *Gilbert Tennent*, 9.

[45] Edwards, 'Personal Narrative' (c.1740), in Edwards, *Works*, vol. 16: *Letters and Personal Writings*, George S. Claghorn (ed.) (1998), 792–793.

[46] Bebbington, *Evangelicalism*, 30.

[47] *BDEB*, 4 (Peter Lineham, 'Thomas Adam').

3. REVIVAL, 1734–1738

Evangelicalism always involved more than the revival of religion but, from the beginning, both revivals and the longing for revival were always central. The kind of religious quickening that proliferated from the mid-1730s was not altogether new, but in frequency, for its publicity and as a replacement for discarded aspects of traditional religion, the evangelical revivals were unusual. They never, however, charted a simple course.

Late 1734 to early 1735[1]

The first in a series of local events that, as their effects rippled outwards, transformed discrete, widely separated phenomena into an interconnected

---

[1] In this chronology, I use conventions of the modern calendar and so begin the year with January 1. The works of most use for constructing the chronicle were *BDEB*; Richard Bennett, *The Early Life of Howell Harris* (1909 in Welsh), trans. G. M. Roberts (London: Banner of Truth, 1962); Milton J. Coalter, Jr, *Gilbert Tennent, Son of Thunder* (Westport: Greenwood, 1986); Dallimore, *Whitefield*; Edwards, *Works*, vol. 4: *The Great Awakening*, C. C. Goen (ed.) (1972); Eifion Evans, *Daniel Rowland and the Great Evangelical Awakening in Wales* (Edinburgh: Banner of Truth, 1985); Heitzenrater, *Wesley*; Derec Llwyd Morgan, *The Great Awakening in Wales*, trans. Dyfnallt Morgan (London: Epworth, 1988); Colin Podmore, *The Moravian Church in England, 1728–1760* (Oxford:

evangelical movement, took place at Northampton, Massachusetts, in late autumn 1734.[2] The event itself cannot be separated from what had been happening in this community over the immediately preceding months: a cyclical return of Puritan seriousness among the laity, special interest by the town's youth in religion, the untimely deaths of two well-regarded young adults, unusual concern for religion in the nearby settlement of Pascommuck and the earnest labours of Northampton's thirty-one-year-old pastor, Jonathan Edwards. Over the course of 1734, Edwards, who had succeeded his grandfather Solomon Stoddard as pastor of the town church only five years before, became convinced that dangerous theological notions were infecting ministers and lay people in the Connecticut River Valley. To counter what he considered the Arminian tendency to rely on self and natural abilities for obtaining salvation before God, Edwards in November preached a two-sermon series on the theme, 'Justification by Faith Alone'. Its doctrine was unequivocal: 'We are justified only by faith in Christ, and not by any manner of virtue or goodness of our own.'[3]

The response, evident by the end of December and growing stronger into the new year, was electric. As Edwards put it in his own first report,

> All seemed to be seized with a deep concern about their eternal salvation; all the talk in all companies, and upon occasions was upon the things of religion, and no other talk was anywhere relished; and scarcely a single person in the whole town was left unconcerned about the great things of the eternal world ... Those that were most disposed to contemn vital and experimental religion, and those that had the greatest conceit of their own reason, the highest families in the town, and the oldest persons in the town, and many little children were affected remarkably; no one family that I know of, and scarcely a person, has been exempt.[4]

Clarendon, 1998); Tyerman, *Whitefield*; Ch. Wesley, *Reader*; Wesley, *Works* (new), vols. 18 and 19: *Journals and Diaries I (1735–1738)* and *II (1738–1743)*, ed. W. Reginald Ward and Richard P. Heitzenrater (1988, 1990); and Whitefield, *Journal*.

2   Essential for these events are Edwards' preliminary account and then the *Faithful Narrative* (1737), in Edwards, *Works*, 4:99–110, 130–211; plus C. C. Goen's masterly annotations in that volume. I have also benefited from George Marsden, *Jonathan Edwards: A Life* (New Haven: Yale University Press, 2003), ch. 9.

3   Edwards, 'Justification by Faith Alone' (1738), in Edwards, *Works*, vol. 19: *Sermons and Discourses, 1734–1738*, ed. M. X. Lesser (2001), 149.

4   Edwards, 'Unpublished Letter of May 30, 1735', in Edwards, *Works*, 4:101.

As part of his effort to fan this spiritual blaze, Edwards followed pietist and High Church Anglican precedents by organizing small groups, divided by age and gender, to meet in private homes for the encouragement of godliness.

By March 1735 other towns in Hampshire County were experiencing the same communal turn to heartfelt, all-consuming faith. News circulated rapidly about the dozens, and then hundreds, who were 'brought to a lively sense of the excellency of Jesus Christ and his sufficiency and willingness to save sinners, and to be much weaned in their affections from the world'.[5] In the towns touched by the revival, unusual concord prevailed, young people gathered to talk about Christ, Scripture was exalted, preaching was attended to with remarkable diligence and people received vivid images of Jesus offering his blood for their sins. In all, about twenty-five communities throughout western Massachusetts and central Connecticut experienced in some measure what Edwards witnessed personally in Northampton. Revival intensity, which began to decline in the spring of 1735, recalled earlier Puritan awakenings. But this 'stir' was more widely spread, more intense, more out of the control of the ministers.

As significant as this revival was for believers in the Connecticut River Valley, it would have remained an isolated occurrence of only local interest, if Benjamin Colman, the respected minister of Boston's Brattle Congregational Church, had not caught wind of events and asked Jonathan Edwards for a report. Edwards' relatively short response, dated 30 May, 1735, became as much a precipitate of the transatlantic evangelical revival as the events in Northampton themselves.

It is important to note, however, that much else was occurring in the English-speaking world in the six months between the first dramatic scenes in Northampton and Edwards' drafting of a report to Colman. On 17 December 1734, August Gottlieb Spangenberg (1704–1792) had arrived in London in order to ask trustees of the new colony of Georgia (established only two years before) if he and a group of his fellow-Moravians could emigrate from Herrnhut to that new settlement in the southern North American mainland. Although there had been little contact between Zinzendorf's Herrnhut and anyone in England for several years, the Moravians knew that the Georgia trustees had offered refuge to exiled Salzburgers and that they actively supported the work of the Anglican SPCK, which itself had offered earlier encouragement to the Moravians and other German pietists.[6] A month

---

[5] Ibid., 104.

[6] On the extensive connections between the German pietists and the SPCK, see Daniel L. Brunner, *Halle Pietists in England: Anthony William Boehm and the Society for Promoting Christian Knowledge* (Göttingen: Vandenhoeck & Ruprecht, 1993).

later, on 23 January 1735, Spangenberg and the first party of Moravians sailed for the new world.

In the spring of 1735 other young men, who at the time meant nothing to the larger world, were also undergoing life-changing experiences. At Oxford a long period of intense spiritual struggle was coming to an end for George Whitefield: 'About this time God was pleased to enlighten my soul, and bring me into the knowledge of His free grace, and the necessity of being justified in His sight by *faith only*.'[7] This illumination, which Whitefield thereafter recognized as his conversion, took place about seven weeks after Easter.

The day when Whitefield reached this spiritual destination may also have been the very day that a similar journey was concluding in the little hamlet of Trevecca (or Trevecka), Breconshire, Wales. Howell Harris, at twenty-one years of age, less than a year older than Whitefield, was a schoolteacher who had been intermittently interested in spiritual matters. Shortly after Easter, Harris took the recommendation of a parish minister and started to read an older devotional work, *The Whole Duty of Man*, by Richard Allestree (1619–1681), an Anglican who had remained loyal to Charles I during the Puritan civil wars. From this reading Harris was led to a period of fasting, self-examination, wrestling against sin and religious despair. At last on the seventh Sunday after Easter, 25 May, during a communion service, Harris received the assurance that God had indeed looked upon him kindly with his grace.

Five days later, on Friday 30 May, Jonathan Edwards finished his letter to Benjamin Colman about Northampton's revival. But before he could send it off to Boston, Edwards' uncle, Joseph Hawley, who had suffered from an extended bout of spiritual melancholy, cut his own throat. That grisly suicide dampened revival enthusiasm in Northampton and would one day provide a cautionary lesson to both Howell Harris and George Whitefield as they too sought the experiences that Edwards described in his letter to Colman.

Mid- to late 1735

Edwards' report reached Benjamin Colman in early June 1735. The latter was so impressed he copied out some of what Edwards had written as an addendum to a letter he was just then posting to John Guyse (1680–1761), a leading Independent minister in London and vigorous opponent of Arminian and Arian teachings. When Guyse received this letter from Colman, he immediately shared Edwards' account with his friend and colleague Isaac Watts and also passed it on

---

[7] Whitefield, *Journals*, 62.

to his congregation in New Broad Street. Guyse's parishioners were so taken by what they heard about events in faraway Massachusetts that they asked their minister if his sermon could be printed. Guyse wrote back to Colman for permission to include details about Northampton, Colman communicated this request to Edwards, Edwards told his Northampton congregation of the request (while exhorting them to hew diligently to the path of righteousness), and (though delayed by illness and other duties) began to prepare a longer account.[8]

While Edwards was still at work on the document that, more than any other single published statement, would define the standard expectations for evangelical conversion and evangelical revival, much else was taking place. Without yet knowing about events in Northampton, others were experiencing in their circumstances something like what Edwards had lived through in his.

In June or July 1735 another young man, twenty-four-year-old Daniel Rowland, an ordained clergyman of the Anglican Church in Wales, but until this time not a serious believer, was converted. His guide to a more active and personal faith was Griffith Jones of Llanddowror. Almost immediately Daniel Rowland's preaching was transformed, and with astonishing effect. To his church in Llangeitho streamed hundreds, and soon thousands, to hear a man in the grip of a spell-binding message, delivered in fluent, impassioned Welsh. Rowland's first sermons after his conversion featured the demands of God's law, but then after about two years he began as well to champion with equal force the mercies of God's grace. The impact of Rowland's preaching was memorialized after his death in a widely circulated poem:

> His name was Boanerges,
> Son of thunder, flaming, true;
> Shaking heaven and earth together
> With a voice both strong and new ...
> These were days like Sinai's glory,
> Sound of trumpet, sight of smoke,
> Storm and lightning, fire and tempest,
> Voice of God that terror spoke ...
> Then he sang with Gospel charm;
> He proclaimed divine salvation,
> Full, complete, sufficient, free,
> Through the death of the Messiah
> Once for ever on the Tree.[9]

---

[8] These details are from Goen's introduction and annotations in Edwards, *Works*, vol. 4.
[9] William Williams, elegy for Daniel Rowland, in Evans, *Daniel Rowland*, 41, 43–44.

Before long Rowland was travelling to preach in other churches. Soon he became the spark of heightened religious interest in a five-county area of central Wales: Cardiganshire, Glamorganshire, Breconshire, Montgomery-shire and Carmarthenshire.

Meanwhile, in the autumn of 1735, George Whitefield, fresh from his evangelical breakthrough at Oxford, was organizing two small societies in his native Gloucester in the west of England, one for men and one for women, with whom he met for prayer and mutual exhortation. John Wesley and Charles Wesley, still pursuing with great diligence the disciplines of their Holy Club, were much preoccupied with the future: should they seek vocations as parish ministers (Samuel Wesley had repeatedly urged John to come to Epworth as his assistant) or carry on as free-floating cleric-scholars (John's fellowship from Lincoln College, which required few official duties, allowed him great freedom to follow his own inclinations, and Charles too had good prospects for a fellowship)? Meanwhile, a second party of Moravians arrived in London and were making preparations to join Spangenberg and their fellows in Georgia. In Wales, Howell Harris began to travel from house to house, often exhorting out of doors, as he urged families to repent of sin and seek God's grace in Jesus Christ. And at Yale College in New Haven, Connecticut, a number of students and recent graduates, including Aaron Burr, who would become a leading Presbyterian minister and a president of Princeton College in New Jersey, were also undergoing decisive personal experiences. In Burr's own account,

> I was brought to the footstool of sovereign grace; saw myself polluted by nature and practice; had affecting views of the Divine wrath I deserved; was made to despair of help in myself, and almost concluded that my day of grace was past … It pleased God, at length, to reveal his Son to me in the Gospel, an all-sufficient and willing Saviour, and I hope inclined me to receive Him on the terms of the Gospel.[10]

In New Jersey Gilbert Tennent was trying to move the Presbyterian churches to more active promotion of the type of godliness he had learned from Theodore Frelinghuysen. Already in the spring of 1734 he had dispatched two overtures to the Synod of Philadelphia in support of efforts to have ministers 'make it their awful, constant, and diligent care, to approve themselves to God, to their own consciences, and to their hearers, [as] serious faithful stewards of the mysteries of God, and of holy exemplary conver-

---

[10] William B. Sprague, *Annals of the American Pulpit*, vol. 3: *Presbyterians* (New York: Robert Carter, 1863), 68.

sions'.[11] Now in 1735 he published his first work, *A Solemn Warning To the Secure World, From the God of Terrible Majesty, Or, the Presumptuous Sinner Detected*. In the style of Puritan 'law work', Tennent urged the preaching of 'terrors' as a way to awaken sinners from complacent trust in themselves so that they could experience the proper 'comforts' of the gospel.

Late 1735 to 1737: Georgia

In late 1735 a decisive conjunction took place between the High Anglican and the Moravian streams that were flowing towards evangelical revival. When in July an official of the SPCK urged John Wesley to accept a call to Georgia in order to serve the English settlers and preach to Native Americans, John speedily canvassed his friends and abruptly decided to go. Charles did not want to accompany him, but John – not for the last time – overrode his brother's objections. To prepare for the journey, Charles rushed through ordination (as deacon, 21 September; as priest, 29 September). The Wesleys then scrambled to make up a party of fellow-workers, but in the end could convince only two others to join them: Charles Delamotte and Benjamin Ingham. The decision by Delamotte (1714–1786) to go with the Wesleys moved his father, a wealthy sugar merchant, to disinherit his son, but it also led Delamotte to the relationships – with the Wesleys, with the Moravians, with Whitefield – that would guide the rest of his life. For Ingham (1712–1772), who had joined the Wesleys' Oxford Holy Club in 1733, the trip to Georgia introduced him to the Moravians, and that introduction was decisive for his later career as a leading itinerant in Yorkshire.

For John Wesley, as he prepared to make the dangerous voyage and begin his poorly defined tasks in a completely foreign environment, there was only continued struggle. On the very eve of departure, he wrote to John Burton, a distinguished scholar and the Georgia trustee who had introduced him to Governor James Oglethorpe, that his 'chief motive' in leaving Britain 'is the hope of saving my own soul'. Wesley pictured the Indians to whom he hoped to minister in idealistic terms, beset by neither 'vain philosophy' nor 'luxurious, sensual, covetous, ambitious' partisanship. From preaching to such primitives he hoped 'to learn the purity of that faith which was once delivered to the saints'. Georgia would be for Wesley a place where he could live simply on 'water and the fruits of the earth', where 'purity of thought' would come from 'see[ing] no woman but those which are almost of a different species from

---

[11] Coalter, *Gilbert Tennent*, 41.

me', and where 'the pride of life' would be extinguished 'in the wilds of America'. As for doing good to others, he hoped that 'if I be once fully converted myself', God would use him to magnify his name.[12] In his new assignment, John Wesley was determined to work very hard indeed to prepare his soul for God. He, Delamotte and Ingham would serve as volunteer missionaries for the SPCK, while Charles was assigned to act as the secretary for Governor Oglethorpe, a military man with extensive service on the Continent and a history of supporting the projects of the SPCK.

When the young and idealistic Oxford graduates took ship in October, they found they were going to be travelling to the new world with the Moravians. The importance of this meeting cannot be over-emphasized. During their sojourn in the colonies, the English clerics would experience a lifetime's worth of incident, but although the effects were obscure at the time, it was connections with the Moravians that mattered most.

Charles Wesley, with much ambiguity surrounding his status as both an Anglican clergyman and the governor's secretary, lasted only a few months. In Georgia, this well-bred, well-educated, earnest High Churchman was completely out of his element. His experiences, including one Sunday (21 March 1736) when his sermon was disrupted by gunshots and an irate matron threatened to blow him up as a religious hypocrite, were mostly discouraging.[13] In late July 1736 he resigned his position and by early August was headed back to England.

John stuck it out longer. He preached with ardour to Indians and British settlers, but with little success. He quarrelled with Dissenters, to whom he would not distribute the Lord's Supper, and also with the colony's magistrates. He also became involved in a badly botched affair of the heart that left him alienated from his would-be intended and sued by the man she had chosen instead of Wesley. Together with Charles, John did publish their first hymnal and also with Charles took very serious notice of the degradation that African slaves endured. In both the promotion of new hymnody and outreach to slaves, the Wesleys were anticipating very important aspects of later Methodist history. But in general, John Wesley's spiritual harvest in Georgia was meagre. As he put it in often quoted words from his journal, 'I left my native country in order to teach the Georgian Indians the nature of Christianity. But what have I learned myself in the meantime? Why ... that I who went to America to convert others was never myself converted to God.'[14]

---

12 Wesley to John Burton, 10 October, 1735, in Wesley, *Letters*, 1:188–190.
13 Ch. Wesley, *Reader*, 68.
14 Wesley, 1 February 1738; in Wesley, *Works* (new), vol. 18: *Journals and Diaries I (1735–1738)*, W. Reginald Ward and Richard P. Heitzenrater (eds.) (1988), 214.

Despite the failure of their mission, the Georgia sojourn was none the less life-transforming.[15] The new-world experience of the Wesleys' colleague Benjamin Ingham suggests why that could be the case, since through his contact with Spangenberg and the other Moravians, Ingham found rest for his troubled soul, an assurance of faith and joy in reconciliation with God.[16]

The influence of the twenty-six Moravians with whom the Wesley party sailed to the new world had become important during the outward voyage. On that trip to America, one of the Moravians taught John Wesley German, Wesley participated eagerly in the Moravians' daily worship services, and, most importantly, he marvelled at their spiritual peace under fire. When violent storms on several occasions almost destroyed their ship, the English passengers cried out in terror and John Wesley himself quailed at the near prospect of death, but the Moravians only sang psalms and waited calmly for the storms to pass.

The Moravians with whom the Wesleys travelled to Georgia differed from the pietists of Halle in a few important details, especially in their conception of salvation. These Moravians, with definite views on the question of Christian assurance, held that it was an ordinary part of ordinary Christian experience to enjoy a firm knowledge of one's acceptance before God. In addition, more than the Halle pietists, they also stressed that conversion could be relatively quick, and that it required neither a protracted season of despair over sin nor extensive exertions in ascetic practice or liturgical duty. In fact, the Moravians sometimes spoke as if care taken in doing godly works, as well as fastidiousness about observing the sacraments, was beside the point for those who were seeking peace with God. (John Wesley would later break with the Moravians over precisely these points.) What most disconcerted Wesley, however, was his direct discussions with Spangenberg, including this brief exchange on 7 February 1736, one day after setting foot on land:

> [Spangenberg] said, 'My brother, I must first ask you one or two questions. Have you the witness within yourself? Does the Spirit of God bear witness with your spirit that you are a child of God?' I was surprised, and knew not what to answer. He observed it, and asked, 'Do you know Jesus Christ?' I paused, and said, 'I know he is the Saviour of the world.' 'True', he replied, 'but do you know he has saved you?' I

---

[15] For assessments of what John Wesley chose to present in his journal and how he presented it, see Heitzenrater, *Wesley*, 58–74; and Rack, *Wesley*, 111–136.

[16] *BDEB*, 590 (E. Alan Rose, 'Benjamin Ingham').

answered, 'I hope he has died to save me.' He only added, 'Do you know yourself?' I said, 'I do.' But I fear they were vain words.[17]

This exchange was only one of many with the Moravians that had the effect of further confusing Wesley's understanding of salvation. Under their teaching he was moving from a straightforward High Church concentration on moral duties as responses to divine revelation towards an experiential reliance on divine grace as both God's free gift and God's enablement for service. In theological terms, he was beginning to get over the extreme fear of antinomianism (thought to spring from too much emphasis on grace) and of enthusiasm (thought to arise from too much interest in God's direct dealing with individuals) that he had inherited as a respectable Anglican of his age. John Wesley would never be in danger of forsaking the energetic path of duty, but from the Moravians he was learning something about the traditional Lutheran understanding of divine mercy and the newer pietist emphasis on the palpable experience of God.

Wesley's Georgia instruction from the Moravians was also intensely practical. Although he worried that Spangenberg and other Moravian leaders exercised religious authority without being properly ordained, he none the less joined eagerly in their society and band meetings, shared their love-feasts and sang with them the hymns they had written about the experiences of grace. When John Wesley left Georgia in December 1737, he seemed worse off than when he had arrived: crossed in love, still anguished in spirit, a failure in his first attempt at a vocation. But his ongoing High Church seriousness was still a rich spiritual soil, and into that soil had now been planted a quickening Moravian seed.

1736–1737: England, Wales, New England

During early 1736, while Jonathan Edwards was preparing his extended account of the Northampton awakening, and the Wesleys were struggling to establish a foothold for ministry in Georgia, evangelical renewal continued apace in other locales. When Howell Harris extended his itinerations as lay exhorter, he began to receive favourable notice from a few Welsh Dissenters, especially Baptists. In May he travelled to Llanddowror for a visit with Griffith Jones, who promptly took the young enthusiast under his wing. Shortly thereafter Harris began to set up small group meetings. The first one, at Trevecca,

---

[17] Wesley, 7 February 1736; in Wesley, *Works* (new), 18: 146.

was in place by September 1736, and within three years thirty more societies were in operation. In December Harris was also reading A. H. Francke's account of how the Halle pietists had set up almshouses and other institutions to assist the poor.

On 20 June 1736, George Whitefield was ordained deacon by the Bishop of Gloucester, Martin Benson, who was measurably less hostile to fervent piety than many of his fellow-bishops. The next Sunday, 27 June, Whitefield preached his first sermon, which Whitefield himself reported was well received – a result, he surmised, from his experience while an Oxford under-graduate in preaching to prisoners and exhorting his friends in the Holy Club. In Whitefield's characteristic mixture of ego and diffidence, he reported, 'I trust I was enabled to speak with some degree of Gospel authority. Some few mocked, but most for the present seemed struck, and I have since heard that a complaint has been made to the bishop that I drove fifteen mad the first sermon.'[18]

Six weeks later, on 8 August, Whitefield journeyed to London for his first sermon in the metropolis, where he continued for two months in a series of temporary assignments. Still later in the year he took a stint of preaching for a friend at a rural parish in Hampshire. From the beginning, Whitefield drew large crowds and attentive listeners. Yet like so many others in his circle he was at sea about permanent prospects. When, therefore, letters began to arrive from the Wesleys in Georgia about the need for workers in that remote corner of the empire, Whitefield was interested. Towards the end of 1736 he received an especially urgent letter from John Wesley, who described a situation where 'the harvest is great, and the labourers so few', and then enquired directly, 'What if thou art the man, Mr. Whitefield', to supply this need?'[19] In December Whitefield resolved to answer Wesley's summons and go to Georgia.

Shortly before Whitefield made that decision, Jonathan Edwards finished the full account of the earlier Northampton revivals and dispatched his manu-script to Benjamin Colman. Colman immediately extracted from it an eighteen-page abridgment, which he appended to two sermons, just then going to the printer, from Edwards' uncle William Williams of Hatfield, Massachusetts, which this veteran pastor had preached around the time of the 1734–1735 awakening. As soon as this work was published, Colman sent a copy to Isaac Watts, who wrote back by return packet in February 1737 (and then again in April) requesting Edwards' full manuscript so that he could publish it in

---

[18] Dallimore, *Whitefield*, 1:97.
[19] Whitefield, *Journals*, 79.

London. As this transatlantic exchange was beginning in December 1736, the dejected and defeated Charles Wesley arrived back in London. Less than a month later, in January 1737, Count Zinzendorf also showed up in that city; within days he was talking to Isaac Watts, Charles Wesley and several more about his own vision for the missionary work of the Moravians.

Charles Wesley was also personally at hand to encourage George Whitefield in his decision to go to America. But before arrangements with Governor Oglethorpe could be finalized and suitable passage secured, a full year passed. During that year Whitefield, the novice young preacher of justification by faith, was transformed into a national sensation. Early in 1737 he preached in the western cities of Bath and Bristol and also in rural Gloucestershire and in London. Beginning in August and continuing through to December he was mostly in London, where unprecedented throngs flocked to hear his sermons.

In London, Whitefield's assignments were varied: 'I was invited to preach at Cripplegate, St. Ann's, and Forster Lane churches ... I also preached at Wapping Chapel, the tower, Ludgate, Newgate, and many of the churches where weekly lectures were kept up.' The pace was frenetic: 'On a Lord's Day, I used to preach four times to very large and very affected auditories, besides reading prayers twice or thrice, and walking, perhaps, twelve miles in going backwards and forwards from one church to the other.'[20] The first of what would rapidly become a flood of newspaper reports broke from the London press in September.

Whitefield's preaching was borne aloft by his spiritual intensity. Once Benjamin Ingham had returned from Georgia in early 1737, for example, Whitefield sought him out to discover how and why Ingham had so 'remarkably grown in grace'. Together, the two talked of Georgia, but even more of God's mercy in Christ: 'At midnight, we would rise to sing praise to God, and to intercede for the whole state of Christ's militant Church here on earth.'[21] Whitefield often met for prayer and singing with other friends as well, at least once carrying these activities through an entire night. The crowds that came to hear such a fervent witness were immense. After Charles Wesley heard him preach on 5 November 1737, he reported that it had not been 'with the persuasive words of man's wisdom, but with the demonstration of the Spirit, and with power. The churches will not contain the multitudes that throng to hear him.'[22]

---

[20] Ibid., 87.

[21] Ibid., 85–86.

[22] Tyerman, *Whitefield*, 1:89.

Whitefield's preaching drew attention in part because of his straightforward message.[23] In 1737 he published one of his earliest signature sermons,
On the Nature and Necessity of Our Regeneration or New Birth in Christ Jesus, which
rapidly went into multiple printings. Its text was 2 Corinthians 5:17 ('If any
man be in Christ, he is a new creature'); it drove home the distinction, rooted
in Puritanism and burnished by the pietists, between nominal and real religion.
To be in Christ was not 'a bare outward Profession, or being called after his
Name'. It was rather 'an inward Change and Purity of Heart, and
Cohabitation of his Holy Spirit'. It was 'to be mystically united to him by a
true and lively Faith, and thereby to receive spiritual virtue from him, as the
Members of the natural Body do from the Head, or the Branches from the
Vine'.[24]

Whitefield's great effect arose from what he proclaimed about the need for
the new birth, but even more from how he proclaimed it – urgently, immediately and as the great question for every hearer *right now*. To Whitefield, formal
doctrine was mostly irrelevant, but not the lived experience of God's grace in
Christ. He preached about these matters like no-one Londoners had ever
heard before. In the pulpit he simply exuded energy; his speech was to the
highest degree dramatic; he offered breathtaking impersonations of biblical
characters and needy sinners; he fired his listeners' imagination; he wept pro-
fusely, often, and with stunning effect. When he was announced as the
preacher, churches were jammed, with some, to be sure, who came to scoff,
but mostly with open-minded enquirers drawn from all classes who knew
great entertainment when they saw it and who were touched by this young
man's message of grace. From August 1737 until he finally departed on 30
December, Whitefield preached over one hundred times (six to seven times
per week), and he had become London's best-known celebrity. Two weeks
before taking ship he observed his twenty-third birthday.

For evangelical religion, the fame of Whitefield's preaching was not,
however, the only noteworthy development in 1737. In New Jersey, Gilbert
Tennent preached in the spring at Maidenhead, but without approval of the
local Presbyterian minister. This offence against old-world propriety provoked
overtures of protest to the Philadelphia Synod. In turn, those protests drew
several other young gospel-preachers into closer fellowship with Tennent.

---

[23]   In the next paragraphs, I am following Harry S. Stout, *The Divine Dramatist: George
       Whitefield and the Rise of Modern Evangelicalism* (Grand Rapids: Eerdmans, 1991), ch. 3,
       'London Boy Preacher', 30–48.

[24]   Whitefield, *A Sermon on Regeneration, Preached to a Numerous Audience in England* (2nd ed.,
       Boston: T. Fleet, 1739), 7–8.

Also in 1737, Howell Harris embraced the doctrine of predestination, which he had previously derided. He also met Daniel Rowland, with whom immediate rapport was established, and he extended his itinerations into ever wider circles. Early in the year his exhorting led to the conversion of Howell Davies (1716–1770), a young schoolmaster who would later enter the Anglican ministry as a curate for Griffith Jones and then become the spark for Calvinistic Methodism in Pembrokeshire at the far western reach of Wales. Late in the year, or perhaps early in 1738, William Williams (1717–1791) was also drawn to Christ by Harris's preaching. Later to be known as Pantycelyn for the Welsh town in which he settled, Williams worked first as Daniel Rowland's curate and then as an itinerant, but his greatest influence came through writings of memorable power, including tracts, poems and hymns (in Welsh and English). In central Wales Daniel Rowland's preaching was expanding its impact; by the end of 1737 crowds of 1,500 to 2,000 were regularly gathering for his sermons, and he was setting up lay-led local societies in Llangeitho and surrounding villages.

Even as more and more Welshmen and women were being touched by Harris, Jones, Davies and Rowland, the progress of evangelical religion also continued in England. John Cennick (1718–1755) of Reading in Berkshire, for example, received an assurance of grace on 6 September 1737. Cennick had been raised in a religiously observant home and had made intense efforts at 'crucifying the flesh', but he was not able to rest in God until at a service in Reading he heard an exposition of Psalm 34:19 and 22: 'Many are the afflictions of the righteous: but the Lord delivereth him out of them all ... The Lord redeemeth the soul of his servants: and none of them that trust in him shall be desolate.'[25] Only after this experience did Cennick, who later brought evangelical preaching to Ireland as a Moravian missionary, make contact with Whitefield, the Wesleys and Howell Harris.

The British event of 1737 that rivalled in importance the emergence of Whitefield was the publication of Jonathan Edwards' *A Faithful Narrative of the Surprizing Work of God in the Conversion of Many Hundred Souls in Northampton, and the Neighbouring Towns and Villages of New-Hampshire* [sic] *in New-England*. Edwards' full account of the earlier Northampton revival, now more than two years past, finally appeared from a London printer in October 1737. Editing by Isaac Watts and John Guyse actually garbled a little of the story (they placed Edwards, for example, in New Hampshire instead of Massachusetts),

---

[25] *BDEB*, 210 (Peter J. Lineham, 'John Cennick'); on Cennick, I am indebted also to Ian Peters for his paper from December 2001 and its information on the circumstances of Cennick's conversion.

but editorial changes were few, and readers first in England and then in Wales and Scotland were soon transfixed by Edwards' report. Philip Doddridge read the *Faithful Narrative* the very week it came out. An Edinburgh edition appeared before the end of the year, and then another soon after. Within fourteen months of its London publication, the *Faithful Narrative* was reprinted in that city, it appeared in a German translation from Magdeburg, Prussia, and Boston's printers rushed three separate editions to New England readers.

The *Faithful Narrative*, like Edwards' edition of David Brainerd's diary, which he prepared for the press in 1749, has never gone out of print. Thus, Edwards' account of the Northampton revival, as well as his account of Brainerd's journey of faith – which Edwards presented as a model spiritual life for all converts – exerted a much broader influence than the sermons Edwards had preached during the revival itself. Five of these sermons were published in 1738 as *Discourses on Various Important Subjects, Nearly Concerning the Great Affair of the Soul's Eternal Salvation ... Delivered at Northampton, Chiefly at the Time of the Late Wonderful Pouring Out of the Spirit of God There*. But this book was never republished as such. It was Edwards' narrative of revival, more than the theology he himself presented as its foundation, that most fired the evangelical imagination.

The *Faithful Narrative* became an instant classic. It was the exemplary exposition of revival, the paradigmatic evangelical event. For impact, it was critically important that the book was published in London, the Mecca of religious intelligence, and that it was vouchsafed by the respected ministers, Watts and Guyse, who were living links to the pious Calvinism of previous generations. With that sanction from that location, Edwards' exposition of the preparation, onset, maintenance, regulation, dangers and effects of revival became normative for many in his generation and even more in the generations that followed. Of first importance was Edwards' stark depiction of the damning reality of human sinfulness ('commonly the first thing that appears ... is a conviction of the justice of God in their condemnation, in a sense of their own exceeding sinfulness and the vileness of all their performances') and his equally powerful account of the palpable reality of divine salvation ('there is wrought in them a holy repose of soul in God through Christ, and a secret disposition to fear and love him, and to hope for blessing from him'). Of nearly equal effect was Edwards' description of the changes wrought upon converts by the Spirit of God:

> It was very wonderful to see after what manner persons' affections were sometimes moved and wrought upon, when God did as it were suddenly open their eyes and let into their minds a sense of the greatness of his grace, and fullness of Christ, and his

readiness to save, who before were broken with apprehensions of divine wrath and sunk into an abyss under a sense of guilt, which they were ready to think was beyond the mercy of God. Their joyful surprise has caused their hearts as it were to leap, so that they have been ready to break forth into laughter, tears often at the same time issuing like a flood and intermingling a loud weeping; and sometimes they han't been able to forbear crying out with a loud voice, expressing their great admiration. In some even the view of the glory of God's sovereignty in the exercises of his grace has surprised the soul with such sweetness, as to produce the same effects.[26]

Similarly, the two conversion stories that Edwards related in full – of a young woman and a four-year-old girl – rapidly became templates for the way many others would picture the normative spiritual journey: from sinful self-despair, through a conversion focused on the excellency of Christ in shedding his blood for the penitent's sin, to a joyful response in God joined with a steady purpose to do good. In sum, Edwards' *Faithful Narrative* was more than the record of a work of God. It was an authoritative description of how, in the words of Watts' and Guyse's introduction, 'our ascended Saviour now and then takes a special occasion to manifest the divinity of this Gospel by a plentiful effusion of his Spirit where it is preached: then sinners are turned into saints in numbers, and there is a new face of things spread over a town or a country'.[27]

By the end of 1737, not only was evangelical renewal visible in several widely scattered locations, but connections were multiplying among early evangelical leaders. Even as they drew on earlier precedents, these leaders were transforming a traditional message of divine grace and traditional patterns of spiritual organization into something substantially new.

1738

After George Whitefield left London in late December 1737 for his new assignment in Georgia, the visible pace of renewal seemed to slow down. But London, as the crossroads of the evangelical world, as well as of the British empire more generally, was soon again the scene of momentous events.

Yet it was never London by itself. By April 1738, Benjamin Ingham had established several local societies in Yorkshire and was guiding them in the practice of a mostly Moravian faith. Howell Harris expanded his Welsh con-

---

[26] Edwards, *Faithful Narrative*, 168, 173, 174–175.

[27] Ibid., 131.

nections to include dissenting Independents. Gilbert Tennent and like-minded Presbyterian colleagues in New Jersey established a New Brunswick Presbytery in May for the purpose of making it easier for evangelical candidates to be ordained. And all over the English-speaking world, even beyond, people were reading Jonathan Edwards' *Faithful Narrative of Surprizing Conversions*. Harris received a copy in February and by November of that year he and Daniel Rowland had come to the conclusion that the Wales of their experience was becoming like the Connecticut River Valley that Edwards described. John Wesley read the book in October and would later make his own abridgement for his itinerants. In Scotland and the American middle colonies additional copies of Edwards' volume were being passed from reader to reader, and the question was being asked with ever greater urgency whether such 'effusions of the Spirit' might possibly appear in these locales as well.

For his part, Whitefield's trip to Georgia was eventful, even if it could not compare with the dramatic scenes he had left behind.[28] During the lengthy outbound voyage, Whitefield succeeded in transforming a rowdy troop-ship into a floating beehive of piety. In Savannah, where there were still barely 500 European settlers, along with a few thousand Native Americans in the vicinity, Whitefield preached, on average, twice daily (four times on Sunday), visited outlying settlements, established several schools, took steps in self-conscious imitation of A. H. Francke to establish an orphanage, and, in contrast to John Wesley's experience, seems to have got on well with almost everyone. His return voyage in the autumn was stormy throughout, but as soon as he landed on the west coast of Ireland (14 November) he was preaching to large and appreciative audiences. By the time he made it to London on 8 December, the news of his coming had prepared the metropolis for more. Shortly after his London return, Whitefield started a correspondence with Howell Harris that resulted in a long and friendly partnership. In the last week of 1738 he preached nine full sermons and expounded the Scriptures informally on at least eighteen other occasions.

The London to which Whitefield returned had been the scene in earlier months of crucial developments for both Moravian visitors and the Wesleys. John Wesley had made it back to London in early February and so was there on the seventh of that month to greet a new party of five Moravians, who were seeking permission to establish a mission among African Americans in the Georgia colony. Their leader was Peter Böhler (1712–1775), a minister who had been converted as a university student under the Wesleys' Georgia friend

---

[28] My account of Whitefield's year away from London is mostly from Tyerman, *Whitefield*, 110–142.

August Spangenberg and who had already worked alongside Zinzendorf in several evangelistic efforts in Germany.[29] Since none in this Moravian group spoke English and since Wesley was eager to continue the spiritual discussions he had begun with Spangenberg, Wesley set them up in London, introduced them to contacts in Oxford and engaged Böhler in intensive discussion. Especially noteworthy was a trip to Oxford of non-stop talk (in Latin and German) on 17 February, after which Böhler wrote to Zinzendorf: 'I traveled with the two brothers, John and Charles Wesley, from London to Oxford. The elder, John, is a good-natured man: he knew he did not properly believe on the Saviour, and was willing to be taught. His brother is at present very much distressed in his mind, but does not know how he shall begin to be acquainted with the Saviour.'[30]

What the Wesleys found particularly difficult was Böhler's assertion that believers ordinarily should experience a full assurance of saving faith. They also balked at his contention that the careful performance of religious duty was mostly irrelevant to achieving such a justifying faith. On 4 March a discouraged John Wesley asked Böhler whether he should end his public ministry, since he was quite sure he did not possess justifying faith. 'By no means,' was Böhler's reply. 'Preach faith *till* you have it, and then, *because* you have it, you will preach faith.' Two days later in a conversation at Oxford with a prisoner, condemned to death, Wesley began to expound as Böhler had recommended. Before the end of March, while Wesley was still struggling with doubts about his own faith, and consequently about his own salvation, he attended this prisoner, who, just before he went to the gallows, rose from prayer to tell his friends: 'I am now ready to die. I know Christ has taken away my sins, and there is no more condemnation for me.'[31]

Meanwhile, in London, the Moravians were formalizing the organization of a religious society whose roots can be traced to a group of German expatriates who wanted to continue the experiences of Herrnhut.[32] Although Böhler and his associates had not come to England intending to missionize the British, they found the interest of people like the Wesleys so intense they began to think it might be helpful to form a society for speakers of English too. Böhler made this decision on 24 April, and one week later on 1 May he

---

[29] See *BDEB*,115–116 (W. R. Ward, 'Peter Böhler').

[30] Böhler to Zinzendorf, in Wesley, *Works* (new), 18:225, n.25.

[31] Wesley, 4 March and 27 March 1738; Wesley, *Works* (new), 18:228, 232–233.

[32] On the details leading to the founding of the Fetter Lane Society and to the Wesleys' experiences of grace in May, see especially Podmore, *Moravian Church in England*, 38–52.

invited a few of his new English friends to join him in setting up such a society. Charles Wesley was ill, but John Wesley joined the group as it followed Böhler's advice and promised to meet weekly to 'confess our faults one to another, and pray for one another that we may be healed'. Two days later Charles Wesley had a long conversation with Böhler, who counselled him, as he had earlier counselled John, to seek God's grace through faith alone. The next day Böhler sailed for Georgia. In his journal, John Wesley wrote, 'O what a work of God hath begun since his coming to England.'[33] The society that commenced under Böhler's guidance, but with a largely Anglican constituency and well-salted with Anglican spirituality, became the hub of emergent evangelical energy. It has always been known as the Fetter Lane Society from the location to which its meetings moved later that year.

After Böhler's departure, but very much in the wake of his teaching, both Wesleys experienced special reassurance of divine grace. For the Wesleys, these powerful, life-changing events were certainly conversions, though perhaps never quite as clear cut as later observers regarded them.[34]

First was Charles who on 11 May met an artisan named Mr Bray, who pressed home the Moravian teachings as these had been outlined by Böhler. In the days that followed, Charles, despite a bout of illness, passed through intense spiritual experiences: 'I waked ... hungry and thirsty after God (12 May) ... I waked without Christ; yet still desirous of finding him (13 May) ... I longed to find Christ, that I might show him to all mankind; that I might praise, that I might love him (14 May).'[35] On Wednesday 17 May, after Wesley with a Moravian friend had pored over the pages of Martin Luther's commentary on the epistle to the Galatians for several hours, he began to think he was finding what he had been seeking: 'I laboured, waited, and prayed, to feel "who loved *me*, and gave himself for *me*". After this assurance that He would come, and would not tarry, I slept in peace.'[36] By the next Sunday, 21 May, Charles was convinced his journey was over: 'I found myself at peace with God, and rejoiced in hope of loving Christ.' Immediately he wrote a hymn, probably 'Christ the Friend of Sinners':

'Where shall my wondering soul begin?
  How shall I all to heaven aspire?

---

[33] 1 May and 4 May 1738; Wesley, *Works* (new), 18:236–237.

[34] For discussion, see Randy L. Maddox (ed.), *Aldersgate Reconsidered* (Nashville: Kingswood/Abingdon, 1990).

[35] Ch. Wesley, *Reader*, 96.

[36] Ibid., 97.

A slave redeem'd from death and sin,
   A brand pluck'd from eternal fire,
How shall I equal triumphs raise,
And sing my greater Deliverer's praise? ...

[7]Come, O my guilty brethren, come,
   Groaning beneath your load of sin!
His bleeding heart shall make you room,
   His open side shall take you in.
He calls you now, invites you home:
Come, O my guilty brethren, come!

[8]For you the purple current flow'd
   In pardons from His wounded side:
Languish'd for you th'eternal God,
   For you the Prince of Glory died.
Believe, and all your guilt's forgiven;
Only believe – and yours is heaven.[37]

Where Charles led, John followed. Through the early days of the very next week, the older Wesley continued to be weighed down by his sense of sin, or as he put it in a letter to a friend: 'All my works, my righteousness, my prayers, need an atonement for themselves. So that my mouth is stopped. I have nothing to plead. God is holy; I am unholy. God is a consuming fire; I am altogether a sinner, meet to be consumed.'[38] On Wednesday 24 May, he awoke at 5am and opened his New Testament to 2 Peter 1:4 ('Whereby are given unto us exceeding great and precious promises: that by these ye should be partakers of the divine nature'.) He attended a service at St Paul's cathedral in the afternoon, where the anthem was from Psalm 130: 'Out of the deep have I called unto thee, O LORD ... O Israel, trust in the LORD: For with the LORD there is mercy, and with him is plenteous redemption. And he shall redeem Israel from all his sins.' In the evening he went 'very unwillingly' to the meeting of a society in Aldersgate Street that had probably originated as a result of Whitefield's preaching the year before but then been regularized by Peter Böhler.[39] One of

---

[37] Ibid., 102–103.

[38] Wesley, c.17 May 1738; Wesley, *Works* (new), 18:242. Annotations and the introductory essay by W. R. Ward (1–119) in this edition of Wesley's *Journal* are critical for a proper understanding of the decisive Aldersgate experience.

[39] Wesley, 24 May 1738; ibid., 249. The Psalms quotation is from the translation in the *Book of Common Prayer*.

the meeting's conveners was reading from Martin Luther's preface to the book of Romans. The Moravians were among the leaders in resurrecting Luther's more directly spiritual, as opposed to his polemical or doctrinal, writings. Wesley did not record the particular part of Luther's preface that struck him so forcibly, but that substantial treatise was in fact one of the roots from which the Moravian conception of Christian salvation had sprung. Wesley's own later account of justifying faith and its effects on the believer would parallel closely what he was hearing from Luther. For example: 'Faith is a living, daring confidence in God's grace, so sure and certain that the believer could stake his life on it a thousand times ... Because of it, without compulsion, a person is ready and glad to do good to everyone, to serve everyone, to suffer everything out of love and praise to God who has shown him this grace'.[40]

While hearing such words Wesley himself felt the touch of God's grace. In his own memorable words,

> About a quarter before nine, while [the speaker] was describing the change which God works in the heart through faith in Christ, I felt my heart strangely warmed. I felt I did trust in Christ, Christ alone for salvation, and an assurance was given me that he had taken away *my* sins, even *mine*, and saved *me* from the law of sin and death.[41]

Nothing ever came easy for John Wesley, so it is not surprising to read what followed next: 'I began to pray with all my might for those who had in a more especial manner despitefully used me and persecuted me. I then testified openly to all there what I now first felt in my heart.' But then 'the enemy' suggested to Wesley that this experience could not be of faith, since he was not overjoyed. Wesley responded with a Scripture and there was brief repose. But only briefly, since when he returned home that same night, 'I was much buffeted with temptations.' This time, however, Wesley 'cried out, and they fled away'.[42]

Often in later life Wesley would return to doubt the conclusive character of his Aldersgate experience. Only months later in early January 1739, for instance, Wesley provided an extended analysis of his spiritual condition in which he concluded, 'I am not a Christian ... I have not the fruits of the Spirit of

---

[40] 'Preface to the Epistle of St. Paul to the Romans' (1522, rev. 1546), trans. Charles M. Jacobs and E. Theodore Bachmann, in *Luther's Works*, vol. 35: *Word and Sacrament I*, Bachmann (ed.) (Philadelphia: Fortress, 1960), 370–371.

[41] Wesley, 24 May 1738: Wesley, *Works* (new), 18:249–250.

[42] Ibid., 250.

Christ.'[43] Periodically throughout the succeeding decades, the same kind of doubt would recur. During one of these bouts he wrote to his brother in June 1766: 'I do not love God. I never did … Therefore I am only an honest heathen.'[44] The Wesley whose preaching brought confident assurance to so many others would sometimes lack that assurance himself.

Despite these later reservations, the experience at Aldersgate, as also Charles Wesley's similar experience the week before, was decisive. Through the influence of Spangenberg and Böhler, the Wesleys had learned a new way of talking about God's redeeming grace, and then they had experienced that grace themselves. This experience unleashed preaching, hymn-writing and society-organizing of tremendous energy. Because of that activity, in turn, the Wesleys' experiences of May 1738 became emblematic for the whole evangelical movement.

After the dramatic breakthroughs of May, John Wesley was eager to probe more deeply into the Moravian vision of the Christian life. And so, impulsive as ever, he proposed a journey across Europe to Zinzendorf's Herrnhut. Benjamin Ingham and several others joined him in looking favourably on this proposal. Thus, while Charles Wesley undertook an energetic round of preaching, personal witnessing and hymn-writing in England, and the Fetter Lane Society continued its weekly meetings, John Wesley, Ingham and six others set off on 13 June for Herrnhut. Their two weeks at the Moravian head-quarters were productive, especially as Wesley had opportunity for extended discussions with several who had been converted in the Moravian way and who had gone on to lives of exemplary preaching and service. As impressed as he continued to be with the Moravian ability to rest with assurance in God's grace, it was probably also on this trip that Wesley began to doubt some expressions of Moravian practice that would soon lead him to break with the movement. A final historical curiosity of this trip is that it took Wesley twice through the Saxon city of Leipzig (27–28 July, 17 August) where Johann Sebastian Bach was music director of the city's churches. Sadly, there is no record that Bach and Wesley met, or that they were even aware of each other's existence.

The party returned to England in mid-September, about the time that Whitefield's ship was leaving the American South for his voyage back to Britain. With John Wesley back in London, an intensified round of society meetings took place at Fetter Lane. Both Wesleys were now more resolutely

[43] Wesley, 4 January 1739; Wesley, *Works* (new), 19:31.
[44] Heitzenrater, *Wesley*, 224; John Wesley to Charles Wesley, 27 June 1766, in Wesley, *Letters* 5:16.

preaching justification by faith, and conversions (with controversy) continued
to multiply.

Whitefield's return to London in December stoked the flames of renewal
to an even higher pitch. The intensity of this early period in evangelical
history – while wonder mingled with awe at the unprecedented manifestations
of the Holy Spirit and before theological, personal and ecclesiastical divisions
divided Calvinists, Arminians and Moravians from each other – climaxed on
the night of 1–2 January 1739. The occasion was a meeting of the Fetter Lane
Society for a love-feast, which entailed a light meal of bread and water followed by a time of testimony, prayer and singing. In attendance were Charles
and John Wesley, George Whitefield, Benjamin Ingham, Westley Hall (who
later married one of the Wesleys' sisters but then degenerated into deism,
polygamy and worse), Charles Kinchin (who would try to resign his living to
become a Moravian, only to die of smallpox in 1742 before he could clearly
discern his own mind), and about sixty others. Whitefield recorded that the
whole night was spent 'in close prayer, psalms and thanksgivings'. Wesley supplied a few more details:

> About three in the morning, as we were continuing instant in prayer, the power of
> God came mightily upon us, insomuch that many cried out for exceeding joy, and
> many fell to the ground. As soon as we were recovered a little from that awe and
> amazement at the presence of his majesty, we broke out with one voice, 'We praise
> thee, O God; we acknowledge thee to be the Lord.'[45]

It was a powerful punctuation mark for the decisive events of 1738, but
also a prelude to years that, against all belief, would be even more remarkable.

---

[45] Whitefield, *Journals*, 196; Wesley, 1 January 1739; Wesley, *Works* (new), 19:29.

4. REVIVAL, FRAGMENTATION, CONSOLIDATION, 1738–1745

Although much in the later history of evangelicalism was still obscure when the Fetter Lane Society gathered to pray on the evening of 1 January 1739, the main emphases and practices of evangelical faith were already coming into view. First in importance was the fact that individuals were being converted to God and to lifetimes of faithful service, and that these individuals regarded their own conversions as anticipations of renewal for entire communities. The preaching that occasioned these conversions represented something new because its practitioners were intending to work directly on the affections and were aiming directly at life-transforming results. This preaching was sometimes provided by itinerants (Whitefield, Howell Harris, and soon many imitators), and sometimes by settled ministers (Daniel Rowland, Jonathan Edwards), but in all forms it sought not simply intellectual communication but also the responsive engagement of the whole person. The power of evangelical preaching lay in its depiction of a severe divine law and a capacious divine gospel. Even the noteworthy intellectuals of the early movement, Jonathan Edwards and John Wesley, used their formidable mental abilities to move the heart rather than simply convince the mind. The search for true religion was ending with palpable experiences of grace.

Much in this nascent evangelicalism reprised themes of the Puritans, except that the time required for conversion was foreshortened, and the scope of reforming interests was narrowed. Compared to the prevailing expectations for religious life, early evangelicalism was also noteworthy for its massive indifference to the institutional structures of traditional religion.

By 1739 Jonathan Edwards had provided evangelicals with a template for how conversions should proceed and how they could effect social renewal. Everywhere evangelical preaching was inspiring the formation of local, predominantly lay-led societies for the spiritual nurture of those who were, or who wanted to be, converted. Evangelicalism was also witnessing a revival of extra-ecclesiastical networks as the circulatory system for tidings of renewal. As Edwards wrote in the *Faithful Narrative*, 'There is no one thing that I know of, that God has made such a means of promoting his work amongst us, as the news of others' conversion.'[1]

In sum, though it was still early in the development of characteristic evangelical practices, still early in the outworking of the main evangelical beliefs, and still early in the careers of the great evangelical leaders, there was definitely an evangelical stirring in the British empire. Typically, as it would turn out for much of later evangelical history, events were out-racing the ability to manage events.

1739

The period following the emergence of Whitefield and Daniel Rowland, the publication of Edwards' *Faithful Narrative* and the fresh experiences of grace in the lives of John and Charles Wesley, Howell Harris and Gilbert Tennent witnessed a great expansion of evangelicalism, but also the first significant clashes of personalities, practices and beliefs among evangelicals themselves. The year 1739 was one of significant transition: some of the key revivalists met each other for the first time; Anglican Evangelicals took unprecedented liberties with time-honoured church traditions; interested parties in Scotland and America harkened with even greater expectation to revival reports coming through London; differences in theology that had been obscured by shared aspirations and the bonds of personal friendship emerged into the open; important new leaders were converted and began to exert an influence; characteristic patterns of evangelical organization crept into view; and more responsibilities were accepted by the evangelical laity.

The events of that year, as signposts to the evangelical renewal that would expand in the 1740s, can only be sketched here. They were, however, indications of an accelerating religious movement.

---

[1] Edwards, *Faithful Narrative of Surprising Conversions* (1737), in Edwards, *Works*, vol. 4: *The Great Awakening*, ed. C. C. Goen (1972), 176.

- In early January, Howell Harris reported to Whitefield that there was 'a great revival in Cardiganshire' under Daniel Rowland.[2]
- On 17 February, after several Anglican rectors in Bath and Bristol forbade Whitefield, as an irresponsible enthusiast, to use their churches, he took the radical step of beginning to preach out of doors. This action – in Luke Tyerman's words, 'a shocking departure from Church rules and usages'[3] – marked a striking willingness to innovate and a fresh break with the Protestant past. Whitefield had become a *bona fide* sensation, harshly censured by some but eagerly sought by many more.
- The very next month, John Wesley followed suit, as did his brother Charles in May. Although the Wesleys and Whitefield considered themselves faithful sons of the Church, their insistence on gospel preaching – wherever, whenever, however – was proving stronger than their respect for traditional ecclesiastical order.
- In March, John, Wesley arrived in Bristol and took over day-to-day care of societies that Whitefield had started in that town and in nearby Kingswood. Whitefield, as soon as his new societies were handed over to Wesley, went on with his itinerant preaching.
- In April, Howell Harris came for the first time to London, where he was deeply moved by witnessing Whitefield's sermons in the open air.
- Also in April, what John Wesley recorded as 'signs and wonders' multiplied during his ministry in Bristol: 'one … cried out aloud, with the utmost vehemence, even as in the agonies of death … Soon after two other persons … were seized with strong pain and constrained to "roar for the disquietness of their heart".'[4] Such phenomena also appeared in response to the preaching of Whitefield and other awakeners. They proved to opponents that Methodism amounted to rank enthusiasm.
- In May, John Cennick joined the Fetter Lane Society, but then almost immediately journeyed westwards to Kingswood, where with Wesley's approval he became the first layman to preach out of doors and, also under Wesley's oversight, took charge of several societies in the Bristol and Kingswood area.
- In August, Whitefield left again for America. Just as he departed, Wesley published a tract on 'Free Grace', which exposed theological differences between Whitefield and himself that had remained latent to this point.

---

[2] Tyerman, *Whitefield*, 1:170–171.

[3] Tyerman, *Wesley*, 1:227.

[4] Wesley, 17 April 1739, in Wesley, *Works* (new), vol. 19: *Journal and Diaries II (1738–1743)*, ed. W. Reginald Ward and Richard T. Heitzenrater (1990), 49. For more on such phenomena, see Watts, *Dissenters*, 1:410–414.

- In October and November, another group of Moravians arrived in England. These were the first of Zinzendorf's associates commissioned to organize a specific mission to Britain. By this time George Whitefield was in New Jersey. He had met Gilbert Tennent and Tennent's venerable father William, and Gilbert Tennent had arranged for Whitefield to preach at a Presbyterian church in New York City after the Church of England commissary refused his request to use the city's Anglican churches. Well before this date much of Scotland had also received news of Whitefield's sensational preaching.
- In mid- to late 1739 Selina, Countess of Huntingdon (1707–1791), daughter of one earl and wife of another, was converted through the witness of a sister-in-law who had been attending Whitefield's sermons and who had also been affected by the preaching of Wesley's colleague, Benjamin Ingham. Soon she was enjoying especially fruitful correspondence with Charles Wesley, and soon she began her lifetime's work of promoting evangelical causes.

From this point it becomes all but impossible to continue a single chronology for an ever-expanding, ever-diversifying story. Developments in England, Scotland, Wales, New England and the middle colonies occurred so rapidly and with such far-reaching consequences that thematic treatment is the only way forward. Yet as we examine some of the most important occurrences of the next years, it is vital to remember that they were not taking place in isolation. Evangelicalism was never tightly coherent, but it did present the characteristics of a movement, albeit diverse and far-flung.

George Whitefield and American evangelicalism (1740)

George Whitefield was present in the American colonies for the whole of 1740. His labours in all the main colonial regions (south, mid-Atlantic, New England) and all of its significant cities (Savannah, Charleston, Philadelphia, New York, Boston) possessed an almost mythic quality, for Whitefield at the height of his powers and in the strong grip of Christian dedication was a marvel. His tours during this single visit from England remain one of the most remarkable events in American religious history, but they were also big with implications for the later course of evangelicalism. Without making the mistake of simply equating Whitefield with early American evangelicalism, it is none the less instructive to examine his activities in some detail, not only for how they shaped American developments but also for how they compared with Whitefield's activities and the development of early evangelicalism in other regions of the Atlantic world.

In late October 1739, Whitefield touched down in Pennsylvania and then preached for several weeks in and around Philadelphia and New York before heading south by land through Delaware, Virginia, North Carolina and South Carolina.[5] He arrived at his orphanage – his colonial home-base – in Savannah, Georgia, on 9 January 1740. After three active months of local preaching, energetic attention to the construction of an orphanage building and sharp quarrelling with Anglican ministers in Georgia and South Carolina, he set off again for the north. Through April and May he preached to audiences numbering upwards of 15,000 in Philadelphia and New York, and to smaller but still substantial gatherings in outlying communities. Crowds would be even larger in New England that autumn, but even in the spring more people were gathering in one place to hear Whitefield than had ever been assembled at one place to that time in the European history of North America. Whitefield returned to Savannah and Charleston for the summer to catch his breath – if overseeing an orphanage that grew to about seventy residents in a very large new building that cost nearly £4,000, supervising the services of Savannah's Church of England congregation (where he was the incumbent) and making short preaching tours into the countryside could be called relaxation. In late August he began the tour that was mentioned in the introduction to this book: Rhode Island in mid-September, then Boston and the surrounding region for a month, proceeding next to Western Massachusetts and down the Connecticut River to Hartford before launching overland again to New Haven, then New York City and Philadelphia for about a week each, and finally off to Savannah on 17 November. And everywhere on this trip, as throughout the year, he was preaching, preaching, preaching. During this ten-week tour of New England, New York and Philadelphia, there were at least 200 formal sermons as well as countless informal exhortations. Through the rest of the year he averaged closer to two sermons per day (instead of three). Long shipboard journeys were for Whitefield not an encumbrance, but a necessity. Otherwise the pace would have killed him.

His message reflected the purpose that drove him to such exertions: 'My one design is to bring poor souls to Jesus Christ.' In his own eyes he pursued that goal judiciously: 'I desire to avoid extremes, so as not to be a bigot on the one hand, or confound order and decency on the other.'[6] With only a few exceptions – James Blair, the Church of England Commissary in Williamsburg, Virginia, was one – Anglican rectors did not allow him to preach in

[5] For this section, I rely especially on Whitefield, *Journals*, 338–505; and Tyerman, *Whitefield*, 1:319–458.

[6] Tyerman, *Whitefield*, 1:433.

their churches. Dissenters, especially the Presbyterians in the middle colonies and the Congregationalists in New England, more than made up for that inconvenience by an eager willingness to open their pulpits. But often crowds were too large for any church, or, for that matter, any building in the colonies, so Whitefield took his message out of doors. Peter Timothy of Boston estimated that 23,000 assembled on the common for Whitefield's farewell sermon on Sunday 12 October – more than the entire population of the city itself.[7]

Characteristically, Whitefield would announce and read a text of Scripture, pray audibly and sometimes also silently (often on his knees), and then begin his discourse. A Boston listener described what happened next on one occasion: 'To have seen him when he first commenced, one would have thought him anything but enthusiastic and glowing; but, as he proceeded, his heart warmed with his subject, and his manner became impetuous, till, forgetful of everything around him, he seemed to kneel at the throne of Jehovah and to beseech in agony for his fellow-beings.' The same observer described Whitefield's verbal agility in once using a passing thunderstorm to compare human life to a transitory cloud, the wrath of God to a lightning bolt, and his divine mercy to the sun emerging after rain. When asked for a text of this particular sermon for the printer, Whitefield replied, 'I have no objection, if you will print the lightning, thunder and rainbow with it.'[8]

After Whitefield had visited Jonathan Edwards in Northampton and preached four sermons and offered two exhortations in three days, Sarah Pierrepont Edwards summed up the mixture of spiritual zeal and raw charisma that created Whitefield's unforgettable presence:

> He makes less of doctrines than our American preachers generally do, and aims more at affecting the heart. He is a born orator. You have already heard of his deep-toned, yet clear and melodious voice. It is perfect music. It is wonderful to see what a spell he casts over an audience by proclaiming the simplest truths of the Bible. I have seen upwards of a thousand people hang on his words with breathless silence, broken only by an occasional half-suppressed sob.[9]

But as he preached, Whitefield also tended to business. He usually travelled with two or three associates, including William Seward, who functioned as business manager, fundraiser, publicist and advance-man extraordinaire. It was,

---

[7] Ibid., 421. Whitefield himself reported 20,000; Whitefield, *Journals*, 472.
[8] Tyerman, *Whitefield*, 1:419–420.
[9] Ibid., 428.

thus, a great personal and professional blow when Seward, sent back to Britain to secure financing for the Savannah orphanage, was killed in the autumn of 1740 during a fracas in Wales brought on by the itinerant preaching of Howell Harris.[10] Seward and others helped Whitefield collect his letters and manage an immense correspondence; during these eighteen months away from England, he wrote an abundance of letters to the Wesleys, Howell Harris, Benjamin Ingham, Charles Delamotte and many others in the broad Methodist networks. He also oversaw an active publishing schedule, which in this trip cemented what became a long-term relationship with Benjamin Franklin and his printing firm in Philadelphia. In addition, Whitefield worked as hard as he could in the odd moments of his frenetic schedule to manage the orphanage, which he modelled on the famous institution that A. H. Francke had built in Halle. Whitefield's travels brought him into contact with many notables: in 1740 alone, with Gilbert Tennent in New Jersey, the Quaker author Anthony Benezet in Philadelphia, and Jonathan Belcher, the royal governor of Massachusetts. With these three, and many, many others whose names have been lost to history, Whitefield established warm, memorable personal contact.

The spiritual effects of his touring were often long-lasting. Many of Whitefield's younger male converts went on to become ministers themselves. More were affected as the layman Nathan Cole was affected after he had rushed from his fields on Thursday 23 October 1740, to hear Whitefield declaim from a scaffold in Middletown, Connecticut, to a crowd estimated at 4,000:

> And my hearing him preach, gave me a heart wound. By God's blessing: my old Foundation was broken up, and I saw that my righteousness would not save me; then I was convinced of the doctrine of Election; and went right to quarrelling with God about it; because that all I could do would not save me; and he had decreed from Eternity who should be saved and who not.[11]

Nathan Cole may have been troubled by more details of older Puritan teaching about predestination than Whitefield intended, but Cole's testimony records accurately both Whitefield's consistently Calvinist emphases and his stirring oratorical force.

Whitefield's influence in America – because of this tour but also his six other visits and the flood of writing by and about him – was momentous. He

---

[10] *BDEB*, 996 (W. R. Ward, 'William Seward').

[11] Michael J. Crawford, 'The Spiritual Travels of Nathan Cole', *William and Mary Quarterly* 33 (January 1976): 93–94.

helped confirm American Presbyterians in a much more consistently evangelical course than their fellow Presbyterians in Scotland and Ireland were pursuing. Similarly, he contributed a strong evangelical note to New England
Congregationalism and so hastened the growth of parties (traditional vs evangelical vs liberal) that soon splintered this once strong establishment. He
inspired many who would later become leaders of Baptist and Methodist
churches. He was also a personal bridge that connected many previously isolated groups, including some Quakers and German immigrant congregations,
with the Dissenting denominations that were his main supporters.

In all his activities, Whitefield combined an extraordinary disregard for
inherited church traditions with a breathtaking entrepreneurial spirit. The willingness to innovate made him immensely popular in the colonies and also
promoted among later American evangelicals a similar disregard for Christian
traditions. Yet his large vision, quick actions and urge to create left an ambiguous legacy, since it was much easier for Whitefield to announce grand plans
than to carry them through. After William Seward's untimely death, for
example, Whitefield could never establish firm control over his orphanage or
bring it to fulfil his lofty goals.[12] This tendency towards insubstantial castle-
building would have a long life among American evangelicals.

Whitefield was both winsomely naïve and casually judgmental in ways that
continue to mark at least some strands of evangelicalism in America. As an
example, he appears to have formed his unfavourable judgment on Harvard
College – 'Discipline is at a low ebb. Bad books are become fashionable
among the tutors and students'[13] – after less than a day in Cambridge, Massachusetts. Similarly, his frequently harsh words about unconverted ministers
probably spoke to a genuine problem, but the supreme self-assurance that
characterized those words and the paucity of hard evidence upon which they
rested amounted to irresponsibility.

Whitefield's all-or-nothing commitment to evangelism at the expense of
well-considered Christian social ethics left an ambiguous legacy as well. His
stance towards the institution of slavery is one example. During 1740, he criticized southern slave-owners for mistreating slaves and took special pains on
several occasions to preach to slaves. But he also decided on the spur of the
moment that, since Europeans were unable or unwilling to work the land supporting his orphanage, it would be 'impracticable' to survive in Georgia

---

[12] For the later history of this institution, see Edward J. Cashin, *Beloved Bethesda: A
History of George Whitefield's Home for Boys, 1740–2000* (Macon: Mercer University Press,
2001).

[13] Whitefield, *Journals*, 462.

without purchasing 'a few Negroes' as slaves.[14] Whitefield, who preached so willingly to slaves, hardly gave a thought when he became a slave-owner himself.

Much of what Whitefield did was admirable by any standard, and his commitment to Christ-centred preaching was a shining beacon. But while his character and purpose possessed great integrity, there was no consistency to his broader actions, no depth to his thinking about culture. Ready-fire-aim was his style. In a word, much that would be best and much that would be worst in the later history of evangelicals in America was anticipated by Whitefield in this one stirring year.

Scottish evangelicalism and George Whitefield (1742)

In Scotland, Whitefield's role, and hence also the development of evangelicalism, was different. Scottish pastors like William McCulloch, James Robe and John MacLaurin, who ministered in Glasgow or its environs, had long prayed for revival, promoted books like *The Marrow of Divinity* and Thomas Boston's *Fourfold State*, and consulted with each other about the renewal of their churches.[15] They also kept alive memories of earlier Scottish revivals that had occurred as a result of field preaching, or even more frequently in connection with the celebration of the Lord's Supper. But into the early 1740s these men and a small handful of like-minded ministerial colleagues were not privileged to witness in Scotland what, they read, was taking place in New England in response to the itinerations of Whitefield. Rather, storm, plague and famine, with much loss of life, seemed to be Scotland's lot through 1739, 1740 and 1741. In the late summer of 1741, Whitefield, fresh from his American return, travelled north to Scotland for thirteen weeks of preaching. The response was good, with large crowds who appreciated the Calvinist accents of his preaching (with which they were very familiar) and his extempore fervency (with which they were not). But overall results did not match the hurricane of grace that Whitefield had brought to New England or even the local tempests that attended his preaching in London, Bristol and other English cities. When, however, Whitefield returned to Scotland in the summer of 1742, many who

---

14 Tyerman, *Whitefield*, 1:444.

15 In this section, I am following Arthur Fawcett, *The Cambuslang Revival: The Scottish Evangelical Revival of the Eighteenth Century* (London: Banner of Truth, 1971); Harry S. Stout, 'George Whitefield in Three Countries', in *Evangelicalism*, 58–72; and relevant articles in *DSCHT*.

were then shaken to the foundation reported that they had been among his auditors the year before.

The future course of Scottish evangelicalism was strongly influenced by the fact that the leading advocates of revival were veteran ministers who took for granted the continuing centrality of the historic Scottish Kirk. In 1742, Robe turned fifty-four years old, McCulloch fifty-one and MacLaurin forty-nine. Moreover, these evangelicals had chosen to stay in the established church when Ralph and Ebenezer Erskine, with whom they otherwise shared many particular convictions, led out their small secession in the early 1730s. Scotland's well-engrained traditions of state-church Calvinism, widespread education and serious theological discussion presented a scene different from that which Whitefield had encountered in America. Yet reports of revival from over the ocean convinced McCulloch and his friends that a similar manifestation of divine grace was possible in their land.

The chain of events that precipitated the longed-for revival began in McCulloch's parish at Cambuslang, just to the south and east of Glasgow. McCulloch was, in the words of Arthur Fawcett, 'a somewhat colourless parish minister', but one whose earnestness and pastoral commitment were appreciated by his parishioners and ministerial colleagues. For most of 1741 he was preaching on the theme of regeneration. In December he stirred his congregation with a message on 2 Corinthians 6:1–2, which includes the apostle Paul's stirring declaration, 'behold, now is the accepted time; behold, now is the day of salvation'. In response, members of the Cambuslang congregation organized themselves into societies for prayer, and expectation began to mount. In February, McCulloch began to preach a mid-week sermon at the request of parishioners who had been touched by Whitefield the previous summer. Then at a memorable sermon on 18 February, the tide began to roll in. The text was Jeremiah 23:6, 'and this is his name whereby he shall be called, THE LORD OUR RIGHTEOUSNESS'. During the sermon many in attendance, especially young men and women, wept; after the meeting over fifty auditors crowded into McCulloch's manse for spiritual counselling. Exhortation, psalm-singing and personal encouragement continued throughout the night. McCulloch was constrained to preach more often; by April he was preaching up to six sermons a week. In a pattern that closely followed the narrative of Jonathan Edwards' *Narrative of Surprizing Conversions*, similar concern for repentance and faith began to spread to neighbouring churches. On 28 April, McCulloch wrote to Whitefield that within the last three months more than 300 had been awakened and perhaps 200 converted.

When Whitefield received McCulloch's letter along with other reports from Scotland, he was in the midst of exciting, if also dangerous, days at the Moorfields in London. This open expanse, a carnival area occupied by many booths for games of chance and refreshments, was regularly thronged with people. To Whitefield it was an ideal location for outdoor preaching. In the spring and summer Whitefield met stiff resistance as he competed head to head with the barkers, pimps, buskers and army recruiters. He was assaulted, his sermons were disrupted and he was at least once set upon by a man with a dagger. But through it all he preached on until he was able to hold huge crowds spellbound; reports multiplied of conversions and lives transformed. But when word arrived from Scotland, Whitefield prepared to head north.

At Kilsyth, a few miles beyond Cambuslang from Glasgow, James Robe began in May to witness some of the same spiritual excitement as in McCulloch's parish. As in Cambuslang, Robe's long-term gospel preaching had turned in the preceding months more directly to the theme of regeneration. In response to his own sermons and to lectures by visitors like John MacLaurin, Kilsyth's people were moving into the same cycle of singing, sermon attendance and personal conferences that, again, followed the narrative originally published by Jonathan Edwards.

Whitefield arrived in Scotland on 3 June, and by the sixteenth he was preaching to very large crowds in Glasgow. His arrival was the occasion for one of the oddest publications of the era, which none the less revealed much about the character of Scotland's religion. Before he journeyed to Scotland in the summer of 1741, Whitefield had enjoyed friendly correspondence with the Erskines and other seceding ministers who were keen to enlist him for two purposes that in their mind amounted to the same thing: preaching the New Birth and joining the seceders in the fight against corruption in the Kirk. Whitefield, however, was interested only in the first of these tasks. In correspondence with Ebenezer Erskine, he very deliberately detached his gospel preaching from questions of denominational strife: 'I come only as an occasional preacher, to preach the simple gospel, to all who are willing to hear me, of whatever denomination ... If I am quite neuter as to [church government] ... I cannot see how it can hinder or retard any design *you* may have on foot. My business seems to be to evangelise – to be a Presbyter at large.'[16] In response, the seceding Associate Presbytery turned harshly against Whitefield. If he could not join them in their plans for reforming the Scottish church, they would not join him in preaching the New Birth. Thus it was that when Whitefield returned to Scotland in 1742, the seceders were ready with a broadside by Adam Gib that was published the very week of his arrival. Its title left little to the imagination: *A Warning Against Countenancing the Ministrations of Mr. George Whitefield ... Together with an Appendix upon the same subject, wherein are*

---

[16] Tyerman, *Whitefield*, 1:505.

shewn, that Mr. Whitefield is no Minister of Jesus Christ; that his call and coming to Scotland, are scandalous; that his practice is disorderly, and fertile of disorder; that his whole doctrine is, and his success must be, diabolical; so that people ought to avoid him, from duty to God, to the Church, to themselves, to their fellow-men, to posterity, and to him. ... By contrast, McCulloch, Robe, MacLaurin and other Church of Scotland evangelicals esteemed Whitefield, made no fuss over his Church of England ordination and were delighted that this Anglican itinerant was willing to help in the revival of the Scottish people as well as of the Scottish church. Scottish evangelicalism would long remain more churchly – and usually more self-consciously Calvinistic and Presbyterian – than evangelicals elsewhere, but the Church of Scotland ministers who welcomed Whitefield were expressing their belief that it was possible to combine a moderate commitment to inherited Presbyterian forms with a full embrace of the modern evangelical spirit.

The climax of this intense period of spiritual renewal came at the mid-July celebration of communion in Cambuslang. Scottish communions were traditionally important affairs, conducted infrequently but with a powerful combination of august solemnity and convivial popular spectacle.[17] Preparatory sermons on the Sunday and Saturday before the communion Sunday were standard. Communion itself was celebrated with sermons, singing and prayers; congregants gathered at long tables where their ministers served them healthy portions of bread and wine. To be admitted, communicants needed to receive a small metal coin, or token, from a regular minister as a sign of good standing. These communion seasons usually occurred in the summer, since crowds were large, and it was necessary to move out of doors; even in ordinary times the service lasted for hours.

The communion celebrated at Cambuslang on Sunday 11 July was anything but ordinary. Whitefield had visited Cambuslang on Tuesday 6 July, and preached at 2 o'clock and 4 o'clock in the afternoon as well as at 9 in the evening. On Saturday he spoke to a crowd estimated reliably at more than 20,000. The next day he and a squadron of Kirk ministers took turns exhorting, distributing the elements at the tables and preaching (seventeen sermons in total!). The meeting lasted for about fourteen hours. Seventeen hundred communicated. As many as 30,000 were in attendance, or almost twice the population of Glasgow and many times the population of Cambuslang. After the communion itself was finished, Whitefield preached for an hour and a half in the lingering Scottish twilight on Isaiah 54:5, 'For thy Maker is thine husband; the Lord of hosts is his name.' Later reports from laymen and lay-

---

[17] For essential background, see Leigh Eric Schmidt, *Holy Fairs: Scottish Communions and American Revivals in the Early Modern Period* (2nd ed., Grand Rapids: Eerdmans, 2001).

women singled out this sermon as the source of extraordinary consolation. During and after the meeting hundreds streamed to the manse, and then to nearby barns, for face-to-face spiritual counsel from McCulloch and other ministers. Throughout the day, many experienced unusual bodily agitations, cried out or fell down as dead. Even remembering Whitefield's penchant for exaggeration, his report to several correspondents that he had never seen anything like this, even in America, is credible.

So great was the impact of this event that McCulloch and his Cambuslang elders arranged for a second communion on Sunday 15 August. Even more people attended, perhaps as many as 50,000. By this time, similar mass gatherings – with mass repentance, mass prayer, mass assurance of salvation – had taken place in James Robe's Kilsyth and at several other venues. In the rush of events younger ministers and probationers were enlisted to assist. One of these was Thomas Gillespie (1708–1774), who had earlier been schooled by Philip Doddridge and who would later lead another group, more evangelical and less punctilious than the earlier Secession, out of the Church of Scotland. Another was John Erskine (1721–1803), who would become the leading figure among Scottish evangelicals during the second half of the century. In his bedazzlement at what he witnessed at Cambuslang, Kilsyth and other revival locations, Erskine rushed to publish a tract of millennial expectation: *Signs of the Times Considered, or the high Probability that the present Appearances in New England, and the West of Scotland, are a Prelude of the Glorious Things promised to the church in the latter Ages.*

For historians, McCulloch and his clerical associates left a priceless legacy by recording the personal testimonies of 106 converts out of the much greater number that came to them for spiritual counsel.[18] The clerical recorders were nervous about the high incidence of dreams, direct words from God and what today might be called charismatic phenomena communicated by these lay people. But they were also obviously filled with gratitude at the opportunity to record such vibrant testimonies to the work of grace. The account of sixteen-year-old Elizabeth Dykes was untypical because of the extended duration of her spiritual struggle, but otherwise representative of what others reported as well. Elizabeth had been reared in a Bible-reading home, where she had memorized the Westminster Shorter Catechism. But she

---

[18] On the importance and use of these manuscripts, see Fawcett, *Cambuslang Revival*, 5–8 and *passim*; Harry S. Stout, *The Divine Dramatist: George Whitefield and the Rise of Modern Evangelicalism* (Grand Rapids: Eerdmans, 1991), 151–154; and Ned Landsman, 'Evangelicals and Their Hearers: Popular Interpretations of Revivalist Preaching in Eighteenth-Century Scotland', *Journal of British Studies* 28 (1989): 120–149.

felt that she had never taken to heart the gospel message. As a result of McCulloch's preaching on the last Sunday of February 1742, she came under conviction, collapsed and was carried to the manse for personal exhortation: 'My sins so pressed upon me, that I could not believe it possible that God would ever pardon my sins, they seemed to me to be so great. I saw nothing before me but hell-fire; and yet my sense of the evil of sin was even greater than my apprehensions of coming wrath.' The oppressiveness of her own guilt continued through this spring and summer of spiritual intensity: 'I saw that there was no relief for me, but in Christ; and yet I seemed to be so great a sinner, as that I could scarcely venture to plead for his mercy.' Through the sermons at the two Cambuslang communions, at which she did not herself communicate because of the crush of people, and through relevant texts of Scripture that came unbidden to her mind, she eventually received a measure of consolation. At the later date when her personal narrative was recorded, she was not yet settled in her faith, but the gospel work was obviously well underway: 'to this day I cannot say that I have an assurance of heaven, but I desire to lay the stress of my salvation on Christ and his righteousness'.[19]

The intense excitement of 1742 soon subsided, Elizabeth Dykes and other converts returned to their ordinary lives, and the millennium did not begin. But a strong evangelical element was now salted into Presbyterian church consciousness. Although it was relatively slow in developing, evangelical emphases in preaching, evangelical concern for personal holiness and evangelical interest in missions grew steadily. Evangelicals contributed a great deal to the Popular Party, in the middle decades of the century, which battled for the rights of congregations and against the Moderates and their patrons. George Whitefield remained a welcome guest during many later trips. But John Wesley, who could not help but admire the Scots' devotion to Scripture and their patient attention to his sermons, continued to find them a cold and unresponsive people. On a preaching mission to Glasgow in 1774, for instance, Wesley twice attended services on a Sunday where the sermons, in his view, 'contained much truth, but were no more likely to awaken one soul than an Italian opera'. Wesley's temperamental distance from the Scots was indicated on that same trip when he recorded his opinion that they were a people 'the greatest part of whom *hear* much, *know* everything, and *feel* nothing'.[20]

In the broader picture, it made all the difference that Whitefield's dramatic preaching was contained by his cooperation with Church of Scotland minis-

---

[19] D. Macfarlan, *The Revivals of the Eighteenth Century, Particularly at Cambuslang* (Edinburgh: Johnston & Hunter, 1847), 143–144, 147.

[20] Wesley, *Journal* (15 May 1774, 12 May 1774), 6:19.

ters, and that the most intense moments of revival in Scotland took place at communion seasons in the established church overseen by senior ministers of the Kirk establishment. The differences with America (where Whitefield functioned like a Dissenting preacher and with almost no attention to the sacraments) and England (where he helped construct a network of Calvinist cells partially in and partially out of the established Anglican church) suggests why Scottish evangelicalism developed along lines different from evangelicalism in these two other regions where Whitefield also exerted such memorable influence.

The organization of publicity (1740ff.)

In the autumn of 1740 an important dimension was added to international evangelicalism when the London printer John Lewis brought out the first number of a new periodical, the *Christian's Amusement containing Letters Concerning the Progress of the Gospel both at Home and Abroad, etc. together with an Account of the Waldenses and Albigenses.*[21] This four-page periodical sold for a penny and survived for only seven months, but it was a sign of significant new developments in the exchange of information and the formalization of communication. Before this first evangelical periodical appeared, books, manuscripts and letters treating the themes of experiential Christianity had already been flowing back and forth across the Atlantic for more than a century. Puritans had sponsored a lively exchange of books that took on a transoceanic dimension after the founding of New England, and the eager bookprinting and bookselling of the Halle pietists had also greatly stimulated the international trade. As part of the rise of modern evangelicalism itself, there had been since the early 1730s a steadily increasing demand for older Puritan classics like Bunyan's *Grace Abounding* and Fisher's *The Marrow of Divinity*, as well as strong interest in the sermons, journals and pamphlets of the era's new evangelical leaders, especially George Whitefield and Jonathan Edwards.

---

[21] In this section, I depend on three outstanding articles by Susan Durden O'Brien, 'A Study of the First Evangelical Magazines', *Journal of Ecclesiastical History* 27 (July 1976): 255–275; 'A Transatlantic Community of Saints: The Great Awakening and the First Evangelical Network, 1735–1755', *American Historical Review* 91 (October 1986): 811–832; and 'Eighteenth-Century Publishing Networks in the First Years of Transatlantic Evangelicalism', in *Evangelicalism*, 38–57. Also useful on revival publications, including the magazines, is Frank Lambert, *Inventing the 'Great Awakening'* (Princeton: Princeton University Press, 1999), 155–179.

The international circulation of literature on experiential Christianity grew from both widespread respect for older writings and the determination of contemporaries to share what they could about the present work of God in their midst. For the latter effort, a particularly important circle of correspondence centred on Whitefield but also drew in other key figures of evangelical Calvinism: Edwards, Benjamin Colman and Thomas Prince, Sr, from New England; James Robe, William McCulloch, John MacLaurin and John Erskine from the Church of Scotland; and Isaac Watts and Philip Doddridge from English Dissent. Anglican Methodists in England as well as Welsh Methodists also took part in the era's active evangelical communication – Howell Harris, for example, regularly passed on copies of John Lewis's magazines to Howell Davies and Griffith Jones,[22] and John Wesley frequently commented in his journal or letters on what he read in the magazines. But the key axis of active communication was constituted by Lowland Kirk Presbyterianism and New England revived Calvinism, with a significant extension to evangelical English Dissent.

John Lewis's *Christian's Amusement* became an important prototype especially for the way in which it put news of revival to use in filling its pages. Lewis's efforts came into their own after Whitefield returned to England from his triumphant American itinerations of 1740 and agreed to supply regular reports to a newly reorganized magazine called *Weekly History: Or, an Account of the Most Remarkable Particulars Relating to the Present Progress of the Gospel By the encouragement of the Rev. Mr. Whitefield*. This particular magazine went through several more name changes in the next few years, but it continued to supply accounts from near and far of revivals and other distinctly evangelical phenomena.

Among the most important of those phenomena were 'Letter Days' and 'Concerts of Prayer'. Letter Days, involving specially designated meetings for reading reports – from private letters, manuscript accounts or published news – about continuing works of conversion, prayer and community reform, were modelled closely on Moravian and pietist gatherings that had become a feature of their commitment to worldwide gospel expansion. They became important especially in England and Wales, where literacy was not as advanced as in Scotland and New England and where greater opportunity existed for evangelicals of different denominations to gather for common purpose. Concerts of Prayer were likewise extending pietist and Moravian practices by trying to link committed believers from various regions in common supplication to God for the extension of gospel work. They also represented a modification of the traditional Puritan days of prayer that had usually been

---

[22] Durden [O'Brien], 'First Evangelical Magazines', 262.

decreed by civic officials or ministerial associations. In this venture, the Scots took the lead in the early 1740s by designating special days to pray for renewed religion, and then in 1744 suggesting to correspondents in England and New England that even more congregations should join together at the same time to pray. Jonathan Edwards seconded this proposal in an influential pamphlet from 1747, *Humble Attempt to Promote Explicit Agreement and Visible Union of God's People in Extraordinary Prayer*, which conveyed the idea to even more interested parties in the English-speaking world.

By the time Concerts of Prayer were widespread, several other evangelical magazines had already come and gone. In Scotland, William McCulloch published his *Glasgow Weekly History* from December 1741 to December 1742 with the specific purpose of reprinting reports from Lewis's London journal. But when revival began at Cambuslang, McCulloch added a great deal of first-hand material from his own experiences. The next evangelical papers represented an advance on efforts by Lewis and McCulloch since they sought to provide a permanent record of the remarkable revivals, which it was apparent from late 1742, had begun to recede. Thus, James Robe brought out his *Christian Monthly History or an Account of the Revival and Progress of Religion Abroad and at Home* from November 1743 to January 1746, and Thomas Prince, Jr, in Boston, with the aid of his father, published the *Christian History, Containing Accounts of the Revival and Propagation of Religion in Great Britain and America* from March 1743 to February 1745. By publishing indexes, by numbering pages consecutively for annual volumes and by carefully editing published material, Robe and Prince showed that they wanted to make their magazines permanent records of what had so recently occurred.

The first issue of Prince's journal set out its purpose to print 'Authentick Accounts from Ministers and other creditable Persons of the Revival of Religion' in New England, 'Extracts of the most remarkable Pieces' published in England and Scotland, 'Extracts of written Letters' from Britain as well as mid-Atlantic and southern American colonies, and occasional digests of 'the most remarkable Passages Historical and Doctrinal' from earlier Christian writers. The magazine would contain 'no Advertisement ... but of Books and Pamphlets or other Things of a religious Importance'. It would feature 'plain & certain Facts' while 'studiously avoiding Personal Reflections and angry Controversy'.[23] The content of the paper's first seven issues was given over entirely to James Robe's narrative of revival in Kilsyth. Prince then set out to publish an extended series on the history of revivals in New England from the period of the founding, but these reports were broken off in the number

---

[23] *The Christian History* (5 March 1743), 1–2.

for 7 May so that he could offer readers extracts from 'some entertaining Letters from the western Parts of Scotland' that reported 'fresh and joyful Occurrences' of revivals.[24] Before the year was out, reports from London, South Carolina and Georgia, often featuring George Whitefield's peripatetic activities, joined those from Scotland and New England. Along the way, *The Christian History* also addressed the particular joys to be found in revived religion, the special problem of 'terrours' and 'faintings' experienced by people under gospel preaching, and proper versus improper understandings of 'grace' in connection with revival exertions.

Journals like Prince's brought international evangelicalism to an important new stage. Revivalistic Calvinism was becoming a public matter, and in so doing was beginning to blur its boundaries with others in the English-speaking world who were uncertain about Calvinism but none the less dedicated to revival. Evangelical self-consciousness increased measurably as articles from the magazines were circulated, read publicly and reprinted in other papers. With these journals, evangelicals were proving that they could compete in the print markets that were burgeoning throughout the Western world. They also demonstrated their ability to organize publicity – in modern parlance, to advertise – with great effect. And they showed they could do so by playing down doctrinal and traditional particularities in favour of religious experiences shared across the denominations. If the magazines displayed what Susan O'Brien has called 'a more instrumental approach to revivalism', in which evangelicals actively sought means beyond preaching to promote their goals, they also promoted a growing weight, again in O'Brien's words, of 'connection, interconnection, and direct assistance', which had long-term consequences for the evangelical movement.[25]

The early magazines themselves died out fairly rapidly, but they remained models for the re-emergence in England of evangelical periodical literature during the 1760s and 1770s with *The Spiritual Magazine* (from 1761), *The Gospel Magazine* (1774) of Augustus M. Toplady, who used it to promote Calvinist convictions, and the Wesleys' answering *Arminian Magazine* (1778), and then for the explosion of periodicals that took place in the 1790s on both sides of the Atlantic, in almost all evangelical groups, and for almost every specific evangelical cause. From the first publications of Lewis, McCulloch, Prince and Robe, the character of evangelicalism as a form of religion identified, driven, expanded, riven, exhorted, challenged, stoked and encouraged by its popular periodicals has never faltered.

---

[24] Ibid. (7 May 1743), 77–80, and continued in subsequent issues.
[25] O'Brien, 'Transatlantic Community of Saints', 830–831.

Theological differentiation

Experiences in this early period within the Church of England illustrate how difficult it would be to unify evangelicals in common theological affirmations, despite their many commonalities of belief and practice. Although Anglicanism remained for many decades the most important centre of evangelical fellowship, conversation and publicity, by the early 1740s harmony within the Church of England among those influenced by Moravian, Puritan and High Church Anglican piety broke down rapidly. An account of these differences, focused on John Wesley's important career, illustrates both the new fractures and the continued synergies of the evangelical movement.[26]

Such an account also anticipates what became a common set of doctrinal tendencies within all of evangelical history, to which we will return in the discussion of evangelical theology in Chapter 9. One strand of evangelicalism has tended to emphasize the importance of right doctrine drawn from Scripture, even the proper form of words to express Christian truths. This strand has often been Calvinistic, as in the 1740s, though many evangelicals branching off from the Calvinist groups have shared the concern for doctrinal precision. Another strand has tended to be so committed to the urgency of preaching Christ and encouraging holy living that it limits concern for doctrine to the existential issues of conversion and sanctification. Both the Calvinist Whitefield and the Arminian Wesley could follow such a course, although Arminians have probably been more consistently drawn in that direction. Yet another evangelical strand has resembled the Moravians in promoting piety so comprehensively as to subordinate doctrine in general to the practices of faith. Still a fourth evangelical strand has rested content with the Christian teachings and church practices inherited in their various traditions. For such ones, like the Scottish Presbyterians who cooperated with Whitefield, respect for historical forms and dogmas plays a large role in theological formation. Anglican developments in the early 1740s do not exemplify these strands exactly, but the broad outlines of each position are clear.

After Wesley returned from his visit to the Moravian centre at Herrnhut in September 1739, he continued for several months to fellowship with the Moravian-led body at Fetter Lane. But unease with the Moravians was the main factor that drew both Wesleys and several of their colleagues to purchase and refurbish an old cannon factory ('the Foundery') in late 1739 and early 1740. By July, the Foundery had become the key centre for the Wesleys'

---

[26] For a helpful overview, see Allan Coppedge, *John Wesley in Theological Debate* (Wilmore: Wesley Heritage, 1987).

preaching, teaching, poor relief, medical provision and organization. By this time, their break with the Moravians was complete.

Despite acknowledging his debt to the Moravians for their emphasis on the personal experience of God's merciful forgiveness of sin, Wesley came to conclude that leaders like Böhler and Spangenberg were promoting two critical errors. First, as Wesley saw it, Moravians spoke out far too strongly against good works and church duties when they preached up justification by faith; to be sure, good works were not by themselves saving, but they were none the less important as steps towards the holiness God requires and provides. Not for Wesley any of the 'stillness' that Moravians seemed to require; he was, by contrast, the champion of 'Christian perfection' as a goal to be sought avidly by all believers. Second, Moravians insisted too strongly that all who truly experienced God's grace would possess a saving assurance of their salvation; Wesley, by contrast, held that 'there are *degrees* of faith, and that a man may have *some degree* of it before all things in him are become new; before he has the full assurance of faith, the abiding witness of the Spirit, or the clear perception that Christ dwelleth in him'.[27] The division with the Moravians involved issues of doctrine, practice and personality. But under the leadership of John and Charles, the Wesleyan movement required more active organization and less passive waiting on the movement of the Spirit than the Moravians seemed to provide.

Despite John Wesley's objections, these Moravian emphases continued to appeal to substantial numbers of Anglicans. Such ones included ministers like Benjamin Ingham, who had been in Oxford, Georgia and Germany with John Wesley, but who from the early 1740s led his societies in Yorkshire from quasi-Anglican associations to full Moravian allegiance. Well into the mid-1740s and beyond, however, party groupings were still fluid, as the career of John Cennick illustrates. In 1739 Wesley had appointed Cennick to guide the Methodist work at Kingswood, near Bristol, but in 1741 Cennick took about fifty members of the Kingswood society into fellowship with Whitefield's network. Over the next few years Cennick, sometimes joined by Whitefield, took part in discussing organizational unity with the Moravians, but then actually left Anglicanism for the Moravian fellowship.

It is important to add that the Moravians did not, of course, view themselves exactly as Wesley did.[28] What he saw as an unwarranted 'stillness', the

---

[27] Wesley, 31 December 1739, in Wesley, *Works* (new), 19:132.

[28] Although their interpretations of Wesleyan–Moravian conflicts differ, Colin Podmore and Frederick Dreyer provide outstanding accounts from the Moravian perspective. See Podmore, *The Moravian Church in England, 1728–1760* (Oxford: Clarendon, 1998), 29–78; and Dreyer, *The Genesis of Methodism* (Bethlehem, PA: Lehigh University Press, 1999), 31–54.

Moravian leaders regarded as a pastoral response to the enthusiasm that flared so easily among Wesley's followers. Where Wesley laboured for years to experience grace (in a pattern approved by the Halle pietists), Moravians felt that conversion should be joyful and might be quick. Following Zinzendorf, Moravians were also coming to celebrate the wounds of Christ and the immense distance that separated 'poor sinners' from a merciful, almighty God, with an intensity that distressed Wesley. Although he continued to publish his own translation of Zinzendorf's hymns, like 'Jesu, thy blood and righteousness/My beauty are, my glorious dress', his ideal of Christian realities and the Moravian ideal had clearly diverged.[29]

In the other theological direction, Wesley's long-standing uneasiness with certain aspects of Calvinism burst forth in a sermon from 1740 entitled 'Free Grace'. The sermon's provenance was a special provocation since Wesley first preached it in Bristol among society members whom George Whitefield, himself in the process of firming up his own Calvinist convictions, had handed over to Wesley for safe-keeping. But to Wesley, the Calvinist insistence that God's electing power was the sole active element in the sinner's conversion verged dangerously close to antinomianism: because Calvinist teaching on predestination so thoroughly emphasized God's actions in bringing the sinner to himself, 'it wholly takes away those first motives to follow after [holiness], so frequently proposed in Scripture, the hope of future reward and punishment, the hope of heaven and fear of hell'.[30] As a committed Christian activist, Wesley could not be persuaded that the Bible taught Calvinist doctrines, especially when those doctrines seemed (to Wesley) to point straight towards a most unChristian inaction.

George Whitefield's response to Wesley's pamphlet inaugurated the most enduring theological conflict among evangelicals, the conflict between Arminian and Calvinist interpretations of Scripture on the nature, motive powers and implications of salvation.[31] To Whitefield it was clear that Wesley was simply misreading the Bible: 'it is plain beyond all contradiction, that St. Paul, through the whole eighth [chapter] of Romans, is speaking of the privileges of those only who are really in Christ ... Had any one a mind to prove the doctrine of *election*, as well as of *final perseverance*, he could hardly wish for a

[29] Wesley, *A Collection of Hymns for the Use of The People Called Methodists* (1780); in Wesley, *Works* (new), vol. 7: *Collection of Hymns*, ed. Franz Hildebrant and Oliver A. Beckerlegge (1983), 309–310.

[30] Wesley, 'Free Grace' (1740), in Wesley, *Works* (1872), 7:376.

[31] For a helpful, succinct treatment, see Alan P. F. Sell, *The Great Debate: Calvinism, Arminianism and Salvation* (Grand Rapids: Baker, 1982).

text more fit for his purpose.'[32] Whitefield's claim for scriptural support was partly in response to Wesley's appeal to texts like 1 Peter 1:2 and Romans 8:29, which, he believed, showed that God's election followed his foreknowledge of what people would do in their God-given freedom.[33] Debate over how best to interpret such passages was and remains extremely important. Yet in this particular dispute, as in other evangelical controversies over theology, characteristic patterns were emerging: Arminians like Wesley held that the realities of Christian experience needed to be taken into account when interpreting Scripture, while Calvinists like Whitefield held that Calvinist biblical interpretations handed down from the Puritans offered the surest support for authentic Christian experience. About most of the evangelical Calvinists of the eighteenth century, it could also be said that they reasoned from their experience of free grace to the doctrines of predestination and election, while Wesleyan Arminians did not follow that path.

In the language of the day, Arminians like Wesley, Calvinists like Whitefield, and Moravians like Ingham and Cennick were still all 'Methodists'. Together they were committed to itineration and the establishment of local societies, while their attitude towards traditional Anglican forms was relaxed. Together they preached first for a true religion of the heart and only secondarily worried about ecclesiastical order. Yet in addition to these common convictions, significant doctrinal differences were dividing evangelicals among themselves.

By this time as well, however, there were a few Anglican ministers who, while not closely identified with Methodist movements as such, had begun to practise evangelical religion. This number included James Hervey (1714–1758) in Northamptonshire, William Romaine (1714–1795) in London, Samuel Walker (1714–1761) of Truro, and William Grimshaw (1708–1763) in Yorkshire, all of whom cooperated to some degree with the Wesleys, Whitefield or both, and yet who were the vanguard of an evangelical Anglicanism that could not be subsumed neatly into any Methodist movement.[34]

Grimshaw was not the only one of these churchmen to experience grace in what might be called a Methodistical way. On Sunday 2 September 1744, Grimshaw became so dizzy and disoriented while preaching that he thought he was dying. He was led from the church to a nearby inn, where he lay in a

---

[32] Whitefield to John Wesley, 24 December 1740, in Whitefield, *Journals*, 574.

[33] Wesley, 'Free Grace', 380.

[34] For summaries, see Kenneth Hylson-Smith, *Evangelicals in the Church of England, 1734–1984* (Edinburgh: T. & T. Clark, 1988), 17–32; and L. E. Elliott-Binns, *The Early Evangelicals* (London: Lutterworth, 1953).

stupor for more than an hour as an icy chill spread over his limbs. In that state, he saw a vision, which that was recorded in the words of a friend:

> He thought he saw as it were a dark foul passage into which he must go: & being entered, saw on the right hand a great high wall on the other side which was Heaven, & another on the left on the other side which was Hell. He overheard God the Father holding a conference with the Lord Jesus Christ concerning him, & for a long time it seemed to go very hard with him, for God the Father would have him to be doomed because he had not wholly relinquished his own righteousness to trust solely & entirely in the merits & righteousness of Christ: but the Lord Jesus pleaded for him. When he had been held in suspense a long time, hoping yet fearing, at last he evidently [i.e., clearly] saw the Lord Jesus thrust down His hands & feet, as it were thro' the ceiling, whilst he particularly observed the wounds in them, & observed the nail-holes to be ragged & bluish, & fresh blood streaming from each of them.[35]

The vision seemed to quicken Grimshaw's body as well as his spirit, because he got up and soon was able to conduct the normal afternoon service at his church. Yet in this experience and through the long career that followed, Grimshaw's conscientious faithfulness to 'regular' church order concerning clerical dress, terms of subscription to the Thirty-Nine Articles, and orderly canonical proceeding kept him securely in the established church.

Romaine's career is particularly interesting since he became the first recognized evangelical to hold a regular benefice in London.[36] Romaine, who came from a wealthy merchant family, had been at Oxford with the Wesleys but had spurned their company. He was already ordained and had served as a curate in Surrey as well as a chaplain to the Lord Mayor of London before he began a multi-year journey that led to his conversion, which probably occurred in 1745 or shortly thereafter. From that time he held various temporary lectureships until in 1766 he was appointed, though only after a legal battle, as the rector of St Andrew's-by-the-Wardrobe and St Anne's Blackfriars in London. Romaine was a Calvinist but he avoided doctrinal strife with Arminians. He worked closely with the Countess of Huntingdon and also maintained a friendship with the Wesleys. Individuals like Romaine, though they might have definite Calvinist, Arminian or even Moravian commitments, found their central doctrinal identity in the forms and traditions of the Church of England, interpreted, to be sure, with as

---

[35] Frank Baker, *William Grimshaw* (London: Epworth, 1963), 72.

[36] See *BDEB*, 953–954 (A. Skevington Wood, 'William Romaine'); and William Romaine, *The Life, Walk and Triumph of Faith*, ed. with introduction by Peter Toon (Cambridge: James Clarke, 1970).

much evangelical emphasis as possible. Romaine might be styled an evangelical Anglican, while John Wesley was an Anglican evangelical, and Charles Wesley, who supported his brother consistently but also held militantly to the Church of England, was somewhere in between.

Organized Methodism (1744)

As important for evangelical history as the emergence of theological parties proved, so too the organizational development of Methodism within the Church of England was a critical occurrence in these early years. Methodism, it must be remembered, was originally a word with broad connotations, since it took in Whitefield, the Countess of Huntingdon, Howell Harris and many more. Yet for the long-term future, the practices and structures associated with John and Charles Wesley's variety of Methodism were of supreme importance.[37]

By the early 1740s, John Wesley was itinerating over more and more territory – in and around London, Wales, the English Midlands and Yorkshire in the north. As he continued to recruit lay itinerant preachers, he also tried to cultivate his clerical friends within the Church of England. In 1743 he published a substantial pamphlet, *The Nature, Design and General Rules of the United Societies*, in which he specified terms for joining the small groups that he modelled on the pietists' *collegia pietatis*. To join a society required people only to show 'a desire to flee from the wrath to come, to be saved from their sins'.[38] Wesley also continued to urge society members to attend their local Anglican churches, and especially to receive the sacrament of communion from their parish ministers. Yet in order to provide preaching stations for himself and other itinerants, he oversaw the construction of meeting houses and the rental of previously constructed buildings. Three of these were functioning in London by 1744, with others in Newcastle and Bristol. While considerable interchange continued with Moravians and Calvinist Methodists, Wesley's associates, disciples and converts were building doctrinal boundaries too. Organizational shape was beginning to emerge as Wesley met regularly with society leaders and his itinerant lay preachers for the promotion of evangelization and parish renewal.

In June 1744, an important landmark was established. With his brother Charles, four other Anglican clergy who were friends of the movement, and

---

[37] In this section, I am following mostly Heitzenrater, *Wesley*, 134–146; Rack, *Wesley*, 237–250; and the articles of John Walsh listed in the Select Bibliography.

[38] Heitzenrater, *Wesley*, 138.

four lay itinerants, Wesley convened what would later be regarded as the first Methodist Annual Conference. Through a series of discussions in which Wesley encouraged open debate, but that ended with the body resolving what he intended, the fledging Connection specified expectations for doctrine and practice. In carefully preserved Minutes, the Wesleyans affirmed the centrality of justification by faith, but also (against the Calvinists) treated repentance and church duties as good works pointing towards justification. They proclaimed the assurance of salvation as a birthright of all Christians, but also (against the Moravians) maintained that believers could expect varying degrees of assurance as they journeyed through life. The Minutes also emphasized how important it was for all believers to advance in holiness towards perfection in Christ.

On questions of practice, the Minutes specified the nature and activities of local cells. No separation from the Church of England was intended; rather, preaching and the organization of converts into societies and bands were meant to rejuvenate the church. For the smooth operation of the societies, the Minutes spelled out the duties of assistants, stewards and leaders in convening the local gatherings, visiting the sick, providing hospitality for itinerant preachers and offering basic schooling to those who needed it. In addition, the Minutes provided guidelines for how the itinerants should structure their sermons, in Richard Heitzenrater's summary, 'to invite, to convince, to offer Christ, and to build up'.[39] Then at the close of the convention, Wesley set up a regular schedule of quarterly meetings (for Newcastle, Bristol and London), and a date for the next general Conference in the summer of 1745. Before they adjourned, Wesley also passed out assignments for the itinerant preachers to cover the next year.

The meeting was important in several ways. Lay preachers were accorded full status alongside the ordained Anglicans. The ligaments of a dynamic organization, preserving both connection and flexibility, were in place. John Wesley was clearly the leader, but he was exerting authority primarily to empower other clergy and laymen, in their turn, to empower society leaders, and all for the purpose of spreading the message of salvation and the prospect of life in the power and blessing of the Holy Spirit. Wesley's Methodism still resembled a large, segmented Anglican voluntary society. But its national extension as well as its effectiveness in promoting gospel preaching gave it a singular solidarity and a unique potential for independent development.

The organizational evolution, which was as rapid as it was effective, should not obscure the essential reasons for the expansion of Wesleyan Methodism.

---

[39] Ibid., 145.

It was not primarily organization but activity, not primarily structure but zeal, not primarily order but sacrifice that made this Methodism a marvel of Christian energy. Wesley was successful at recruiting itinerants because no-one, with the exception of George Whitefield, travelled more incessantly himself. Wesley inspired others to preach a gospel message because he took the claims of the gospel upon himself with utter, even obsessive, seriousness. The Wesleyan movement reached out to unbelievers bypassed by both Anglicans and Dissenters because it was committed to reaching the poor wherever they were found. Above all else, Wesleyan Methodism worked because its leaders were conscious that God had worked upon themselves.

No-one has ever described the source of Wesleyan effectiveness more evocatively than John Walsh:

> Perhaps the most characteristic image of the English movement is, not that of John Wesley preaching to great crowds in the sunken outdoor amphitheater at Gwennap in Cornwall, but Wesley as he is described in John Barrit's diary, standing in a barn with a knot of shabby people around him, explaining the love of God in the process of regeneration. Would they recognize the presence of God's love? Yes, they would. For how did wives and husbands recognize the love they bore each other, or children know that they were loved by their parents? They *felt* it in their hearts. And so too it would be with God's grace.[40]

The outer history of Wesleyanism as an organized religious movement had only just begun in 1744. But in the activities of the Wesleys, the few Anglican clergy who cooperated with them, and most of all in the swelling ranks of lay itinerants, its inner spirit was already surprisingly well formed.

International revived Calvinism

After renewal within Anglicanism, the second centre of evangelicalism by the mid-1740s was the network of revived Calvinists who, though attuned to the doings of Whitefield and his Calvinist associates in the Church of England, were linked to each other even more strongly by their position as, in various ways, outsiders to the established Church of England. This network did include the English Dissenters Watts, Doddridge and their associates, who were especially important for the access they provided to London publishers.

---

[40] John Walsh, '"Methodism" and the Origins of English-Speaking Evangelicalism', in *Evangelicalism*, 34.

But its greatest spiritual advances were taking place among the Calvinist awakeners in Britain's outlying established churches – Welsh Anglicans, Scottish Presbyterians and New England Congregationalists – and among the Presbyterians in the ecclesiastical open spaces of the American middle colonies. The critical importance of George Whitefield for the early history of evangelicalism is suggested by the fact that he was the only major figure as completely at home in this Calvinist internationale as among the Church of England revivalists.

In parallel with English evangelicals, Welsh Methodists were beginning to organize their own network of local societies. The first meeting of what would eventually become the Calvinist Methodist Association took place on 7 January 1742 at Dugoedydd under the chairmanship of Daniel Rowland, and with Howell Harris and about twenty mostly lay exhorters in attendance.[41] Later that year a set of guidelines was issued to govern these meetings and to encourage further evangelical activity within the established church in Wales. Organizationally, Welsh evangelicals moved slowly in pressing differences with accustomed practices in their Anglican state church. But as more and more people attended to the ministries of Rowland, Harris, William Williams and like-minded preachers, pressure grew towards the development of a powerful Calvinistic Methodism.

Similarly in Scotland, the great results of 1742 drew together a significant phalanx of dedicated evangelical labourers, but separate evangelical emphases took shape only slowly within the established Kirk. Evangelical sentiments were also present in the Associate Presbytery, but although sermons and poems by Ralph and Ebenezer Erskine were read, translated and re-preached elsewhere in Britain's Celtic fringe, especially by Welsh Methodists, sharpened ecclesiastical competition kept Secession and Kirk evangelicals from cooperating with each other. Because of the strength of inherited Presbyterian traditions, there was almost no Methodism as such in Scotland.

In America the Great Awakening had left a strong evangelical presence in New England, with active networks of ministers who welcomed itinerant evangelists, followed Whitefield's career with interest, read the sermons and tracts of Jonathan Edwards and urged their fellow-ministers to greater concentration on the realities of heart religion. As elsewhere in the North Atlantic region, however, revival generated considerable opposition, some to the new stress on evangelical theology, but more to what seemed like disruptive excesses from revival enthusiasts.

---

[41] See Eifion Evans, *Daniel Rowland and the Great Evangelical Awakening in Wales* (Edinburgh: Banner of Truth, 1985), 177–180.

The leader of the opposition in New England was Charles Chauncy (1705–1787), at that time still the young pastor of Boston's First Church, where he would remain through a long and much-noticed pastorate.[42] Chauncy was as quick to espy the brambles of enthusiasm as some of the revival's supporters were to spot the fruits of the Spirit. Beginning in 1742, he began to collect materials for what he and a network of other 'Old Lights' (or defenders of settled, inherited ways) considered antinomian and enthusiastic excesses. While Jonathan Edwards was publishing a series of works that defended the revival by sorting its positive, God-given blessings from its negative, human-manufactured excesses, Chauncy and his allies denounced the movement as a whole. He first passed on unfavourable reports of New England's revivals to Scotland and then, in an effort to tar by association, published a tract on the French Prophets, a body of extreme Huguenots who had spun off into bizarre fanaticism at the end of the seventeenth century. But Chauncy's most extensive assault on the emerging evangelicals was a lengthy book, *Seasonable Thoughts on the State of Religion in New England*, which was published in the fall of 1743 as an antidote to Edwards' *Some Thoughts Concerning the Present Revival of Religion in New England*, which appeared in the spring of that year. To Chauncy, what friends of the revival regarded as God's good actions were nothing more than wild-eyed delusion:

> The true Account to be given of the *many* and *great* Mistakes of the present Day, about the SPIRIT's Influence is not the *newness* of the Thing ... but a *notorious* Error generally prevailing, as to the *Way* and *Manner* of judging in this Matter. People, in order to know, whether the Influences they are under, are from the SPIRIT, don't carefully examine them by the *Word of GOD*, and view the *Change* they produce in the *moral State* of their *Minds* and of their *Lives*, but hastily conclude such and such *internal Motions* to be *divine Impressions*, merely from the *Perception* they have of them ... This is the Error of the present Day; and 'tis indeed the *proton Pseudos*, the first and grand Delusion.[43]

James Davenport (1716–1757), minister of a Congregational church on Long Island, but then from 1740 a manic itinerant, was one of Chauncy's prime neg-

---

[42] For Chauncy's activity in the 1740s, see E. S. Gaustad, *The Great Awakening in New England* (New York: Harper & Bros., 1957), 80–101; and Edwards, *Works*, 4:61–65, 80–86, 308–312.

[43] Chauncy, *Seasonable Thoughts on the State of Religion* (1743), in Alan Heimert and Perry Miller (eds.), *The Great Awakening* (Indianapolis: Bobbs-Merrill, 1967), 293.

ative examples. For about three years, Davenport abrasively denounced regular parish preachers and whipped up extraordinary bodily reactions among his humble auditors. In March 1743 at New London, Connecticut, he conducted a book-burning of traditional Christian classics that Davenport denounced as the mere husks of genuine religion.[44] Although Davenport was soon corralled – shortly thereafter he publicly repented of his errors – critics of the New England establishment who were less extreme continued to decry the spiritual weakness of the established-church system inherited from the Puritans.

An important result of counter-charge and defence was to divide the partisans of evangelical revival among themselves. Thus, 'New Lights' (which in America, but not Britain, meant pro-revivalists) included some congregations that continued in the establishment, but also some in separating congregations whose members broke with the established system in order to found churches where true believers could commune with each other in the purity of the gospel. By 1745 there were perhaps thirty to thirty-five of these separated congregations, which, though still a relatively small number, did anticipate what eventually became, in the words of C. C. Goen, 'a permanent shattering of the Congregational establishment in New England'.[45]

Among Presbyterians of the middle colonies evangelicalism was now securely rooted, but, as in New England, with disruptive ecclesiastical results.[46] A party of Scots-Irish revivalists associated with the Tennent family eagerly promoted preaching as exemplified by George Whitefield, but they were opposed by a party of traditionalists, also mostly from Scotland via Ireland, who felt that Whitefield and his ways threatened everything sound in their church. The latter group initially prevailed and in 1741 expelled the Tennent, or 'New Side', faction from the Synod of Philadelphia. Four years later, however, a more cautious group of ministers, many trained in New England, joined the Tennents and colleagues from New York, New Jersey and Pennsylvania in forming a thoroughly evangelical Synod of New York as an alternative to the Old Side Synod of Philadelphia.

---

[44] See Harry S. Stout and Peter Onuf, 'James Davenport and the Great Awakening in New London', *Journal of American History* 70 (1983): 556–578.

[45] C. C. Goen, *Revivalism and Separatism in New England, 1740–1800* (2nd ed., Hamden: Archon, 1969), ix, with 302–306 enumerating the separate congregations.

[46] On these events, see Leonard J. Trinterud, *The Forming of an American Tradition: A Re-examination of Colonial Presbyterianism* (Philadelphia: Westminster, 1949), 109–134; and for an updating, Thomas H. L. Cornman, 'Securing a Faithful Ministry: Struggles of Ethnicity and Religious Epistemology in Colonial American Presbyterianism' (PhD dissertation, University of Illinois at Chicago, 1998).

The crucial New England faction was led by Jonathan Dickinson (1688–1747), one of the most effective American church leaders of his generation.[47] Although Dickinson was a friend of revival and had welcomed Whitefield to his church at Elizabethtown, New Jersey, in November 1739 and April 1740, he also feared the excesses of enthusiasm, especially the tendency of the awakened to think that they no longer needed to pay attention to the requirements of God's law. Dickinson's most characteristic, and also effective, work was a dialogue published in 1742, *A Display of God's Special Grace*, in which he attempted to defend revival while maintaining the church's need to promote order, discipline and stable holiness.

As a leading mediator between the warring Scots–Irish factions, Dickinson was especially concerned about ministerial training. One of the Old Side's first efforts, in fact, had been to disenfranchise students who had gained their education at the 'Log College' conducted by Gilbert Tennent's father, William, in Neshaminy, Pennsylvania. After the establishment of the New York Synod in 1745, Dickinson consulted with several of his colleagues about how they could meet the need for ministers in new settlements, many of which were being set up by immigrants from Ulster. Yale, because of coolness toward Whitefield, was now suspect, and the 'Log College' had closed with William Tennent's retirement (he died in 1746). With three other ministers, including Aaron Burr of Newark, New Jersey, and three wealthy laymen from New York, Dickinson secured a charter in late 1746 for a new institution of higher learning called the College of New Jersey. In 1748 this charter was strengthened when Jonathan Belcher, Whitefield's old friend, was transferred from his post as governor of Massachusetts to become governor of New Jersey. The new college was designed by New Sides for New Sides, but the charter language was broad enough to provide education for young men from several denominations and for careers other than the ministry. To no-one's surprise, Dickinson was asked to be the first president. Although his death in late 1747 meant that he served only briefly at that post, the work he began in his parsonage at Elizabethtown slowly developed through changes of location (first to Newark and then to Princeton) until it became a mainstay of classical education accessible for evangelicals through the rest of the eighteenth century. The Princeton Theological Seminary, which spun off as a separate institution in 1812, would extend the impact of these earlier educational initiatives much further in the evangelical world.[48]

---

[47] For welcome treatment of a neglected figure, see Bryan F. LeBeau, *Jonathan Dickinson and the Formative Years of American Presbyterianism* (Lexington: University of Kentucky Press, 1997).

[48] For fuller accounts, see Mark A. Noll, *Princeton and the Republic, 1768–1822* (Princeton:

The American Presbyterians were not as close to their fellow-Presbyterians in Scotland as the Scots were to selected Congregational clergy in New England, particularly Jonathan Edwards. Yet the surge of revival among American Presbyterians did exert an evangelical influence back to the more liberal Presbyterianism of Ireland, even as influences from Britain continued to flow to the new world. As a result, these historic bonds across the Atlantic helped American Presbyterians maintain a style of evangelicalism that was more churchly, clerical and confessional than became the American norm.

The refinement of evangelical preaching

By the mid-1740s, evangelical preaching had also emerged as a distinct form of Christian proclamation. Whitefield was critical in this process, since he influenced so many people in so many places by what he said, as well as how he said it. Forthright preaching of repentance, the redemptive work of Christ, the necessity of faith and the privileges of holy living were Whitefield's sermonic stock-in-trade. But because he usually dispensed with a written-out sermon text, because he preached intentionally for emotional as well as intellectual effect, and because he called upon individuals to respond *as individuals* to his message, these traits also became characteristic of evangelical preaching in general.[49]

Early in the 1740s, several types of characteristic evangelical sermons were securely in place. Gilbert Tennent's blast, 'The Danger of an Unconverted Ministry' (1740), represented the kind of denunciatory sermon that evangelicals could level against what they considered traditionalistic or formalistic counterfeits of true religion. Jonathan Edwards' famous 'Sinners in the Hands of an Angry God' (1741) provided the premier illustration of the hell-fire and damnation sermon. This sermon, however, has been caricatured more often than it has been copied.

Princeton University Press, 1989); and Noll, 'The Founding of Princeton Seminary', *Westminster Theological Journal* 42 (1979): 72–110.

[49] On the broad cultural implications of Whitefield's dramatically new form of preaching, see Harry S. Stout, 'Religion, Communications, and the Revolution', *William and Mary Quarterly* 34 (1977): 519–541; Frank Lambert, *'Pedlar in Divinity': George Whitefield and the Transatlantic Revivals* (Princeton: Princeton University Press, 1994); and Timothy D. Hall, *Contested Boundaries: Itinerancy and the Reshaping of the Colonial American Religious World* (Durham, NC: Duke University Press, 1994), 32–39, 97–99.

Just as representative as either denunciation or damnation was a strong sermonic strand that expatiated upon the consolations of the gospel. In this
regard, Edwards' less frequently quoted 'The Excellency of Christ' (1738) was
just as representative of the new evangelicalism as his 'Sinners in the Hands of
an Angry God'. In the former, Edwards detailed at length why the repentant
sinner could hope in Christ:

> If you are a poor distressed sinner, whose heart is ready to sink for fear that God
> never will have mercy on you, you need not be afraid to go to Christ, for fear that he
> is either unable or unwilling to help you: here is a strong foundation, and an
> inexhaustible treasure, to answer the necessities of your poor soul; and here is infinite
> grace and gentleness to invite and embolden a poor unworthy fearful soul to come to
> it. If Christ accepts of you, you need not fear but that you will be safe; for he is a
> strong lion for your defense; and if you come, you need not fear but that you shall be
> accepted; for he is like a lamb to all that come to him, and receives them with infinite
> grace and tenderness.[50]

But perhaps the most characteristic of evangelical sermon-types were
those that described the origin, nature and process of saving faith in Jesus
Christ. Among the most reprinted of these most characteristic sermons were
the discourses that John Wesley in 1746 gathered as his *Standard Sermons* and
then reprinted regularly as a guide for his movement. The first sermon in this
collection was entitled 'Salvation by Faith'. It had been preached for the first
time at Oxford in June 1738, less than a month after Wesley's memorable
experience at Aldersgate. Its text was Ephesians 2:8 ('By grace ye are saved
through faith'). It began with bold assertions:

> [T]here is nothing we are, or have, or do, which can deserve the least thing at God's
> hand...
> [The human] heart is altogether corrupt and abominable...
> If then sinful man find favour with God, it is 'grace upon grace!' ... Grace is the
> source, faith is the condition, of salvation.

The sermon itself was divided into three sections, in which Wesley's exposition was as forthright as his opening phrases: 'I. What faith it is through which
we are saved. II. What is the salvation which is through faith. III. How we may

---

[50] Edwards, 'The Excellency of Christ' (1738), in Wilson M. Kimnach, Kenneth P.
Minkema and Douglas A. Sweeney (eds.), *The Sermons of Jonathan Edwards* (New Haven:
Yale University Press, 1999), 184–185.

answer some objections'.[51] The countless sermons that have been preached by evangelicals since the 1740s have ventured far in every direction. But they have been most faithful to the original springs of evangelicalism itself when they have remained connected to this Wesleyan home-base.

By the mid-1740s evangelical impulses were well rooted in the established churches that accounted for the vast bulk of organized religion in Britain and the colonies. At this point evangelicalism could still be most easily defined as a movement of spiritual renewal within these dominant state churches. Hints of the later and much wider diffusion of evangelicalism in groups far beyond the boundaries of establishment religion could be glimpsed by 1745, but that diffusion would mostly occur in years to come.

In 1745, organized evangelicalism was still not too much more than an informal network of correspondents who eagerly shared books promoting true religion, passed on news to each other of extraordinary effusions of the Holy Spirit and cooperated in producing magazines that chronicled local revivals. The proponents of revival in the English state church and the widely dispersed network of revivalistic Calvinists (with Whitefield as the key figure linking these two groups) represented the main institutional venues.

By 1745, sparks from the Anglican evangelical centre and from the more widely spread Calvinist revival network had also fallen among Baptists in both the old and new worlds, as well as more generally into Ireland, the American southern colonies, the Canadian Maritimes and the West Indies. But at this early date in those far-flung regions evangelical faith was still more incipient than realized. Evangelicalism as a whole had entered into a particularly unstable situation where the strength of the movement was found within established churches that were, at best, lukewarm in their welcome. But that particular situation did not last for long.

Before going on to trace developments after 1745, however, it would be well to address directly a most important but also most complex question: why did it happen?

---

[51] Wesley, 'Salvation by Faith' (1738); in Wesley, *Works* (new), vol. 1: *Sermons I: 1–33*, ed. Albert C. Outler (1984), 118.

5. EXPLANATIONS

Historians have offered many explanations for the outbreak of evangelical revival, as well as for the more general upsurge of evangelicalism throughout the English-speaking world in the 1730s and 1740s. A difficulty in sorting through such explanations is that many of them are convincing for only some regions in which evangelicalism emerged, or for only some aspects of evangelical experience, or from only some angles of interpretation. Some explanations that work well for individual revivals do not help much with the general rise of evangelicalism, and vice versa. The more useful particular explanations are for specific situations, the harder it can be to understand what one historian has called 'the mystery of how it was that so many evangelicals in different parts of England and Wales [as well as New England, the middle colonies, and soon Scotland, the southern colonies and Canada] began to preach the same kind of message independently of one another'.[1] To put the issue more broadly: in 1730, while many evangelical elements were present in the churches of Britain and the colonies, there was no discernible evangelical movement. Twenty years later, by contrast, although considerable intellectual and organizational confusion existed among evangelical groups, a diverse, variegated and sometimes competitive but also distinctly discernible evangelical movement had come into existence. Later chapters examine the sources of

---

[1] David Hempton, 'Religion in British Society, 1740–1790', in Jeremy Black (ed.), *British Politics and Society from Pitt to Walpole* (London: Macmillan, 1990), 214.

evangelical diversity, variety and competition. In this chapter the question is how evangelicalism came about.

The rise of evangelicalism does not pose exactly the same challenge as the occurrence of evangelical revivals, though the two matters are closely related. Participants at the time and observers later spoke of revivals or awakenings in three or four overlapping senses. An awakening might mean, first, an experience of 'revival' at a particular place for which local preachers or circumstances were the primary visible agents. This is the sense of awakening provided by Jonathan Edwards' *A Faithful Narrative of Surprising Conversions* (1737) and also by accounts of the extraordinary communion seasons of 1742 in Scotland. Second, the term 'revival' could be used for the excitement generated by a travelling preacher, supremely George Whitefield, but also many of his imitators. A third sense of awakening referred more generally to positive spiritual good arising from durable local cells and broader interconnected networks created for the promotion of holiness. The various Methodist societies, especially those connected by John Wesley's ceaseless itinerancy, were the prime examples of this form of awakening, but parallel movements were found among the Calvinistic Methodists of Wales, some Moravian bodies in England and Ireland, and a few groups in America. A fourth use of the concept occurred when observers described specific regions or populations as so thoroughly affected by gospel preaching as to be transformed socially or culturally in the direction of Christian ideals. The various senses of revival or awakening were of course not mutually exclusive. They were linked not only by circumstances – for example, the establishment of Methodist classes sometimes seemed to transform entire regions, Whitefield was often welcomed by promoters of local revivals, and notable preaching moments often led to the creation of local societies. They were linked as well by a common set of expectations attending virtually all usages: that a revival or awakening would be marked by the conversion of individuals, that it would be notable in a more general sense for its impact on many lives, and that because of its effects there would be increased adherence to churches and voluntary religious societies.

Over time it became clear that for evangelicalism to take root, the longing for revival was more important than revival itself. Over the course of the eighteenth century and beyond, evangelical revivals waxed and waned, even as evangelicalism grew steadily apace. Evangelicalism did indeed come to be marked by the kind of preaching featured in the awakenings. It was a preaching aimed directly at popular affections, expecting life-changing results, emphasizing the message of divine grace as the God-given remedy for sin, and often (though not always) dispensing with elaborate ratiocination. Evangelicalism did flourish where strong local societies, with strong lay leadership, provided spiritual nurture and religious community for women and men who were, or would be, converted. Its revivalistic practices did provide a common set of assumptions about how best to address the problems of society: the conversion of individuals to God and to lives of faithful service offered a template for how renewal would work upon entire communities. Evangelicalism also tended towards the same indifference to tradition and inherited ecclesiastical institutions that marked revival practice. Yet if evangelicals regularly prayed for awakenings and understood revival as the norm for ordinary religious life, by the 1740s and 1750s there was more to evangelicalism than evangelical revival. Asking why evangelical revivals took place, whether in Britain or North America, is, thus, only part of a broader question about the rise of evangelicalism itself.

A movement of the Spirit

Explanations for the rise of evangelicalism do well to begin where the evangelicals themselves began. If, out of respect for these early evangelicals and a due sense concerning the limits of later observers, their voices are allowed to come first among a series of explanations, it restores balance to the task of interpretation. Other, later, accounts certainly need to be heard, but to explain the revivals without the testimony of revivalists is an act of sheer hubris.

As historians themselves, the early evangelicals were deeply impressed with the role that extraordinary effusions of the Holy Spirit had played in the entire pilgrimage of the church. When Jonathan Edwards contemplated the way in which God worked in history, his conclusion was that 'from the fall of man to this day wherein we live the Work of Redemption in its effect has mainly been carried on by remarkable pourings out of the Spirit of God'.[2] Because of the importance of revival to evangelical consciousness, Edwards' assessment rapidly became standard.

Joseph Milner (1749–1797), an Anglican schoolmaster and the first general church historian from the evangelical movement, began his history of the early Christian centuries in typically evangelical fashion by proclaiming that it would focus on 'men who have been REAL, not merely NOMINAL Christians', and do so without paying attention to the 'EXTERNAL church' of their adherence or to 'their rites and ceremonies, or forms of Church-government'. Milner's work was preoccupied, rather, with what he called

---

[2] Edwards, *History of the Work of Redemption* (preached 1739, published posthumously), in Edwards, *Works*, vol. 9: *A History of the Work of Redemption*, ed. John F. Wilson (1989), 143.

'those EFFUSIONS of the Spirit of God, which from age to age have visited the earth, since the coming of Christ', and which Milner described as 'a remarkable display of the Divine Grace, at some particular season'.[3] In the terms of Edwards and Milner, the rise of evangelicalism was the manifestation of a special outpouring of the Holy Spirit.[4]

The first thorough historian of the American Great Awakening, Joseph Tracy (1793–1874), shared this general view about the origins of evangelicalism, but formulated his convictions quite specifically with respect to New England. In his opinion, the most fundamental explanation for the revival was the fresh 'prominence and power' given to 'the idea of the "new birth" as held by the Orthodox Congregationalists of New England, and to others who harmonize with them; the doctrine that in order to be saved, a man must undergo a change in his principles of moral action, which will be either accompanied or succeeded by exercises of which he is conscious'. As Tracy read the past, 'The history of the "Great Awakening" is the history of this idea, making its way through some communities where it had fallen into comparative neglect, and through others where it was nearly or quite unknown.'[5]

John Wesley's assessment of the rise of Methodism offered for Britain something similar to what Tracy provided for New England. Writing in the mid-1760s, Wesley maintained that Methodism as a movement had arisen in response to preaching drawn from the Scriptures and featuring the doctrine of 'justification by faith'.[6] With Tracy, Wesley took for granted that the Holy Spirit worked with particular efficacy where the Bible's genuine teaching came to the fore. Preached truth promoted true religion.

Efforts at discerning spiritual causes and providing spiritual evaluations for both awakenings and the emergence of a general evangelical faith were not, however, limited to the friends of revival. Christians who thought the new

---

[3] Joseph Milner, *The History of the Church of Christ*, vol. 1 (2nd ed., Cambridge: Cambridge University Press, 1800), ix–x, 3–4. Another important early work that carried this view of history right up to the time of the revivals was John Gillies, *Historical Collections Relating to Remarkable Periods of the Success of the Gospel, and Eminent Instruments Employed in Promoting It*, 2 vols (Glasgow: R. & A. Foulis, 1754).

[4] For learned commentaries on this theme, see Michael J. Crawford, *Seasons of Grace: Colonial New England's Revival Tradition in Its British Context* (New York: Oxford University Press, 1991), 248; and John Walsh, 'Joseph Milner's Evangelical Church History', *Journal of Ecclesiastical History* 10 (1959): 174–187.

[5] Joseph Tracy, *The Great Awakening: A History of the Revival of Religion in the Time of Edwards and Whitefield* (Boston: Charles Tappan, 1845), ix, xiii.

[6] Wesley, 'A Short History of Methodism' (c.1764), in Wesley, *Works* (1872), 8:349.

evangelical emphases were taking the church in the wrong direction were also quick to isolate spiritual causes and effects. For example, a 1743 convention of Massachusetts clergy dominated by ministers who opposed the revivals sounded very much like John Wesley and Joseph Tracy, but in reverse. This group held that 'the pure Doctrines of the Gospel' contradicted claims about holiness that were not backed by a holy life; that it was 'contrary to the *Scriptures*' for itinerants to preach without the permission of parish pastors; that it was a violation of 'the Rule of the Gospel' for disenchanted parishioners to separate from their churches; and that the practice of indiscriminate judging, censuring and condemning others (especially ministers) on the basis of a sup-posed spiritual knowledge was 'most contrary to the Spirit and Precepts of the Gospel, and the Example of Christ'.[7] In their judgment, the excesses of revival proved that it came, not from the Holy Spirit, but from enthusiasm.

Spiritual interpretation of both particular revivals and evangelicalism more generally was common throughout the eighteenth century, and it has remained persistent to this day in some religious circles. As the testimony of the disaffected Massachusetts ministers indicated by their opposition to revival practices, and as much theological in-fighting among the friends of revival also indicated by its willingness to think the worst of fellow evangeli-cals, there could be great differences among spiritual interpretations. But what all who look to explain things in such a spiritual way have assumed is that they could understand clearly the ways of God in the world. In offering such views, they have not been oblivious to evidence, but it is a use of evidence strongly influenced by theological convictions concerning how God does, or even must, act. Other interpretations of the rise of evangelicalism also reflect the influence of worldviews, but spiritual interpretations are singular because of the close fit between evangelical experiences and evangelical explanations.

Agents and agency

A spiritual account of the rise of evangelicalism would, however, be distorted if it were assumed that the work of the Holy Spirit, teaching about the New Birth or a desire for conversion spread spontaneously and without agents. The same judgment applies to non-spiritual accounts that look only to large-scale

---

[7] *The Testimony of the Pastors of the Churches in the Province of Massachusetts-Bay ... May 25. 1743. Against several Errors in Doctrine, and Disorders in Practice* (1743), in Richard L. Bushman, *The Great Awakening: Documents on the Revival of Religion, 1740–1745* (1970; Chapel Hill: University of North Carolina Press, 1989), 127–128.

social forces as the cause of revival. By contrast, a full explanation must not back away from agency, for the early evangelical preachers were powerful, early evangelical communicators were effective and early evangelical organizers were successful. By taking note of the agents who, whether perceived as servants of God or merely adept shapers of culture, historical explanation adds the sphere of human responsibility to realms of theological principle, religious conviction or social tectonics.

Whatever else might be said about them, the young men who preached the sermons, generated public attention, founded the magazines, established the local classes, built the connections and wrote the books, pamphlets and articles were social actors of unusual force. It is, of course, relevant to note that they were young, with most of the major leaders during the 1730s still in their 20s or, if older, like John Wesley, still unsettled in vocation. Evangelicalism, in fact, gave a whole cohort of energetic but relatively insecure young spiritual adepts not only causes to champion but jobs to perform.

It is similarly relevant to note that the shaping of early evangelicalism was very much a male affair. Women might provide exemplary narratives of conversion, as in Edwards' early account of events at Northampton or the life-stories taken down at Cambuslang. They regularly offered critical personal or financial support, whether John Wesley's mother Susannah, Jonathan Edwards' wife Sarah Pierrepont Edwards or George Whitefield's friend and backer the Countess of Huntingdon. And they certainly provided a major proportion, which rose steadily after the 1740s, of participants in evangelical congregations and societies. Yet important as women always were for evangelicalism on the ground, the public movement was driven by men.

They were, however, unusually gifted men: one of the greatest public orators of the century (Whitefield), one of the most effective organizers for one of the longest periods of effectiveness (John Wesley), one of the pioneers in the management of publicity (William Seward), one of the most compelling popular troubadours (Charles Wesley), one of the most powerful thinkers (Edwards), several of the critical forerunners of printed mass communication (John Lewis, Thomas Prince, William McCulloch), and then scores of others who in their local spheres were sometimes even more memorable as preachers, networkers, hymnwriters, theologians and communicators.

It is not excessive to claim that the early evangelicals created evangelicalism.[8] What they made it out of, for what ends, in response to what conditions

---

[8]   For sophisticated discussion about such 'creation', see Crawford, *Seasons of Grace*, 13–15 and *passim*; and Frank Lambert, *Inventing the 'Great Awakening'* (Princeton: Princeton University Press, 1999).

and in what relation to God and his ways are all questions worthy of the most serious discussion. Yet create it they did, and the human agency must always be a large factor in interpretations of early evangelical history.

The flow of history

It is also relevant to note that fresh spiritual energy was working its effects at a particular point in the religious history of the English-speaking people. Evangelicalism emerged just as the very last living witnesses of the Puritan Revolution (1640ff.) and Royal Restoration (1660) were passing from the scene. Fear of enthusiasm and its disastrous effects, which remained a critical legacy of that mid-seventeenth century, was by no means dead. Even some entirely orthodox and attractively pious observers in the late 1730s and early 1740s joined critics in viewing the revivals as perilous sources of presumptuous spiritual pride. But time had passed, legal freedom had opened up in the British Isles and entirely new religious challenges faced the colonists in North America. In short, enough had changed from 1660 that some respectable leaders were now willing to risk a charge of enthusiasm in order to promote forms of faith they felt that they themselves, as well as the larger public, required. Nervous responses did include new fears about unchecked behaviour (i.e., antinomianism) and unregulated zeal (i.e., enthusiasm), but such challenges to the new evangelical preaching were not as strong as had been the case in 1660, 1688 or even in 1714, when the House of Hanover succeeded the House of Stuart as Britain's ruling monarchs.

A religious menace to social wellbeing certainly loomed large as a spectre in the period when evangelicalism appeared, but increasingly that menace was identified, not with Protestant religious enthusiasm, but with the Church of Rome in league with Britain's imperial enemies. Beginning with the reign of William and Mary in 1688, Britain found itself involved in an on-going series of wars with France (there was also a short period of hostility against Spain in the late 1730s). France, it happens, was also the foreign sponsor of the ousted royal line of the Catholic James II, whose supporters were known as Jacobites (from James = Jacobus). Twice in the first half of the century, France backed efforts by descendants of James II to recover the British throne – a worrying invasion in 1715 and then the incursion by Bonnie Prince Charlie in 1745 that swept through Scotland and advanced deep into England before it was checked. For ever-growing numbers of Britons, these threats to Hanoverian rule, as also the threats conveyed by Britain's foreign wars, were also threats to the inherited Protestantism of

Britain and its colonies.[9] To mention only one of many possible examples showing these connections, Thomas Prince preached a memorable sermon in Boston in late 1746 in which he looked back on 'the Most Remarkable Salvation of the Year Past, Both in Europe and North-America'. To Prince, who had only shortly before ended publication of his periodical, the *Christian History*, with its accounts of evangelical revivals in the colonies, Britain and Europe, the defeat of Bonnie Prince Charlie in April 1746 simply had to be placed alongside New England's victory over the French fortress at Louisbourg, Nova Scotia, in June 1745 (one of the many far-flung engagements in that round of warfare between France and Britain). These victories were literal Godsends. In those battles, 'all our civil and religious Liberties, our Privileges, Properties and the Lives of Multitudes seemed under God to be depending'. The threat was contributed particularly by the 'Empire, Power, and Influence of the popish, cruel, ambitious, restless' rulers of France and especially by 'the popish spirit [that] made them in Affairs of Religion *cruel*'.[10] Prince, as virtually all Protestant ministers did in such sermons, urged repentance and faith before God as the only sure way to safety in times of trial and as the best path to bring a divine blessing upon the body politic. What incorporated British foreign policy into the era's religious history was the opportunity the Catholic threat opened up for specifically evangelical proclamation. While preaching about justification by faith, the assurance of salvation and the direct witness of the Holy Spirit might still convey a whiff of enthusiasm, it also provided the sharpest, clearest and most fruitful antidote to the doctrines of works righteousness and hierarchical tyranny that most Britons saw in Roman Catholicism. Britain's interminable wars with Catholic France did not manufacture English-speaking evangelicalism, but they did stimulate a social and religious environment in which evangelical religion could flourish.

The same conclusion must be drawn about the specific juncture in formal church history during which evangelicalism emerged. In all regions of the empire the decade of the 1730s was disquieting for the established churches, which, it is helpful to remember, were the churches for well over 90% of the

---

[9] For full development of this theme, see Linda Colley, *Britons: Forging the Nation, 1707–1837* (New Haven: Yale University Press, 1992), 11–54.

[10] Thomas Prince, *The Salvation of God in 1746. In Part Set Forth in a Sermon at the South Church in Boston, Nov. 27, 1746. Being the Day of the Anniversary Thanksgiving in the Province of the Massachusetts Bay in N. E. Wherein the Most Remarkable Salvation of the Year Past, Both in Europe and North-America, as Far as They Come to Our Knowledge Are Briefly Considered* (Boston: D. Henchman, 1746), 11, 17.

population. In England, leading Anglicans worried about what seemed to be a rising tide of influential deist propaganda, as illustrated by Thomas Woolston and Matthew Tindal mentioned in Chapter 1. They worried as well about new efforts by Dissenters to remove the civil disabilities of the Test Act (defeated by Parliament in 1736 and again in 1739) and also about possible support for such proposals from political Whigs with their own reasons for subverting the established church.[11] What one historian has called 'the contemporary Anglican crisis of authority' was helping create both the uncertainties confronting the rising leaders of evangelicalism and a receptivity for their message.[12]

It was much the same in Scotland, where the uncertainties of the 1720s – especially from the Marrow Controversy and the heresy trials of Professor John Simson – were exacerbated by a small withdrawal from the Kirk led by John Glas (1695–1771), a learned proponent of the spiritual church and an intellectualist view of faith, who became leader of the Glasites, or Sandemanians as they were known in England and America after Glas's son-in-law Robert Sandeman. Then in the 1730s came the well-publicized succession of the Erskine brothers and their Associate Presbytery. In New England during this same period, Jonathan Edwards thought he could see Arminianism undermining the theological foundations, while many others held with Edwards that expanding opportunities for material gain alongside growing commercial contact with the mother country were sapping the region's moral fibre.[13] Elsewhere in the colonies, churches did not seem to be keeping up with the spread of population or the multiplying tasks of Christian civilization, even if they were growing in numbers and sometimes in spiritual seriousness as well.

For the course of English-speaking church history, in other words, it was a propitious moment for a new religious movement like evangelicalism. Old fears of enthusiasm were fading, new challenges from imperial Roman Catholicism were pressing and manifold uncertainties were besetting the

---

[11] For more on these problems, see John Walsh and Stephen Taylor, 'Introduction: the Church and Anglicanism in the "long" eighteenth century', in *The Church of England, c.1689–c.1833* (Cambridge: Cambridge University Press, 1993), 1–64. For the enduring public opinion that simply assumed the necessity of an orthodox church establishment, see J. C. D. Clark, *English Society, 1660–1832* (2nd ed., Cambridge: Cambridge University Press, 2000).

[12] Henry D. Rack, 'Religious Societies and the Origins of Methodism', *Journal of Ecclesiastical History* 38 (October 1987): 589.

[13] See especially Mark Valeri, 'The Economic Thought of Jonathan Edwards', *Church History* 60 (March 1991): 37–54.

church establishments of the day. The times were ripe for a message that
echoed trusted themes from the past but that also articulated them with a
sensibility for the present. Yet the times and seasons of ecclesiastical history
are still only part of the story.

Shifting structures

To turn attention away from what participants experienced self-consciously
towards what students of history may perceive more clearly than the actors
themselves is to provide necessary complication for understanding the rise
of evangelical religion in the English-speaking world. However it is viewed spiritually, evangelicalism must also be seen as fully participating in broad movements of eighteenth-century social, ecclesiastical, intellectual and psychological
life, as part of a new configuration of material, intellectual and religious practices and institutions even then coming into view. Perceived within these contexts, evangelicalism was an answer to accelerating economic and demographic
change. As such, it offered a solution to structural religious crisis. It represented
also a religious response to the new mental world of the Enlightenment. And it
presented internal, psychological resources to meet the external, social challenges of the century.

Social-ecclesiastical

Over the first fifty years of the eighteenth century, British society at home and
in the colonies was in process of transformation. Almost all historical periods
witness multiple alterations of some sort, but the English-speaking people in
this period were undergoing an unusual concatenation of rapid social
changes.[14] Population had begun the steady growth that would accelerate even
more rapidly during the second half of the century. The expansion of parliamentary British power was even more rapid, especially in the North American
colonies and the West Indies, but also for previously neglected parts of
Ireland and the Scottish Highlands (particularly after the climactic defeat of
the Jacobites and Bonnie Prince Charlie in 1746). Imperial expansion always

---

[14] For helpful treatment of these concerns, see two of the essays in P. J. Marshall (ed.), *The
Oxford History of the British Empire*, vol. 2: *The Eighteenth Century* (New York: Oxford,
1998): Patrick K. O'Brien, 'Inseparable Connections: Trade, Economy, Fiscal State, and
the Expansion of Empire, 1688–1815', 28–52; and Jacob M. Price, 'The Imperial
Economy, 1700–1776', 78–104. Many of the other chapters in this volume also bear
directly on the themes of this chapter.

had a political aspect, but for this period attachment to the British empire meant even more for commerce and communication. Precisely in this half-century, developments in manufacturing, banking, politics, naval technology and transportation were being matched with new movements of taste, life-style, culture and entertainment to construct the great juggernaut of British trade that would conjoin, enrich and inspire significant portions of the planet for the next two hundred years.[15] Evangelicalism grew up as a religious move-ment, in other words, at roughly the same time as the beginning of England's Industrial Revolution, the rise of the commercial middle classes, the establish-ment of the first British empire and the idealization of British parliamentary freedom in constant warfare with France.

In the midst of demographic, commercial and imperial change, the dynamics of English-speaking societies were also being altered. Throughout the British empire there was more space (social as well as physical) for indi-vidual initiative. 'Individualism' as a word was not coined until Alexis de Tocqueville used it in the 1830s to describe what he witnessed during his famous trip to America, but ways of acting that relied less on given expecta-tions and more on personal action were well established before there was a word to describe the phenomenon. Similarly, voluntary organization, which linked individuals as a result of freely chosen commitments, was increasingly common in spheres of commerce (e.g., the corporation), politics (e.g., the political faction) and intellectual culture (e.g., the autonomous publisher of books and newspapers). The beginnings of what sociologists now call 'civil society' – self-standing organizations that bind individuals together for public purposes but without tight governmental control – were widely visible throughout Britain and her colonies by the 1750s. For social change pointed in the direction of self-created voluntary organization, Britain's imperial arrangement was ideal. In London and other English regions, as well as in lowland Scotland and the north of Ireland, personal and group initiatives were creating many new commercial opportunities. In the col-onies, the opening up of unprecedented amounts of space and the fragility of the formal social arrangements carried from the mother country evoked other kinds of personal and group initiative. Britain was still in many ways a traditional society, but the opening of that society for all manner of com-mercial, political and personal opportunity marked a new stage of social development.

---

[15] For cultural implications of this commercialization, see T. H. Breen, 'An Empire of Goods: The Anglicization of Colonial America, 1690–1776', *Journal of British Studies* 25 (1986): 467–499.

Such changes bore directly on religion and the churches. The ideal of a uniform state church that, by providing well-regulated spiritual services, unified the nation in its worship of God, remained strong. But practical shortcomings in fulfilling the potential of that ideal were becoming increasingly obvious. Historians have described these shortcomings in various ways. With England and Ireland in view, it is possible to speak of 'the pastoral inadequacy of the Established Church in those geographical areas where demographic and manufacturing growth exposed serious weaknesses in the Church's parochial structures'.[16] In these terms, the intent of the early evangelicals 'was not to create new denominations but to found voluntary associations which might leaven the lump of existing churches, and charge them with fresh energy'.[17]

The situation in the colonies was structurally different but with the same favourable conditions for new forms of the old religion. 'Church hierarchies ... were undeveloped, clerical authority in most major denominations was weak, lay control over religious matters was extensive and relations between ministers and congregations often conflicted, anticlericalism was widespread, and a shortage of trained ministers among several denominations left many newly settled areas without ministers'.[18] The number of churches was growing rapidly in the new world, but expansion was not rapid enough to reach all in the opening areas, nor did its success compensate for weaknesses in settled regions. The outbreak of evangelical religion in the colonial revivals was in part an answer for those who longed for vital religion on the frontier; even more, it was an answer for 'those who already belonged to churches but were unhappy with their religion'.[19] The appeal of evangelical faith 'strongly suggests existing religious institutions were failing in important respects to meet the spiritual needs of colonial populations, who in significant numbers turned to an alternative and, for them, more emotionally satisfying form of religious belief that emphasized the importance of conversion, the centrality of the individual in the conversion experience, and the primacy of religious beliefs in daily life'.[20]

---

[16] Hempton, 'Religion in British Society', 217.

[17] John Walsh, 'Origins of the Evangelical Revival', in G. V. Bennett and J. D. Walsh (eds.), *Essays in Modern English Church History in Memory of Norman Sykes* (New York: Oxford University Press, 1966), 161.

[18] Jack P. Greene, *Pursuits of Happiness: The Social Development of Early Modern British Colonies and the Formation of American Culture* (Chapel Hill: University of North Carolina Press, 1988), 202.

[19] Richard Hofstadter, *America at 1750: A Social Portrait* (New York: Knopf, 1971), 218.

[20] Greene, *Pursuits of Happiness*, 203.

When the rise of evangelicalism is viewed against the background of rapid social and commercial expansion and in combination with the inability of creaking church–state structures to keep up, then it becomes apparent why historians bring in this larger picture to explain religious developments. From the broadest angle, 'the eighteenth-century Evangelical Revival had more to do with adaptations to structural changes in society, in particular, those conducive to religious voluntarism, than with the death and rebirth of evangelical piety'.[21] A similar conclusion can be drawn from the activities of the leading evangelists: 'In the revivalists' view, the religious market on both sides of the Atlantic had too long been overregulated, dominated by principles other than those of experiential religion.'[22]

Awakeners were not cynical manipulators artificially crafting a new message for the sake of merely personal gain. They were, rather, adapters who themselves had found 'true religion' hidden within the older establishmentarian Protestantism, but who then displayed an almost intuitive ability to analyse the desires of others for whom the inherited ecclesiastical structures were proving irrelevant or inadequate. That intuition sustained their efforts at communicating the religious authenticity they themselves had experienced in a spiritual landscape starved of vital personal piety. The 'essential effect' of the new evangelicalism 'was the internal reinvigoration of Protestantism through more popular styles of worship'. Its attraction was strongest for those 'who were eager to explore the limits of the Protestant drive toward individualized piety and conviction'.[23] For the new configuration of eighteenth-century British life the leading revivalists had a word in season. The effectiveness of George Whitefield, for instance, 'lay in integrating religious discourse into this emerging language of consumption. In the fields of London he discovered, in effect, how to ply a religious trade in the open air of the marketplace.'[24] By setting aside earlier religious forms, the evangelicals did not think they were setting aside the faith once delivered, but rather adjusting it to the new social realities of the age. 'Revivalists continued to propagate in varying degrees a much different model of the social world, one that their civilized opponents persisted in reading as chaos approaching barbarism.' As itinerants moved from place to place, their preaching 'came to symbolize an openness to the work of God's free Spirit in a mobile, expansive world'. Revivalists and reports of revival that circulated throughout the Atlantic region underscored 'the close relationship

---

[21] Crawford, *Season of Grace*, 14.

[22] Lambert, *Inventing the Great Awakening*, 111–112.

[23] Hofstadter, *America at 1750*, 218.

[24] Harry S. Stout, 'George Whitefield in Three Countries', in *Evangelicalism*, 59.

between the new evangelical itinerancy of the Great Awakening, the explosion of the century's revolution in commerce, and the unprecedented human mobility throughout the empire'.[25]

When historians explain early evangelicalism by reference to such social conditions, they are not necessarily denying its spiritual reality. They are saying, rather, that however the work of God is pictured, there existed a natural congruence between the spiritual ideals proclaimed by evangelists and the social realities experienced by the people who responded to that proclamation. The same relationship obtained for connections between evangelicalism and the major intellectual movements of the day.

Intellectual

As an eighteenth-century movement, evangelical Christianity coexisted with the Enlightenment, that elusive construct of principles and practices that historians depict as succeeding earlier ages of intellectual traditionalism and leading on to various forms of romanticism.[26] In its general stance, evangelicalism clearly opposed some expressions of the Enlightenment – like the extreme scepticism of the Scottish philosopher David Hume, the atheism of French *philosophes* who contributed to the *Encyclopédie* (1751ff.), the doubts about the Bible found among a number of Enlightenment thinkers or the religious-style egotism paraded by Jean-Jacques Rousseau in his *Confessions* (1782). Yet in other significant ways, evangelicalism was itself an authentic expression of Enlightenment principles. Evangelicals, for example, followed the path marked out by John Locke in his *Essay on Human Understanding* (1689), since they held, with Locke, that the self's personal experience was foundational for obtaining reliable knowledge. 'True religion', for evangelicals, might be recommended by tradition and by formal authorities, but until people personally experienced the love of God in their hearts, evangelicals held that their standing before God had to be in doubt. As that conviction suggests, evangelicals also shared the Enlightenment's trust in the affections. Later evangelicals would contrast bare cognitive apprehension ('head knowledge') with genuine religious life ('heart knowledge') in a form that followed Enlightenment thinkers like Francis Hutcheson of Glasgow, who devoted his career to describing the nature and capacities of 'the moral sense'. Evangelicals also acted in accord

---

[25] Timothy D. Hall, *Contested Boundaries: Itinerancy and the Reshaping of the Colonial American Religious World* (Durham, NC: Duke University Press, 1994), 130–131.

[26] Two very helpful accounts are Henry F. May, *The Enlightenment in America* (New York: Oxford University Press, 1976); and Roy Porter, *The Creation of the Modern World: The Untold Story of the British Enlightenment* (New York: Norton, 2000).

with the Enlightenment when their desire for practical results drove them beyond the boundaries of acceptable received tradition. They reflected standard Enlightenment commitments by preferring knowledge based on their own experience rather than knowledge authenticated by historical precedent, by tradition, or by an inherited state church. So it was, among evangelicals, that the personal experience of God's grace always held a privileged place, that injunctions urging laypeople to read the Bible for themselves proliferated and that wide use was made of natural theology (step-by-step reasoning moving from ordinary experience to proof for the existence of God).

The place where evangelicalism revealed its closest affinities to the Enlightenment was in a dramatically heightened concern for the assurance of salvation. In the words of historian David Bebbington, Jonathan Edwards and other early evangelicals who preached and wrote about the means through which people could truly know they were redeemed derived their 'confidence about salvation from the atmosphere of the English Enlightenment'.[27] John Wesley's famous statement from early 1738 was a heart-cry of evangelicalism as a whole: 'The faith I want is, "a sure trust and confidence in God, that through the merits of Christ my sins are forgiven, and I reconciled to the favour of God"... I want that faith which none can have without knowing that he hath it.'[28] Such words had been heard before in the history of Christianity, but not nearly so often and without the intensity with which they were sounded at the dawn of evangelicalism. Since evangelicals, who placed such stress on religious experience, did retain allegiance to Scripture and the classical doctrines of Christianity, it is inappropriate to view the Enlightenment as 'creating' evangelicalism in any simple sense. Yet failing to pay full attention to the early evangelicals' exploitation of Enlightenment thought-forms would short-circuit explanations for the rise of evangelicalism as much as failing to recognize how deftly evangelicalism spoke to the shifting social landscape of the period.

Psychological

Psychological explanations provide a mechanism for suggesting how the fit between evangelicalism and its contexts actually worked. The best historical psychology is multi-valent and tentative, since it is impossible ever to gain exhaustive understanding about any one action in the past and since the weight of contemporary psychological assumptions easily overwhelms the

---

[27] Bebbington, *Evangelicalism*, 48; see 42–74 for fuller discussion of the Enlightenment character of eighteenth-century evangelicalism.

[28] Wesley, 29 January 1738; in Wesley, *Works* (new), vol. 18: *Journals and Diaries I (1735–1738)*, ed. W. Reginald Ward and Richard P. Heitzenrater (1988), 215–216.

ability to understand the past in its own terms. Yet when handled with sensitivity, hypotheses suggesting how the extrinsic forces of social reality and the
intrinsic appeal of the evangelical message came together can be illuminating.
One of the most interesting of such psychological explanations was provided
by the historian Richard Bushman for the events of the Great Awakening in
New England. In his view, 'two conditions prepared men for conversion: an
increased desire for material wealth that ministers called worldly pride or cov-
etousness, and the growing frequency of clashes with authority entailed in the
pursuit of wealth'. As Bushman describes the situation, the expanding commercial possibilities of the British empire in the 1720s and 1730s were grating
against the moral restraints of New England's Puritan past. Awakening
preaching was the new element that released the psychological tension: 'In the
converts' minds the escape from guilt was possible because of God's grace.
The idea that the law could not condemn if God justified contained the
deepest meaning of the Awakening.'[29]

As with all such proposals concerning cause-and-effect relations, there is
more than one way to interpret an explanation. Does Bushman mean that
the most basic meaning of the Great Awakening was the release of social-
psychological pressure? Or might he mean that God used social-psychological
pressures to prepare needy sinners to receive the message of divine grace? And
why would similar preaching in the middle colonies, the South, England and
parts of Scotland and Ireland eventually yield similar religious results, yet in situations where the psycho-social dynamics were at least somewhat different?

From a different angle, Bruce Hindmarsh has suggested that it was the
combination of new evangelical preaching and the era's shifting cultural
values that provided an unusually satisfying sense of psychological stability.[30]
The awakeners preached God's moral law and divine judgment to people who
still believed in these traditional Christian doctrines. Yet because Anglo-
American society had loosened – because people believed they now had more
control over their own destinies – this new awareness of personal agency
could also heighten insecurity. If I have the power to act, I have also the
potential to doom myself to failure in this life and for eternity. To that insecurity the promise of the direct experience of divine grace in Christ became
almost literally 'living water'. It brought the spiritually dead to life and gave

---

[29] Richard L. Bushman, *From Puritan to Yankee: Character and the Social Order in Connecticut,
1690–1765* (New York: Norton, 1970), 188, 194.

[30] Hindmarsh, personal correspondence. But see D. Bruce Hindmarsh, '"My chains fell
off, my heart was free": Early Methodist Conversion Narratives in England', *Church
History* 68 (December 1999): 925–926, which draws upon Watts, *Dissenters*, 1:394–421.

them direction, purpose and real spiritual energy. The content of Christian notions of law, sin, guilt, judgment, promise, faith and hope was not altered *per se*, but the psycho-social landscape in which the evangelicals preached these concepts had changed considerably.

As for all explanations of the revival, questions raised by the psychological explanations of Bushman and Hindmarsh stimulate the best kind of discussion since they call for careful attention to the ways in which social, ecclesiastical, intellectual and psychological factors may have entered into the actual religious history of the English-speaking world in the middle decades of the eighteenth century.

Conclusion

The result – from a commingling of factors, agents and influences – was evangelicalism. But a commingling it certainly was, and beyond any human capacity to disentangle. As a prime example, George Whitefield became a defining figure for early evangelicalism because he was a heartfelt preacher of New Birth communicated by the work of the Holy Spirit, but also because he was an expert marketer of the gospel in the new open spaces of British imperial commerce, a notable example of *petit bourgeoisie* self-fashioning and an effective purveyor of divine grace as balm to personal psychological distress. Similarly, in England and Wales, Methodism brought spiritual, emotional, economic and psychological support to a great number of individuals whom the established church could not or did not reach; for an even larger number in North America, Methodism was to master the ambiguous openings of Revolutionary and post-Revolutionary American life and so provide both assured standing before God and satisfying relationships with other humans. Evangelicals, whose message offered peace with God, also cannily grasped the dynamics of an expanding market economy.

There can be no single statement that 'explains' the rise of evangelicalism. As appropriate as it is for a historian of the Catholic Reformation of the sixteenth century to 'underscore the role played by geography, national sentiment, and international politics in shaping the experience of Catholic renewal', so can a historian of the eighteenth century highlight the role played by economic change, ecclesiastical capacity and international conflict in shaping evangelical renewal.[31] However one regards the work of the Holy

---

[31] R. Po-Chia Hsia, *The World of Catholic Renewal* (Cambridge: Cambridge University Press, 1998), 7–8.

Spirit in the evangelical movement, the Spirit was certainly putting to use channels of influence from the domains of ordinary history. Those channels were many, but why they worked to different effects in different regions and on different individuals only the closest attention to sources and the most multi-dimensional explanations can say.

In the simplest sort of summary, evangelicalism grew out of earlier forms of heart-felt British Protestantism and was stimulated by contact with heart-felt continental pietism. It was grounded religiously in the innovative preaching of justifying faith. It was promoted and maintained by the effective exertions of capable spiritual leaders. It offered a compelling picture of direct fellowship with God for believers as individuals and in groups. It represented a shift in religiosity away from the inherited established churches toward spiritual communities constructed by believers themselves. It featured a form of conversion as much focused on personal experience, as much convinced of the plasticity of human nature and as much preoccupied with claims of certainty as any manifestation of the Enlightenment. And because its spirituality was adjusted to an opening world of commerce, communications and empire, that spirituality effectively resolved the psychological dilemmas created by this opening world.

Such a multi-dimensional explanation for the rise of evangelicalism is neither easy to summarize nor simple to apply. It may, however, offer a way forward for those who hope to respect the spiritual realities of early evangelical movements while also situating them in the actual circumstances where they emerged.

6. DEVELOPMENT, 1745–1770

In the quarter century between 1745 and 1770, evangelicalism underwent a dramatic expansion and diversification. The death of George Whitefield on 30 September 1770, in Newburyport, Massachusetts, while on his seventh extended visit to the colonies, was an important landmark, since Whitefield had been the acknowledged prototype of the evangelical preacher, the only early evangelical at home in Scotland and America as well as in England, and the prime mediator between evangelicals in established churches and those who were Dissenters. With or without Whitefield, evangelicalism remained predominately a movement within the established churches of England, Wales, Scotland and New England. But extension into the Scottish Highlands, Ireland, the southern mainland colonies and the West Indies also took place in this quarter century, even as evangelicalism in the established churches underwent marked changes and as significant evangelical inroads were made among Dissenters. The evangelical propensity for responding to social disruption was also manifest in these years, which witnessed a series of dramatic public shocks:

- the final defeat of the Stuarts in their effort to re-take the British throne (1745–46);
- two major wars with France: in the mid-1740s King George's War, or the War of the Austrian Succession, and in the late 1750s to the early 1760s the Seven Years, or French and Indian, War;
- the first public violence (the 'Boston massacre' of 1770) anticipating the American War for Independence.

Anglican evangelicalism

In England, the key institutional development was movement within the established church towards more sharply defined organization for both Arminian
(Wesley) Methodists and Calvinistic (Whitefield) Methodists. Although Methodists only occasionally spoke out in favour of separation from the state church,
and although some like Charles Wesley protested vehemently against any move
even hinting at separation, solidification as quasi-independent movements went
on.[1] John and Charles Wesley continued to guide their Connexion through
annual conferences for the lay itinerants whom John Wesley appointed and tried
to control; in 1746 Wesley formalized the annual assignment of itinerants in
seven well-mapped circuits; in the early 1750s he disfellowshipped itinerants who
were eager to leave the established church and came close to authorizing his lay
itinerants to administer the Lord's Supper (which, as his brother reminded him,
would have meant schism); in 1760 John Wesley rebuked itinerants in Norwich,
but with restraint, for administering the sacrament; in 1763 he published a
'Model Deed' to formalize his own ownership and use of Methodist chapels;
and in the mid-1760s he failed in an effort to broaden cooperation between his
movement and ordained evangelical ministers in the Church of England.

For the history of Wesleyan doctrine and practice, the middle decades of
the century were especially important for new controversies over the doctrine of Christian perfection.[2] Wesley had maintained this teaching from early
in his public career, but gave more care to careful definition in these years.
For example, from 1756: 'Christians are called to love God with all their
heart, and to serve him with all their strength; which is precisely what I
apprehend to be meant by the scriptural term perfection.' Or again from
1767: 'By perfection I mean the humble, gentle, patient love of God and man
ruling all the tempers, words, and actions, the whole heart by the whole life.'[3]
In the late 1750s the doctrine once again came to the fore when more
Methodists in local societies claimed, in Wesley's phrase about a group in
Yorkshire, to have been 'cleansed from all unrighteousness'.[4] As excitement

---

[1] For clear discussion, see Rack, *Wesley*, 291–305.

[2] In this section, including material on Bell and Maxfield, I am following Rack, *Wesley*,
    333–342; for clear discussion of the doctrine as taught by Wesley, see Kenneth J. Collins,
    The Scripture Way of Salvation: The Heart of Wesley's Theology (Nashville: Abingdon, 1997),
    171–182.

[3] Wesley, *On Christian Perfection: To the Rev. Mr. Dod* (1756), in Wesley, *Works* (1872), 11:449;
    Wesley to Charles Wesley, 27 January 1767, in Wesley, *Letters*, 5:38.

[4] Wesley, *Journal* (16 February 1760), 4:366.

rose on Methodist circuits, two local leaders verged on enthusiasm. George Bell not only claimed to have experienced perfection, but he also conducted wildly uproarious meetings and claimed to exercise the gift of healing. Thomas Maxfield pursued his own version of perfectionism into an acrimonious public dispute with Wesley and then the take-over of a Wesleyan chapel. In response, Wesley moderated his own rhetoric but did not abandon the doctrine. Other responses were fraught with longer-term consequences. Regular Evangelical ministers in the Church of England drew back with nervousness about spiritual and social disorder. Closer to home, Charles Wesley also reacted conservatively. While continuing to agree with John on the possibility of Christian perfection in this life, Charles now urged greater caution against excesses and stressed continual discipline rather than a single act of faith as the path to perfection. Charles Wesley, who had married happily and then by 1756 mostly stopped itinerating, remained his brother's chief counsellor, but from this period he became increasingly wary of all separatistic impulses in their movement.

The way in which Wesleyan Methodism was developing as an increasingly distinct evangelical association within Anglicanism, though not yet a formally separated, independent denomination, is well illustrated by the early career of John Fletcher.[5] Fletcher was born in Switzerland, migrated to England as a young man and then, through contact with Methodists, including Charles Wesley, underwent a profound conversion. In 1757 he took Anglican orders after consulting John Wesley, but Wesley was displeased when in 1760 he chose to settle as the vicar of Madeley, Shropshire, instead of continuing to itinerate. His work was successful at this location, but as a friend of both Wesleys, George Whitefield and many other early evangelicals, his influence extended much wider. In the early 1770s he did emerge as an articulate theological spokesman for Wesleyan positions in opposition to fresh Calvinist polemics, but even in these writings he remained almost as irenic as Whitefield. John Wesley urged him on several occasions to take up supervision of his itinerants as a full-time calling, but Fletcher chose rather to continue his combined efforts as regular Anglican clergyman and loyal friend of the Methodist movement.

Calvinistic Methodists within the Church of England were undergoing a transition very much like the Wesleyans, but for this period it is important to recognize the increasingly important association between George Whitefield and Selina, Countess of Huntingdon.[6] After her conversion, the Countess at

---

[5] For a reliable introduction, see *BDEB*, 393–394 (Patrick Streiff, 'John William Fletcher').

[6] For an outstanding introduction, *BDEB*, 585–586 (Peter J. Lineham, 'Selina, Countess of Huntingdon'). Three recent books have cast welcome light on this previously under-

first cooperated with evangelicals of all sorts, even to the extent of skipping rapidly from one favourite to another. But after the death of her husband in 1746, she entered an enduring alliance with the Calvinists. In 1748 she appointed Whitefield as her chaplain, in part because he was more willing than John Wesley to expend time and energy in her short-lived efforts at evangelizing her aristocratic friends. Even before she established a firm tie with Whitefield, Selina had already encouraged the work of itinerant preachers. Soon she was also appointing Methodists as her personal chaplains. This option, which was reserved for the nobility, she exploited as a convenient way of supporting evangelical preaching while short-circuiting the normal placement procedures of the Church of England that were firmly in the control of patrons mostly hostile to the evangelicals.

In 1760 the Countess sold off some of her jewellery to finance the construction of a chapel in Brighton. This building and a number of others that soon followed were intended as preaching posts to supplement the ministrations of the established church. They differed from the Wesleys' chapels in being reserved primarily for regularly ordained Anglican clergy. Despite her own Calvinist leanings, Selina remained on good terms with a wide range of Methodists, especially Charles Wesley and John Fletcher. She also attempted to enlist both Calvinists and Wesleyans (including Fletcher) in the leadership of a training school for clergy that she established in 1768 at Trevecca in Wales on property owned by Howell Harris. This new venture was a direct response to the expulsion from Oxford in 1768 of several evangelical students whose crime was to meet privately for singing and extempore prayer. This expulsion, as it happened, provoked a strong response from Whitefield, who testified to the increasingly political character of the times by claiming that the students were dismissed only because they were 'Methodists' (as he had been 'for about thirty-five years') and by testifying that 'every additional proselyte to true Methodism, is an additional loyal subject to King George the Third'.[7]

In the event, Lady Huntingdon's attempt at evangelical ecumenicity foun-

---

studied figure: a strongly archival interpretation, Edwin Welch, *Spiritual Pilgrim: A Reassessment of the Life of the Countess of Huntingdon* (Cardiff: University of Wales Press, 1995); a more secular account, Boyd Stanley Schlenther, *Queen of the Methodists: The Countess of Huntingdon and the Eighteenth-Century Crisis of Faith and Society* (Durham: Durham Academic Press, 1997); and a more evangelical account, Faith Cook, *Selina, Countess of Huntingdon: Her Pivotal Role in the Eighteenth-Century Evangelical Awakening* (Edinburgh: Banner of Truth, 2001).

[7] George Whitefield, *A Letter to the Reverend Dr. Durrell, Vice-Chancellor of the University of*

dered on the shoals of theological conflict, which burst out afresh in 1770 between Arminians and Calvinists. Still, the Countess continued to devote most of her wealth to evangelical causes, she was a critical factor in bringing an evangelical witness to the English aristocracy, and for many years she provided the non-Wesleyan Methodists with the same kind of support that the Wesleys offered to others through their movement. Selina's manner was sometimes imperious, her life was marked by many personal and family difficulties and she did not always control her formidable temper. Yet in her own way she was as important for the development of English evangelicalism in the middle decades of the century as the Wesleys and Whitefield.

Evangelical expansion in England was not limited to the Methodist Connexions. An increasing number of beneficed Anglican clergymen were promoting evangelical views, either after being converted while already in the ministry (like Henry Venn [1724–1797] of Huddersfield in Yorkshire) or by coming into the ministry as evangelicals (like Thomas Haweis [1734–1820] of Aldwincle in Northamptonshire). In Cornwall, Samuel Walker (1714–1761) came to evangelical views about the time he was installed as curate of Truro (1746). His local ministry, which included small groups in the parish and a monthly gathering of clerics, as well as his published sermons, effectively promoted an irenic, church-based and non-perfectionistic form of evangelicalism. The conversion in 1748 of the slave captain John Newton eventually led to a powerful evangelical voice in the Church of England, especially after his ordination and installation as the rector of Olney, Buckinghamshire, in 1764.[8] Such properly ordained clergy were usually friendly with Methodists of several varieties; until the 1790s there was, in fact, no hard-and-fast barrier between them and the Methodists, except that they insisted on carrying on the regular work of clergy within a parish. This growing evangelical element within the established church was of great long-term significance, not least for differentiating the history of English evangelicalism from the story on the other side of the Atlantic.

Through these middle decades Anglican evangelicalism was also still linked closely to the Moravian movement.[9] The early Moravians considered themselves only visitors, but by the early 1740s so many Englishmen and women had

---

Oxford; Occasioned By a late Expulsion of Six Students from Edmund-Hall (Boston: Thomas & John Fleet, 1768), 23, 33.

[8] *BDEB*, 1137–1138 (W. J. Clyde Ervine, 'Henry Venn'); 536–537 (A. Skevington Wood, 'Thomas Haweis'); 1152–1153 (Arthur Pollard, 'Samuel Walker'). For more on Newton, see below, 184–187.

[9] See especially Colin Podmore, *The Moravian Church in England, 1728–1760* (Oxford:

been drawn to the Moravians' Christ-centred piety, their Lutheran stress on justification by faith and their missionary passion that a separate English branch of the movement developed. Zinzendorf himself never advocated a distinct English church, but urged repeatedly that Moravian societies should put themselves under the jurisdiction of an Anglican bishop and function as voluntary societies within the comprehensive state church. But when respected leaders like Benjamin Ingham insisted on setting up as Moravians, there was little that Zinzendorf could do. The Moravian appeal was deep, with at least six members of the Wesleys' original Holy Club at Oxford eventually joining the movement. An Act of Parliament from 1749, which offered official recognition to the Moravians as 'an antient Protestant Episcopal Church' and which allowed Moravians in Britain and the colonies to affirm rather than swear judicial oaths, gave further recognition.[10] But soon thereafter a temporary change in English public opinion occurred, in part because of tracts from the Continent that accused the Moravians of sexual irregularities, doctrinal heresy and public disruption. George Whitefield, who had many friends going to and from the Moravians, chimed in with a pamphlet from 1753 that charged Zinzendorf with financial chicanery and religious indiscretion. The result was that the English bishops turned on the Moravians and prevented known adherents of their movement from gaining official church positions. Although the reputation of the Moravians recovered by the end of the century, their general influence was much reduced by comparison to the early years of evangelicalism.

English Dissent

England's older Dissenting churches were also being drawn in an evangelical direction during the middle decades of the century, though the movement was slow. The deaths of Isaac Watts in 1748 and of Philip Doddridge in 1751 removed the two Dissenters who had done the most to publicize evangelical breakthroughs and encourage evangelical efforts. The course of English church history since the Restoration of 1660 had left the Dissenters wary of enthusiasm, distrustful of public show and strongly committed to reasoned forms of discourse. Doddridge – with congenial connections to Whitefield, John Wesley and the Countess of Huntingdon – was somewhat unusual as a

---

Clarendon, 1998); and J. C. S. Mason, *The Moravian Church and the Missionary Movement in England, 1760–1800* (Woodbridge: Boydell, 2001).

[10] Podmore, *Moravian Church in England*, 228.

Dissenter open to the new evangelical concerns. In addition, where traditional Christian orthodoxy had been preserved among Dissenters, as with the Particular Baptists, it was sometimes a form of rigid dogmatism rather than the experiential faith so characteristic of the revival movement. English Presbyterians never did accommodate to the new evangelicalism. Rather, their leading figures in the second half of the century would become Richard Price (1725–1791) and Joseph Priestley (1735–1804), both of whom gave up traditional belief in the Trinity and in the reality of a divine atonement, even as they joined their liberal theology to radical political sentiments.

Baptists and Independents proved more receptive to evangelical emphases, but at first mostly by indirection. The path towards evangelicalism took shape in several different ways. When the Methodist movements within the Church of England left some ministers and laity dissatisfied with the pace of revival in the established church, or when the Anglican hierarchy expelled evangelicals for insubordinate disruption, the only open route was Dissent.[11] So it was that a trickle of Wesleyan societies began in the early 1750s to constitute themselves as Baptist churches, and several societies that did not accept the Wesleys' Arminian theology turned Independent. The well-known itinerant John Bennet (1715–1759) is a striking example of this pattern. Bennet was converted under Moravian influence in 1742 and then in 1743 became an unusually effective itinerant for John Wesley in the north of England. But as his own theology turned in a Calvinist direction and after a contretemps with Wesley (Bennet married Grace Murray, whom Wesley had considered his betrothed), Bennet left the Methodists in 1752 for an Independent chapel at Bolton, Lancashire. Two years later he was named the minister of an Independent church in Cheshire.[12] Many of the converts of the Evangelical Anglican clergy likewise moved with Bennet to positions of influence among the Independents.

Some Independents also moved towards revival by withdrawing from the ministry of unorthodox ministers. At Shrewsbury, as an example, the Independent and Presbyterian churches united in 1741 under Job Orton

---

[11] Watts, *Dissenters* 1:452, with 450–464 describing the contemporary picture more generally; and John Walsh, 'Methodists at the End of the Eighteenth Century', in Rupert Davies and Gordon Rupp (eds.), *A History of the Methodist Church in Great Britain*, vol. 1 (London: Epworth, 1965), 293–296.

[12] See Simon Ross Valentine, *John Bennet and the Origins of Methodism and the Evangelical Revival in England* (Lanham: Scarecrow Press, 1997); and Henry D. Rack, 'Survival and Revival: John Bennet, Methodism, and the Old Dissent', in Keith Robbins (ed.), *Protestant Evangelicalism: Britain, Ireland, Germany and America, c.1750–c.1950: Essays in Honour of W. R. Ward* (Oxford: Blackwell, 1990), 1–24.

(1717–1783) who maintained the religion of the Puritans.[13] When, however, this congregation appointed an Arian as Orton's successor, a substantial group withdrew and appointed as their minister Robert Gentleman, who, as R. Tudur Jones records, was 'possest of a spirit of Methodism'.[14] Under Gentleman this new congregation became a strong evangelical force throughout Shropshire.

The most direct stimulus for evangelical Dissent, however, was provided by the Calvinistic Methodism of Whitefield and the Countess of Huntingdon. From the start, Whitefield's ardent but indiscriminate piety was appreciated in Dissenting circles, where Puritan influence lingered, and his willingness to preach from Baptist and Independent pulpits eventually overcame much of the Dissenting wariness about revival. Because he devoted less energy than the Wesleys to maintaining the societies and co-workers that sprang up from his influence, tabernacles and society buildings built for and by Whitefield were easily transformed into Dissenting chapels. As early as 1764, Whitefield cut through thickets of ecclesiastical ambiguity by registering two of his prominent London preaching stations – Moorfields and Tottenham Court – as Independent meeting houses. The same process was at work among the ministers and gathering places sponsored by the Countess of Huntingdon. Her training school at Trevecca was set up to prepare evangelicals excluded from Oxford and Cambridge for Anglican orders, but many of its students became Independent ministers instead. Dissent, in the end, was powerfully shaped by evangelical impulses originating within the Anglican church.

The origin of evangelicalism among English Baptists involved an internal theological evolution as well as participation in the new religious currents of the era. In 1770 there was a small-scale revival among Arminian Baptists guided by the former Methodist Dan Taylor (1738–1816) that led to the founding of the New Connexion of General Baptists.[15] This evangelical movement enjoyed considerable success in the East Midlands and West Yorkshire, but its influence would soon be eclipsed by the evangelical turn of the Particular Baptists.[16] These Baptists had remained doctrinally orthodox, but often in an extreme

---

[13] BDEB, 845 (J. H. Y. Briggs, 'Job Orton').

[14] R. Tudur Jones, Congregationalism in England, 1662–1962 (London: Independent Press, 1962), 156–157. My thanks to David Bebbington for this information on the Shrewsbury evangelicals.

[15] BDEB, 1082 (E. F. Clipsham, 'Dan Taylor').

[16] General Baptists held that Christ's atonement was effective for all humans in general; Particular Baptists held that, strictly speaking, Christ's death atoned only for the elect.

Calvinist form that discouraged active evangelism and that placed more stress on correct doctrinal formulas than on active piety. Some Particular Baptists were pushed towards evangelical activism through contact with Philip Doddridge in the 1740s; more were drawn in the same direction by the foundation of the Northamptonshire Baptist Association in 1764, which drew ministers from far beyond this one county; and still others received a decisive evangelical impulse by reading the works of Jonathan Edwards. One of those readers was Caleb Evans (1737–1791) of Bristol, who, with his father, the Welsh-born Hugh Evans (1712–1781), promoted a more experiential and practical form of the Baptist faith.[17] The Evans' interest in itinerancy, missions and hymn-publication led naturally to the founding of the Bristol Educational Society in 1770, which exerted an even more direct evangelical influence on a wide variety of Dissenting students. The crucial doctrinal move impelling Baptists into broader fields of service came when a few leaders concluded that it was not inconsistent with a high view of God's sovereign grace actively to encourage all hearers of the gospel to repent and believe. Baptists, with Independents, were slower than Anglicans in responding to the evangelical appeal, but by 1770 an evangelicalization of Dissent had begun that would eventually exert a worldwide influence.

With multiple strands of vigorous development, England in 1770 was unquestionably the centre of the evangelical world. Revival within the established church of the imperial homeland drove evangelicalism as a whole. London remained the critical clearing-house for literature, hymns, information and the framing of contested questions. To be sure, evangelical beliefs and practices were expanding rapidly in other parts of the empire, sometimes with dramatic force, and sometimes with distinctive shape. In addition, evangelical impulses from the centre were migrating rapidly to the margins and often undergoing significant alteration as they rebounded back to the centre. Yet the preaching of Whitefield, the connexions of the Wesleys and the Countess of Huntingdon, and the debates over doctrine and church order stimulated by these Anglican leaders remained the decisive engines of the movement.

Wales

Of course, it is not as though events elsewhere were insignificant. In Wales, for a start, although the Calvinistic Methodist Association did not develop the

---

[17] *BDEB*, 366–337, 378–369 (Roger Hayden, 'Caleb Evans' and 'Hugh Evans').

self-standing character of the Wesleyan conferences, itinerants within the Welsh counties early met for regular monthly meetings. Soon Quarterly Associations were established for North and South Wales to receive reports from these monthly gatherings. Leadership for the Welsh movement was provided by Howell Harris and Daniel Rowland until 1750, at which time there were over 400 local Welsh societies. But tensions between these two dynamic preachers, which had been building for some time, broke out into the open that year.[18] Harris accused Rowland of unseemly 'levity'; Rowland thought Harris was running off into extremes of doctrine and personal conduct. Other responsible leaders joined Rowland in holding that Harris was concentrating so much on the blood of Christ that proper Trinitarian balance was lost, that he was exalting his own authority as a kind of divinely revealed fact and that he had entered into an unwise partnership with a prophetess (Sidney Griffith) not his wife. The result was a division of leadership and also a division among the Methodists. Most of the active work of preaching and monitoring societies fell to Rowland and his associates. Harris retreated to his property in Trevecca, where he built a spacious house for those who still sought his ministry. Rowland and Harris would be reconciled in 1762, but Harris never regained the influence of his early years.

Under Rowland's preaching, and sparked also by a new collection of hymns from William Williams, a fresh outbreak of revival occurred at Llangeitho in 1762. As in earlier pulses of Welsh revival, again there were 'signs and wonders', meetings of pentecostal fervour and a great deal of raucous lay activity.[19] This time the upsurge of evangelical feeling snapped the patience of Rowland's bishop, who expelled him from his curacy. Thereafter Rowland ministered in a chapel built especially for his use, but this fissure within Welsh Anglicanism went no further. Williams' hymns, however, remained an enduring inspiration, whether depicting the seriousness of sin:

'Twas they betrayed Thee, blessed Lamb,
    They were the thorny crown,
They were the nails, the scourge, that bowed
    Thy suffering body down

---

18 For a thorough account, see Eifion Evans, *Daniel Rowland and the Great Awakening in Wales* (Edinburgh: Banner of Truth, 1985), 269–280.

19 On these aspects of the evangelical revival in Wales, see especially Derec Llwyd Morgan, *The Great Awakening in Wales*, trans. Dynfnallt Morgan (London: Epworth, 1988), 22–30, 88–101.

or the transports of redemption:

> Nature hath no joys to offer,
>   Whatso'er its sweetness be,
> That are equal to the accents
>   Of forgiveness full and free;
> Let me hear Thy words, so tender,
>   Words of power from Heaven that sound,
> In the heart a bliss creating,
>   Which in naught below is found.[20]

Sometimes Williams' verse became powerful poetry as well as confident affirmation:

> Hard were the nails and cruel,
>   To pierce that form of grace;
> But now they hold the compass
>   Of heaven in its place:
> The hope of Adam's children
>   Flows from that awful hour,
> When earth beheld its Maker
>   Abused by human power.[21]

And soon Williams was joined by many others, like Morgan Rhys (1716–1779) and John Williams (1726–1806), who by the appeal of their hymn-writing worked a permanent transformation in Welsh spiritual life.

By the early 1760s, Methodism in Wales, though still loosely contained within the established church, was also being promoted by a number of other capable preachers like Howell Davies (1716–1770) in Pembrokeshire, Peter Williams (1723–1796) of Llandyfaelog and David Jones (1736–1810) of Llangan, who secured his charge through the good efforts of the Countess of Huntingdon. Peter Williams was an especially important figure for preparing the first complete translation of the Bible into Welsh (published 1770) and writing the first Welsh commentary on the whole of Scripture. In virtually every feature of the work in Wales, skilful and impassioned use of the Welsh language not only built sturdy evangelical networks, but also laid

---

[20] *Hymns of the Welsh Revival*, ed. and trans. R. Parry (Wrexham: Hughes & Son, n.d.), 53, 59.

[21] H. Elvet Lewis, *Sweet Singers of Wales* (London: Religious Tract Society, 1900), 50.

the foundation for the distinctly evangelical Welsh culture that flourished in the next century.[22]

Scotland

In Scotland, evangelical expansion continued within the established Kirk along the lines begun during the communion revivals of 1742, but it also entered the Highlands under dramatic, if also tragic, circumstances. In lowland Scotland as the first generation of evangelical leaders passed from the scene (James Robe in 1753, John Maclaurin in 1754, William McCulloch in 1771), fresh energy was provided by John Erskine (1721–1803), who ministered in Edinburgh from 1758. Erskine had from the start defended the communion revivals of 1742 and soon became a promoter of anti-patronage as also of evangelical theology. His English correspondents included Philip Doddridge and, towards the end of his life, the Cambridge Anglican, Charles Simeon. He was also in regular touch with Jonathan Edwards and several of his students in New England; after Edwards' death Erskine became one of the chief agents in promoting his works, including in the Netherlands, where Erskine enjoyed several correspondents, as well.[23] Evangelical convictions in lowland Scotland, which remained mostly within the borders of the established church, began in the 1760s to be distinguished clearly as a theological platform separate from the anti-patronage defence of congregational rights.[24] The publications of John Witherspoon (1723–1794) suggest the way in which anti-patronage and doctrinal orthodoxy mingled in those years. Witherspoon, who migrated to America in 1768 to become president of the College of New Jersey at Princeton, published in 1753 a satire on Moderate churchmanship and theology (e.g., 'all ecclesiastical persons ... suspected of heresy, are to be esteemed men of great genius, vast learning and uncommon

---

[22] See, in general, Morgan, *Great Awakening in Wales*; and more specifically, D. W. Bebbington, 'Religion and National Feeling in Nineteenth-Century Wales and Scotland', in Stuart Mews (ed.), *Religion and National Identity* (Oxford: Blackwell, 1982), 492–493.

[23] For Erskine's connections with Edwards, see Christopher Wayne Mitchell, 'Jonathan Edwards's Scottish Connection and the Eighteenth-Century Scottish Evangelical Revival' (PhD dissertation, St Mary's College, University of St Andrews, 1997), 203–204, 220–221, 231–240.

[24] See especially John R. McIntosh, *Church and Theology in Enlightenment Scotland: The Popular Party, 1740–1800* (East Linton: Tuckwell, 1998).

worth').[25] It included denunciation of the Moderates for eagerly accepting the intrusive authority of patrons. Witherspoon also published treatises on justification and good works (1756) and on regeneration (1764), which William Wilberforce later brought back into print. They were marked by the measured, moderate and ecclesiastical Calvinism characteristic of Kirk evangelicalism as a whole.[26]

The one new break of evangelicals from the established Kirk occurred in the early 1750s, when the General Assembly cracked down on opponents of patronage.[27] The central actor this time was Thomas Gillespie (1708–1776), who had studied with Philip Doddridge in England before ordination in the Church of Scotland and who had then helped William McCulloch edit the conversion narratives from Cambuslang. When in the late 1740s Gillespie resolutely defended the church session of Inverkeithing after it rejected a new patronage appointment, and when he insisted on standing with the local presbytery in its support of Inverkeithing, he was deposed from the Kirk. At this point, Gillespie could have joined the Secession Presbytery of Ralph and Ebenezer Erskine, but he did not find the Seceders' exclusionary Calvinism and their defence of a confessionally pure national church compelling. Instead he ministered as a kind of independent until in 1761 he joined with a few other colleagues to form a Presbytery of Relief for those who could not abide the Kirk's exercise of authority but who did not want to join the Seceders. Within fifteen years there were about twenty congregations in the 'Relief Church'. Gillespie's wide range of evangelical friendships, including Whitefield, John Erskine and (by correspondence) Jonathan Edwards, as well as his theology of moderate Calvinism aimed at the evangelization of individuals, marked out an increasingly common position. Not strict churchmanship but theology and ecclesiology in service to gospel proclamation was the key.

Evangelicalism in the Scottish Highlands represented something very different.[28] Well into the eighteenth century, religion in this Gaelic-speaking region

---

[25] John Witherspoon, *Ecclesiastical Characteristics* (1753), in *The Works of John Witherspoon*, 4 vols (Philadelphia: Wm. Woodward, 1802), 3:211.

[26] For a solid survey, see L. Gordon Tait, *The Piety of John Witherspoon: Pew, Pulpit, and Public Forum* (Louisville: Geneva, 2001).

[27] In this paragraph, I follow Kenneth B. E. Roxburgh, *Thomas Gillespie and the Origins of the Relief Church in 18th Century Scotland* (Bern: Peter Lang, 1999).

[28] Authoritative introductions are provided by D. E. Meek, 'Highlands', *SDCHT*, 402–407; and John MacInnes, *The Evangelical Movement in the Highlands of Scotland, 1688 to 1800* (Aberdeen: Aberdeen University Press, 1951).

had been a matter of lightly worn Episcopalianism or Roman Catholicism, interwoven with a great deal of ancient paganism. Against this hereditary background, evangelicalism advanced in the wake of the British army. The specific opportunity was supplied by Parliament's determination to destroy the clan system because of its support for Jacobite efforts at retaking the British throne. When the last of these attempts was finally and decisively crushed at the Battle of Culloden, near Inverness, in April 1746, the government decreed massive changes in Highland life. Roads were built into previously inaccessible glens, cash and lease replaced clan control of land, the tartan and bagpipe were banned, and the 'clearance' of agricultural property began that drove tens of thousands of Highlanders out of Scotland. Into this scene of cultural disorientation, Presbyterian evangelism came as a revolutionary force. Central to the rise of strong evangelical Calvinist churches was the activity of 'the Men', lay-exhorters and catechists who provided public readings of the Scriptures in Gaelic and organized converts into small Methodist-like classes.

Almost as important was a band of poets whose powerful lyrics were every bit as significant for Highland evangelism as the hymns of William Williams and his associates were for the spread of Calvinistic Methodism in Wales. Chief among the poets was Dugald Buchanan (1716–1768), who had heard Whitefield preach at Cambuslang in 1742 and who, after conversion two years later, became an itinerant teacher and exhorter.[29] It is reported that shortly before his death Buchanan engaged in conversation with David Hume, during which the philosopher opined that a scene from Shakespeare's *The Tempest* was the most sublime passage in all of literature. To that claim, Buchanan immediately responded by quoting Revelation 20:11–13: 'And I saw a great white throne, and him that sat on it, from whose face the earth and the heaven fled away; and there was found no place for them. And I saw the dead, small and great, stand before God...'[30] Buchanan's Gaelic verse owed much to Isaac Watts; to his fellow-Highlanders it conveyed evangelical realities with startling effect:

> At midnight, when a slumber deep
> Wraps all the world in rest profound,
> Mankind shall be aroused from sleep
> By the last trumpet's awful sound...
> A ruddy blush along the sky,

---

[29] See *BDEB*, 159 (D. E. Meek, 'Dugald Buchanan').

[30] Lachlan Macbean, *Buchanan, the Sacred Bard of the Scottish Highlands: His Confessions and His Spiritual Songs Rendered into English Verse* (London: Simkin, Marshall, Hamilton Kent, 1919), 39.

Like dawn of morning rising red,
Now shows the Christ Himself is nigh,
Bringing the day of doom and dread...
Then shall a glorious angel raise
Christ's blood-marked banner waving free,
To gather those that loved His ways,
And made His sufferings their plea...
To Jesus flee without delay,
Thy sins abhor, their ways abjure,
With real faith His voice obey,
As heard in His commandments pure.[31]

In the words of John MacInnes, historian of Buchanan and the evangelical movement he represented, Highland evangelicalism 'succeeded in moulding the life and character of a whole race, albeit a small one. It was their guide and support during the hard and difficult pilgrimage from medieval ways of thought and life to an outlook more consistent with the world in which they had to live.'[32] Buchanan notably assisted that pilgrimage in 1767 by supervising the first publication of the New Testament in Gaelic. To indicate the extent of international evangelicalism at this time, that translation project was sponsored by the Scottish Society for the Propagation of Christian Knowledge, which had been founded in 1709 to provide charity schools in the Highlands, and which also supported missionaries, including David Brainerd in his work among Native Americans in North America. Highlanders were not spared the clashes over Moderatism and the battle between patronage and anti-patronage forces that took place in the Scottish church generally, but the evangelical faith that grew up in the aftermath of Culloden has remained to this day a formative influence on the whole of Highland culture.

Ireland

In Ireland, where a distinctly evangelical witness arrived at about the same juncture as in the Scottish Highlands, the results were muted. Ireland's three main religious bodies – Anglican, Presbyterian, Catholic – constituted highly self-conscious and largely self-contained religious communities. Their own internal fixations, as well as intense competition with each other, offered only modest

---

[31] Buchanan, 'The Day of Judgment' (ET), in ibid., 41, 44, 50, 62.
[32] MacInnes, *Evangelical Movement in the Highlands*, 1.

scope for evangelical expansion.[33] John Wesley made the first of his twenty-one visits to Ireland in 1747, but since his work on that island (in contrast to his practice in England) was directed more towards aristocratic land-owners and British soldiers, he did not gain the kind of following among the middle and labouring classes that his movement enjoyed in England. Wesley, who was usually moderate in his stance toward Roman Catholicism, became more fiercely anti-Catholic in Ireland after what he called 'popish mobs' disrupted his preaching.

The most effective early evangelist in Ireland was not a Wesleyan but a Moravian, John Cennick, who arrived in Dublin in 1746 and who was fairly successful at the usual combination of itinerant preaching and society formation. Cennick's entry was eased by cooperation with one group of Dublin Baptists and with a few Anglicans and other Dissenters. Soon Moravian colleagues of Cennick were also active in Ulster, despite the opposition of Presbyterians who questioned the Moravians' doctrinal soundness and the disruption they feared from Cennick's enlistment of laypeople, women as well as men, for the work. Irish Moravianism represented an intriguing link back to continental pietism, but it was soon mostly absorbed into Wesleyan Methodism, which gained ground as a result of John Wesley's frequent visits. Early Baptist reactions to Methodists or Moravians were hardly more favourable than those from Anglicans or Presbyterians. One local Baptist church complained about the 'tumults', the 'wild promiscuous assemblies', and the 'pretense of religion' that Methodists spread in their wake. But the same Baptists also conceded that 'there may be something of imitation among the Methodists', who gathered so regularly for 'prayer and admonishing' and who kept up such a 'constant correspondence' with their spiritual brothers and sisters throughout the rest of the British empire.[34] These kinder words did not signal a notable Irish welcome for evangelicalism in the middle decades, but they did hint at why evangelicalism began to expand in Ireland only a short time thereafter.

The dynamism of British evangelicalism in 1770 was still very much centred in the established churches of England (with Wales) and Scotland. Methodist

---

[33] I rely here especially on David Hempton and Myrtle Hill, *Evangelical Protestantism in Ulster Society, 1740–1890* (London: Routledge, 1992), 3–19; and David Hempton, 'Noisy Methodists and Pious Protestants: Evangelical Revival and Religious Minorities in Eighteenth-Century Ireland', in George A. Rawlyk and Mark A. Noll (eds.), *Amazing Grace: Evangelicalism in Australia, Britain, Canada, and the United States* (Grand Rapids: Baker, and Kingston and Montreal: McGill-Queen's University Press, 1994), 56–72.

[34] Cork Baptist Church Book, as quoted in Hempton, 'Noisy Methodists and Pious Protestants', 63–64.

movements, functioning as parachurch societies within the establishment, remained the key to evangelical expression and expansion. Even as these Methodist movements evolved in different directions, something of where they were headed could be glimpsed among evangelicals in the new world.

African Americans

The one truly revolutionary development in evangelicalism during the middle decades of the century was the beginning of an enduring Christian presence among African Americans. In these beginnings evangelicalism was moving out to a group with no social standing, no strong tradition of Christian faith, no stake in church establishments and no heritage of European civilization. Yet both the missionary future of evangelicalism and the later rooting of evangelicalism in places far beyond the borders of Western society were visible more clearly in these African-American developments than anywhere else in the eighteenth century. The rise of evangelical faith among black communities in the new world did not represent revival in the old sense of the term – understood as the promotion of 'true religion' in contrast to the husks of an inherited nominal religion. But it was revival in a new form – as evangelization and then the formation of new communities of fellowship where Christianity had been all but unknown before. No-one in the eighteenth century realized that the spread of Moravian, Methodist and Baptist influence among African Americans would be so important, since these events received very little attention compared to interest in the dynamic awakeners at work in the established churches. But for the history of evangelicalism as it would develop in the twentieth and twenty-first centuries, what happened in St Thomas, Antigua, the Virginia Tidewater and the Low Country of South Carolina and Georgia was the wave of the future.[35]

Again the Moravians were pioneers.[36] In the early 1730s a black servant at the court of the King of Denmark, by the name of Anton, was brought to Herrnhut by Count Zinzendorf so that he could plea for volunteers willing to go to his native St Thomas (Virgin Islands). Anton hoped in particular that

---

[35] For this orientation towards the broader history of evangelicalism, see Andrew F. Walls, 'The Evangelical Revival, The Missionary Movement, and Africa', in *Evangelicalism*, 310–330.

[36] The following paragraphs rely heavily upon Sylvia R. Frey and Betty Wood, *Come Shouting to Zion: African American Protestantism in the American South and British Caribbean to 1830* (Chapel Hill: University of North Carolina Press, 1998), 80–117.

they could share the gospel message with his enslaved sister Anna. In response, Johann Leonhard Dober and David Nitschmann left Germany for St Thomas, where the work they began in 1732 produced almost immediate results. The Moravian missionaries, who functioned as Methodists would also do a few years later, presented a very different gospel from what the slaves in the West Indies or the North American mainland had heard from Anglican ministers. From its founding in 1701, the Anglican Society for the Propagation of the Gospel (SPG) had tried to promote ministry to new-world slaves, but without much effect. Anglican Christianity remained resolutely hierarchical, made much of status and hereditary roles, sharply limited the voice of women and maintained sharp racial divisions in church seating and the administration of the sacraments. Moravians, though they did not speak out against slavery as such, offered what seemed like a different religion. They encouraged blacks to sing with whites, preached spiritual equality before God and welcomed the expression of religious emotion from everyone and on almost all occasions. So radical were the Moravians for their time that one of their early workers in St Thomas actually took a mulatto bride, a step that brought down the wrath of the island's white planters but that also demonstrated to the slaves the advantages of stable, regular matrimony.[37] Undeterred by opposition, the Moravians went on. In 1738, they set apart five slave 'helpers' to assist in the numerous cells and congregations that had grown up in response to their message. When the Moravians provided instruction in reading and when they encouraged black exhorters to take on more responsibilities, the movement only accelerated. For their part, St Thomas's masters tried to suppress this voluntaristic, lay-led form of Christianity, even going to the extreme of burning Christian books. But they could not stop what the Moravian missionaries began and the African-American converts carried through.

Shortly thereafter Moravians came also to the British islands of Jamaica (1754), Antigua (1756) and Barbados (1765). Though forced to work under the close supervision of the planters, their labours were fruitful. On Antigua there was special response, with over 11,000 gathered in Moravian churches by the end of the century. Such Moravian efforts also provided an opening that Baptists and Methodists, who arrived in the 1780s, would exploit to establish their own active congregations.

Not long after the Moravians began their work in the Virgin Islands, the Wesleys arrived in Georgia, where they provided a foretaste of later Methodist approaches to African Americans. On 1 August 1736, John Wesley enjoyed his first personal meeting with black slaves; it included a serious conversation on

---

[37] Ibid., 84.

the nature of the soul with a female slave. Wesley closed his account, as recorded in his *Journal*, by expostulating: 'When shall the Sun of Righteousness arise on these outcasts of men, with healing in his wings!'[38] Later in his Georgia stay Wesley preached on the estates of several believing planters who allowed, or even encouraged, preaching to their slaves. From these early experiences Wesley took away a revulsion against slavery itself as well as an awareness of the need for Christian work among the enslaved population. For his part, Charles Wesley was also especially interested in Christian outreach to Africans, as when he preached at Newgate Prison in July 1738 to a group of condemned inmates, including 'a poor black that had robbed his master'. Wesley grieved when the prisoners were executed soon afterwards, but not without also rejoicing 'with my poor happy Black; who now *believes* the Son of God loved him, and gave himself for him'.[39]

The Wesleys' commitment to evangelization among Africans did not die as their Georgia experience faded in time. In 1758 John preached to a small group in England that included a planter, Nathaniel Gilbert, recently returned from Antigua. With him were three black slaves, including two women whom Sylvia Frey and Betty Wood identify as Sophia Campbell and Mary Alley.[40] Some months later Wesley baptized two of these slaves: 'One of these is deeply convinced of sin, the other rejoices in God her Saviour and is the first African Christian I have known. But shall not our Lord, in due time, have these heathens also "for His inheritance"?'[41] The Wesleys' eagerness to preach to blacks, their disregard for questions of social standing and their open welcome for fellowship in Christ to all who believed also marked the Methodism that emerged strongly in Antigua when the Gilbert retinue returned to that tiny island shortly after their encounter with Wesley.

George Whitefield was also an effective preacher to slaves in his many journeys to Georgia, South Carolina, and elsewhere in the colonies. As we have seen, Whitefield at first attacked the slave system, but then eventually came to accept it and even to own slaves himself. None the less, his preaching continued to resemble the Wesleys' by addressing black men and women as spiritual equals and by encouraging the formation of informal Methodist societies on plantations. His encouragement of open emotional responses to his messages,

---

[38] Wesley, 31 July 1736 (which includes events for 1 August), in *Works* (new), vol. 18: *Journals and Diaries I (1735–1738)*, ed. W. Reginald Ward and R. P. Heitzenrater (1988), 169.

[39] Ch. Wesley, *Reader*, 122–123.

[40] Frey and Wood, *Come Shouting to Zion*, 242.

[41] Wesley, *Journal* (29 November 1758), 4:292.

no less than his subordination of social distinctions to the imperatives of preaching, likewise made him an effective stimulus of African-American faith.

A similar pattern was witnessed in the ministry of Samuel Davies (1723–1761), the Presbyterian awakener in Virginia. Davies was not a social radical, and in fact, like Whitefield, became a slave-owner himself. But he was also a determined advocate of literacy among blacks and he had no qualms about admitting converted slaves to full church membership. His sermon from 1754, 'The Duty of Christians to Propagate their Religion Among the Heathens, Earnestly Recommended to the Masters of Negro Slaves in Virginia', defended African Americans as fully human, especially for the purposes of education and religion. By 1755, Davies had baptized over one hundred slaves and regularly preached to 200 more. Many decades later, a professor of theology at Princeton Seminary, Archibald Alexander, who had grown up in Virginia, wrote that he knew personally several individuals 'born in Africa, who were baptized by Mr. Davies, and by his care had been taught to read: and have seen in their hands, the books given to them by this eminent preacher'.[42]

The impact of such evangelical outreach received an unusual memorial in what was probably the very first publication by an African American. Phillis Wheatley (c.1753–1784) was an African-born slave who had been purchased by a merchant family in Boston, which then manumitted her in recognition of her precocious literary abilities. When Whitefield died, Wheatley, who had heard him preach, wrote a memorial poem that featured lines representing Whitefield's address to the slaves:

'Take him, ye *Africans*, he longs for you,
Impartial Saviour is his title due:
Wash'd in the fountain of his redeeming blood,
You shall be sons, and kings, and Priests to God.'[43]

The poem also offered condolence to Lady Huntingdon as Whitefield's patron. Then when Wheatley later published a book of poems, including the memorial

---

[42] Archibald Alexander, 'Instruction of Negro Slaves', *Biblical Repertory and Princeton Review* 15 (January 1843): 26–27.

[43] Phillis Wheatley, 'On the Death of the Rev. Mr. George Whitefield. 1770', in *The Poems of Phillis Wheatley*, Julian D. Mason, Jr (ed.), (Chapel Hill: University of North Carolina Press, 1966), 10. These lines are from the version as printed in Wheatley's *Poems on Various Subjects, Religious and Moral* (1773). When the memorial was first published as a separate broadside, the third line quoted had read, 'If you will chuse to walk in grace's road' (ibid., 68).

to Whitefield, she dedicated it to the Countess. Selina and other English evangelicals responded by publicizing the poem and the book, and John Wesley reprinted some of her poems in the *Arminian Magazine* as well. As a northern ex-slave, Wheatley was not the typical African-American believer, but her response to Whitefield did suggest the depth of sentiment that linked the heralds of an evangelical gospel to the Christian conversion of African Americans.

By 1770, a significant start had been made by Moravians and Methodists in evangelizing new-world African Americans, forming African-American religious societies and encouraging black religious leadership. By this date a parallel movement was also at work among what would became the first generation of black Baptists as well. Baptist expansion in the upper South led to some fruitful preaching by whites to blacks, while scraps of Christian faith from Anglican liturgies and Methodist preaching also provided raw materials for the take-off of African-American Baptist faith. Baptists offered a direct, emotional, egalitarian religion that may have been even more subversive of inherited social distinctions than that of the Methodists. White Baptist example and general evangelical preaching combined in the 1760s to create not only an evangelistic movement, but also a movement that encouraged black religious leadership. By around 1770 a black preacher, known only as Moses, had gathered a significant congregation in the Virginia capital, Williamsburg. Shortly thereafter, George Liele in Georgia, after hearing a sermon by a white Baptist, experienced a classically evangelical period of conviction, repentance and rebirth. Liele, in turn, became a powerful exhorter on Georgia plantations and in cities like Savannah and Silver Bluff, South Carolina. About 1770, a slave in the latter place, David George, heard Liele preach shortly after he had been warned by another slave, Cyrus, that if he continued his dissolute life 'he should never see the face of God in glory'. George, who at the time was illiterate, sought spiritual relief but without fruition until Liele arrived and preached on Matthew 11:28: 'Come unto me all ye that labour, and are heavy laden, and I will give you rest.' In a later autobiographical account, George reported what happened next: 'I went to him and told him so; that I was weary and heavy laden, and the grace of God had given me rest.'[44] Before the outbreak of the American War of Independence in 1775, George had helped form a black Baptist congregation in Silver Bluff and others were emerging in Savannah and several other Low Country locations.

The movement of evangelicalism beyond the boundaries of British society had begun. As often in the evangelical story, the prompting of continental

---

[44] Grant Gordon, *From Slavery to Freedom: The Life of David George, Pioneer Black Baptist Minister* (Hantsport, Nova Scotia: Lancelot, 1992), 22–24.

pietists was critical. But even more vital was the evangelical understanding of the gospel as free – that is, as broader, deeper and higher than the conventions of both British Christendom and Western civilization. Evangelicals in their early decades were not social radicals, yet the message that moved them to action was beginning to have radical effects.

Most important for the introduction of evangelicalism to African Americans were African Americans themselves. Slaves who responded to the message from white Moravians, Methodists and Baptists, or from exhorters of their own race, were doing an apparently simple thing by understanding the evangelical message of divine reconciliation as if it were a sincere offer meant truly for them. Yet no circumstance in the early history of evangelicalism has meant more for the world history of Christianity than that deceptively simple first step.

The North American mainland

For British settlements on the North American mainland the key developments in the middle of the century were another series of beginnings. Revival of the spectacular, preacher-centred type had flourished in the years 1740–1742 whenever Whitefield appeared, and also at quite a few locales where his imitators did their work. But although Whitefield continued to travel in America, and although effective preaching for revival by no means ceased after the early 1740s, religion in the colonies witnessed few dramatic moments like the sensations of the early years. In the generation from 1745 to 1770, the number of Protestant churches continued to grow, but not as fast as the population.[45] In some ways the evangelical story in North America resembled what happened on the British side of the Atlantic. Thus, the Moravians were early promoters of evangelical practices in America, especially at their settlement in Bethlehem, Pennsylvania, to the north of Philadelphia, which grew from less than one hundred in 1740 to over 600 in 1759.[46] But since the geog-

---

[45] Information on numbers of churches in the following paragraphs are taken from Edwin Scott Gaustad, *Atlas of American Religious History* (rev. ed.; New York: Harper & Row, 1976), 4, 43; Edwin Scott Gaustad and Philip L. Barlow, *New Historical Atlas of Religion in America* (New York: Oxford University Press, 2001), 8; and Stephen A. Marini, 'The Government of God: Religion in Revolutionary America, 1764–1792', an unpublished manuscript for the use of which I am grateful to Professor Marini.

[46] Beverly Prior Smaby, *The Transformation of Moravian Bethlehem: From Communal Mission to Family Economy* (Philadelphia: University of Pennsylvania Press, 1988).

raphy of North America was much more expansive and the population much thinner than in the old world, evangelical personalities, emphases and practices were at first much circumscribed by denominational traditions. Moravians in the new world, as an instance, remained a mostly separated people who did not exert the general influence that they did upon almost all aspects of the evangelical movement in England.

Congregationalists

An indication of larger trends is suggested by the career of Jonathan Edwards, whose high hopes for the renewal of true Christianity in his Northampton, Massachusetts, parish did not survive the decade of the 1740s.[47] Edwards, to be sure, continued to publish books that were eagerly read in Scotland, Wales and some corners of England and New England. They included *A Treatise Concerning Religious Affections* (1746), which provided Edwards' last defence of the reality of the early Awakenings but also his most rigorous effort at distinguishing true religion from its enthusiastic counterfeits; *An Humble Attempt to Promote Visible Union of God's People in Extraordinary Prayer for the Revival of Religion* (1747), which seconded suggestions from Scotland that 'Concerts of Prayer' be held at specifically stated times to allow believers on both sides of the Atlantic to pray together for awakenings; and his edition of the diary of David Brainerd (1749), which offered a close-up view of the earnest evangelical spirituality for which Edwards had preached. Yet even as Edwards extended his international circle of correspondents and forged ahead with private study and public exhortation, there was trouble at home. Edwards' desire to restrict the sacraments to those who made credible professions of faith represented a break with his grandfather Stoddard's practice and so alienated a large and influential segment of his congregation.[48] His own personality, which could be stiff, did not help ease the conflict, and so in 1750 he was dismissed by the same congregation that he had publicized in the much-read *Narrative* as a paradigmatic instance of revival. Scottish friends offered to secure a pulpit for him in their country, but he chose to move to the frontier town of Stockbridge, Massachusetts, and minister to two small congregations, one white and one Native American. The change of scene allowed Edwards the personal leisure to complete several important theological treatises before he died in 1758, just weeks after assuming the presidency of the

---

[47] For a full account of these difficulties, see George M. Marsden, *Jonathan Edwards: A Life* (New Haven: Yale University Press, 2003).

[48] The documents, with a most helpful introduction, are found in Edwards, *Works*, vol. 12: *Ecclesiastical Writings*, ed. David D. Hall (1994).

College of New Jersey in Princeton. But troubles in Northampton indicated that his view of consistent Christianity, which combined powerful revivalism and strong Calvinism, was not necessarily a religious ideal for other New Englanders.

More generally, the tumults of the revival years seemed to have slowed the momentum of renewal in New England. Where Congregational churches had annually admitted as many as twenty-five new members upon profession of faith during the peak revival years of the early 1740s, the average soon fell off considerably and did not rise to over five per year until the 1790s.[49] In addition, the once unified phalanx of New England Congregationalism was now rent into competing factions. New Light pro-revivalists stood with Edwards and his students, like Joseph Bellamy (1719–1790) of Bethlem, Connecticut, and Samuel Hopkins (1721–1803) of Great Barrington, Massachusetts, in promoting revival and maintaining the ecclesiastical *status quo*. A few more Separates left the established church in order to practise a faith untainted by corrupted traditions. Old Lights may have approved much in revival preaching and New Light theology, but they were traumatized enough by disruption in the churches to defend militantly New England's church–state traditions. A small band of liberal thinkers, impressed by advanced views from figures of the British Enlightenment and led by Charles Chauncy, were beginning to inch away from the doctrines of the Puritans. New England Calvinism remained a great force: it would empower the most important movements of Christian social action in North America into the early years of the next century and set the agenda for formal American theology into the 1850s. But on the ground it was a denomination so strongly influenced by the old New England Way that adjustment to the commerce, expansion, warfare, democratization and voluntarism of the coming age proved quite difficult.

Baptists

The great beneficiary of the Great Awakening in New England turned out to be the Baptists. In fact, Baptists throughout America – whether in the South, the region surrounding Philadelphia or in New England – embraced evangelical practices and beliefs more rapidly than their counterparts in England.

The experiences of Isaac Backus (1724–1806) were representative of the evangelical zeal and evangelical success that from the 1740s energized Baptists

---

[49] These numbers are from Richard D. Shiels, 'The Methodist Invasion of Congregational New England', in Nathan O. Hatch and John H. Wigger (eds.), *Methodism and the Shaping of American Culture* (Nashville: Kingswood, 2001), 260.

in North America.[50] Backus was converted on 22 August 1741, as he worked in the fields outside his native Norwich, Connecticut. At the time he was a member of Norwich's Congregational church, in which he had been baptized as an infant. The converted Backus moved quickly into a New Light orbit and always considered Jonathan Edwards' main theological position as a perfectly satisfactory statement of his own convictions, sacraments and ecclesiology excepted. From the awakened Congregationalism of the Great Awakening, Backus took the principle that God worked visibly by his grace to convert individuals and then to link them with others into genuine Christian fellowship. Yet he was also among the still small number of New Englanders who were coming to doubt the coercive element in the New England Way that forced citizens to support the Congregational state churches.

Those opinions provide the context for what was the second decisive event in Backus's spiritual pilgrimage, which occurred in the spring of 1748. He was by then the minister of a Separate Congregational church in Titicut, Massachusetts, when he refused, with most of his congregation, to pay a town tax levied on all citizens for the construction of a meeting house for the local established church. For his pains, Backus was threatened with imprisonment and several of his members actually lost property or were put in jail.

Hard on the heels of this disillusioning experience came another crisis, now in the form of a dispute within his flock about infant baptism. When several of his congregants challenged the practice, Backus studied the issue for himself in the Scriptures and soon came to the conclusion that believer's baptism by immersion, on the basis of a public profession of faith, was the biblical norm. Backus's third critical turning point then followed. His Titicut church included those like himself who accepted believer's baptism, as well as some who supported the historic Puritan practice of baptizing infants. For several years Backus and his congregation pursued the path of charity and tried to maintain a church that allowed for baptism in both modes. But the experiment did not work, and the church dissolved early in 1756. Isaac Backus was a convinced convert and supporter of New Light religion. He was resolutely opposed to state coercion in religion. Now he knew as well that he was an evangelical Baptist.

When Backus was ordained and installed in June 1756 as the minister of the First Baptist Church of Middleboro, Massachusetts, there were just thirty-six

---

[50] For Backus, I have relied on William C. McLoughlin (ed.), *Isaac Backus on Church, State, and Calvinism: Pamphlets, 1754–1789* (Cambridge, MA: Harvard University Press, 1968); and McLoughlin, *Isaac Backus and the American Pietist Tradition* (Boston: Little, Brown, 1967).

Baptist churches in New England, with most of those located in Rhode Island. Soon that situation changed as Backus led an energetic band of eager evangelists in an effort to convince New England of the need for spiritual rejuvenation and the truth of Baptist polity. The Warren Baptist Association, created in 1767, became a powerful vehicle for those purposes. Baptists preached for conversion, they maintained evangelical Calvinist theology, they encouraged young men to step forth as pastors, they offered women full participation in the rites and deliberations of local congregations and they badgered the New England establishment for full religious liberty. When Backus died in 1804, New England was home to 312 Baptist churches.

A different set of circumstances brought Baptists into the South. The main Baptist organization in the colonies had been the Philadelphia Baptist Association, which dated from 1707. Its members were somewhat less fixated on dogma than their English counterparts and somewhat more active in promoting evangelism. Yet this Philadelphia Association still reflected the pattern of old-world Dissent by being relatively passive in its practice and relatively traditional in its emphasis on the details of correct belief. The Philadelphia Association helped sponsor the first evangelical Baptists in the southern colonies, but that work turned out to be more actively evangelistic than the Association expected; it also brought emphases entirely different from those that were present among the few Freewill or General (Arminian) Baptists who had earlier arrived as immigrants from England. The new work was led by brothers-in-law from Connecticut, Shubal Stearns (1706–1771) and Daniel Marshall (1706–1784).[51] Both had been deeply affected by the preaching of George Whitefield and both had adopted Baptist principles in the early 1750s. In 1754 Stearns heard about appeals for church work from settlers in the Piedmont region of North Carolina and immediately set out. He was soon joined by Marshall, whose move to the Carolinas had been punctuated by brief stops in Pennsylvania and Virginia, where he had planted Baptist churches. Stearns was a particularly effective itinerant who oversaw the start of numerous churches and also the creation of the Sandy Creek Baptist Association. Marshall worked with Stearns for several years but then in 1772 pushed further south into Georgia to found the first Baptist churches in that state. Preachers connected with Stearns and Marshall were among the influences that brought the Christian message to George Liele, David George and other African Americans. Marshall and Stearns were self-consciously Separate Baptists, whom the Regular Baptists of the Philadelphia Association

---

[51] For background, see *BDEB*, 745–746, 1046 (Bruce Shelley, 'David Marshall' and 'Shubal Stearns').

at first regarded as too emotional and too uncultured. But after local Baptist churches and associations were well and thoroughly established, full cooperation was established in 1787 between the main contingents of Baptists in the mid-colonies and in the South.

The key matter for evangelical history is that from the awakenings of the 1740s, most Baptists in the colonies wholeheartedly embraced revival teachings about the direct call of God, the reality of a personally experienced Christian faith and the urgency of proclaiming that message to others. Occasionally Baptists verged on sectarian extremes, as when some refused to acknowledge the validity of any baptism, adult or infant, if not administered within their own local congregation. But this kind of in-group self-sufficiency was a natural reaction to the intense opposition their work received from established Congregationalists in New England and established Anglicans in the South. Persecution from the establishment – which ran to fines in New England and physical assault in the South, especially Virginia – was a steady fact of Baptist life into the 1770s.[52] But, for the opening geography of the colonies as well as for a society with opening ideology, the self-starting, lay-oriented, Bible-centred and thoroughly active work of the evangelical Baptists made them the mainland's most dynamic religious movement between the revivals of the 1740s and the Revolution of the 1770s. They were the primary beneficiaries of the Great Awakening. In the colonies of North America there were fewer than one hundred Baptist churches in 1740, but almost 500 by the outbreak of the war with Britain in 1776.

Presbyterians

The 1741 schism of the Presbyterians, which was described in Chapter 4, came to an end in 1758. In the intervening years, and despite the death of Jonathan Dickinson in 1747, the New Sides' combination of moderate revivalism and evangelical Calvinist theology had advanced rapidly, in marked contrast to the lassitude prevailing among the ecclesiastically and socially conservative Old Sides. During the seventeen years of the schism, the number of Old Sides ministers declined from twenty-eight to twenty-three, while the number of New Sides' clergy climbed from twenty-two to seventy-three, with many of the New Sides' recruits having enjoyed an evangelical education at Yale or one of the classical academies conducted by mid-colony ministers.[53] These local

---

[52] For documentation, see Rhys Isaac, *The Transformation of Virginia, 1740–1790* (Chapel Hill: University of North Carolina Press, 1982), 161–163, 172–77, 200–203.

[53] Leonard J. Trinterud, *The Forming of an American Tradition: A Re-examination of Colonial Presbyterianism* (Philadelphia: Westminster, 1949), 150–151.

schools were the closest American counterpart to the Dissenting Academies conducted by such important English ministers as Philip Doddridge. During these middle decades colonial Presbyterians were much more consistently evangelical and much more self-consciously orthodox than their counterparts in England, Ulster or even Scotland. Led by a number of articulate, learned but also active ministers, they enlivened their inherited Calvinist dogma with effective revival preaching. Gilbert Tennent, the key Presbyterian during the Great Awakening, grew more acceptable to the defenders of ecclesiastical propriety after he became minister of Philadelphia's chief Presbyterian church in 1743, but he remained a firm friend of Whitefield and a stalwart proponent of evangelical emphases even as he chaired the conference of reunion that brought Old Sides and New Sides back together in 1758. By that time a number of younger ministers had added considerable momentum to the evangelical cause. Samuel Finley (1715–1766), a native of Ireland and student at William Tennent's 'Log College' before settling in Nottingham, Maryland, and Aaron Burr (1715–1757), a Yale graduate who took the Presbyterian church in Newark, New Jersey, in 1736, were two of the leading preacher-evangelists of their era.[54] Both were thoughtful advocates of a pious Calvinism, both served as trustees of the College of New Jersey and then as presidents (Burr 1748–1757, Finley 1761–1766), and both prepared scores of young men for the ministry in the principles of evangelical Calvinism. Burr's connections with New England and New Light Congregationalism – begun during his time at Yale and solidified by his marriage to Jonathan Edwards' daughter Esther – suggested also the bearing of his theological convictions and those of many Presbyterian contemporaries. For her part, Esther Edwards Burr was an unusually articulate laywoman who worked consistently at discerning the Christian meaning of her overwhelmingly busy domestic round.[55]

Samuel Davies, who like Burr and Finley ended his career as the president of the College of New Jersey (1759–1761), was an even more influential promoter of evangelical Calvinism in the Presbyterian Church.[56] Davies' special task was to initiate a Presbyterian presence in Virginia, where, until his suc-

---

[54] For introductions, see *BDEB*, 387–388 (Richard Pointer, 'Samuel Finley'), 175 (Randall Balmer, 'Aaron Burr').

[55] See *The Journal of Esther Edwards Burr*, ed. Carol F. Karlsen and Laurie Crumpacker, (New Haven: Yale University Press, 1984).

[56] For introductions, see George William Pilcher, *Samuel Davies: Apostle of Dissent in Colonial Virginia* (Knoxville: University of Tennessee Press, 1971); and Mark A. Noll, 'Samuel Davies', *American National Biography*, 24 vols (New York: Oxford University Press, 1999), 6:159–161.

cessful negotiation with the colony's Anglican establishment, there had been considerably less liberty for Dissenters than in the mother country. Davies settled permanently in Virginia in 1748 and began itinerating among small clusters of back-country settlers who had appealed for spiritual nurture. But Davies was at pains to register his presence with the colonial government and to claim the protection of Britain's Act of Toleration from 1689, which had accorded some legal rights to most English Dissenters. He was immediately successful as a church planter, but it was not until Davies preached rousingly patriotic sermons at the start of the French and Indian War in 1754–1755 that the Anglican establishment grudgingly granted legal status to the new Presbyterian churches. Davies thus pried open a door that first Baptists, then Methodists and finally many denominations went through in promoting evangelical faith in the southern Anglican colonies. When he left Virginia for Princeton in 1759, each of his seven preaching stations had become a regular church, and he had been joined by ten other ministers who were carrying an evangelical message to the Carolinas and further into the Virginia frontier. As an indication of how successful all Presbyterians were in Davies' era, it is significant that the number of colonial Presbyterian churches rose from about 160 in 1740 to nearly 600 by 1776. Two factors were primarily responsible for spurring that growth: a burst of immigration from Ulster to the middle and southern colonies that created a strong demand for new congregations, and an energetic ministry that blended active evangelicalism with traditional Presbyterian Calvinism.

Civil religion

Davies' prominence in these middle decades points to an important feature of American history that, even at this early period, prepared the way for significant contrasts with British evangelicalism. Put in simplest terms, by the time of the French and Indian War (1754–1763), most evangelicals in America were far more willing to embrace a republican picture of the political world than most evangelicals in Britain.[57] In the mid-eighteenth century, republicanism meant a distrust of centralized political power, a commitment to checks and balances in government, a fear of political enslavement and belief in an interlocking relationship among liberty, law and natural rights. Republican theory also drew a close connection between the morals of a people and the safety of its government – virtue in the public made it more likely that

---

[57] For details, see the discussion of 'Christian republicanism' in Mark A. Noll, *America's God, from Jonathan Edwards to Abraham Lincoln* (New York: Oxford University Press, 2002), 53–92.

government would flourish, vice more likely that it would become tyrannical. Republicans were not necessarily committed to democracy, but where democratic principles were at work, these principles invariably coalesced with republican convictions. In Britain, by contrast, republicanism was regularly associated with doctrinal heresy. The people who spoke most of rights, the corruption of government and the dangers of political slavery were the same who held exalted views of inherent moral potential, denied the doctrines of original sin and a substitutionary atonement, and trusted as much in natural human reason as in Scripture.[58] An elderly John Wesley, when faced with the desire of his classes to select their own leaders, put starkly what was, if often in more moderate form, a typical assertion of British evangelicalism: 'We are no republicans, and never intend to be.'[59]

In America it was different. As early as King George's War in the 1740s, American clergymen had already begun to link opposition to Catholic France, the enjoyment of British liberty and the proclamation of freedom in Christ to a republican analysis of the political world. That linkage was strengthened during the French and Indian War, and by no-one as powerfully as Samuel Davies. In 1755 Davies preached the first of several stirring patriotic sermons that interwove orthodox theology and republican politics. While the purpose of the sermon was to exploit the calamities of war as a goad to repentance and faith, Davies spent a great deal of his time building a republican view of the conflict: 'Our religion, our liberty, our property, our lives, and everything sacred to us are in danger', especially of being 'enslaved' by 'an arbitrary, absolute monarch' enforcing conformity to 'the superstition and idolatries of the church of Rome'.[60] A few American evangelicals, particularly the Baptists, remained apolitical during the French and Indian War, but evangelicals who joined the war effort, whether Congregationalists in New England or Presbyterians in the middle and southern colonies, sounded much like Davies.

The long-term implications of this ideological development were large. In part that development explains why such a large proportion of American evangelicals so readily and so actively supported the later War for American Independence, since in the colonies the perceived threat of parliamentary 'tyranny' was simply equated with an assault on the gospel as well. Even more they indicate that decades before American evangelicals abandoned church-

---

[58] For these connections, see especially J. C. D. Clark, *English Society, 1660–1832* (2nd ed., Cambridge: Cambridge University Press, 2000).

[59] Wesley to John Mason, 13 January 1790, in Wesley, *Letters*, 8:196.

[60] Samuel Davies, 'God the Sovereign of All Kingdoms' (5 March 1755), in *Sermons on Important Subjects*, 3 vols (4th ed., New York: J. and J. Harper, 1828), 3:173.

state establishments, they were being drawn closer to republican and democratic habits of mind than their counterparts in Britain. It is true that some British Dissenters, like the Baptist Caleb Evans, and Scottish Presbyterians, like Charles Nisbet of Montrose, joined American evangelicals in this way of thinking.[61] But their political and social views remained a minority position in England, Scotland and even in much of Wales and Ireland, while at the same time more advanced political views were rapidly becoming the majority norm in the American colonies.

Methodists
A final North American development of great future significance, though hardly noticed at the time, was the arrival of the Methodists. George Whitefield was already very well known in the colonies, but converts and others influenced by his preaching were usually drawn to Congregational, Presbyterian and Baptist churches rather than to parachurch societies as in Britain. The Wesleys' early work in Georgia had anticipated the later work of Methodists, but their brief tenure in the new world did not leave a sustained Wesleyan presence.

The American situation for Methodism was also unusual because of the nature of new-world Anglicanism. In an odd reversal that did not sit well with English bishops and American rectors, Anglicanism in the new world had to function as a Dissenting body. The Society for the Propagation of the Gospel (SPG) and the Society for Promoting Christian Knowledge (SPCK) had been active in North America and the West Indies from the earliest years of the century, but their work had an ambiguous effect. These societies did a great deal to provide ministers for new-world parishes, including the sponsorship of John Wesley in Georgia, and to supply colonists with literature. They even made a few preliminary, though ineffective, attempts at mission work among native Americans. But non-Anglican colonists were not overly impressed. Rather, Congregationalists, Presbyterians, Baptists and other Dissenters who were filling up the countryside mostly resented the work of the Anglican societies. They looked upon their agents as interested primarily in establishing the same Anglican superiority in the colonies as existed in England. The Anglicans never succeeded in putting a bishop in the colonies, a step that

---

[61] For a lucid general account, see James E. Bradley, *Religion, Revolution and English Radicalism: Non-conformity in Eighteenth-Century Politics and Society* (New York: Cambridge University Press, 1990); and one on this Scottish case, James H. Smylie, 'Charles Nisbet: Second Thoughts on a Revolutionary Generation', *Pennsylvania Magazine of History and Biography* 98 (1974): 189–205.

would have done wonders for communication, morale and teaching. It would also have saved lives and much money, since American candidates for Anglican ordination had to make the long and hazardous Atlantic crossing to receive the episcopal laying-on of hands. But whenever proposals were advanced to name an Anglican bishop for the colonies, colonial Dissenters of all sorts resisted with all their might and main. From the 1760s, when the SPG made several particularly inept efforts to plant 'missionaries' in places like Boston, resentment against Anglicanism fed directly into more general colonial antagonism to the mother country.[62] Moreover, when colonists did switch church allegiance in order to become Anglican, which happened with some regularity in New England from the 1720s, these newly minted Anglicans tended to deprecate the Calvinist theology of the Puritans and also the evangelical emphases that fuelled revival in England's established church.[63]

Given these new-world realities, it is not surprising that evangelical renewal movements within Anglicanism had much more difficulty getting underway in the colonies than in the old world. As we have seen, when Whitefield was in North America, he worked more closely with Dissenters and received less cooperation from fellow-Anglicans than was the case in England. American Anglicans who welcomed Whitefield were few indeed. One exception was Devereux Jarratt (1733–1801), a Virginian who experienced an evangelical conversion in 1752 and then after study and the required trip to England was ordained to the Anglican ministry in 1763.[64] Jarratt was an active preacher of grace; he itinerated widely from his home parish in Bath, Virginia, encouraged the work of Wesley's itinerants after their arrival in the colonies, and was one of the rare Anglican ministers explicitly acknowledged as a colleague by the later American Methodist Church. Yet it is an indication of the general situation that Jarratt's Anglican colleagues for long considered him a fanatic and only in the last decade of his life offered him even a measure of respect.

These Anglican conditions explain much about the beginnings of Methodism in North America. The earliest Methodist initiatives in the new world were uncoordinated, unplanned and lay-led. They did, however, benefit from

---

[62] The classic study remains Carl Bridenbaugh, *Mitre and Scepter: Transatlantic Faiths, Ideas, Personalities, and Politics, 1689–1775* (New York: Oxford University Press, 1962).

[63] The case of the most notable convert from Congregationalism to Anglicanism is told in Joseph Ellis, *The New England Mind in Transition: Samuel Johnson in Connecticut, 1696–1772* (New Haven: Yale University Press, 1973).

[64] See *BDEB*, 604–605 (Gillis Harp, 'Devereux Jarratt'); and Marvin Bergman, 'Public Religion in Revolutionary America: Ezra Stiles, Devereux Jarratt, and John Witherspoon' (PhD dissertation, University of Chicago, 1990), 155–210.

the kind of connections to the Continent that had been so important in England.

American Methodism began when immigrants from Ireland – several themselves earlier immigrants from the German Palatinate – started in the 1760s to set up local classes in New York City and in rural Maryland.[65] Philip Embury and his cousin Barbara Ruckle Heck had been converted under John Wesley's preaching in Ireland in the early 1750s. After they crossed the ocean to New York in 1766, they established a Methodist society with their families and a few others, including at least one black servant woman. About the same time, Robert and Elizabeth Strawbridge, who had also been associated with Methodists in Ireland but disciplined for pushing too hard for lay ordination, were itinerating from their Maryland homestead and working at forming local societies. Even before the founding of the New York cell-groups, the Strawbridges built a small preaching chapel on their property. The New York and Maryland Methodists were not connected, but they and several other pro-moters of *ad hoc* societies were soon tapping into two large populations of potential converts: the swelling tide of immigrants from all four British prin-cipalities, among whom were many connected to Moravian, Calvinist or Wesleyan varieties of British Methodism; and the vast numbers in America who had responded to the ceaseless itinerant preaching of George Whitefield.

A decisive boost forward was provided by a military veteran of the French and Indian War, Captain Thomas Webb (c.1725–1796), who had been con-verted by Moravian preaching in England in 1765. After Webb returned to America, he began to itinerate out of his base in Albany, New York. Webb served as the personal link between Methodist societies in New York, Philadelphia, Wilmington (Delaware) and several sites in New Jersey. Under Webb's guidance, the American Methodists also began to let John Wesley know what was going on. Soon they could report that 250 contributors, including women and several slaves, had given enough money to construct a substantial preaching chapel on John Street, New York City, a building desig-nated by its location but also as a 'Wesley Chapel'. John Wesley at first reacted with relative indifference, but when the trickle of reports swelled to a torrent, it was time to act. In 1769 he commissioned Robert Williams, a Welsh itiner-ant, who had been active in Ireland, as well as two English itinerants, Richard Boardman and Joseph Pilmore, to represent his interests in America. The

---

[65] On the much debated sequence of early Methodist developments in America, I am following the authoritative account in Dee E. Andrews, *The Methodists and Revolutionary America, 1760–1800: The Shaping of an Evangelical Culture* (Princeton: Princeton University Press, 2000), 32–42.

latter two were formally appointed to what became the fiftieth circuit of the Wesleyan Connexion. Almost immediately Wesley's agents were successful in gathering crowds, forming societies and instituting Wesleyan practices such as love feasts, the circulation of conference minutes and the singing of Charles Wesley's hymns. They reported to Wesley a field white unto harvest.

George Whitefield's death in September 1770 indirectly precipitated one of the key early developments in American Methodist history. The Countess of Huntingdon, upon hearing of Whitefield's demise, moved to appoint one of her other chaplains to take his place as the coordinator of Calvinistic Methodist activities in the colonies. When that news reached the Wesleys, they rushed to recruit more workers for their own Connexion. One of the young men who responded to this appeal was Francis Asbury, who eventually arrived in America in October 1771 as a young (twenty-six-years-old) but already experienced itinerant. When he first set foot in America, there were about 300 people enrolled in American Methodist societies. At his death forty-five years later, there were over 300,000.[66] Asbury was not the only person responsible for this dramatic upsurge, but his role as organizer, encourager, preacher, delegater and mediator of John Wesley's form of evangelical Christianity was critical.

The passing of Whitefield in September 1770 and Francis Asbury's arrival in America one year later marked an important transition point in evangelical history. Never again would there be a single individual who, like Whitefield, enjoyed such full and beneficial connections with such a wide range of evangelicals. Whitefield's death also weakened the prominence of Calvinism in the movement as a whole; various forms of moderate Calvinism and Arminianism became more widely embraced in the decades that followed, especially in America. The passing of Whitefield (an ordained Anglican) and the great American Methodist future signified by Asbury (a person with no clerical training) symbolized also the weakening of establishments as the centre of the evangelical interest.

By 1770–1771 evangelical religion had also begun a process of accelerating diversification that has never slowed. The fact that evangelicalism had taken hold in the Scottish Highlands, in Ireland, in the three main regions of the American colonies, among African Americans and in several islands of the West Indies – and that evangelical converts were beginning to exert real influence among Dissenters in England as well as among Baptists and

---

[66] *Minutes of the Annual Conferences of the Methodist Episcopal Church for the Years 1773–1828* (New York: T. Mason & G. Lane, 1840).

Presbyterians in America – meant that, even if it was not always apparent, evangelicalism was changing the face of religion in the English-speaking world as a whole. Connections with continental pietism remained significant as well, whether as a factor in the evangelization of Yorkshire, Methodist activities in America or mission outreach in the West Indies. Whitefield, the Grand Itinerant, was dead, but the religion he preached was very much alive, and nowhere more so than among the tiny band of new-world Methodists, whose expansion would be the most dramatic event in the next generation of evangelical history.

7. DIVERSIFICATION, 1770–1795

The quarter century after the death of Whitefield in 1770 witnessed another period of dramatic expansion and diversification in the history of evangelicalism. Most obviously important was the growing strength of the movement outside the boundaries of church establishments. Evangelicalism began as an effort to revive religious practice in the state churches of the British empire, but within two generations the pursuit of true religion had carried evangelicals beyond traditional patterns centred on inherited ecclesiastical forms and, in fact, was beginning to push them into unevangelized areas of the globe, where first-time proclamation rather than revival was the central concern. As this process advanced, critical masses of determined evangelicals were adding strength to strength in the established churches of England and Scotland, and there remained also considerable evangelical vitality in the established Congregational churches of New England. But the evangelical surge was definitely breaking the mould in which it had first been cast, as an abridged chronology for the years leading up to 1795 suggests:

1778:   The Wesleyan superintendent, Thomas Coke, circulates an appeal for Methodist volunteers to undertake a mission to Africa, which follows in the train of similar appeals made earlier by the Moravians and leads on to a growing concern for foreign missionary effort.

1779:   During Holy Week personal faith is kindled in Charles Simeon, who would become the central figure among Anglican evangelicals for the next generation.

1784:   American Methodists organize as a separate church not related to any Anglican body and, for practical purposes, independent of John Wesley's influence.

1785:   Publication of Andrew Fuller's *The Gospel of Christ Worthy of All Acceptation* marks the triumph of evangelicalism among England's Particular Baptists.

1787:   In Dublin a General Evangelical Society is founded to pool recruits, energy and funds from all interested Protestants for the evangelization of Ireland.

1790–92:   Advocates, many female, of a 'New Dispensation' in the Annapolis River Valley of Nova Scotia break free from traditional Baptist and Congregational churches to pursue a passionate form of New Light evangelical faith.

1791:   The deaths of John Wesley on 2 March and of the Countess of Huntingdon on 17 June effectively complete the separation of the Wesleyan and Calvinistic Methodists from the Church of England (though in both cases the process of separation is long, messy and drawn out).

1792:   Among several hundred African Canadians transported from Nova Scotia to Sierra Leone is the Baptist preacher David George, who immediately founds the first Baptist churches on the African continent. This same year the English Baptist William Carey publishes a dramatic appeal for missionary outreach and brings to birth a new Baptist Missionary Society, which in the next year dispatches Carey with John Thomas and their families to the Indian sub-continent as its first missionaries.

1792 or 93: Richard Allen and a fellow-African American are expelled from Philadelphia's St George's Methodist Church; Allen with other blacks then founds Bethel African Methodist Episcopal Church as the first black Methodist congregation in America.

1794:   Samuel Marsden, an Anglican minister, arrives in Sydney, New South Wales (Australia), to take up his duties as a minister in that new British penal colony but also as an agent for possible missionary outreach into New Zealand and the Pacific islands.

1795:   In Scotland, Robert and James Alexander Haldane are converted and almost immediately begin to use their considerable inherited wealth for promoting parachurch and Dissenting education and evangelism. In England, paedobaptist Calvinists found the Missionary Society (later London Missionary Society) as a nondenominational voluntary society for the recruitment, commissioning and supporting of cross-cultural missionaries.

The decades immediately following the death of Whitefield were also filled with dramatic political events that, even as they refashioned the geo-political landscape of the North Atlantic, created for evangelicals new situations, new challenges, new openings and new alliances. The American War for Independence (1775–1783) dramatically shrank the first overseas British empire but also turned British attention to possibilities for colonial expansion in other parts of the world. The Gordon Riots of June 1780, which began as protests against parliamentary legislation easing legal restrictions on Roman Catholics and ended with hundreds dead and much of London in ashes, underscored the fragility of social order at the centre of English-speaking civilization. The storming of the Bastille on 14 July 1789, along with the outbreak of the first wars of the French Revolution in 1792 and the guillotining of Louis XVI in January 1793, traumatized all regions of Britain. The decades of unprecedented military mobilization that followed until the final defeat of Napoleon in 1815 decisively shaped British politics, economic life, ideology and social attitudes. It also led eventually to the war of 1812 between Britain and the United States, which became a conflict that powerfully affected the political future of Canada as well.

These major events in political and social history were also major events in the history of evangelicalism. The American Revolution forced North American evangelicals to test the adaptability of their faith to circumstances that were much more republican and democratic than anything experienced before that time. It also led to a new experiment in disestablishment, which fundamentally altered the religious environment in which evangelicals were carrying on their work. The Gordon Riots spoke for the enduring strength of anti-Catholic sentiment, which touched evangelicals as strongly as other British Protestants. Charles Wesley took special pains to disassociate Methodists from the violence, but other evangelicals were active supporters of Lord George Gordon, whose Protestant Association precipitated the riot.[1] The outbreak of war with Revolutionary France created the unsettling circumstances in which several notable evangelicals, like the Haldanes in Scotland, were converted. It also inspired Anglican Evangelicals to stress their loyalism to the Crown, a profession in which most Wesleyans and Old Dissenters soon

---

[1] On connections with Lord Gordon in Lady Huntingdon's circle, see Boyd Stanley Schlenther, *Queen of the Methodists: The Countess of Huntingdon and the Eighteenth-Century Crisis of Faith and Society* (Durham: Durham Academic Press, 1997), 164–165.

joined. After the example of the American and French Revolutions sparked an unsuccessful revolt in Ireland in 1798, evangelicals for the first time made rapid gains among Irish Presbyterians and Irish Anglicans. And the international diplomacy connected to British–French strife that brought on the war of 1812 also redirected the evangelical history of North America, since it pushed Canadians back towards Britain and a more formal evangelical faith while confirming Americans in their ecclesiastical democratization. Throughout these years the strengthening of the British navy and the expansion of Britain's post-Revolutionary overseas empire created the conditions in which foreign missionary efforts took hold. Evangelical history, in other words, was very much part of the broader history of the period. In the accounts that follow, the ever-present realities of diplomacy, war, economic opportunity, economic crisis, ideological stress and strain, as well as imperial contraction and expansion, are not in the foreground. But, for the larger story, they were nearly as important as directly spiritual and ecclesiastical developments.

It is artificial to structure evangelical history from roughly 1770 to roughly 1795 by any one rubric, but since this is a period when evangelical dynamism moved so decisively beyond inherited patterns, it is not entirely inappropriate to describe the growing variety within evangelicalism as taking shape in six discernibly different forms: *as* the establishment, *out of* the establishment, *alongside* the establishment, *after the end* of establishment *against* establishment and *completely beyond* establishment.[2]

As the establishment

In 1795, when John Newton (1725–1807) paused to survey the religious life of England, he was not altogether displeased by what he saw. Newton's own life course, in turn, opens a window into the progress of evangelicalism in the English established church.[3] Newton had been converted during his service as

---

[2] Compared to the wealth of literature available for the 1740s, major studies of evangelicalism during the last quarter of the eighteenth century are rare, with the exception of two magisterial accounts for the situation in England: John Walsh, 'Methodism at the End of the Eighteenth Century', in Rupert Davies and Gordon Rupp (eds.), *A History of the Methodist Church in Great Britain*, vol. 1 (London: Epworth, 1965), 277–315; and W. R. Ward, *Religion and Society in England, 1790–1850* (New York: Schocken, 1973), 1–69.

[3] The essential study is Bruce Hindmarsh, *John Newton and the English Evangelical Tradition Between the Conversions of Wesley and Wilberforce* (Oxford: Clarendon, 1996), but Arthur

a slave captain. He first fellowshipped with Independents before undertaking an intensive course of self-study and seeking Anglican ordination, and he eventually repudiated the slave-trade along with the institution itself. Newton's path to preferment in the Church of England was prepared by a host of evangelicals, each of whom had come to exert some influence on or within the establishment. In his early post-conversion years during the 1750s he made friendly contact with George Whitefield and John Wesley. He was encouraged by several Anglican ministers from Yorkshire, including Henry Venn, William Grimshaw and Henry Crook (1708–1770). After he had written an autobiography of his conversion, *An Authentic Narrative of Some Remarkable and Interesting Particulars in the Life of *********, the manuscript was read by Thomas Haweis before being published in 1764. Haweis, in turn, informed Lord Dartmouth about the promise of the author. Dartmouth (1731–1801), who would later serve as President of the Board of Trade and Secretary of State for the Colonies and also become a confidant of George III, was active in placing evangelicals in the established church.[4] With the advowson (or right to name the minister) he had purchased for Olney, Dartmouth secured a position for Newton as curate-in-charge and also persuaded the Bishop of Lincoln to ordain the former slave captain. Since the Olney position brought with it only a small annual stipend, the pious London merchant John Thornton (1720–1790) supplemented Newton's salary with a generous annual donation.

Newton served at Olney for sixteen effective years. He preached with conviction and visited his parishioners faithfully; he cultivated good relations with nearby Dissenting pastors; he diligently catechized the children of his parish; he exercised a wide-ranging ministry of spiritual counsel through correspondence and personal conversation; and with William Cowper (1731–1800) he wrote hymns for mid-weekly and special meetings of the parish. Of those hymns, the most famous has been 'Amazing grace! how sweet the sound, /That saved a wretch like me!' Newton presented this hymn to his congregation for the first time on Friday 1 January 1773, as the keynote to a New Year's

---

Pollard's excellent introductory article in *BDEB*, 824–825, is helpful for charting the networks of Anglican Evangelicals in which Newton became central. See also the useful new biography, William E. Phipps, *Amazing Grace in John Newton: Slave-Ship Captain, Hymnwriter, and Abolitionist* (Macon: Mercer University Press, 2001).

[4] In 1769 the American evangelist Eleazar Wheelock named his Indian school in Lebanon, Connecticut, after Lord Dartmouth, a name it retained after moving as 'Dartmouth College' in 1769 to its current location in New Hampshire. See *BDEB*, 1178 (David Kling, 'Eleazar Wheelock').

Day service. As it happened, that day marked William Cowper's last appearance at an Olney church service. Soon thereafter Cowper suffered a renewed attack of melancholic depression, in which he felt he had been reprobated by God to eternal damnation. Though Cowper went on to write much notable poetry, he never entirely recovered from that depression.[5] Some of Newton's most intense pastoral labour at Olney was directed towards Cowper, whom he urged to believe what Newton wrote in one of the stanzas of 'Amazing Grace' that is now often omitted from hymnbooks:

> The Lord has promised good to me,
>   His word my hope secures;
> He will my shield and portion be,
>   As long as life endures.[6]

In 1780 John Thornton procured for Newton the living of a London parish where he served with even greater effect on a broad evangelical constituency. Among the most innovative of Newton's London initiatives was the creation of the Eclectic Society, an informal group started in 1783 that included a few laymen and Dissenters as well as other Evangelical Anglican clergy in the London area. Its times of discussion, prayer and mutual support embodied Newton's own ideal, which Bruce Hindmarsh nicely summarizes as 'a non-partisan group of evangelical believers, gathered in a spirit of friendship for "improving" spiritual conversation'.[7] Although he would have been

---

[5] Cowper is such a fascinating as well as such a complex character that his life all but demands multiple perspectives. For a solid introduction, see *BDEB*, 262–263 (Arthur Pollard, 'William Cowper'); then (academic-literary) James King, *William Cowper: A Life* (Durham, NC: Duke University Press, 1986); (historical-theological), D. Bruce Hindmarsh, 'The Olney Autobiographers: English Conversion Narratives in the Mid-Eighteenth Century', *Journal of Ecclesiastical History* 49 (1998): 61–84; and (spiritual) John Piper, *Tested by fire: The Fruit of Suffering in the Lives of John Bunyan, William Cowper, and David Brainerd* (Leicester: Inter-Varsity Press, 2001), 81–119.

[6] For details of composition and first presentation, see Steve Turner, *Amazing Grace: The Story of America's Most Beloved Song* (New York: HarperCollins, 2002), 79–86.

[7] Hindmarsh, *John Newton*, 313. More than a century and a half later, John Stott would revive the Eclectic Society in London, where it became instrumental in evangelical renewal within the contemporary Church of England; see Timothy Dudley-Smith, *John Stott: The Making of a Leader* (Leicester: Inter-Varsity Press, 1999), 305–308; and Dudley-Smith, *John Stott: The Later Years* (Leicester: Inter-Varsity Press, 2001), 82–83, 151–152.

mortified if anyone at the time had said such a thing, Newton's own personal influence was a major reason why in 1795 he could record a growing evangelical presence within the Church of England:

> The times are dark; but perhaps there were darker in *England* sixty years ago, when, though we had peace and plenty, the bulk of the kingdom lay under the judgment of an unregenerate ministry, and the people were perishing for lack of knowledge ... [Now] every year the gospel is planted in new places – ministers are still raising [*sic*] up – the work is still spreading. I am not sure that in the year 1740, there was a single parochial minister [i.e., Anglican parish clergymen], who was publicly known as a gospel preacher, in the whole kingdom: now we have, I know not how many, but I think not fewer than four hundred.[8]

Further testimony to the rising fortunes of Anglican evangelicalism was illustrated during the latter years of Newton's career (he died in 1807), for Newton became a trusted confidant to several distinguished Anglican leaders, both lay and clerical. He encouraged Charles Simeon (1759–1836), well-born and Cambridge-trained, when in 1783 Simeon became the rector of Holy Trinity Church, Cambridge, and began his half-century of preaching, networking and encouraging evangelical clerical candidates. Newton was even more directly helpful to Hannah More (1754–1833), the popular writer who corresponded with Newton from about 1780 and whom Newton encouraged in her faith, which in turn became the basis for energetic labours as a writer of Christian, anti-radical tracts in the 1790s and beyond. Newton also had multiple opportunities to support William Wilberforce (1759–1833), the MP for Hull and then Yorkshire, who was converted in the mid-1780s and who then went on, with Newton's explicit encouragement, to the two great labours of his life: reforming the morals of England and attacking slavery. John Newton's life did not stand in any simple way for the course of evangelicalism in the established church, but it none the less indicated how far the promotion of heart religion, Bible-centred piety and zealous holiness had come within the establishment. Antagonistic bishops still derided evangelicals as 'Methodists' or 'serious clergy', but it was not long until evangelicals were themselves becoming bishops.[9]

---

[8] Quoted in Hindmarsh, *John Newton*, 327. John Walsh estimated the number at between 300 and 500 by the end of the century; Walsh, 'Methodism at the End of the Eighteenth Century', 291.

[9] Quotations from Kenneth Hylson-Smith, *Evangelicals in the Church of England, 1734–1984* (Edinburgh: T. & T. Clark, 1988), 67.

The situation was similar in Scotland. Within the established church evangelical convictions gradually became even more important among the Popular Party than anti-patronage convictions.[10] In this process, John Erskine, correspondent of Edwards and friend of several English evangelicals, played a key role, especially with the publication in 1765 of a *Dissertation on the Nature of Christian Faith*. That work differentiated between intellectual assent to the truth of Christianity and a 'saving faith' involving the actual experience of God. New stress on the possibility of the Christian's assurance followed in the wake of Erskine's signal work. A steadily rising evangelical tide became even stronger when the French Revolution precipitated a sharp turn to evangelical principles and evangelical experience within the Kirk. New publications, new agencies for reform and missions, and new schools were only some of the results.[11] Evangelicals in the Church of Scotland did not yet enjoy the broad social influence that they gained in the first half of the nineteenth century under Thomas Chalmers, but a very significant mobilization of evangelical energy had now grown from the seeds planted at Cambuslang and Kilsyth in the early 1740s.

By contrast to the situation in Britain, evangelicalism in the established Congregational churches of New England was merely hanging on. Although the Constitution of the new United States (implemented 1789) forbade national church establishments, states were free to do as they chose. Connecticut clung to its preferential place for the Congregationalist churches until 1818, Massachusetts until 1833. During the last third of the eighteenth century, evangelical efforts were yielding mixed results within this last bastion of Protestant church establishments in the new world. Students and spiritual progeny of Jonathan Edwards continued to push for revival, but the social earthquake of the American Revolution and a preoccupation with the metaphysical implications of benevolent Calvinism worked to restrict their effectiveness. Quarrels with Old Light traditionalists and the growing drift towards Unitarianism in some Massachusetts congregations were likewise enervating. Several of Edwards' students became consequential theologian-pastors in their own right, but none succeeded in either promoting or explaining renewed Christian experience with their teacher's effectiveness. Joseph Bellamy enjoyed an influential ministry in rural northwestern Connecticut and as the mentor of many pastoral apprentices, even as his own theology became preoccupied with God

---

[10] I am following John R. McIntosh, *Church and Theology in Enlightenment Scotland: The Popular Party, 1740–1800* (East Linton: Tuckwell, 1998).

[11] See especially David Alan Currie, 'The Growth of Evangelicalism in the Church of Scotland, 1793–1843' (PhD dissertation, University of St Andrews, 1990).

as divine law-giver and as he engaged in lengthy polemics defending Edwards' ideal of a spiritually pure local church.[12] After Samuel Hopkins moved from Great Barrington, Massachusetts, to Newport, Rhode Island, where merchants could make a fortune in the slave-trade, he courageously expanded insights from Edwards' theological ethics into a sophisticated attack on slavery itself. Hopkins' *System of Doctrine Contained in Divine Revelation* from 1793 represented the most comprehensive theology published by an American evangelical since Edwards. This work became a key textbook for a number of New England Congregationalists, styled the 'New Divinity' by their opponents. Its strength was its careful attention to the logical implications of main Calvinist doctrines; its weakness an adjustment of classical Christian doctrines to the rationalism of the American Enlightenment.[13] Jonathan Edwards, Jr (1745–1801) tried to maintain his father's principles in a pastorate at New Haven, Connecticut, but the pall of theological disputation and his own inflexibility led to the near vanishing of his congregation.[14] Timothy Dwight (1752–1817), a grandson of Edwards and student of Jonathan Edwards, Jr, was more effective as a minister and as an educator as well. After a successful pastorate, he was called to be president of Yale College in 1795, where steady preaching and a winning personality soon resulted in revivals among the student body.[15] By the time Dwight came to Yale some other New England churches were beginning to experience fresh instances of revival and to take steps for promoting missionwork on the American frontier.[16] Yet loyalty to the prerogatives of establishment and an inability to fight themselves clear from tangled theological disputations limited the effectiveness of Congregational evangelicalism.

In general, New England Congregationalists were being whip-sawed by the cultural transformation worked by the American Revolution. Most Congregationalists had warmly supported the War for Independence as a necessity to

---

[12] See Mark Valeri, *Law and Providence in Joseph Bellamy's New England: The Origins of the New Divinity in Revolutionary America* (New York: Oxford University Press, 1994).

[13] See Joseph A. Conforti, *Samuel Hopkins and the New Divinity Movement* (Grand Rapids: Eerdmans, 1981).

[14] See Robert L. Ferm, *Jonathan Edwards the Younger, 1745–1801: A Colonial Pastor* (Grand Rapids: Eerdmans, 1976).

[15] See John R. Fitzmier, *New England's Moral Legislator: Timothy Dwight, 1752–1817* (Bloomington: Indiana University Press, 1998).

[16] For solid treatments, see David W. Kling, *A Field of Divine Wonders: The New Divinity and Village Revivals in Northwestern Connecticut, 1792–1822* (University Park: Penn State University Press, 1993); and James R. Rohrer, *Keepers of the Covenant: Frontier Missions and the Decline of Congregationalism, 1774–1818* (New York: Oxford University Press, 1995).

preserve what they considered their hard-won freedoms. But when 'the contagion of liberty' spread out of their control, they were nonplussed.[17] In
response to Revolutionary ideology, evangelical Congregationalists made
adjustments. Bellamy, for example, tried to protect God from being pictured
as an 'arbitrary tyrant' by teaching a governmental view of the atonement
instead of the classical doctrine of penal substitution. Hopkins tried to underscore the reality of human freedom by teaching that sinfulness lay in sinful
acts themselves and not in an inherited sinful nature. But these adjustments and the Congregationalists' residual sense of entitlement provided
neither compelling theology nor a particularly effective approach to post-
Revolutionary society. Only by turning to voluntary organizations and less
clearly Calvinistic forms of revivalism would Congregationalists regain some
energy in the early years of the nineteenth century, but by then Baptists and
Methodists had replaced the Congregationalists as the most dynamic evangelical forces in the new United States and even in some parts of New England.[18]

In England and Scotland, evangelicals were bringing fresh energy to the
renewal of their nations' inherited establishments. By the end of the century
(1799), evangelical Anglicans had even succeeded in founding an agency to
support foreign missions, though in Scotland similar attempts were beaten
back by a 'Pastoral Admonition' from the Kirk, which in the same year cau-
tioned against itinerancy, lay-run Sunday Schools and missionary exuberance.
Unlike the situation in the United States, evangelicalism in Britain had
received a second lease on life within the state churches, both of which have
continued to provide a significant base for evangelical witness to the present.

It bends chronological boundaries to mention Canadian developments at
this point, but they are pertinent to the continued history of establishment
forms of evangelicalism – or, more accurately for Canada, quasi-establishmentarian evangelicalism. The war of 1812 – to Americans, 'The Second War
for Independence', to Canadians, 'The First War of American Conquest' –
drew Canadian evangelicals closer to establishment ways and practices. This
war frightened most Canadian Protestants so severely that they turned back
towards British models of church life as they turned away from the democracy, entrepreneurial creativity and disregard for tradition of American evangelicals. Thus, during and after the war of 1812, Canadian Presbyterianism

---

[17] The phrase is from Bernard Bailyn, *The Ideological Origins of the American Revolution*
(Cambridge, MA: Harvard University Press, 1967), 230–319.

[18] These post-Revolutionary developments are explored in Mark A. Noll, *America's God,
from Jonathan Edwards to Abraham Lincoln* (New York: Oxford University Press, 2002),
209–292.

became more closely attached to the forms of the Scottish Kirk; some Canadian Presbyterians went on contending for an ideal of organic, comprehensive church life even after their evangelical Scottish contemporaries had given it up.[19] Evangelical Anglicans in Canada worked for state-church comprehension, as well as for state funding, just as actively as their High Church and Broad Church fellow-Anglicans, at least into the 1860s.[20] And Canadian Methodists, led by master organizer Egerton Ryerson (1803–1882), guided his co-religionists in paths of conservative Loyalism, respectable education and calmly balanced evangelical conviction.[21] Although these developments took place after the 1790s, they reflected Canadian efforts at perpetuating different varieties of quasi-establishmentarian evangelicalism that flowed from patterns defined in the latter years of the eighteenth century.[22]

Out of the establishment

Despite its central place in the 1730s and 1740s, establishment evangelicalism by the 1790s had become considerably less important for the entirety of the movement, at least in part because ambiguity about the Methodist Connexions was being resolved in favour of Dissent. For the English movements of the Wesleys and the Countess of Huntingdon, as well as for a new breed of Scottish evangelicals, the perceived imperatives of the gospel were at last trumping the claims of traditional church order.

Wesley's long battle to maintain his movement both as a flexible, lay-empowering and accommodating agency of evangelistic Christian holiness and also as a parachurch ministry loyal to the Church of England collapsed during the last decade of his life. The precipitating cause was an incessant plea from Methodists in America, who had no practical way of enjoying baptism

---

[19] See Richard W. Vaudry, *The [Presbyterian] Free Church in Victorian Canada, 1844–1861* (Waterloo, Ontario: Wilfrid Laurier University Press, 1989).

[20] See William Westfall, *Two Worlds: The Protestant Culture of Nineteenth-Century Ontario* (Kingston and Montreal: McGill-Queen's University Press, 1989), 19–49.

[21] See *BDEB*, 964–965 (Marguerite Van Die, 'Egerton Ryerson'); John Webster Grant, *A Profusion of Spires: Religion in Nineteenth-Century Ontario* (Toronto: University of Toronto Press, 1988), 68–70, 74–77; and Neil Semple, *The Lord's Dominion: The History of Canadian Methodism* (Kingston and Montreal: McGill-Queen's University Press, 1996), 42–99.

[22] As the next volumes in this series will show, quasi-establishments exerted an influence in other far-flung parts of the British empire throughout the nineteenth century.

and the Lord's Supper unless itinerants, almost all of whom were laymen, provided these sacraments themselves.[23] Wesley had faced similar pleas from his
English and Irish itinerants for at least thirty years, but had always taken
refuge in the availability of Anglican parish churches and regular Anglican
services to meet these needs. Even in England and Ireland, the growth of the
Wesleyan Connexion, not to speak of frequent Anglican opposition to the
Methodists on principle, had made Wesley's insistence on the lay functioning
of his non-ordained itinerants a nearly impossible situation. In America,
where spaces were huge and Anglicans of any sort often scarce, it was completely unworkable. On 1 September 1784, practicality triumphed over principle; Wesley personally ordained two Methodists for service in America, and
then shortly thereafter ordained Thomas Coke, who was already an Anglican
priest, as a 'superintendent' with the power of conducting ordinations of
others. In other words, Wesley took upon himself the prerogative of a bishop,
and he commissioned Coke to act with similar episcopal powers. Coke and the
newly ordained Methodist clergy were then sent to America with instructions
to ordain Francis Asbury as Coke's fellow 'superintendent' (a term that
quickly became 'Bishop' once the Atlantic was safely crossed). Charles Wesley,
whom John did not consult before taking this step, was predictably furious:

> So easily are Bishops made
>   By man's, or woman's whim?
> W——— his hands on C——— hath laid,
>   But who laid hands on Him?…
> It matters not, if Both are One,
>   Or different in degree,
> For lo! ye see contain'd in John
>   The whole of Presbytery.[24]

The die, however, was cast. John Wesley continued to urge his British itinerants not to hold society meetings at the same time as Anglican parish services,
but the aged Wesley's authority was flagging and the demand from his British
itinerants for ecclesiastical self-direction was insistent. At his death in 1791,
there was considerable confusion, since Wesley had left a number of contradic-
tory instructions. It was indicative of the future that when Charles Wesley had

---

[23] There are unusually clear discussions of the process in Heitzenrater, *Wesley*, 285–292;
and Dee E. Andrews, *The Methodists and Revolutionary America, 1760–1800: The Shaping of
Evangelical Culture* (Princeton: Princeton University Press, 2000), 31–72.

[24] Ch. Wesley, *Reader*, 430–431,

died in 1788 he was buried in an Anglican churchyard, but when John died in 1791 he was buried beside a Methodist chapel. Several years passed, with much conflict between the central Methodist Conference and local societies and local trustees as well as among those still fighting the battle between Church and Dissent, but by 1795 the Wesleyan Methodists had for most purposes become a new Dissenting denomination. In the words of Richard Heitzenrater, 'Over a period of more than sixty years, Wesley had developed methods and procedures that, while intended to "reform" the Church of England, in fact gave the Methodists a self-conscious identity distinct from the Church.'[25]

These strivings bore fruit. The number of Methodists in society totalled over 55,000 in 1790. Within ten years the number had climbed to nearly 90,000 Wesleyan members (many more were associated but not fully in society) and an additional 5,000 in the breakaway Methodist New Connexion.[26] In Ireland, there were about 6,100 members in society in 1780, over 14,000 in 1790, and over 19,000 in 1800.[27]

Separation from the Church of England had proceeded even earlier for the Countess of Huntingdon's Connexion. During the latter years of his life, George Whitefield, whose Calvinist theology and casual approach to ecclesiastical tradition continued strong in the Countess's Connexion, had already spun off several of his chapels as Dissenting meeting houses (usually Independent). In 1779 Selina reacted to a dispute over the opening of a large new preaching station in Spa Fields, London, by registering all of her chapels as Dissenting places of worship and ordering the preachers at these chapels to declare themselves Dissenters. Several of her chaplains who were ordained as Anglicans refused to do so. Shortly before her death the Countess then made provision for carrying on the Connexion as a separate denomination, but without her drive, determination and money the plan did not flourish. Although the Connexion continues to this day, most of her chapels and her remaining ministers, as in turn much of Whitefield's legacy, ended with Dissent and in so doing added to the expansion of evangelicalism in British Nonconformity.

Outside of England, Methodist movements in Wales and Scotland were also moving towards denominational status, though at different rates of separation. Welsh Methodism did not reach its ecclesiastical fork in the road until 1810–1811, when the wholly Welsh-speaking Calvinistic Methodist Connexion

[25] Heitzenrater, *Wesley*, 312.

[26] Robert Currie, Alan Gilbert and Lee Horsley, *Churches and Churchgoers: Patterns of Church Growth in the British Isles since 1700* (Oxford: Clarendon, 1977), 139.

[27] David Hempton and Myrtle Hill, *Evangelical Protestantism in Ulster Society, 1740–1890* (London: Routledge, 1992), 38.

began to conduct its own ordinations. After this juncture the great stream of Welsh evangelical Calvinism, which became in the nineteenth century so important for the Welsh language and Welsh nationalism, as well as for the cause of gospel Christianity, flowed mostly as a Dissenting movement separate from the Anglican Church of Wales.

In Scotland, the evangelical energy of Robert and James Alexander Haldane could not be contained for long in the Kirk after the brothers were converted in 1795. At first they attempted to promote explicitly evangelical ventures within the Kirk, but soon they founded a Society for the Propagation of the Gospel at Home (1797), entered into active cooperation with English evangelicals, both Anglican and Dissenter, and began to drain off parishioners from Church of Scotland parishes. As wealthy landowners with minds of their own, the Haldanes were not easily pressed into anyone else's mould, but their work eventually fuelled a considerable expansion in Scotland of both Independents and Baptists. In their turn, the small number of already existing Old Scots Independents and Scots Baptists had already been mobilizing before the Haldane conversions and would continue to become ever more evangelical over the course of the next century.

One of the unexpected results of the rise of 'Methodism' was, thus, a great strengthening of evangelical Nonconformity. Whether as new denominations in England and later Wales, or through its assistance to Old Dissent throughout Britain, the Methodism that began as a renewal of establishmentarian Christianity became, in the end, and in several forms, a critical factor in the spread of evangelicalism alongside the establishment.

Alongside the establishment

Into the 1770s, Protestant Nonconformity in England, Ireland and Wales continued as a penumbra in the background of British religion. The turn of Dissent to evangelicalism changed that situation dramatically. With a direct bestowal of energy from Moravianism and the converts of Whitefield, with a quickening of faith among Baptists and Independents, with a significant stimulus from America and with a wholesale borrowing (especially itinerancy) from the Methodists, Nonconformity entered a period of dynamic evangelical expansion that lasted for at least a century. In the graphic phrase of John Walsh, 'Dissent had drawn an enormous blood-transfusion from the veins of the Evangelical Revival.'[28]

---

[28] Walsh, 'Methodism at the End of the Eighteenth Century', 293.

The change under way among Independents was strikingly illustrated by the career of David Bogue.[29] Bogue was a Scot who, after preparing for ministry in the Kirk, moved instead to England, where he took an Independent church in Hampshire. From the start of this ministry he exemplified the outward-looking spirit of an evangelical activist. He founded an academy aimed at training young men for the ministry, added itinerant preaching as a regular feature of his curriculum, explored the possibility of missionary service in the Far East under the sponsorship of the East India Company (but the Company denied permission) and eagerly cooperated with other Dissenters and some Anglicans in a wide variety of enterprises. He wrote for the *Evangelical Magazine*, whose founding in 1793 by a trans-denominational group of moderate Calvinists was itself a sign of quickening evangelical activism. Through articles published in this magazine as well as by assiduous cultivation of a wide circle of personal associates, Bogue was one of the key figures in the 1795 founding of the London Missionary Society, the interdenominational agency that Calvinist paedobaptists formed to promote evangelization in the Pacific and other places far from Britain. It was a sign of an evangelical 'Catholic spirit' that Independents and Calvinist Methodists joined with some evangelical Anglicans and Presbyterians in this venture. Bogue also played a role in the conversion of the Haldane brothers and helped stimulate their enthusiasm for voluntary religious organizations. And Bogue was far from being alone as a Congregationalist of 'the strong earnest evangelical breed', as his colleague with the Missionary Society, James Boden of Sheffield, was called.[30] Rather, Bogue was the vanguard of a new evangelical urgency that greatly revived the religion and long-term fortunes of his denomination.

The move towards evangelicalism was nearly as strong among the Particular Baptists. With the Northamptonshire Association as the critical clearing house for theological and personal inspiration, Baptists turned with increasing energy to outwardly directed tasks of evangelization and mission. John Sutcliff (or Sutcliffe, 1752–1814), Baptist minister in Olney, cooperated with the Anglican John Newton in preaching and pastoral ministry. Robert Hall, Sr (1728–1791) published a treatise in 1781, *Help to Zion's Travellers*, that argued for a full measure of human activity alongside the Particular Baptists' traditional trust in God's sovereign direction of salvation. His son, Robert Hall, Jr (1764–1831), came to Cambridge as a Baptist pastor not long after Charles Simeon became the rector at Holy Trinity Church, and in that office Hall presented a strong

---

[29]   See *BDEB*, 115 (J. H. Y. Briggs, 'David Bogue'). For a general account of this
      quickening, see Watts, *Dissenters*, 2:1–22, 110–158.
[30]   *BDEB*, 114 (J. H. Y. Briggs, 'James Boden').

evangelical challenge to the university and the city. Robert Hall, Jr, was somewhat unusual for the Baptists of his day for being a faithful advocate of civil
freedom and the lifting of legal disabilities for Dissenters. John Ryland, Jr
(1753–1825), Baptist pastor in Northampton and then president of the Bristol
Academy, was one of several pastors who read the works of Jonathan Edwards
with great appreciation. After receiving a parcel of Edwards' books from John
Erskine in Scotland, Ryland read Edwards' *A Humble Attempt to Promote Visible
Union of God's People in Extraordinary Prayer for the Revival of Religion* (1747), which
was directly instrumental in Ryland's organization in 1784 of a cell whose
purpose was to pray for the evangelization of England and the world. The
senior Robert Hall was another avid reader of Edwards.

Hall's recommendation of Edwards' *Freedom of the Will* to Andrew Fuller
(1754–1815) led to a critical moment in Baptist history.[31] Fuller's own spiritual
struggles and his observations of others as a young minister stimulated an
intense inner debate on issues of human responsibility in relationship to
divine sovereignty. In Dissenting terms, Fuller was wrestling with 'The
Modern Question', so called after a pamphlet from 1737, *A Modern Question
Modestly Answered*, by Matthias Maurice, a Congregationalist pastor who argued
that it was 'the duty of poor unconverted sinners, who hear the Gospel
preached or published, to believe in Jesus Christ'.[32] To Baptist traditionalists,
this proposition seemed to negate the force of God's sovereign call of election, since how could it be the duty of an ordinary sinner to repent if God
was the sole agent in bringing unbelievers from spiritual death to spiritual life?
More and more Calvinist Dissenters in the half century of debate that followed the publication of Maurice's work were coming to believe that he was
right – the gospel should be preached freely to all, and all hearers of the
gospel should be implored to turn to Christ. Yet the suspicion lingered that to
take this step was to set aside what seemed to most Particular Baptists clear
biblical teaching about God's electing grace and the true path of salvation.
Andrew Fuller was struggling with this issue when he was guided to Jonathan
Edwards. In Edwards' *Freedom of the Will*, Fuller was impressed with Edwards'
distinction between 'moral ability' (the desire to turn to God) and 'natural
ability' (the capacity to turn to God). With Edwards, Fuller came to embrace
the conviction that all people should and could turn to God if they would do
so – thus justifying free and full gospel preaching. But in addition Edwards

---

[31] A useful introduction is Phil Roberts, 'Andrew Fuller', in Timothy George and David S.
Dockery (eds.), *Theologians of the Baptist Tradition* (Nashville: Broadman & Holman, 2001),
34–51.

[32] Watts, *Dissenters*, 1:457.

showed him how he could also continue to believe that redemption required God's gift of 'a new sense of the heart' to change the character lying behind all human choices. At least to Fuller's satisfaction, and also the satisfaction of many other Baptists, Edwards had solved the conundrum of how to believe in the scriptural teaching of predestination while also following the scriptural mandate for worldwide evangelism.

And worldwide it certainly was, for the circle of Northamptonshire Baptists nurtured a growing number of individuals, both lay and clerical, who felt an increasing burden to take the gospel message to unbelievers wherever they might be found. One of these was William Carey (1761–1834), a shoemaker, schoolteacher and pastor who, after being inspired by accounts of Captain Cook's voyages in the Pacific, began to think seriously about the mandate for Christian witness in such parts of the world.[33] After several years of discussion with Baptist colleagues, in 1792 Carey published a short tract that exerted a huge impact: *An Enquiry into the Obligations of Christians, to Use Means for the Conversion of the Heathens: in which the religious state of the different nations of the world, the success of former undertakings, and the practicability of other undertakings, are considered.* What Carey meant by 'means' he made clear at the outset: 'As our blessed Lord has required us to pray that his kingdom may come, and his will be done on earth as it is in heaven, it becomes us not only to express our desires of that event by words, but to use every lawful method to spread the knowledge of his name.'[34] Spurred on by Carey, Baptist leaders including Fuller and Ryland later in 1792 founded the Particular Baptist Society for Propagating the Gospel Among the Heathen (or Baptist Missionary Society). Although this society was not the first British venture to undertake foreign missions, Carey and his Baptist colleagues have been correctly described as the key promoters of modern missionary service in an evangelical form.[35]

The innovation that meant most for the revitalization of Dissent was not, however, foreign missions but evangelistic initiative at home. The two, of course, were closely related. The same motives that drove Carey and the Baptist Missionary Society to contemplate self-sacrificing missionary service abroad nerved many other Baptists and Independents to self-sacrificing itineration in

---

[33] For a reliable recent treatment, see Timothy George, *Faithful Witness: The Life and Mission of William Carey* (Worcester, PA: Christian History Institute, 1998).

[34] William Carey, *An Enquiry into the Obligation of Christians, to Use Means* (Leicester: Ann Ireland, 1792), 3.

[35] For authoritative treatment, see Brian Stanley, *The History of the Baptist Missionary Society, 1792–1992* (Edinburgh: T. & T. Clark, 1992).

the British Isles.[36] When Dissenters took this page from the manual of standard Methodist procedure, the result was fresh energy for expansion. A tradition of Dissenting itinerancy extended back into the seventeenth century, but it had been stifled first by governmental regulation and then by the cooling of Nonconformist zeal. It revived through the influence of Whitefield's public preaching, the Wesleyan itinerations, the Countess of Huntingdon's patronage and also from the same theological sources that were encouraging mission work. Village preaching, field preaching, evangelistic forms of lay exhorting, cottage prayer meetings – all were new means appropriated by Independents and Baptists for proclaiming the gospel and, incidentally, reviving their own denominations. The success of Dissenting itinerancy eventually raised political suspicions, especially the fear that these mostly humble ministers and lay preachers were part of a conspiracy inspired by French Revolutionary radicalism to undermine British order. That suspicion, which came to a head after the start of the new century, was not so much a sign of actual political threat as a tribute to the successful and thoroughly evangelical revival of British Dissent.

After the end of establishment

Revival of another kind was under way in America during the same years of Dissenting rejuvenation and Methodist reorganization in Britain. The period of the American Revolutionary War (1775–1783) had been favourable for only one kind of 'religion' in the breakaway British colonies, a 'civil religion of independence' that devoted considerable spiritual energy towards advancing the patriot cause.[37] That civil religion carried much further the republican–Christian bond that had first appeared in earlier colonial wars. It stimulated intense but fanciful preoccupation with apocalyptic texts of the Bible and offered religious reassurance for those who took up arms against the mother

---

[36] The key study is Deryck W. Lovegrove, *Established Church, Sectarian People: Itinerancy and the Transformation of English Dissent, 1780–1830* (Cambridge: Cambridge University Press, 1988).

[37] See John F. Berens, *Providence and Patriotism in Early America, 1640–1815* (Charlottesville: University Press of Virginia, 1978), 81–164; Ruth H. Bloch, *Visionary Republic: Millennial Themes in American Thought, 1756–1800* (New York: Cambridge University Press, 1985); Nathan O. Hatch, *The Sacred Cause of Liberty: Republican Thought and the Millennium in Revolutionary New England* (New Haven: Yale University Press, 1977), 97–175; and Mark A. Noll, *Christians in the American Revolution* (Grand Rapids: Eerdmans, 1976), 49–78.

country, but it did little to promote active Christian life. The war, with its dislocation of the economy, forced movements of people, and appropriation and sometimes destruction of churches, was a trial for all denominations. It was a particular disaster for colonial Anglicans, who suffered the loss of much property, but who were also stigmatized by their church's loyalism to King and Parliament. Anglicans reorganized in 1785 as the Protestant Episcopal Church in the United States of America, but it would be many years before the new denomination regained momentum and even more years until in the 1810s a strong evangelical movement also arose.[38]

Congregationalists and Presbyterians, who mostly supported the patriot war effort, were not damaged as badly. But Congregationalists, as we have seen, were suffering under the pressure of a growing Unitarian movement and also from an inability to adjust establishmentarian habits to the new realities of a republican United States. Presbyterians, for their part, were well positioned for advance, but they were held back by problems of denominational leadership and by uncertainties in meeting the challenge of a western-moving population.[39] John Witherspoon, the Scottish-born president of the College of New Jersey at Princeton, won renown as the only clergyman to sign the American Declaration of Independence (1776), but his advancing age greatly reduced the stimulation he had brought to the church in the years immediately after his arrival in 1768. Princeton, which had seen almost half its students enter the ministry in Witherspoon's first years as president, saw that number drop to less than one-fifth in his latter years.[40] In the period before Witherspoon's death in 1794, American Presbyterians were split into three different parties. One was represented by the work of Samuel Stanhope Smith (1751–1819), Witherspoon's son-in-law and successor as president of Princeton, who seemed to be following English Presbyterianism into Enlightenment latitudinarianism. Another was led by Ashbel Green (1762–1848), pastor of Philadelphia's Second Presbyterian Church and key member of the Princeton board, who struggled to combine traditional Presbyterian concern for education, traditional Presbyterian confessionalism and anything-but-traditional mobilization for the frontier. The third was headed by energetic preachers in the American West – like James McGready (c.1758–1817) and Barton W. Stone (1772–1844) – who were following the

---

[38] See the early pages of Diana Hochstedt Butler, *Standing Against the Whirlwind: Evangelical Episcopalians in Nineteenth-Century America* (New York: Oxford University Press, 1995).

[39] Noll, *America's God*, 124–130.

[40] Mark A. Noll, *Princeton and the Republic, 1768–1822* (Princeton: Princeton University Press, 1989), 53.

movement of Scots-Irish immigrants into the western Carolinas, Kentucky and Tennessee, and adjusting received Presbyterian traditions in order to provide a Christian witness on the rapidly developing frontier.[41] Not until after the turn of the century was it clear that American Presbyterians would promote both a generally historical Calvinism and a modestly activistic voluntarism; not until then did the Presbyterians' contribution to the expansion of evangelical influence in the United States come into its own.

American historians speak rightly of a 'Second Great Awakening' that revived commitment to Christianity, drove church expansion to unprecedented levels and went a considerable distance towards Christianizing many of the institutions and social habits of the new nation. But they regularly misconstrue its timing and its provenance by focusing on local Congregational revivals in New England from the mid-1790s or on the emergence of large-meeting revivalism in upstate New York during the 1820s under the Presbyterian-Congregationalist Charles Grandison Finney. In point of fact, the revitalization of religion after the American Revolution began in the mid-1780s; it took place principally in the South and rural New England; the agents of its renewal were almost exclusively Methodists, Baptists and even more radical evangelicals; and a large proportion of its constituency was black.[42]

Baptists were probably the only American denomination to advance during the war years, and almost all of that advance was evangelical. Methodists, by contrast, were hamstrung during the conflict by the taint of Loyalism – not only were they suspect for their connection with the Anglican Church, but John and Charles Wesley, along with other British Methodists, had made widely publicized comments denouncing the American rebellion as a cynical assault on Britain's mild and godly authority. It did nothing for Methodists in America, for instance, when the Wesleys' trusted theological lieutenant, John Fletcher, wrote in 1776 that the 'groans' of African Americans 'upbraid the hypocritical friends of liberty [in America], who buy, and sell, and whip their fellow men as if they were brutes, and absurdly complain that *they* are enslaved' by Parliament.[43] When patriotic feeling rose against the Methodists

[41] *BDEB*, 718–719 (Thomas T. Taylor, 'James McGready') and 1060 (C. Leonard Allen, 'Barton Warren Stone').

[42] The clearest account of this situation is in the unpublished manuscript of Stephen A. Marini, 'The Government of God: Religion and Revolution in America, 1764–1792', which informed my own effort to describe 'the evangelical surge' in *America's God*, 161–186.

[43] John Fletcher, 'The Bible and the Sword' (1776), in Ellis Sandoz (ed.), *Political Sermons of the American Founding Era, 1730–1805* (Indianapolis: Liberty Press, 1991), 567.

because of such commentary, all of the itinerants whom Wesley had recruited for service in America, except Francis Asbury, returned home, and Asbury was forced to lie low in the Delaware countryside. As soon as active fighting ceased, however, Methodism was immediately on the march. With the Baptists they seemed instinctively to understand how as Christians they could exploit the new social economy of the new American nation.

The American War for Independence was a revolutionary war as much for freeing space, liberating ideology and empowering the marginalized as it was for the political break with Great Britain. The country that emerged from the war in 1783 and that after a few false steps was refashioned in the Constitution of 1789 was open for immediate migration over the Appalachians into Kentucky, Tennessee and points beyond. It was formally committed to republican government and to the rejection of inherited authority. It had announced in the Declaration of Independence that 'all men are created equal', a notion that in the context of the eighteenth century was preposterous and yet that more and more Americans – including unpropertied males, women and slaves, none of whom had been in the minds of the Founding Fathers – took very seriously indeed. In the Constitution the federal government both guaranteed the free exercise of religion and prohibited a national religious establishment.[44] Tax support for Congregational churches hung on in Connecticut and Massachusetts, and several of the new states initially required office holders to be Christians, or even Protestants. But the organization of American life was clearly moving in a direction that no European country had experienced before.

That direction was towards the uncoupling of religious adherence from direct state interest. Americans soon found many informal ways of supporting religiously inspired practices – whether restricting public activity on Sunday, holding Christian worship services in the United States Capitol building, enlisting public funding for missionaries to Native Americans or reading the Bible in tax-supported schools.[45] But these marks of an unofficially established Protestant faith were considered non-sectarian and so could be supported for general social purposes rather than out of deference to inherited

---

[44] For complexities of how that 'freedom of religion' actually operated, see Thomas J. Curry, *The First Freedoms: Church and State in America to the Passage of the First Amendment* (New York: Oxford University Press, 1986); and Derek Davis, *Religion and the Continental Congress, 1774–1789: Contributions to Original Intent* (New York: Oxford University Press, 2000).

[45] On these establishment-like practices, see especially James H. Hutson, *Religion and the Founding of the American Republic* (Washington: Library of Congress, 1998), 75–97.

religious authority. Old-world assumptions that ruled out the possibility of a stable, honourable society without a formally established church did not pass away as rapidly as some American ideologues suggested. But compared to any other civilized nation in Europe, they were dying, and they were dying fast. Within two decades of the American founding, religion – and much else that in Europe had functioned by inherited right – was being handed over to the people at large and to market forces. The liberal character of the American Revolution was nowhere more evident than in the new assumptions that if enough people with enough competing interests were given enough freedom, they could take care of themselves.

In such an environment forms of evangelicalism not dependent on state-church support spread like wildfire. Baptists had never asked for government help, but in the old country they had been hemmed in by the Church of England, the establishmentarian restrictions of parliamentary legislation, and their own self-understanding as Dissenters (with all that such self-understanding implied about the acknowledged prerogatives of the establishment). By contrast, in America after the War, Baptists in the middle and southern regions found no state church, they were completely free to organize as they chose and they were committed first of all to the gospel message they proclaimed. Baptists had come into the southern colonies only in the 1760s; by 1790 half of all American Baptists lived in the five most southern states. Baptists founded an average of about 50 new churches each year during the 1780s.[46] Although historiography on Baptists is not as advanced as it should be, there is no doubt that evangelical energy drove Baptist preaching into the open spaces of post-establishment America.

Important as Baptist action was, the great engine behind what has been called 'the phenomenal advance of evangelical Protestantism' that began in the mid-1780s was Methodism.[47] After the end of the War, Methodists

---

[46] For the numbers, Sylvia R. Frey and Betty Wood, *Come Shouting to Zion: African American Protestantism in the American South and British Caribbean to 1830* (Chapel Hill: University of North Carolina Press, 1998), 120; and Noll, *America's God*, 166, 181.

[47] Frey and Wood, *Come Shouting to Zion*, 120. Important general accounts include Andrews, *The Methodists and Revolutionary America*; Nathan O. Hatch and John H. Wigger (eds.), *Methodism and the Shaping of American Culture* (Nashville: Kingswood, 2001); Christine Leigh Heyrman, *Southern Cross: The Beginnings of the Bible Belt* (New York: Knopf, 1997); Cynthia Lynn Lyerly, *Methodism and the Southern Mind, 1770–1810* (New York: Oxford University Press, 1998); Russell E. Richey, *Early American Methodism* (Bloomington: Indiana University Press, 1991); and John H. Wigger, *Taking Heaven by Storm: Methodism and the Rise of Popular Christianity in America* (New York:

regrouped under Asbury. They were given a definite boost by John Wesley's provision of an ordained ministry in 1784. They gave themselves an even greater boost in that same year at the famous 'Christmas Conference' in Baltimore at which they constituted American Methodism as a separate ec-clesiastical body. That gathering, which was a general meeting of American itinerants, did not simply accept Wesley's directives, but rather made a con-scious decision to vote for Asbury and Thomas Coke as their 'superintendents' (soon 'bishops'). The new Methodist Episcopal Church was still respectful of 'Daddy' Wesley, but to all intents and purposes it was now acting on its own.

Only the excitement attending Whitefield's early preaching can match what happened next when the Methodists were unleashed on the new American nation. Coke and especially Asbury led by example through indefatigable travel and insistent gospel proclamation. Asbury's favourite texts were Luke 19:10 ('For the Son of man is come to seek and to save that which was lost') and 2 Corinthians 6:1–2 (which reads in part, 'behold, now is the accepted time; behold, now is the day of salvation').[48] Asbury preached on these and similar evangelistic passages virtually everywhere in the new country. And as he preached he organized. Beginning in the 1780s Asbury regularly made a giant circuit each year throughout the whole United States to convene local Methodist conferences, assign itinerants to their own circuits, recruit new preachers and encourage his veterans.

From the start he was joined by a host of itinerating evangelists as dedic-ated to the cause as he was. They included stalwarts like Freeborn Garrettson (1752–1827), who survived hostility against his pacifism during the American Revolution to become an extraordinarily effective itinerant, first in the south-ern states, then to the Canadian Maritimes and then back to New York State. When he was an old man, Garrettson ruminated on the work of more than half a century. For him, it was critical that Methodists had proclaimed 'the *essentials* of the gospel'. Those essentials were crystal clear in his mind:

> The design of preaching is to awaken sinners and to bring them to Christ; to urge believers to the attainment of holiness of heart and life – to show sinners the turpitude of their hearts and sinfulness of their practice, and to bring them to the foot of the cross, stripped of self and of all self dependence; to press the old

Oxford University Press, 1998). For connections to the Methodist story in Britain, see especially David Hempton, *The Religion of the People: Methodism and Popular Religion, c.1750–1900* (London: Routledge, 1996).

[48] Elmer T. Clark (ed.), *The Journals and Letters of Francis Asbury*, 3 vols (Nashville: Abingdon, 1958), 2:818–842 ('Index of Sermon Texts').

Methodistical doctrines of justification by faith; the direct evidence from God, through faith in the merits of Christ, of the forgiveness of sin; and the adoption into his family. Nor are we to be ashamed of that unfashionable doctrine, Christian perfection.[49]

As Methodist itinerants, most of whom were young men, urged this message on all who would listen, they were denounced as ecclesiastical upstarts, destroyers of families, agents of social upheaval and worse.[50] But even more, they were welcomed by an increasingly restless people as offering words of eternal life and guidance for practical Christian living.

As the American population burst from the sea coast, Methodist itinerants marched along stride for stride, even as other Methodists worked just as assiduously in settled areas for the conversion of the lost and the organization of the convicted. Wherever they went the itinerants introduced the panoply of Methodist 'discipline': regular class meetings for spiritual examination and mutual exhortation, larger society gatherings for preaching from local elders and ordained itinerants, monthly and quarterly conferences for celebrating the sacraments and taking part in the sacrament-like love feast and everywhere the production, distribution and constant use of hymnbooks.[51]

The statistics that Asbury and his colleagues diligently collected year by year tell part of the story. In 1780 there were forty-two itinerants ministering to 8,500 society members in twenty-one circuits. Ten years later it was 227 itinerants for almost 58,000 society members in 101 circuits. Almost one-fifth of the society members were African American.[52] By that year as well, the number of American Methodists in the still thinly populated regions of the United States pushed past the number in Wesley's British Connexion.[53] (When considering such numbers, it is necessary to observe that in both Britain and America the number of individuals taking part in Methodist activities in some form was always several times that of those who became full members of a

---

[49] Garrettson, 'Substance of the Semi-Centennial Sermon' (1827), in Robert Drew Simpson (ed.), *American Methodist Pioneer: The Life and Journals of the Rev. Freeborn Garrettson, 1752–1827* (Rutland: Academy, 1984), 399.

[50] For a full catalogue, see Heyrman, *Southern Cross*.

[51] For details, see Russell E. Richey, *The Methodist Conference in America: A History* (Nashville: Kingswood, 1996); and Lester Ruth, *A Little Heaven Below: Worship at Early Methodist Quarterly Meetings* (Nashville: Kingswood, 2000).

[52] *Minutes of the Annual Conference of the Methodist Episcopal Church for the Years 1773–1828* (New York: T. Mason & G. Lane, 1840).

[53] Heitzenrater, *Wesley*, 264.

AMERICAN METHODISTS
Numbers of Society Members and Preachers 1773–1791

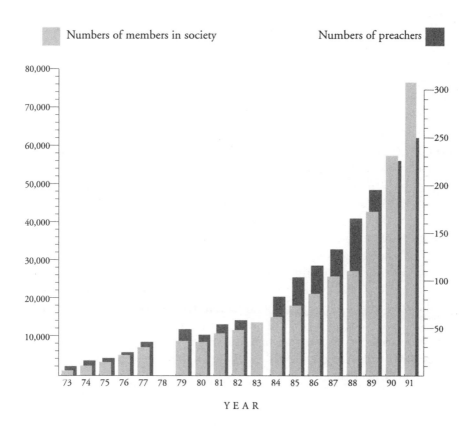

Numbers of members in society   Numbers of preachers

YEAR

Source: *Minutes of the Annual Conference of the Methodist Episcopal Church for the Years 1773–1828, vol. 1* (New York: Mason & G. Lane, 1840)

society.) The surge of Methodist growth did tail off during the decade of the 1790s, in part because of a schism in 1792 precipitated by James O'Kelly's demand for more democracy in naming preachers to circuits and in checking Asbury's general authority. O'Kelly's self-described Republican Methodists were only the first of what would be several later schisms. But the majority of Methodists, with loyalty to Asbury intact, went on. By 1800 the earlier pattern of spectacular expansion resumed. Fifty years later more than one in three Americans who belonged to a church were Methodist.

The story of the Methodists in large measure defined American religious history during the two generations after independence. For broader evangelical history, American Methodists demonstrated the adaptability of evangelicalism to new conditions. The United States deliberately replaced the authority of tradition with the workings of the market. It deliberately opened up new land, in effect begging people to leave settled communities on the Atlantic Coast and beckoning newcomers from Europe. It offered the prospect of new freedoms, new standards of culture and new institutions of civilization. It embraced republican government with open arms. It dismissed the idea of inherited authority. In this environment evangelicalism, which had come into existence to revive true religion in established churches, found itself transformed into an affecting religion of the heart for a people on the move. Much about evangelicalism remained the same in the transition from aristocratic Britain to republican America: Francis Asbury and Freeborn Garrettson embraced John Wesley's theology and Charles Wesley's hymns with the same commitment as Wesleyans in Britain. But much was also changed. American Methodists, and to a lesser extent American Baptists, were constructing a new type of civilization as well as preaching the gospel. For several decades this transformation of evangelicalism led to more conversions and greater social influence than had been enjoyed by either establishment or Dissenting evangelicals in Great Britain.

Against establishment

By the 1790s, evangelical experiences were in a few instances combining with evangelical principles into a justification for whole-hearted resistance to church tradition. Evangelicals in general sat more lightly to tradition than did other Christians in the eighteenth century, but most agreed with leaders like Whitefield, the Wesleys, Jonathan Edwards, John Erskine and even Andrew Fuller that evangelical revival should aim at reviving, not replacing, inherited forms of Protestant faith. But a few voices were now going further. Full-blown 'Restorationism', in which Spirit-empowered believers professed to 'read the Scriptures as though no one had read them before me' and which led to the renunciation of all denominational names except New Testament 'Christians', was still a few years in the future.[54] Yet already by the 1790s it was clear that some evangelicals were prepared to carry the relativizing of church tradition a very long way indeed.[55]

This kind of radicalism disturbed the Wesleyan movement on both sides of the Atlantic. In 1795, English Methodists adopted a Plan of Pacification that gave much authority to trustees of local chapels, along with stewards and leaders, over the decision to offer the sacraments or not.[56] To Methodists still attached to the Church of England, this seemed like a precipitously radical step. But to the Methodists' real radicals, like Alexander Kilham (1762–1798), this measure did not go nearly far enough. In that same year, Kilham published *The Progress of Liberty Among the People Called Methodists*, which used historic language about the rights of free-born Englishmen to demand a much expanded role for ordinary lay Methodists in the Connexion. The times, with visions of French Revolutionary violence disturbing many levels of British society, were not ripe for such an appeal. Kilham was called a Leveller (with reference to the enthusiastic extremists of the Puritan Revolution) and a Painite (with reference to Tom Paine's deistic and politically egalitarian tracts, which were then at the height of their influence), and in 1796 he was expelled from the Connexion. One or two other itinerants and several thousand lay Methodists left with him. But Kilham's main effect was to move the great body of Methodists closer to each other in professing their loyalty to King George III and in forming a moderate, stable and non-threatening vehicle of religious renewal.

In the United States, the course of James O'Kelly's 'Republican Methodism' bore striking similarities to Kilham's 'New Connexion', except that O'Kelly's warrants for protesting against the tyranny of Francis Asbury came

---

[54] The quotation is from Alexander Campbell, 'Reply' (to an Episcopal bishop who had rebuked Campbell for breaking with tradition), *Christian Baptist* 3 (3 April 1826): 204. For a full discussion of these tendencies, see Nathan O. Hatch, *The Democratization of American Christianity* (New Haven: Yale University Press, 1989).

[55] Besides Hatch, *Democratization of American Christianity*, key studies are Stephen A. Marini, *Radical Sects of Revolutionary New England* (Cambridge, MA: Harvard University Press, 1982); Deborah Valenze, *Prophetic Sons and Daughters: Female Preaching and Popular Religion in Industrial England* (Princeton: Princeton University Press, 1985); and George A. Rawlyk, *The Canada Fire: Radical Evangelicalism in British North America, 1775–1812* (Kingston and Montreal: McGill-Queen's University Press, 1994).

[56] I am here following David Hempton, *Methodism and Politics in British Society, 1750–1850* (2nd ed., London: Hutchinson, 1987).

from the republican rhetoric of the American Revolution.[57] O'Kelly was a veteran of the Continental Army who felt that Asbury and Coke were acting like arbitrary despots in making yearly assignments for itinerants, of whom he was one. In the face of this episcopal power, O'Kelly's supporters charged that the movement was 'far gone into POPERY' and that Asbury, 'through a species of tyranny', was making itinerants 'slaves for life'.[58] When Asbury did not give in, and when the main body of Methodists stood with Asbury, O'Kelly and his followers, who were concentrated in Virginia, broke off in 1792 as the Republican Methodist Church. This schism was proportionately larger than Kilham's in England and was one of the reasons for the relatively slow net growth of American Wesleyans during the 1790s. But, as in England, the Methodists under Asbury soon regrouped and went on in their effort to construct what they considered a gospel-centred, people-oriented, lay-empowering but still disciplined evangelical church.

By the time the Methodist schisms occurred, other evangelicals, or others strongly influenced by evangelical movements, were also using the authority of personal religious experience and personal appropriation of Scripture to attack inherited religious authority. In rural New England a pot-pourri of sectarian movements had gained strength from the 1770s, inspired in nearly equal parts by the itinerating evangelism of George Whitefield and the heady politics of the revolutionary era. Universalists were led by John Murray (1741–1785), who emigrated from Britain to New England in 1770 and who claimed that the Scriptures taught the universal salvation of all people. Free-Will Baptists gained recruits by labelling traditional Calvinist doctrine concerning God's sovereignty in redemption as a species of spiritual tyranny. Benjamin Randall (1749–1808) of New Hampshire, who was convicted of his sin by hearing one of George Whitefield's last sermons, set up his own church in 1780 in order to promote the principle of local congregational autonomy (a traditional Baptist idea) and the unrestrained free agency of humans to choose salvation (which was not). Universalists, Free-Will Baptists and a few other groups like the Shakers of Mother Ann Lee were taking advantage of opened geography and political liberty, but doing so by stretching the emphases on personal religious experience and personal scriptural authority that were becoming standard in other religious movements of the day.

One of the local New England preachers who imbibed the spirit of anti-traditional spiritual freedom most thoroughly was Henry Alline (1748–1784), a figure of importance for carrying evangelical emphases into yet another part

---

[57] See Hatch, *Democratization of American Christianity*, 69–82.

[58] For these and other accusations, see Noll, *America's God*, 339–340.

of the English-speaking world.[59] Alline was born in Rhode Island, but moved with his family as a youth to Falmouth, Nova Scotia. After he experienced a powerful conversion in 1775, Alline began to preach with considerable effect in the sparsely populated settlements along the Bay of Fundy. Alline's lack of interest in politics was one of the factors that kept Nova Scotia from joining American patriots in their War for Independence, but Alline's influence was much more directly spiritual than political.[60] To a frontier population, which was being augmented by 35,000 British Loyalists expelled from the thirteen revolting colonies, Alline preached the New Birth as passionately as Whitefield, but without Whitefield's Calvinist theology. His fiery sermons, his denunciation of religious form and church tradition, his many popular hymns and his passionate plea for a nearly mystical vision of God created a 'New Light stir'. John Wesley did not like what he heard about Alline from Methodists on the scene in Nova Scotia: 'Mr. Alline may have wit enough to do hurt; but I fear he will never have wit enough to do good.'[61] But in the Maritimes, Alline prepared the way for an influx of evangelical Baptists, Methodists and Presbyterians who would make this the most thoroughly evangelical region in Canada, and he did so, in the title of his major theological work (1783), as *The Anti-Traditionalist*.

A final example of evangelicals being pushed by evangelical convictions to protest against inherited ecclesiastical order is provided by the rise of the African Methodist Episcopal Church.[62] Richard Allen (1760–1831) was born a slave in Delaware and as a youth came under the preaching of Methodist itinerants. 'Shortly after', in the words of his autobiography, 'I obtained mercy through the blood of Christ, and was constrained to exhort my old companions to seek the Lord.'[63] Allen's conversion testified to the effectiveness of

---

[59] See Maurice Armstrong, *The Great Awakening in Nova Scotia, 1776–1809* (Hartford: American Society of Church History, 1948); and George A. Rawlyk (ed.), *Henry Alline: Selected Writings* (New York: Paulist, 1987).

[60] See Maurice Armstrong, 'Neutrality and Religion in Revolutionary Nova Scotia', *New England Quarterly* 9 (March 1946): 50–62; and Gordon Stewart and George Rawlyk, *A People Highly Favored of God: The Nova Scotia Yankees and the American Revolution* (Toronto: Macmillan, 1972).

[61] Wesley to William Black, 13 July 1783, in Wesley, *Letters*, 7:182.

[62] See Carol V. R. George, *Segregated Sabbaths: Richard Allen and the Emergence of Independent Black Churches, 1760–1840* (New York: Oxford University Press, 1973).

[63] *The Life Experience and Gospel Labors of the Rt. Rev. Richard Allen, To Which Is Annexed the Rise and Progress of the African Methodist Episcopal Church in the United States of America* (1833; New York: Abingdon, 1960), 15.

Methodist evangelists among African Americans, a success that had already produced in Harry Hosier (c.1750–1806) one of the great public orators in American Methodist history.[64] Soon Allen joined a Methodist society and, while still enslaved, began to preach. Around 1780 Allen's master was challenged directly by the itinerant Freeborn Garrettson about his slave-holding; as a result, Allen and his family were allowed to purchase their freedom. Then, with Francis Asbury's encouragement, Allen preached as an itinerant himself throughout Delaware, New Jersey and Pennsylvania until in 1786 he settled in Philadelphia, where his preaching was welcomed by whites and a growing number of African Americans. Asbury encouraged this work, but white trustees of Methodist churches often made life difficult. The famous incident when Allen and his praying friends were expelled from St George's Methodist Church led to the formation in 1794 of the Bethel African Methodist Episcopal Church. This congregation was approved by Asbury, who remained friendly throughout, but its leaders were persistently harassed by other Methodist stewards and trustees. The story of how in response to that harassment this local congregation evolved into the headquarters of the African Methodist Episcopal denomination extends past the turn of the century (1816). Allen's importance lay in how he combined intense loyalty to the teachings of Methodism with unstinting efforts at African-American self-government. 'We are beholden to the Methodist, under God, for the light of the Gospel we enjoy', was his constant testimony.[65] But as an African American daring to strike off in the creation of churches by and for African Americans, he was leading where no-one else had gone before, but where many would follow. Such ones included George White (1764–c.1830), a freed slave who helped establish the first independent African-American Methodist church in New York City, and John Jea (b. 1773), a Nigerian-born slave who was manumitted in New York State and then exercised an influential ministry through preaching, publishing and hymn-writing in England.[66]

Dissident Methodists, Free-Will Baptists, African Americans and those who were caught up in Nova Scotia's 'New Light stir' were all motivated by what they took to be the principles of gospel-renewal, 'true Christianity' and authentic scriptural authority. Their willingness to follow these principles, even if leading to a break with forms of Christianity established by law, precedent, designated authority or racial traditions added a new dimension to the

---

[64] *BDEB*, 573–574 (Charles W. Brockwell, 'Harry Hosier').

[65] *Life Experience and Gospel Labors of Richard Allen*, 30.

[66] Graham Russell Hodges (ed.), *Black Itinerants of the Gospel: The Narratives of John Jea and George White* (Madison: Madison House, 1993).

history of evangelicalism. In the more than two centuries since, many varieties of evangelicals have embraced a certain measure of Christian tradition. But evangelicalism has also powerfully contributed to the actions of some who, like Alexander Kilham, Henry Alline and Richard Allen, were led by their evangelical convictions to break as thoroughly with tradition as they could imagine.

Completely beyond establishment

Another kind of evangelical innovation, which by the mid-1790s was manifesting itself in many directions, arose from the missionary motive.[67] Questions about supporting or abandoning established institutions, traditions, procedures, techniques and church–state arrangements became secondary when the challenge was to plant, rather than revive, the Christian faith. The great age of evangelical missionary exertion still lay in the future, but by the time of Wesley's death there already existed a remarkable evangelical trajectory into the wider world.

The rise of evangelicalism in the world, of which the rise of missionary interest was a central factor, involved a complex, multi-dimensional story. Anglicans played a part through the SPG and the SPCK, as did newly converted Africans in America and the West Indies as well as the Society in Scotland for Propagating Christian Knowledge (SSPCK). Whitefield, the Countess of Huntingdon, Samuel Davies, Jonathan Edwards and several prominent Methodists also contributed. Increased awareness of exotic locales far beyond Europe and North America was stimulated by tremendous publicity given to the Pacific voyages of Captain James Cook (1768–1779) and to the 1788 parliamentary trial of Warren Hastings, Governor-General of India, who was accused by Edmund Burke and others of various crimes in the regularization of Britain's rule over India. Growing concern about the slave-trade and the slave populations in the West Indies and North America also stimulated missionary interest. Once again, however, it was an impetus from pietism on the Continent that probably acted as the most important precipitating agent.[68]

---

[67] For overviews, see Walsh, 'Methodism at the End of the Eighteenth Century'; Watts, *Dissenters*, 2:5–22; and Stanley, *Baptist Missionary Society*, 1–6.

[68] For that judgment and much of the material on the Moravians in the following paragraphs, I rely on J. C. S. Mason, *The Moravian Church and the Missionary Awakening in England, 1760–1800* (Woodbridge: Boydell, 2001), which expands and corrects Johannes van den Berg, *Constrained by Jesus' Love: An Enquiry into the Motives of the*

That impetus, in turn, led on to a significant evangelical break-out into the world through black migrations, through the expansion of the British empire, through the influence of key books and through the exertions of new voluntary mission societies.

During the first generation of evangelical revival, several initiatives took the gospel message beyond the traditional bounds of British civilization. In the mid- to late-1740s, David Brainerd followed the example of earlier Puritan missionaries to the Indians like John Eliot (1604–1690) and tried to preach to the Mahicans of New York State and then to the Delawares in New Jersey. Brainerd's brother, John, took over the work with the Delawares in 1748 and stayed with it for many years.[69] In Virginia, Samuel Davies included Native Americans in his first preaching forays. The Brainerd brothers were sponsored by the SSPCK, which, closer to home in Scotland, began the important work of translating the Bible into Gaelic.[70] Meanwhile, Anglicans, including some evangelicals, had from 1728 been supporting a mission in Tranquebar, India, that had been launched by Halle pietists a quarter-century earlier. Yet evangelicals remained mostly fixated upon renewing the inherited churches and religious life of British and colonial Christendom until the Moravians, in W. R. Ward's apt phrase, 'bridge[d] the gap between revival and missions'.[71]

Missionary Awakening in Great Britain in the period between 1698 and 1815 (Kampen: J. H. Kok, 1956). For other important statements about continental influence on the beginnings of evangelical missionary interest, see W. R. Ward, 'Missions in their Global Context in the Eighteenth Century', in Mark Hutchinson and Ogbu Kalu (eds.), *A Global Faith: Essays on Evangelicalism and Globalization* (Sydney: Centre for the Study of Australian Christianity, 1998), 108–121; Andrew F. Walls, 'The Protestant Missionary Awakening in Its European Context', in *The Cross-Cultural Process in Christian History* (Maryknoll: Orbis, 2002), 194–214; and Daniel L. Brunner, *Halle Pietists in England: Anthony William Boehm and the Society for Promoting Christian Knowledge* (Göttingen: Vandenhoeck & Ruprecht, 1993).

[69] The negligible results of David Brainerd's actual work as a missionary is a different subject from the broad impact of David Brainerd's diary; on the two brothers' actual missionary service, see Henry Warner Bowden, *American Indians and Christian Missions: Studies in Cultural Conflict* (Chicago: University of Chicago Press, 1981), 152–157.

[70] Donald E. Meek, 'Protestant Missions and the Evangelization of the Scottish Highlands, 1700–1850', *International Bulletin of Missionary Research* 21 (April 1997): 67–72.

[71] Ward, 'Missions in Their Global Context', 116.

For Moravians to make an impact on evangelical missionary efforts, however, two things were necessary: missionary ventures that could demonstrate at least some success and a renewal of the Moravian image in the English-speaking world. The first task was accomplished very early on. As we saw in Chapter 6, Moravians left for missionary service in the West Indies in 1732, only five years after the revivalistic renewal of the 'Unity of the Brethren' at Herrnhut. In 1740, several years before the arrival of David Brainerd, Christian Heinrich Rauch (1718–1763) was achieving some success with Mahican Indians on the New York-Connecticut border.[72] After Brainerd came and went, Rauch brought some of his Mahican converts into a Moravian Indian settlement near Bethlehem, Pennsylvania (Friedenshutten, or 'a shelter of peace'). A few years later, but thirty years before English Methodists arrived, Rauch moved to Jamaica to assist in the Moravian mission on that island.[73]

The work in Bethlehem, Pennsylvania, had begun in 1744 under David Zeisberger (1721–1808), who used the Moravians' characteristically Christ-centred piety to carry out what was probably the most effective Protestant witness to Native Americans in the whole century.[74] Zeisberger maintained a flourishing Indian settlement at Friedenshutten until pressure from land-hungry settlers forced a move to a new settlement, Gnadenhutten (or, 'a shelter of grace'), in the Ohio Territory. Tragically, in 1782 American patriot marauders, worried about Indian ties with British troops, slaughtered ninety of the Moravian Indians at Gnadenhutten while Zeisberger was away in Detroit trying to convince British authorities that the Indians of his settlement were pacifists like the rest of the Moravians. By that date, Moravian missions had been expanded in the West Indies and started in Greenland, Labrador, Newfoundland, the Cape of Good Hope (South Africa) and Tranquebar (India).

Moravians were themselves people without a country, uprooted as the Unity of the Brethren from Bohemia, living as wayfarers on the Zinzendorf estates in Saxony, sitting lightly both to material possessions and to the historic differences that divided Protestants, curious about foreign customs (including foreign languages), committed to the potential contribution of women in active Christian service and powerfully motivated by gratitude to

---

[72] For an account of how and why the Moravians succeeded, see Rachel Wheeler, 'Women and Christian Practice in a Mahican Village', *Religion and American Culture* 13 (winter 2003): 27–68.

[73] *BDEB*, 917–918 (Wade A. Horton, 'Christian Heinrich Rauch').

[74] *BDEB*, 1225 (Richard Pointer, 'David Zeisberger').

God for the experience of grace in Jesus Christ. Because of life experiences and religious conviction, they were ideal missionaries.

Yet even with remarkable missionary ventures under way, the Moravians would not have exerted much influence on the English-speaking world if their reputation had not revived (for earlier problems, see Chapter 6). This recovery of reputation did in fact take place after Zinzendorf died in 1760. It was managed at the centre by August Gottlieb Spangenberg, the Wesleys' friend and guide from long-ago Georgia days. As the Moravians' new leader, Spangenberg paid off debts, toned down the extremes of Zinzendorf's 'blood and wounds' piety, worked at restoring good relations with Protestant state churches, and re-emphasized the strictly spiritual goals of Moravian mission-ary service. As a key British ally in all of these efforts, Spangenberg worked closely with Benjamin La Trobe (1728–1786), who had been born in Dublin and brought into Moravian circles by John Cennick's early preaching in that city.[75] After several trips to Herrnhut and service as a Moravian pastor in Yorkshire, La Trobe became the designated leader of British Moravians in 1768, the same year he helped to establish the Society for the Furtherance of the Gospel as the British wing of the Moravian missionary programme. La Trobe's relations were somewhat cool with John Wesley, but increasingly from the 1770s he enjoyed warm fellowship with the Welsh academy at Trevecca, with Methodists of both Arminian and Calvinistic leanings, and with several influential evangelicals in the Church of England. From 1783 he was a regular participant in John Newton's Eclectic Society. Most importantly, the persistent labours of La Trobe and his British Moravian colleagues overcame the suspi-cion that had built up concerning the movement and so made possible a much fuller circulation of news and exhortation between Moravians and their friends in all English-speaking regions. In turn, Moravian connections of one sort or another played a key role in founding the three great mission agencies of the 1790s: the Baptist Missionary Society (1792), the London Missionary Society (1795) and the evangelical Anglican Church Missionary Society (1799).

Of all evangelical ventures into the broader world, Moravians had the least direct influence on the significant efforts by converted Africans to take a gospel witness to their homelands. Manumitted slaves early entertained visions of a missionary approach to Africans. An early leader in these efforts was Olaudah Equiano (1745–1797), who had been kidnapped and enslaved in West Africa as a youth, but who then purchased his own freedom in 1766. In 1774, after persistent contact with evangelical believers, he experienced a con-

---

[75] On La Trobe, see Mason, *Moravian Church and the Missionary Awakening*, 63–79.

version while meditating on Acts 4:12: 'I saw the Lord Jesus Christ in his humiliation, loaded, and bearing my reproach, sin, and shame.'[76] Almost immediately thereafter Equiano began an active campaign that combined agitation against slavery with proposals for Christian activity in West Africa. In 1779 he approached the Bishop of London with a request to be ordained and commissioned as a missionary to Africa. When that request was refused, he continued to publicize the plight of African slaves throughout the British Isles; later he also journeyed to America for the express purpose of thanking Quakers for their consistent stand against slavery. *The Interesting Narrative of Olaudah Equiano*, which he published in 1789, recounted both his spiritual pilgrimage and his labours against slavery; in turn, this book became a much-republished weapon in the anti-slave arsenal.[77]

Similar impetus to evangelical concern for the world came from the forced immigration of African Americans who remained loyal to Britain during the American Revolution. Of this group David George was the main leader.[78] The war's reach into South Carolina and Georgia disrupted the infant congregations that George and other redeemed slaves had begun in the 1770s. Because George and a large group of slaves and ex-slaves felt their chances were better with Britain than the newly independent United States, they joined the liberating British forces.[79] George continued to preach during the war itself, but then, when his liberators were defeated, accepted transport to loyalist Nova Scotia, where he founded the second black church to be established in that province. While in Nova Scotia, George seems to have been touched by the radical evangelicalism flowing from the ministry of Henry Alline, but this British colony proved in the end almost as unfriendly to free black settlers as the American slave-holding states had been. Thus, in 1792, after a decade in Nova Scotia, George removed to Sierra Leone with part of his congregation and became the leading black minister in that new British colony. Much philanthropy along with British evangelical concern was poured into the Sierra

---

[76]   *The Interesting Narrative of the Life of Olaudah Equiano, or Gustavus Vassa, the African. Written by Himself* (1789), as abridged in Adam Potkay and Sandra Burr (eds.), *Black Atlantic Writers of the 18th Century* (New York: St Martin's, 1995), 244.

[77]   Lamin Sanneh, *Abolitionists Abroad: American Blacks and the Making of Modern West Africa* (Cambridge, MA: Harvard University Press, 1999), 24–31.

[78]   See Grant Gordon, *The Life of David George: Pioneer Black Baptist Minister* (Hantsport, Nova Scotia: Lancelot, 1992).

[79]   On George's place in the political, racial and religious history of the British occupation, see Sylvia R. Frey, *Water from the Rock: Black Resistance in a Revolutionary Age* (Princeton: Princeton University Press, 1991), 37–39.

Leone venture, but on the ground the pioneering work of actual Christian ministry was accomplished mostly by African Canadians like George.[80]

As George's experience suggests, the scope for evangelical missionary effort grew as the second British empire expanded. British imperial advance in West Africa, South Africa, India, Botany Bay (Australia) and other points in the South Pacific opened up new opportunities for trade and new dimensions for a colonial extension of European power politics. It also opened up new vistas for Christian missions.

The experience of Charles Grant (1746–1823) illustrates how imperialism, trade and missionary interests would advance together.[81] Grant was a well-born merchant who sailed for India in 1767 as an employee of the East India Company. Before he was finished, he would become a director, and then chairman, of the company. During his first years in India he lived a life of some dissipation, but then was converted and, significantly, from the mid-1770s began to have contact with Moravians. Soon he was arguing against the company's policy of prohibiting Christian outreach to Indian groups, which had been instituted in order to make trading as inoffensive as possible. In 1787 he wrote a long letter to the British government urging it to support a Protestant mission to India. When he returned to England in 1792, he spoke out against Britain's policy of Indian military conquest, he gained William Wilberforce's cooperation in a campaign for the 'Christianization of India', and he supported the individuals who were working towards the creation of the interdenominational LMS and the Anglican CMS. In partial response to the publicity generated by Grant, Thomas Coke in 1786 proposed an Indian mission for the Methodists and in 1789 the SPCK sent Abraham Clarke to Calcutta as a missionary to the Indians. Even if the Wesleyans did not act on Coke's proposal and Clarke soon shifted over to become a chaplain for the East India Company, the message promoted by Grant was beginning to make a difference.

The pattern in India was replicated also in South Africa, where the British takeover of the Cape of Good Hope from the Dutch in 1795 followed the appearance of Moravian missionaries some years earlier and led almost immediately to the arrival of Johannes van der Kemp (1747–1811) as an agent of the LMS. Between 1797, when van der Kemp offered himself for service to the

---

[80] See Andrew F. Walls, 'A Christian Experiment: The Early Sierra Leone Colony', in G. J. Cuming (ed.), *The Mission of the Church and the Propagation of Faith* (Cambridge: Cambridge University Press, 1970), 107–129.

[81] See Ainslie T. Embree, *Charles Grant and British Rule in India* (New York: Columbia University Press, 1962).

LMS, and 1801, when the size of his large Khoi (Hottentot) congregation in the Cape drew nervous criticism from other European colonists, van der Kemp also helped form the Netherlands Missionary Society and inaugurate the work of the South African Missionary Society. In those years he also established a fruitful partnership with Ntsikana (1760–1820), a dynamic prophet-evangelist from the Xhosa tribe whose effectiveness among his own people marked out the path that much later evangelization would take in the Two-Thirds World.[82]

In Australia and the Pacific, Britain's immediate goals were to scare off the French and establish a penal colony for the excess prison population of the British Isles. No sooner had these plans been announced, however, than William Wilberforce, John Newton and other evangelical Anglicans lobbied Prime Minister Pitt to appoint a chaplain for the colony to be established in New South Wales. Richard Johnson (1755–1827) was this man, who sailed with the first fleet in 1787 and persevered through great difficulties for more than a decade. The assistant whom Wilberforce and his friends later secured for Johnson turned out to make a much broader impact on both Australian church history and mission outreach in the Pacific. Samuel Marsden (1765–1838) left for the nearly eight months' voyage to Australia in July 1793.[83] Even before he left England, he had supported the idea of a mission to Tahiti, which had been made famous through Captain Cook's diaries. As the child of a Methodist-leaning home, a product of Joseph Milner's evangelical instruction at the Hull Grammar School, a student under evangelical teachers at Magdalene College, Cambridge, and a young minister recruited by Wilberforce and Newton, Marsden was an evangelical thoroughbred. His work in Australia led to the founding of influential churches, businesses and voluntary societies – all amid the raucous controversies characteristic of small colonial societies. For broader purposes, he was the key supporter in the Pacific when in 1796 the LMS dispatched its first expedition of thirty missionaries to Tahiti. He was also the one who tried to put the pieces together when that mission imploded. Even more significantly, in 1813 he initiated a landmark mission to the Maori of New Zealand that soon expanded to other islands of the South Pacific. Marsden has been censured for his callousness to Australia's own aboriginal population, but most observers credit him with unusual cultural sensitivity toward the Pacific islanders and with playing a key

---

[82] *BDEB*, 834 (Andrew C. Ross, 'Ntsikana'), and 1133 (Andrew C. Ross, 'Johannes van der Kemp').

[83] For outstanding treatment, see A. T. Yarwood, *Samuel Marsden: The Great Survivor* (Melbourne: Melbourne University Press, 1977). I thank Mark Hutchinson for providing a copy of this illuminating book.

role in the great movements of evangelization that occurred in that part of the world during the nineteenth century. Marsden's career speaks to the dramatic results that occurred when Moravian initiatives sparked evangelical missionary activity in the first stages of Britain's new imperial expansion.

A further connection was established between British imperial politics and missionary interest by the campaign against slavery, which is discussed in the next chapter. As anti-slavery grew, so also did closer attention to conditions in the West Indies, the North American mainland and the slave-gathering catchments in West Africa. That attention led almost naturally to a rise in missionary concern for societies ravaged by the slave-trade as well as for the slaves themselves.

In the surge of evangelical missionary interest during the last third of the eighteenth century, several landmark publications did much to make the case for cross-cultural evangelism. William Carey's *Enquiry* of 1792 was the climactic and the most influential, but by the 1790s there existed a small shelf of works of nearly equal influence. Jonathan Edwards' edition of David Brainerd's diaries (*The Life of David Brainerd*, 1749) presented a figure of intense introspective zeal who reported surprising receptivity to the gospel message he preached (through translators) to Native Americans. Of considerable importance for turning the English-speaking world to the actual do-ability of cross-cultural missions was David Cranz's *The History of Greenland: Containing a Description of the Country, and Its Inhabitants, a Relation of the Mission Carried on for Above Thirty Years by the Unitas Fratrum* (ET, 1767), which described a pioneering Moravian mission in convincing, attractive detail. In 1783, Thomas Coke's appeal to Methodists in *A Plan of the Society for the Establishment of Missions among the Heathen* was matched by a similar appeal to all Anglicans from the Bishop of London, *A Sermon Preached Before the Incorporated Society for the Propagation of the Gospel*. Both of these works proclaimed the need for Christian witness among West Indian slaves, but also pushed further to contemplate the goal of missionary activity beyond the reach of British imperial rule. Two influential books in the 1780s by A. G. Spangenberg provided the kind of practical detail, theological support and calm encouragement that had become the Moravian stock-in-trade: *Instructions for Members of the Unitas Fratrum who Minister in the Gospel among the Heathen* (ET, 1785), and *An Account of the Manner in Which the Protestant Church of the Unitas Fratrum, or United Brethren, Preach the Gospel and Carry on Their Missions Among the Heathen* (ET, 1788). After Carey's *Enquiry* appeared to great effect, the tide rolled on. A stirring appeal by the Anglican Melville Horne, *Letters on Missions* (1794) was particularly effective in mobilizing missionary endeavour within the Church of England. At a time of increased international opportunity, such works presented the necessity as well as the attractiveness of missionary service with telling force.

The upshot of much activity, thought, prayer and overseas experience was the foundation of the voluntary mission societies by the Baptists in 1792, the interdenominational moderate Calvinists in 1795 (LMS), and the evangelical Anglicans in 1799 (CMS). The Wesleyan Methodists, who had done so much to promote effective evangelism in Britain, organized a little later in 1813. John Wesley was not uninterested in foreign missions but thought that there was sufficient work for the moment in the unevangelized parts of the British Isles. Thomas Coke, who had called for missionaries as early as 1777 and who had worked diligently to send Methodists to the West Indies, West Africa, North America and other far-flung regions, provided the most consistent push for Methodist missionary labours. It was, thus, sad but fitting when Coke himself, at sixty-six years of age, volunteered for the first Methodist mission to India, but died and was buried at sea before his ship reached its destination. The evangelical turn to voluntary associations as the vehicle for channelling, as well as stimulating, missionary interest marked a decisive move away from the establishmentarian instincts that many of the first evangelical leaders had brought with them into their work.

Within only a few years after John Wesley's death in 1791, his bold and reckless claim as a young man, 'I look upon the world as my parish',[84] was no longer quite so ridiculous. Not Wesley himself or even just the Methodists, of course, but evangelicalism as a whole had begun to move around the globe, even as it was moving deeper into British, American, Canadian and West Indian societies. For quite some time, the main evangelical developments would continue to occur within the bounds of the English-speaking world as known in the eighteenth century. But a process of globalization was definitely under way. From the perspective of the early twenty-first century and an awareness of how widely evangelical types of Christian faith are now spread in the world, that earlier globalization with its initiatives in Sierra Leone, the Cape of Good Hope and the South Pacific seems just as important as what was happening at 'home'.

---

[84] Wesley to James Hervey, 20 March 1739, in Wesley, *Letters*, 1:286. And for almost the same phrase ('The whole world is now my parish') at virtually the same time (10 November 1739), see George Whitefield to R. D., in *A Select Collection of Letters of the Late Reverend George Whitefield*, 3 vols (London: Edward and Charles Dilby, 1772), 1:105. My thanks to Bruce Hindmarsh for these citations.

8. IN THE WORLD

Evangelicalism in its origins was overwhelmingly a movement of spiritual renewal. The first evangelicals concerned themselves with social, political, institutional or intellectual arrangements only as these matters seemed to promote or threaten personal faith. From this perspective, traditions of Christian social engagement, political practice, institutional loyalty and intellectual principle could easily be viewed as contributing to the stultifications of formal faith that had to be overcome in order to find true religion. Evangelicalism was a pietistic movement in which the relationship of the self to God eclipsed all other concerns. The views of Henry Alline – who posed a stark antithesis between 'the injury of Tradition, the Prejudice of Education, the Distress and Torment of the Slavery thereby', and 'some small experience of Redemption ... the Sweetness of divine Life, the Joys of immortal Love, and attracting Views of the Nature and Perfections of the Deity' – represented an extreme opinion, but one that was recognizable in some form for almost all evangelicals.[1] Yet the otherworldliness of self-conscious evangelical piety was never by any means the whole story.

Many of the early evangelicals retained an interest in the broader affairs of the world simply because it was second nature by upbringing to do so. Others moved naturally, almost irresistibly, to broader action in the world as they

---

[1] Henry Alline, *The Anti-Traditionalist* (1783), in George A. Rawlyk (ed.), *Henry Alline: Selected Writings* (New York: Paulist, 1997), 268.

began the pursuit of gospel holiness. Still others took up activistic practices that had been promoted by the religious streams flowing into evangelicalism, whether the comprehensive concern for social order of the Puritans, the reform of manners pursed by high Anglicans, or the widely ranging philanthropic exertions of the continental pietists. Ministry to convicts, care for orphans, the provision of schooling for the unattended poor, sharp-eyed commentary about the exercise of political or economic power, and even protests against slavery were, thus, all a natural and early part of evangelical attention to the world. That attention became even more prominent as the movement developed, for the swelling tide of conversions meant also a swelling tide of the converted. To be evangelical inevitably meant a great stress on conversion, but from the start it also meant a great interest in what the converted should be doing. Thus it was that evangelical attention to society, politics, institutions and intellectual life expanded throughout the latter decades of the eighteenth century, though usually in response to problems, needs or crises thrust upon the evangelicals. To these situations they reacted with a combination of overtly evangelical spiritual reasoning, tentative moves towards the formulation of self-consciously evangelical ethics and much conventional wisdom rooted in the particulars of region, social class, or partisan interest. Evangelicals, in other words, were never as successful at 'fleeing the world' as they thought they should be. The ironic result of that 'failure' was a rich, if also complex, record of social, political, institutional and intellectual engagement.

Characteristic approaches

In the absence of a unitary social programme, evangelicals pursued varied approaches to life in the world. Throughout this period and for all of later evangelical history, the tendency to pull back from secular engagement for the sake of narrowly spiritual goals remained strong. But alongside this tendency quickly emerged what might be called patrician, bourgeois and plebeian strategies, each driven by basic evangelical beliefs but each also conforming to the conventions of particular segments of eighteenth-century society.

The tendency to contrast pious, ennobling concentration on God and venal, debasing attention to the practices of ordinary daily life remained an often colourful aspect of evangelical experience. The extreme otherworldliness of the 'anti-traditional' Henry Alline or the book-burning James Davenport was not necessarily typical. But many other evangelicals still did consistently promote world-denial. John Wesley, for instance, published several pamphlets on marriage throughout his career in which his attitude, perhaps influenced by his own unfortunate marriage to the widow Mary (Molly) Vazeille, ranged from serious caution to outright promotion of the single, celibate life.[2] His attitude was seconded by John Berridge, an itinerating Anglican minister friendly with the early revivalists, who expressed an oft-quoted though unfair opinion on the marriages of the Methodists' early leaders: 'Matrimony has quite maimed poor Charles [Wesley] and might have spoiled John [Wesley] and George [Whitefield] if a wise Master had not graciously sent them a brace of ferrets.'[3] This spirit also characterized other early evangelical expressions. In the early stages of evangelical development in Scotland, its leaders regularly criticized their opponents for betraying the gospel through over-involvement in worldly affairs. Similarly in North America, Francis Asbury led the early Methodist movement away from political or social engagement. George Whitefield's lifelong phobia of ostentation in dress, food or housing revealed a similar wariness about worldly affairs.

Despite frequently heard appeals to forsake the world for Christ, however, evangelicals regularly went back into their worlds with Christ, and increasingly so as the movement spread into more churches, more regions and more social circumstances during the second half of the century. By the 1790s the spectrum of evangelical approaches was clearly established. On what might be called the extreme right, with greatest strength in establishmentarian Anglicanism, was a stance of conservative, aristocratic, activistic and humane paternalism. On the extreme left, with greatest strength among those who objected most strenuously to traditional church–state establishments, was a position of democratic, participatory and congregational or family-based populism. Between these poles arose also a variety of middle-class positions, with greatest force among British Dissenters and evangelicals in the new United States, which were marked by self-mobilizing, voluntary efforts to create a new kind of civil society.

Patrician

The patrician position has received a great deal of attention because of the visibility of the Countess of Huntingdon at mid-century, the well-publicized

---

[2] As an example, *Thoughts on a Single Life* (1765), in Wesley, *Works* (1872), 11:456–463. For discussion, see Henry Abelove, 'The Sexual Politics of Wesleyan Methodism', in Jim Obelkevich, Lyndal Roper and Raphael Samuel (eds.), *Disciplines of Faith: Studies in Religion, Politics and Patriarchy* (London: Routledge & Kegan Paul, 1987), 86–99; and Rack, *Wesley*, 251–269.

[3] Quoted in Rack, *Wesley*, 253. The comment was unfair because Whitefield's marriage, though not ideal, was relatively serene compared to John Wesley's truly unfortunate liaison.

reforming work of William Wilberforce and Hannah More in England at the
end of the century, the strenuous efforts by Timothy Dwight to retain the
hereditary privileges of established Congregationalism in post-Revolutionary
America, and even the labours of John Erskine to evangelize the entire life of
the Scottish Kirk. In work as pastor of the established Congregational church
in Greenfield, Connecticut (1783–1795), and then president of Yale College
(from 1795), Timothy Dwight tried to demonstrate why a comprehensive
Christian society needed to preserve the colonial state-church establishments
even as it embraced the blessings of liberty secured by the American War for
Independence. In Dwight's view, a vibrant state church would provide the
necessary Christian guidance for the new American nation, while the republican principles of the Revolution would keep establishments from the kind of
imperial excess practised by the British. As it worked out, Dwight's vision
could not be fulfilled, since American evangelicals were turning resolutely
away from the principle of establishment and towards voluntary means for
organizing churches and promoting public morality. Yet his efforts show that
top-down social ordering regulated by evangelical zeal was not restricted to
the British Isles.[4]

In Scotland, John Erskine was somewhat more successful than Dwight at
incorporating an active evangelical element into a traditional church-state
establishment. Erskine was no aristocrat, but during his service in two
different Edinburgh churches (1758–1803), he exerted tireless efforts at coor-
dinating evangelical personnel, activities and aspirations in the established
church. Throughout, Erskine took for granted, as many Scottish evangelicals
would for a long time, that the most effective sanctification of society would
come from the top downwards and in the shape of the inherited structures of
the traditional Kirk.[5]

Even more than in Scotland, evangelical Anglicans succeeded at sustaining
a paternalistic vision of Christian social order in England. The activism of
such Anglicans was rooted in a distinctly evangelical sense of Christian duty:
because God had graciously rescued them from bondage to sin, they would
respond in gratitude by providing others with parallel opportunities for spiritual liberty and vital holiness. But it also moved instinctively to support hierarchical institutions like the Anglican Church itself, to picture a healthy society
in terms of inherited social distinctions and to distrust anything smacking of
democracy, republicanism or individualism.

---

[4]   See John R. Fitzmier, *New England's Moral Legislator: Timothy Dwight, 1752–1817*
      (Bloomington: Indiana University Press, 1998).
[5]   *DSCHT*, 300–301 (N. R. Needham, 'John Erskine').

John Wesley's social practice retained much of this hierarchical paternalism.[6] He was as reluctant to share control over Methodist orphanages and schools as he was over the direction of Methodist preaching circuits. He remained deeply sceptical about democracy. At least in his own eyes, his loyalty to the King and the principle of monarchy never wavered. He hoped that his movement would revitalize the state church and enable it to recover godly leadership for all of English society. He worked hard to keep his lay itinerants on a short leash and to distinguish them clearly from the properly ordained clergy. It is an important comment on widespread assumptions of the period that Wesley's aristocratic management of the Methodists was – for the most part and with only a few exceptions – accepted quite cheerfully.

Yet much in Wesley's most characteristic activity worked against his instinctive High Church establishmentarianism. He asked laymen, and sometimes even laywomen, to take on tasks that had for centuries been restricted to the clergy. He extended significant responsibilities to many who enjoyed neither ordination nor a university education. He worked ceaselessly at encouraging converts and itinerants to study. He gave a voice in cell and band meetings to the humblest, most downtrodden citizens of the realm. To the day of his death, he lived an abstemious life that remained a public rebuke to luxurious pretence, whether aristocratic or bourgeoisie. He sought in hymnody, spiritual nurture and education to provide uplifting substitutes for what he considered the destructive dissipations of drink, cards and the theatre. In sum, while Wesley remained in many ways a representative upperclass Englishman, he was just as authentically a reformer of the stratified social order that he had inherited and that he professed always to uphold.

Compared to Wesley, the energetic publicist, author and educator Hannah More (1745–1833) presented a less complicated example of top-down, establishmentarian Anglican evangelicalism. But even her case, as also the situation of her friend William Wilberforce, offers much more than simply evangelical rhetoric sanctioning an aristocratic vision of ideal society.

Hannah More was the product of a middling home but gained financial independence from a suitor who dallied long before finally deciding not to marry. By the mid-1770s she was accepted in a high-minded circle of London artists and writers that included David Garrick, Dr Samuel Johnson and Sir

---

[6] For orientation, see David Hempton, 'John Wesley and England's "*ancien régime*"', in Hempton, *The Religion of the People: Methodism and Popular Religion, c.1750–1900* (London: Routledge, 1996), 77–90; Rack, *Wesley*, 360–380; and John Walsh, *John Wesley, 1703–1791: A Bicentennial Tribute*, Friends of Dr Williams's Library Lecture (London: Dr Williams's Trust, 1993), 16–17.

Joshua Reynolds. Even as she made a name for herself as poet and author of tragic dramas, she displayed a sober realism about the course of her life. In 1776 she met Charles Middleton, a navy man who would later be an important influence with Wilberforce, and soon joined the attack on the slave-trade that Middleton engineered. From the early 1780s her increasingly serious thoughts about religion were guided into explicitly evangelical paths by gentle advice from John Newton. As an indication of how her convictions had settled, she published in 1790 *An Estimate of the Religion of the Fashionable World*. This forthright tract included a stiff defence of Anglican liturgy and hierarchy but was even more specifically aimed at what she considered 'a visible decline of piety among the higher ranks' of British society. More's characteristic interests were evident when she spelled out why that decline was so important: 'the notorious *effect* of the decay of this religious principle … corrupts our mode of education, infects domestic conduct, spreads the contagion downwards among servants and inferiors, and influences our general manners, habits, and conversation'.[7] More's great contribution to public advocacy began in the early 1790s with the publication of tracts – strongly plotted, decisively moral and written to be read – that championed traditional Christianity and traditional social order as the necessary antidote to the radical religion and radical politics she associated with the French Revolution. These tracts, along with the schools she and her sisters organized for reaching out to the poor children of a rapidly changing Britain, established her reputation as a busy, controversial defender of settled ways in church and society.

More has been pilloried as a mouthpiece for the reactionary forces of wealth and aristocracy.[8] But it is closer to her actual situation to interpret her work as a complex dialectic made up of conservative religious principle, fearless female assertion and creative response to rapid social change.[9] More

---

[7] *An Estimate of the Religion of the Fashionable World* (1790), from *The Works of Hannah More: First Complete American Edition*, 2 vols (New York: Harper and Brothers, 1835), 1:278.

[8] For a recent, sophisticated example, see Mona Scheuermann, *In Praise of Poverty: Hannah More Counters Thomas Paine and the Radical Threat* (Lexington: University Press of Kentucky, 2002).

[9] I am here indebted to helpful personal communications from Professor Shirley Mullin, as well as accounts provided by Christine L. Krueger, *The Reader's Repentance: Women Preachers, Women Writers, and Nineteenth-Century Social Discourse* (Chicago: University of Chicago Press, 1992), 94–124; Patricia Demers, *The World of Hannah More* (Lexington: University Press of Kentucky, 1996); and Robert Hole (ed.), *Selected Writings of Hannah More* (London: William Pickering, 1996).

praised the virtues of patriarchal society, with its stability rising from the deference of wives to husbands, servants to masters, inferiors to superiors – yet
as a single woman she carved out a memorable career of public advocacy,
exhortation and evangelism. She defined the essential task of reforming
Britain as a matter of the social elite recovering religion and then letting it
trickle down to the lower orders. But she also redefined what it meant for the
great to be great by championing the virtues of humility, self-giving and altruism. That More gave up writing dramatic tragedies because she came to doubt
the heroic ideals of the classical world shows how much she was influenced
by evangelical religion. Hannah More did offer a top-down, traditional and
anti-democratic solution to the crises of her age, but by comparison with
other social conservatives among her contemporaries, like Edmund Burke or
leading bishops of the Church of England, her stance represented a clearly
evangelical approach to public life and its duties.

Even more visible as representatives of a patrician Anglican stance
towards life in this world was the network of fairly well-born and fairly
wealthy evangelicals who in the 1790s gathered around the Anglican parish
church in Clapham, a few miles southwest of London, and who would many
decades later be called the 'Clapham Sect' or Clapham 'saints'.[10] The centre
of this group was William Wilberforce (1759–1833), whose work against
slavery is noted below, but the many influential figures associated with
Clapham also took on many other demanding tasks. Much of Clapham's
activity came somewhat later, like promoting a Christianization of British
interests in India (from the mid-1780s), organizing the Church Missionary
Society (1799), founding the evangelical flagship periodical *The Christian
Observer* (1802) and helping to create the British and Foreign Bible Society
(1804). But already by the early 1790s the drive against slavery had resulted in
sponsorship of a free colony in West Africa (Sierra Leone) and several other
creative initiatives in public affairs. Besides Wilberforce, the key figures at
Clapham were Henry Thornton (1760–1815), a banker and MP who became
his era's most active philanthropist, and the rector in Clapham from 1792,
John Venn (1759–1813), whose father Henry Venn had earlier brought an
effective evangelical witness to several parishes including Clapham (served
1754–1759). The 'saints' also included several other high-placed civil servants, merchants, bankers and at least one titled lord, all of whom shared an

---

[10] An up-to-date account of the complicated family networks at Clapham in the 1780s
and 1790s is provided by the early sections of Christopher Tolley, *Domestic Biography:
The Legacy of Evangelicalism in Four Nineteenth-Century Families* (Oxford: Clarendon,
1997).

active evangelical faith and an active concern for doing good in England, West Africa, India and beyond. The religious style of this group has been well summarized by phrases once written about the ministry of Henry Venn: 'theological moderation, Anglican regularity, and liturgical commitment'.[11] Their philanthropy was equally establishmentarian, but in its dedication to helping members of several marginalized groups, the Clapham saints were far ahead of their time.

Plebeian

Plebian, democratic and populist forms of evangelical public life were slower to develop than the patrician. However egalitarian the spiritual message of the Wesleys, Jonathan Edwards, George Whitefield, Daniel Rowland and Gilbert Tennent may have been, these early evangelical leaders did not intend to subvert traditional social order. Only Howell Harris among the earliest evangelicals, and then only indirectly, anticipated the type of populism that became more visible by the 1780s and 1790s, and then burgeoned after the start of the new century throughout the English-speaking world.[12]

Individuals and groups that were unambiguously evangelical and fully democratic, or even radical, had only begun to emerge by the time Wesley died in 1791. But in scattered English, American and Canadian locations they were already pushing towards an extensive renovation of evangelicalism from below. In North America, it was the example of Whitefield's boundless itineration, the movement of people away from the settled East into the hinterlands and the ideological impact of the American Revolution that promoted a more thoroughly democratized evangelicalism. In England, the same result occurred primarily in the penumbra of the Methodist movements where the centrifugal force of empowering conversion overcame the centripetal force of John Wesley's and the Countess of Huntingdon's personal authority.

---

[11] *BDEB*, 2:1138 (W. J. Clyde Ervine, 'Henry Venn').

[12] Key works on this strand of evangelicalism are Stephen A. Marini, *Radical Sects of Revolutionary New England* (Cambridge, MA: Harvard University Press, 1982); Deborah M. Valenze, *Prophetic Sons and Daughters: Female Preaching and Popular Religion in Industrial England* (Princeton: Princeton University Press, 1985); Nathan O. Hatch, *The Democratization of American Christianity* (New Haven: Yale University Press, 1989); G. A. Rawlyk, *The Canada Fire: Radical Evangelicalism in British North America, 1775–1812* (Kingston and Montreal: McGill-Queen's University Press, 1994); and Catherine A. Brekus, *Strangers and Pilgrims, 1740–1845: Female Preaching in America* (Chapel Hill: University of North Carolina Press, 1998).

Converted Baptists like Isaac Backus, as well as leaders of New England's separating Congregationalist congregations, pioneered in charting this kind of populist religion.[13] But they were joined as well by English and Irish lay itinerants like John Cennick, for whom the dynamism of Wesleyan, Calvinist or Moravian revival burst the bounds of conventional religious practice. When the evangelical message began to attract slaves, and when converted African Americans began to organize churches for themselves, the result was even more intense movement towards genuinely people's churches. The conversion during the 1770s of populist leaders like Henry Alline and Richard Allen laid the groundwork for significant democratization in the decades that followed. Also by the 1770s, connections were increasing between evangelical converts and representatives of older movements, like the Quakers, that enjoyed a long history of resisting centralized religious authority.

In an over-simplified picture, populist evangelicalism can be viewed in four main manifestations. First were the African Americans, who had begun to form churches in the American middle and southern states by the 1790s, and who were active as well in the West Indies, Nova Scotia and the west coast of Africa. More obviously unconventional were the flourishing tribes of radical New England sectarians, among whom the ministry of Henry Alline was closest to main evangelical emphases and would leave the longest evangelical legacy.

On both sides of the Atlantic, Methodism was a prime source of still other attempts to new-model the Christian faith on radical principles of personal and social liberty. Some Methodists, like Freeborn Garrettson and William Black (1760–1834) of Nova Scotia, pushed conventions to the limit as young itinerants, but then came back to calmer, more cooperative, more institutional faith. Those who could not conform to Wesley, his successors or Francis Asbury left the movement, like James O'Kelly, Alexander Kilham and Hugh Bourne (1772–1852), who founded 'the Primitive Methodists' in England. And then there were those who, while remaining loosely in the Methodist orbit, found constraint of whatever sort an undue burden. The most notable representative of such free-form Methodism was Lorenzo Dow (1777–1834), who, despite a reputation for eccentricity (his nickname was 'Crazy' Dow) and persistent reliance on dreams and visions, became a widely known preacher in Canada, Britain, the West Indies and the United States, and an effective

---

[13] For full treatment, see William G. McLoughlin, *New England Dissent, 1630–1833: The Baptists and the Separation of Church and State*, 2 vols (Cambridge, MA: Harvard University Press, 1971), 1:340–693; 2:695–786.

pioneer of Christian witness in many frontier regions of the English-speaking world.[14]

A final variety of populist, free-form evangelicalism developed towards the end of the century among a few energetic souls who believed that the liberating power of the gospel contradicted the entirety of inherited ecclesiastical organization. Elias Smith (1769–1846), who was converted as a teenager and originally served as a Baptist minister, was one important leader who shared this belief.[15] After several disillusioning episodes where he felt that the gospel was being squelched by oppressive habits of political power and ecclesiastical convention, Smith eventually determined to be called simply a 'Christian'. His restlessly peripatetic career anticipated the 'Restorationist' movements that multiplied after the turn of the century and that would find even more effective leadership from the founders of other 'Christian' and 'Disciples' movements like Barton W. Stone and Alexander Campbell.

The radical and democratizing effect of such evangelical movements is indicated perhaps most clearly by the fact that in their early decades they made room for public preaching by women. The Free-Will Baptists Sally Parsons and Mary Savage Card, as also the Methodists Abigail Leister, 'Sister' Mills and Sarah Riker, were all active in the northern and middle United States during the 1790s as public exhorters, revival preachers or co-preachers with their husbands.[16] At just about the same time women were beginning to engage in similar activity in areas of Britain where radical Methodist teaching was strongest.[17] For an understanding of evangelicalism as a whole, the most notable thing about these women revivalists was not that they preached only rarely about equal rights or female liberation, but rather that they were driven to public activity by the transforming effects of personal evangelical experience.

By the 1790s, populist or radically democratic forms of evangelicalism had taken root in many regions. The leaders of these movements almost always had undergone a life-redirecting experience of conversion, a surprisingly large

---

[14] On Dow, see Nathan O. Hatch, *The Democratization of American Christianity* (New Haven: Yale University Press, 1989), 36–40, 130–135; George A. Rawlyk, *The Canada Fire: Radical Evangelicalism in British North America, 1775–1812* (Kingston and Montreal: McGill-Queen's University Press, 1994), 110–112; and David Hempton, *Methodism and Politics in British Society, 1750–1850* (2nd ed., London: Hutchinson, 1987), 94–95.

[15] See especially Michael G. Kenny, *The Perfect Law of Liberty: Elias Smith and the Providential History of America* (Washington: Smithsonian Institution Press, 1994).

[16] Brekus, *Strangers and Pilgrims*, 343–346.

[17] See Valenze, *Prophetic Sons and Daughters*, 29–34, 187–204.

number of them had been touched by the ministry of George Whitefield, most had received little formal education but often exerted prodigious self-discipline in mastering the Bible, and most also recognized a natural synergy between the evangelical message of spiritual liberation and the era's many movements of political liberation. As a group, these radicals were strongly anti-Calvinistic, not so much as a result of direct biblical exegesis as from their sense that the Calvinists' God looked suspiciously like an inflexible tyrant. They were drawn to public ministry through an internal, personal 'call' instead of external, ecclesiastical summons. As fervent advocates of itinerant revival preaching, they prepared the way for the camp-meetings that would play such an important part in nineteenth-century evangelical history throughout Canada, the United States and parts of Britain. Most also featured singing as a crucial public activity in which all could participate. As all-out pietists, radical evangelicals could be completely indifferent to politics, or on some occasions translate egalitarian spiritual principles into democratic political action. Radical movements remained a subordinate theme in eighteenth-century evangelical-ism, but they had none the less become important by the 1790s and so would offer a significant precedent for at least some other evangelical activity in the centuries that followed.[18]

Bourgeois

Distinctly middle-class forms of evangelical life in the world also began slowly. But by late in the century they were beginning to suggest what, in the centuries to come, would be the predominant approach by evangelicals to society. Characteristically middle-class evangelicalism would take over some of the patterns initiated by their patrician fellow-evangelicals, but would also follow closely the pattern of social engagement pioneered by continental piet-ists, especially for promoting missions, education, self-improvement and social reform.

---

[18] The history of radical evangelical populism has been obscured. In some instances, mature denominations and organizations are embarrassed by the extremes of their founders: see Nathan O. Hatch, 'The Puzzle of American Methodism', in Hatch and John H. Wigger (eds.), *Methodism and the Shaping of American Culture* (Nashville: Kingswood, 2001), 23–40. In other instances modern radical scholars have been disinclined to recognize how much early evangelicals contributed to the movements they cherish: for a discussion along these lines concerning the most important of modern radical historians, see David Hempton and John Walsh, 'E. P. Thompson and Methodism', in Mark A. Noll (ed.), *God and Mammon: Protestants, Money, and the Market, 1790–1860* (New York: Oxford University Press, 2002), 99–120.

The key was the voluntary society, supported by voluntary contribution and publicized by a voluntary press.[19] As voluntarists, evangelicals were following in the steps of high-church Anglicans, German pietists and the Scottish Society for the Propagation of Christian Knowledge (SSPCK). As English Dissent became more thoroughly evangelical, as evangelicalism spread in the disestablished landscape of the United States, and as Evangelical Anglicans and Scottish Presbyterians became impatient with the creaking mechanisms of their established churches, the pace of self-mobilizing voluntarism quickened dramatically.

The efforts of Robert Raikes (1725–1811) to promote Sunday schools among the urban poor offered a paradigm for many later evangelical ventures.[20] Raikes was a newspaper publisher who turned his *Gloucester Journal* into an agent for many philanthropic causes. In 1780, with the help of Anglican associates, he began a school on Sundays for young people who were not being reached by normal church activities and who were otherwise occupied during the week. The curriculum of Raikes' Sunday schools featured Christian instruction, but also aimed directly at promoting literacy and basic scientific knowledge in general. He was, in effect, transporting the goals of Griffith Jones' earlier Welsh-language schools into urban England. As Raikes publicized the work of the Sunday schools in his newspaper – thereby using publicity as a tool for recruiting volunteers – and as in 1785 he helped set up a London-based society for promoting Sunday schools throughout the country, Raikes took the steps that countless evangelical voluntarists would later follow with countless other endeavours. Significantly, the wealthy MP and Clapham 'saint', Henry Thornton, was one of the first trustees of the London society, which indicates how easily patrician and bourgeois evangelicals could cooperate in such work. By 1797 there were 1,000 Sunday schools in England with nearly 70,000 scholars.

The kind of evangelical social engagement represented by Sunday schools differed from the earlier philanthropies of George Whitefield, which had been largely *ad hoc* and personal, and even those of John Wesley, which had been controlled closely by his all-seeing eye. It also represented a different approach than plebian social engagement because the middle-class evangelicals valued elite education, trusted in the power of extensive organization, wanted leaders who enjoyed respect in society at large, did not treat wealth as inherently cor-

---

[19] Critical orientation is provided by Andrew F. Walls, 'Missionary Societies and the Fortunate Subversion of the Church', in Walls, *The Missionary Movement in Christian History: Studies in the Transmission of Faith* (Maryknoll: Orbis, 1996), 241–254.

[20] Orientation is provided in *BDEB* 2:913–914 (V. H. H. Green, 'Robert Raikes').

rupting and worked more to infiltrate than to overthrow inherited structures of power. Yet as 'formalists' who opposed the radical democratization of the 'anti-formalists', bourgeois evangelicals flourished in the absence of establishments (United States) or as an alternative to establishmentarian monopolies (England, Ireland, Scotland, Canada).[21]

The missionary societies that appeared in the 1790s were the pace-setting organizations, but they were joined by societies for distributing the Bible, reforming manners, promoting education, reforming prisons, improving hospitals, abolishing the slave-trade and many more, which in the century after 1770 transformed the shape of Protestantism in English-speaking parts of the world.

That new shape, for which evangelicals were largely responsible, can be described socially, in the terms of theorist Jürgen Habermas, as promoting fundamental alterations in 'commodity exchange and social labor' when citizens took it upon themselves to construct 'the bourgeois public sphere' or 'the sphere of private public come together as a public' for themselves. For Habermas, Britain led 'the developmental history of civil society as a whole in which commodity exchange and social labor became largely emancipated from governmental directives'. But that situation was even more evident in the United States, where a civil society constituted by middle-class participants for their own purposes came to flourish during the early decades of the nineteenth century. For this process, evangelical religion communicated above all a system of inner motivation, at the same time as it bypassed traditional aristocratic political authority and imposed a self-discipline on the new middle-class managers of social exchange.[22]

Religiously, the bourgeois evangelical approach sprang from a dialectic of disillusionment and empowerment. Disillusionment concerned the capacity of inherited, statist, communal and comprehensive established churches effectively to promote true religion in the altered social and intellectual conditions of the eighteenth century. Empowerment came from the conviction that God in Christ palpably redeemed individuals and that God the Holy Spirit actually

---

[21] On the distinction between 'formalists' and 'anti-formalists', see Curtis D. Johnson, *Redeeming America: Evangelicals and the Road to the Civil War* (Chicago: Ivan Dee, 1993), 7–8.

[22] Jürgen Habermas, *The Structural Transformation of the Public Sphere: An Inquiry into a Category of Bourgeois Society*, trans. Thomas Berger (Cambridge, MA: MIT Press, 1989), 27–29, 73–75. For further elaboration along these lines, see George M. Thomas, *Revivalism and Cultural Change: Christianity, Nation Building, and the Market in the Nineteenth-Century United States* (Chicago: University of Chicago Press, 1989).

indwelt the redeemed so that they might *do* his will. In an important alteration from what had gone before, evangelicals looked upon that indwelling as pertaining particularly to themselves and to their voluntary associations rather than to inherited church institutions. In this respect, bourgeois evangelicalism represented the Methodist-ization, not just of the church, but of life as a whole.

With Americans of all denominations and English Dissenters in the vanguard, but also with surprising support from English, Scottish, Irish and Canadian establishmentarians, evangelical voluntarism represented a powerful approach to society linked directly to the effective power of evangelical preaching, conversion, sanctification and fellowship. For evangelical life in the world, this voluntarism was the wave of the future.

Anti-slavery

The evangelical mobilization against the slave-trade offers the best example from the late eighteenth century of how patrician, proletarian and bourgeois evangelicals took significant social action in connection with their heartfelt personal religion. Although early evangelicalism was highly unusual in the eagerness of leaders to preach to enslaved Africans and also in the effectiveness of that preaching, first-generation evangelicals either held slaves themselves (Edwards, Whitefield, Samuel Davies) or simply accepted the slave system as a given in the British empire. In the second evangelical generation, by contrast, the attack on the slave-trade became an important evangelical cause.

The pioneers of that activity were former slaves themselves. Although they were not usually in a place to mount effective public persuasion about the system as a whole, they were definitely in a position to demonstrate how fruitful the combination of spiritual New Birth and liberation from slavery could be. So it was in Delaware that after Richard Allen was converted and, after Freeborn Garrettson had preached directly against slavery to Allen's master, Allen was able to purchase his own freedom and to embark immediately on a wide-ranging ministry of itinerant preaching.[23] Similarly, David George and Thomas Peters in Georgia and North Carolina, respectively, took advantage during the mid-1770s of the offer of freedom from occupying British troops and also preached effectively the power of the New Birth that they had ex-

---

[23] *The Life Experience and the Gospel Labors of the Rt. Rev. Richard Allen ... Written by Himself* (Abingdon: Nashville, 1960), 15–18.

perienced.[24] Olaudah Equiano's *Life* from 1789 added considerable fuel to the flickering flame of evangelical anti-slave sentiment. In New England, the black Congregationalist minister, Lemuel Haynes, likewise joined seamlessly a dedicated defence of Jonathan Edwards' Calvinist theology with militant opposition to slavery.[25] Free black evangelicals were usually too busy with other tasks to devote themselves completely to anti-slavery work, but they were always a chief element in that effort.

In America, anti-slavery sentiments, which had long been at work among the Quakers, emerged even more sharply in the labours of Anthony Benezet (1713–1784) of Philadelphia, whose family background included contact with the Moravians. The anti-slavery works he published from the early 1760s had an almost immediate resonance with several evangelical leaders.[26] Yet when a distinctly evangelical anti-slavery emerged in America it came not from contact with Quakers, but through an application of the theology of Jonathan Edwards.[27]

In 1770 Samuel Hopkins, Edwards' closest student, became the minister of a Congregational church in Newport, Rhode Island, where he could witness the realities of slave-trading close up in this northern shipping centre. Repelled by what he saw, Hopkins joined other local Congregationalists in setting up a society to return converted slaves to Africa as missionaries. In 1776 he broadcast his opinions with a forthright pamphlet that applied Edwardsean theology directly to contemporary events, *A Dialogue Concerning the Slavery of the Africans: Shewing it to be the duty and interest of the American colonies to emancipate all their African slaves: With an address to the owners of such slaves. Dedicated to the Honorable the Continental Congress.* In this work, Hopkins attacked the system for its general dehumanizing of both slaves and slavers. He then charged that slavery violated express commands of Christ by promoting ill treatment of the oppressed, whom Jesus had singled out for special mercy.

---

[24] Grant Gordon, *From Slavery to Freedom: The Life of David George, Pioneer Black Baptist Minister* (Hantsport, Nova Scotia: Lancelot, 1992), 30–32; and Lamin Sanneh, *Abolitionists Abroad: American Blacks and the Making of Modern West Africa* (Cambridge, MA: Harvard University Press, 1999), 50–53.

[25] See John Saillant, *Black Puritan, Black Republican: The Life and Thought of Lemuel Haynes, 1655–1833* (New York: Oxford University Press, 2003).

[26] For example, *Observations on the Inslaving, Importing, and Purchasing of Negroes* (1760); and *A Caution or Warning to Great-Britain and her Colonies in a Short Representation of the Calamitous State of the Enslaved Negroes in the British Dominions* (1767).

[27] For expert recent orientation, see Harry S. Stout and Kenneth P. Minkema, 'The Edwardsian Tradition and Ante-Bellum Anti-Slavery', forthcoming.

And then he turned to the specific concept of 'benevolence', which he had developed from Edwards' description of the ideal Christian life as 'love to Being in General'. According to Hopkins, the spirit of the age had blinded people to the essential humanity of Africans, which led to a most unfortunate result: 'This has banished all attention to the injustice that is done them, and any proper sense of their misery, or the exercise of benevolence towards them.'[28] The concept of 'benevolence' remained central to Hopkins' ethics, so that nearly twenty years later, when he wrote another hard-hitting pamphlet, he used similar arguments against the evils of the slave system.[29] By finding in his teacher's metaphysical theology a motive for attacking slavery, Hopkins was joined by several other students and admirers of Jonathan Edwards, including Levi Hart and Edwards' own son, Jonathan Edwards, Jr, Congregational ministers in Connecticut and Jacob Green, a New Englander converted under Whitefield, who became a Presbyterian minister in New Jersey.[30] As an indication of how far-reaching such anti-slavery could be, Hopkins in 1776 extended his Edwardsean thinking to what was for the time a truly radical position. Against a tide of religious opinion that viewed Britain (or the British colonies) as singularly chosen by God, Hopkins contended that the unique status of Israel 'is now at an end, and all nations are put upon a level; and Christ ... has taught us to look on all nations as our neighbours and brethren'.[31]

In Britain, opposition to the slave-trade did not usually lead to such theological conclusions, but there as well it became a prominent feature of the maturing evangelical ethic. For his part, John Wesley had brooded over the lot of slaves since his time in Georgia during the mid-1730s. What finally seems to have moved him to action on the subject was a book by Anthony Benezet, which he read in early 1772. This volume convinced Wesley that the modern trade in slaves to the new world represented the 'execrable sum of all villainies', and was far worse than 'whatever Christian slaves suffer in Mahometan countries'.[32] Only a short time later he published a pamphlet in which he

---

[28] Hopkins, *A Dialogue Concerning Slavery* (Norwich, CT: Judah Spooner, 1776), 34.

[29] Hopkins, *A Discourse upon the Slave-Trade, and the Slavery of the Africans* (Providence: J. Carter, 1793).

[30] On this Edwardsean anti-slave party, see Mark A. Noll, *Christians in the American Revolution* (Grand Rapids: Eerdmans, 1977), 92–102; and Noll, 'Observations on the Reconciliation of Politics and Religion in Revolutionary New Jersey: The Case of Jacob Green', *Journal of Presbyterian History* 44 (1976): 217–237.

[31] Hopkins, *Dialogue*, 21.

[32] Wesley, *Journal* (12 February 1772), 5:445–446.

addressed the slave-holders of North America and the West Indies with characteristic directness:

> You know [slaves] are procured by a deliberate series of more complicated villainy (of
> fraud, robbery, and murder) than was ever practised either by Mahometans or Pagans
> ... Now, it is your money that pays the merchant, and through him the captain and
> the African butchers. You therefore are guilty, yea principally guilty, of all these
> frauds, robberies, and murders ... therefore, the blood of all these wretches who die
> before their time, whether in their country or elsewhere, lies upon your head.[33]

Largely because of such opinions, the Methodists in Britain and, into the
1790s, also of North America, would not allow slave-holders to become full
members of their societies.

Evangelical activity against slavery climaxed in the patient work of William
Wilberforce and his associates, who from the 1780s developed a systematic
series of reforms aimed at eradicating first the slave-trade and then slavery
itself.[34] The eventual success of those ventures, culminating in Wilberforce's
bills in Parliament against the slave-trade and then against slavery itself, will be
treated in volume two of this series, but here it is important to see how a variety
of evangelical influences came together to create the British evangelical assault.

The Wilberforce circle included several individuals who had been turned
against slavery by first-hand experience in the West Indies. Zachary Macaulay
(1768–1838) had been sent as a sixteen-year-old to work as a book-keeper in
Jamaica, where he was appalled by the human bondage he saw. Upon returning
to England, he threw himself into reforming causes, becoming in 1793 the
governor of Sierra Leone and devoting much of the rest of his life to providing research on slavery to Wilberforce and other public opponents of the
system. As an indication of how ties of kin connected with religious reform,
Macaulay's sister was married to Thomas Babington (1758–1837), a banker,
philanthropist and abolitionist who, as an MP, helped Wilberforce and Henry
Thornton in many of their public battles. Another evangelical reformer with
West Indian experience was James Stephen (1758–1832), a barrister who inherited property in St Christopher, where he lived from 1783 to 1794 and where he
was turned into a committed opponent of slavery. During a trip back to
England in 1788–1789, he visited Wilberforce and pushed him to be more

---

[33] Wesley, *Thoughts on Slavery* (1774), in Wesley, *Works* (1872), 11:78.

[34] On Wilberforce, I have been guided by John Pollock, *Wilberforce* (London: Constable,
1977); and John Wolffe, 'William Wilberforce', *Oxford Dictionary of National Biography*
(Oxford: Oxford University Press, 2004).

active in the anti-slave cause; a few years later, after returning permanently to England, he married Wilberforce's widowed sister Sarah. James Ramsay (1733–1789) was even more important in forging the evangelical anti-slave alliance. After service as a physician in the British fleet and in St Kitts, Ramsay returned to England, where he was ordained in the Church of England and provided with a benefice by Sir Charles Middleton, under whom he had served in the navy. Ramsay's 1784 book, *Essay on the Treatment and Conversion of African Slaves in the British Sugar Colonies*, moved Wilberforce towards aggressive involvement in the cause. Even more importantly, Ramsay's influence helped secure his patron's engagement against the slave- trade.

Charles Middleton (1726–1813), an admiral and MP later ennobled as Lord Barham, was a Scot whose genius for administration played a key role in British triumph over the French navy in the wars that began in 1793. From the influence of his wife Margaret (d. 1792), who had been touched by the ministry of Whitefield, Middleton became an active evangelical. When his wife and his friend James Ramsay urged him to use his seat in Parliament as a platform for opposing the slave-trade, Middleton agreed that the cause needed a champion, but held that he was not the one to take up the challenge. In Middleton's opinion, Wilberforce was that man.

Wilberforce had sought spiritual and personal purpose from his youth as part of a wealthy and newly landed family in Hull, through his years as a Cambridge undergraduate and at his entrance into Parliament in 1780 shortly after his twenty-first birthday. Wilberforce's aunt Hannah Thornton and Wilberforce's schoolmasters, Joseph Milner and Isaac Milner of the Hull Grammar School, had planted an evangelical seed that finally grew in the mid-1780s after Wilberforce took Isaac Milner along on two lengthy excursions to the Continent. A reading of Philip Doddridge's *The Rise and Progress of Religion in the Soul* had also made a difference. As a typical evangelical, Wilberforce in the first flood of redemptive experience resolved to abandon his life as a parliamentarian in order to serve God in the church. But a chorus of older evangelicals, including John Newton, urged him not to give up his place as a rising young politician who, among other advantages, enjoyed a close friendship with the younger William Pitt (Prime Minister from 1783). As Wilberforce solidified both his evangelical convictions and his political career, so too did he look for causes to which he might devote himself. He found the first of these in the reform of public morals, an effort that led to the foundation of the Society for Giving Effect to His Majesty's Proclamation Against Vice (so named for a royal proclamation by George III in 1787). Wilberforce's landmark book, *A Practical View of the Prevailing Religious System of Professed Christians in the Higher and Middle Classes in this Country, Contrasted with Real Christianity*, which appeared in 1797, was intended to further this particular cause.

This volume created a sensation when it was published, both for its forth-right arguments in favour of historic Christianity and for being written by a young and influential MP. The book's popular natural theology and its outline account of Protestant history provided background support for Wilberforce's main goal, which was to turn Britons from the 'very inadequate conception which they entertain of the importance of Christianity in general' and from 'the commonly received opinion' that, if people simply admitted the general truth of Christianity and avoided gross moral faults, 'we have no great reason to be dissatisfied'.[35] By contrast, the proper basis of what Wilberforce termed 'the true nature of Religion' or 'real Christianity' was solidly evangelical. That basis required individuals to acknowledge honestly the true burden of sin and to recognize that those sins 'must finally sink us into perdition' unless they responded joyfully to 'the gracious invitation, "Come unto me, all ye that labour and are heavy laden, and I will give you rest" [Matthew 11:28]'.[36] But once having received that invitation, the true Christian is in place to answer the 'call on us for vigorous and continual resolution, self-denial, and activity'. Moreover, 'the promotion of the glory of God' furnishes 'a vigorous, habit-ual, and universal principle of action'.[37] If such springs of action could be multiplied and flow together, the effects would be visible throughout the land: 'It is a truth which will hardly be contested, that Christianity, whenever it has at all prevailed, has raised the general standard of morals to a height before unknown.'[38] On the basis of these arguments, Wilberforce posed a choice for his countrymen: did they want to follow the path of France, with 'manners corrupted, morals depraved, dissipation predominant, above all, Religion dis-credited, and infidelity grown into repute and fashion'? Or did they want a moral, stable and godly social order? If so, the means was at hand: 'the Christianity which can produce effects like these must be real, not nominal, deep, not superficial. Such then is the Religion we should cultivate, if we would realize these pleasing speculations, and arrest the progress of political decay.'[39] In short, the book represented a memorable effort at translating the evangelical principle of 'true religion' into vigorous social practice.

Wilberforce's work against the slave-trade was marked by the same dedica-tion, and by an even more remarkable assemblage of willing helpers. The

---

[35] Wilberforce, *A Practical View of Christianity* (1797), Kevin Charles Belmonte (ed.) (Peabody: Hendrickson, 1996), 1, 77.

[36] Ibid., 87, 182, 35.

[37] Ibid., 49, 89.

[38] Ibid., 191–192.

[39] Ibid., 200, 209.

Middleton circle, which introduced Wilberforce to the cause, included not only the Admiral's far-flung naval connections and his wife's wide evangelical network, but also Bishop Beilby Porteus (1731–1808), who had first-hand experience of slavery in his native Virginia; Benjamin La Trobe, the Moravian itinerant and promoter of missions; Granville Sharp (1735–1813), whose radical political views did not keep him from active support of the parliamentary campaign; and Thomas Clarkson (1760–1846), whose *Essay on the Slavery and Commerce of the Human Species* from 1786 inspired the nascent anti-slavery crusaders and also drew Clarkson into their ranks. In addition, from his first ventures into public life, Wilberforce was sustained by his Clapham friends and he enjoyed the support of well-known evangelical leaders like John Newton. The last letter that John Wesley wrote in a life of incessant correspondence was to Wilberforce, whom he urged to 'Go on, in the name of God and in the power of His might, till even American slavery (the vilest that ever saw the sun) shall vanish away before it.'[40]

William Wilberforce's persistent testimony against the slave-trade represented the finest hour for social involvement in early evangelical history. But it is vital to realize that he was never alone in his effort. Rather, Wilberforce benefited from earlier and parallel evangelical efforts, and he was supported by a vast array of eager helpers, most of whom were motivated in their abolitionist activity by life-changing evangelical experience.

Limitations of evangelical anti-slavery

As exemplary as the anti-slavery testimony was, however, it is also important to recognize the limits of this activity, and by so doing to perceive important limits more generally with evangelical involvement in society. Evangelicalism never amounted to a full-blown religious tradition, but was rather a style of personal living everywhere combined with conventional attitudes and actions. Wilberforce and his circle drew energy, endurance, steadfastness and unusual altruism from their Christian experience as evangelicals, but they remained elite, paternalistic Anglicans. Samuel Hopkins and his fellow-students of Jonathan Edwards were infused with similar evangelical energy, but they remained Congregational New Divinity pietists. Richard Allen, Olaudah Equiano and David George found religious security in the evangelical message of salvation, but however much evangelical conviction bore them up, they still approached life in the world from the vantage point of former slaves.

---

[40] Wesley to Wilberforce, 22 February 1791, in Wesley, *Letters*, 8:265.

As a *revival* movement, in other words, evangelicalism transformed people within their inherited social setting, but worked only partial and selective transformation on the social settings themselves. A harsh, but none the less accurate, statement by the Marxist historian Eric Williams is indicative of much evangelical activity: 'Wilberforce was familiar with all that went on in the hold of a slave ship but ignored what went on at the bottom of a mine-shaft.' In other words, the vision that drove Wilberforce and his associates to heroic lengths on behalf of the enslaved failed to grasp the degradation that was descending upon Britain's own labouring poor. Williams extended his indictment by noting that Wilberforce was in favour of the Corn Laws, which protected the income of Britain's landed classes by prohibiting the importa-tion of cheap grain, was callous towards the working-class complaints that surfaced in the depression following the end of war with France in 1815 and was convinced that the Reform Bill of 1831, which sought the elimination of 'rotten boroughs' and extended the franchise to more middle-class British men, was too radical.[41]

The story for other evangelicals was not the same as with Wilberforce, but for the evangelical movement in general, approaches to society tended to be tactical, personal and *ad hoc* rather than strategic, structural and systematic. Above all they relied on the recruitment of volunteers for all causes – whether for evangelism, church renewal and missionary outreach, for influencing Parliament and Congress, or for establishing voluntary societies to change the social order. Compared to the reliance on inherited structures that characterized earlier Protestant life, voluntary organization unleashed tremendous energy. But voluntarism, of course, relied on the character of volunteers. The difficulties in this arrangement were revealed most clearly in the American struggle against slavery.[42] Into the 1790s, evangelicals of many kinds, especially Methodists and Edwardsean Congregationalists, spoke out forcefully against slavery. But even as they did so, voluntaristic energy was at work for evangelism and church renewal in the slave-states. Soon those efforts were succeeding beyond hope, but when it came to the anti-slave cause, success carried a high price. As more and more slave-owners were won to Christ, it became harder and harder to insist upon the manumission of slaves (even though many slaves were also

---

[41] Eric Williams, *Capitalism and Slavery* (Chapel Hill: University of North Carolina Press, 1944), 182.

[42] I am here following James D. Essig, *The Bonds of Wickedness: American Evangelicals Against Slavery, 1770–1808* (Philadelphia: Temple University Press, 1982); and Donald G. Mathews, *Slavery and Methodism: A Chapter in American Morality, 1780–1845* (Princeton: Princeton University Press, 1965).

being evangelized). So it was that in the slave- states the success of evangelical-ism was marked also by a muting of the evangelical complaint against slavery. The voluntaristic effort that worked so well at recruiting new believers was not effective in convincing enough slave-holders that slavery was an evil to be removed. In this tragic situation, voluntaristic inspiration, voluntaristic mobil-ization and voluntaristic reform could accomplish great things, but such pro-cedures lacked a mechanism to change the social framework that volunteers simply took for granted. British anti-slavery eventually worked in Britain because the slave-holders of the West Indies represented a small (and not very thor-oughly evangelized) portion of the British body politic – and also because British courts refused to recognize the legality of slavery on British soil. In America, evangelical anti-slavery failed because there were so many slave-holders and so many of them were evangelicals. Much was gained when evangelical vol-untarism took the place of earlier coercive establishmentarian Protestantism, but this transition also lost the possibility of using undemocratic coercion to do what 'the people' could not or would not choose to do for themselves.

In the world

The strengths and weaknesses of evangelical approaches to the world were, thus, fully displayed by the mid-1790s. Evangelicalism was proving to be flexible, people-oriented and energetic; it was effectively reaching out to troubled consciences and conveying through its message genuine transforma-tion of life. In fact, so effective was the transforming power of the gospel that John Wesley and other leaders began to worry that sober evangelical diligence was creating too many newly affluent citizens with too much wealth for their own spiritual well-being.[43] For social problems requiring the mobilization of volunteers, evangelicalism was especially successful. The spread of evangelical convictions and the social responsibility evangelicalism encouraged in response to the gospel may even have had something to do with dampening the potential for revolution in England during the 1790s.[44] Evangelical values

---

[43] For discussion, John Walsh, 'Methodism at the End of the Eighteenth Century', in Rupert Davies and Gordon Rupp (eds.), *A History of the Methodist Church in Great Britain*, vol. 1 (London: Epworth, 1965), 308–313.

[44] The thesis was first proposed in articles (1906) and a book (1913) by Elie Halévy. See Elie Halévy, *The Birth of Methodism in England*, ed. and trans. Bernard Semmel (Chicago: University of Chicago Press, 1971); and for discussion, John D. Walsh, 'Elie Halévy and the Birth of Methodism', *Transactions of the Royal Historical Society* 25 (1975): 1–20.

certainly had much to do with making self-government work in the new United States.[45]

At the same time, evangelicalism did not fashion worldviews, push towards fundamental intellectual insight or show great understanding of the structures of British and North American life. It was a movement that, with respect to inherited social situations, could renew and reform, but (apart from the voluntary society itself) not create. The dynamism of evangelicalism was revealed most clearly in its missionary activity, its innovations that reached those whom established churches had passed by and its ability to mobilize ordinary women and men who had experienced the extraordinary operations of God's Spirit. The limitations of evangelicalism appeared most clearly in challenges requiring either systematic and comprehensive analysis or cooperative and coercive actions. Brief comments on how leading evangelicals approached intellectual life and issues of war and peace illustrate both strengths and weaknesses of the movement.[46]

It remains an oddity that the greatest intellectual in the whole history of evangelicalism was also its first great intellectual. Jonathan Edwards, in his intense labours as a philosophical theologian, subjected the best thought of his era to extraordinary painstaking analysis.[47] Thus, he borrowed notions of epistemology from John Locke, but also repudiated Locke's preference for self-verified knowledge over divinely revealed knowledge. Edwards recognized, and even celebrated, the achievements of Sir Isaac Newton's science, but also reconceptualized the entire nature of the cosmos in order to make God, rather than self-standing matter, the basis for all scientific progress. He

---

[45] For this argument, Mark A. Noll, *America's God, from Jonathan Edwards to Abraham Lincoln* (New York: Oxford University Press, 2003), 187–208.

[46] Both subjects deserve much more attention than they receive here. For hints on intellectual life, see David W. Bebbington, 'Science and Theology in Britain from Wesley to Orr', and Mark A. Noll, 'Science, Theology, and Society: From Cotton Mather to William Jennings Bryan', in David N. Livingstone, D. G. Hart and Noll (eds.), *Evangelicals and Science in Historical Perspective* (New York: Oxford University Press, 1999), 120–141, 99–119. For balanced, sensitive treatment of a similar situation in literature and the arts, see Doreen Rosman, *Evangelicals and Culture* (London: Croon Helm, 1984).

[47] Outstanding treatments include Norman Fiering, *Jonathan Edwards's Moral Thought and Its British Context* (Chapel Hill: University of North Carolina Press, 1981); Edwards, *Works*, vol. 6: *Scientific and Philosophical Writings*, ed. Wallace E. Anderson (1980); and George M. Marsden, *Jonathan Edwards: A Life* (New Haven: Yale University Press, 2003).

read with appreciation ethicists like Francis Hutcheson, who described the affections as foundational for human understanding and human morality. Yet he also argued in words as subtle as they were vigorous that only traditional views of sinful human nature and saving divine grace could provide a reliable basis for truly virtuous action. He pored over the most advanced theological reasoning from the colonies, Britain and several continental sources, but in response constructed his era's most thorough reformulation of Calvinist theology. For more than a century after his death, Edwards remained the one figure from the 1730s and 1740s who demanded attention from serious theologians of whatever stripe. During the last fifty years he has been the only early evangelical figure to inspire prolonged attention from modern students of ethics, metaphysics, cosmology, religious psychology, philosophy of science and philosophical theology.[48]

Yet once beyond Edwards, the intellectual life of evangelicalism looks less impressive. The emphasis on conversion and on the active presence of the Holy Spirit has led at least some evangelicals to deny the value of intellectual effort itself. The distrust of inherited authorities – both ecclesiastical and educational – means that evangelicals have repeatedly attempted to invent intellectual first principles for themselves. The strong tendency to define the church as the voluntary product of voluntary effort has undercut the ability to learn from earlier Christian generations. And while the distrust of establishments has liberated many evangelicals from a thralldom to meaningless forms, it has also deprived them of the benefits of inter-generational intellectual nurture. At its best, much evangelical thought reflects savvy practical wisdom rather than thorough foundational reasoning.

John Wesley's dalliance with the ideas of John Hutchinson illustrates the more ordinary pattern of evangelical savvy. Early in his career Wesley sometimes recommended the work of Hutchinson (1674–1737), a steward to the Duke of Somerset who distrusted the science of Newton as materialistic and instead argued that a true view of nature could be derived from the study of

---

[48] On the multiplication of scholarship, see Nathan O. Hatch and Harry S. Stout (eds.), *Jonathan Edwards and the American Experience* (New York: Oxford University Press, 1988), 3. For recent perceptive assessments of what might be called 'the Jonathan Edwards phenomenon', see Michael J. McClymond, 'The Protean Puritan: *The Works of Jonathan Edwards*, Volumes 8 to 16', *Religious Studies Review* 24 (1998): 361–367; Bruce Kuklick, 'An Edwards for the Millennium', *Religion and American Culture* 11 (2001): 109–117; and Leigh E. Schmidt, 'The Edwards Revival: Or, the Public Consequences of Exceedingly Careful Scholarship', *William and Mary Quarterly* 58 (2001): 580–586.

Old Testament Hebrew construed without the vowel points.[49] Hutchinson's reliance on the Bible alone appealed to Wesley as did also his willingness to critique the intellectual establishment. But Wesley was no mean reasoner himself, and he came eventually to the conclusion that Hutchinson's arguments 'have no foundation in Scripture or sound reason'.[50] In his own wide reading and ceaseless writing, however, Wesley did not advance his own foundational critique of the age's scientific and philosophical reasoning as his contemporary Jonathan Edwards had done. In this respect, Wesley was much more typical of later evangelical history than was Edwards.

On questions of war and peace, by contrast, Wesley moved at least somewhat beyond conventional views, while most other evangelicals remained tied to the ordinary norms of their day. The era in which modern evangelicalism was born, it is helpful to remember, was an age of nearly constant warfare between Britain and France, as well as of armed rebellion (Jacobites in Britain 1715 and 1745, rebels in America 1776 and United Irishmen in Ireland 1798) and significant police action by British troops (India, Minorca, French Senegal, Martinique, Grenada, Cuba and the Philippines).[51] For the most part evangelicals tended to follow the pattern of their own locations when they addressed war and peace. Samuel Davies in Virginia actually won legal standing for Presbyterians in that Anglican colony through his vigorous anti-French and anti-Roman Catholic sermons during the French and Indian War. Jonathan Edwards spoke with a little more Christian discernment during King George's War (1740–48), when New England backed an expedition to take Louisbourg on Cape Breton Island from the French. George Whitefield usually took advantage of times troubled by war to press the urgency of the New Birth, but when he did stoop to address contemporary events, he was consistently patriotic in a conventional way. Only occasionally, as with Henry Alline and Freeborn Garrettson during the American Revolution, did pietistic convictions lead evangelicals to resist the war spirit and hold out for pacifism.

On the issue of warfare, John Wesley was the most interesting evangelical figure of the eighteenth century, because he actually examined the issue at some depth. During the American Revolution, it was not surprising that

---

[49] On Hutchinson's limited appeal to evangelicals, see Noll, 'Science, Theology, and Society', 105–108.

[50] Wesley, *Journal* (31 July 1758), 4:280.

[51] This listing is from Samuel J. Rogal, 'John Wesley on War and Peace', in Roseann Runte (ed.), *Studies in Eighteenth-Century Culture*, vol. 7 (Madison: University of Wisconsin Press, 1978), 329. This subject is well treated in Rogal's article (329–344) and in Briane K. Turley, 'John Wesley and War', *Methodist History* 29 (January 1991): 96–111.

Wesley, as a conservative Anglican committed to the virtues of the monarchy, criticized the American patriots in harsh terms. But it was just as characteristic for Wesley to bemoan the outbreak of war, whenever it occurred, as an impediment to the gospel. At the start of the American war, for example, he wrote in a letter that, 'wherever war breaks out, God is forgotten, if He be not set at open defiance. What a glorious work of God was at Cambuslang and Kilsyth from 1740 to 1744! But the war that followed tore it all up by the roots and left scarce any trace of it behind.'[52]

Wesley also escaped the normal pattern of the early evangelicals by making strong statements against the evil of warfare itself. The most extensive of such comments came in his long book on *The Doctrine of Original Sin*, which he published in 1757 as a response to earlier work by John Taylor that softened traditional Christian teaching on the nature and extent of human sinfulness. To defend that traditional teaching, Wesley paraded a long list of reasons from, as he said, 'Scripture, Reason, and Experience', why Christians should consider original sin a very serious and continuing universal condition of humankind. Among the 'greater and more undeniable' proofs to show that 'the very foundations of all things, civil and religious, are utterly out of course in the Christian as well as the heathen world', was the fact of warfare. Wesley was astounded that anyone would attempt to 'reconcile war, I will not say to religion, but to any degree of reason or common sense'. As Wesley under- stood it, warfare existed mostly for base reasons – because, for example, people could not live with differences of opinion on religious questions or because various factions tried to extend their power over other peoples. His conclusion, at least at that time, was that 'Men in general can never be allowed to be reasonable creatures, till they know not war any more'.[53]

The timing of this statement is noteworthy, for it was made while war was under way with France and while other evangelicals, like Samuel Davies and George Whitefield, were expressing with much less reservation the necessity of fighting off the French as representatives of tyranny and false religion.

Yet it is clear from the scope of Wesley's career that he was not a pacifist and that he did not object to warfare in principle when it was mandated by a legally installed ruler. In early 1756 when Englishmen were just beginning to feel the effects of the new war with France that had been under way for two years in the colonies, he even briefly considered trying to raise a troop of 200 Methodist volunteers for the defence of London against an anticipated French attack. Two decades later, near the start of the American war, Wesley

---

[52] Wesley to Thomas Rankin, 19 May 1775, in Wesley, *Letters*, 6:151.

[53] Wesley, *The Doctrine of Original Sin* (1757), in Wesley, *Works* (1872), 9:221–223.

included some comment on the general subject in a hard-hitting pamphlet directed against the practice of slavery. In the pamphlet he attacked the ancient Justinian position that it was legitimate to enslave prisoners of war. 'War itself is justifiable only on principles of self-preservation', he held, but those principles do not allow for the enslavement of defeated soldiers and their families.[54] At other times, Wesley justified warfare as part of necessary loyalty to one's sovereign, for the purpose of 'self-preservation', and when it was necessary to restore internal order.[55]

Wesley, in sum, remained a conventional Christian of the eighteenth century in proposing no general principle against participation in warfare. None the less, for an evangelical of his time and place his understanding of war as a gross example of humankind's original sin was unusual, and his ability to see the individual human cost of warfare an exception to the rule.

John Wesley's commentary on warfare, as also Jonathan Edwards' extraordinary labours on intellectual questions and the Wilberforce circle's attacks on slavery, demonstrate that evangelicals were capable of creative responses to the challenges of living in the world. Yet these instances, admirable as they appear, were not necessarily typical of early evangelicalism. For life in the world, evangelicals experienced the weaknesses of their strengths.

If evangelicals were strong in personal reassurance before God, they were weak in the formation of worldviews. If they stripped away other considerations to focus on the need for a Saviour, they sometimes also stripped away the urgency to think generally about responsible Christian life in the world. The remarkable effects from concentrating on Christian experience as depicted in Scripture were often matched by the deliberate devaluation of intellectual tradition. At the end of the day, evangelical concern for society reflected the character of the movement as a whole. It was a pietistic movement that did much good in the world. But as a pietistic movement its focused attention on the spiritual tended to edge aside, rather than stimulate, self-conscious attention to the social.

---

[54] Wesley, *Thoughts Upon Slavery* (1774), in Wesley, *Works*, 11:71,
[55] Turley, 'John Wesley and War', 109–110.

9. TRUE RELIGION

Changing the world was never as important for the early evangelicals as changing the self, or as fashioning spiritual communities in which changed selves could grow in grace. Already in the eighteenth century, evangelicalism was exerting a broad influence on cultural and social values, and for both Britain and North America it would do so even more in the nineteenth century. But throughout this period, and far beyond, the heart of evangelicalism was the quest for True Religion – what it was, how to obtain it, why it was often obscured, what to do with it. Evangelicals became an important force in Western societies and began to exert an impact on the world as a whole, above all because of their commitment to the ideal, and to the practice, of genuine Christianity.

Evangelical ideals concerning true – as opposed to formal, inherited, nominal, simply traditional, or corrupted – Christianity came to expression most clearly in the great surge of hymn-writing that marked the first two generations of the movement. Yet however important a common set of standard themes was for expressing those ideals in song among all evangelicals, important differences did divide them into separate sub-movements, streams or groups. Mostly unremarked at the time, but now very much a concern of contemporary historians, were differences between male and female versions of evangelical experience. Very much noticed in the eighteenth century, and still of continuing interest, were theological differences among evangelicals in their attempts to describe the ways of God among his people and in the world. Questions of gender, issues in theology and the development of hymnody deserve much more attention than is provided by the sketches that follow, but since each of these topics is rooted in evangelical Christian experience, it will be appropriate to end this chapter on the main spiritual themes of eighteenth-century evangelicalism with a brief treatment of religious experience itself.

Gender

For almost all of its enterprises, evangelicalism regularly attracted more women than men. Except at colleges and universities, which were still all-male institutions, almost every other important venue of evangelical life witnessed the majority involvement of women. The meaning of the new evangelical religion for women has thankfully been the subject of expert modern attention, though this is a subject that is still in the process of being opened up.[1]

Among the other disruptions brought about by the evangelical revivals of the eighteenth century was a disruption of traditional gender roles. When men and women were converted, often in life-shaking moments of great crisis, gender distinctions receded or were reversed. When individuals were born again – 'swallowed up in God' or 'wrapped up in God' were phrases used more than once – everything changed.[2] Those changes affected gender boundaries differently depending on who and where the born-again evangelicals were. Evangelical movements within the Church of England, Scottish or new-world Presbyterianism and New England Congregationalism experienced a loosening of tight gender expectations – women might occasionally give voice in public to their experiences of grace, pastors paid more attention to what might be learned from women about the ways of God and leaders encouraged household, private and outside-of-church religious activities by both men and women. Such activities once again followed along lines that the

[1] Key works include Susan Juster, *Disorderly Women: Sexual Politics and Evangelicalism in Revolutionary New England* (Ithaca: Cornell University Press, 1994); Deborah M. Valenze, *Prophetic Sons and Daughters: Female Preaching and Popular Religion in Industrial England* (Princeton: Princeton University Press, 1985); and Catherine A. Brekus, *Strangers and Pilgrims: Female Preaching in America, 1740–1845* (Chapel Hill: University of North Carolina Press, 1998). For an earlier treatment of this theme, some of which is repeated here, see ch. 6, 'Gender', in Mark A. Noll, *American Evangelical Christianity: An Introduction* (Oxford: Blackwell, 2001).

[2] For the use of these phrases, see George A. Rawlyk, *'Wrapped Up in God': A Study of Several Canadian Revivals and Revivalists* (Burlington: Welch, 1988); Juster, *Disorderly Women*, 57–62; and Brekus, *Strangers and Pilgrims*, 42.

Moravians had pioneered.[3] In his Congregational Church in Northampton, Massachusetts, Jonathan Edwards regularly singled out women (and girls) as offering models for the kind of spirituality he felt the Bible described. Women of status and wealth, like the Countess of Huntingdon, could become powers behind the scenes, and contributions by communicators like Hannah More or women hymn-writers were usually well received. Yet within the formal, established churches long-standing traditions of Western Christendom ensured that only men were ordained, men were the ones who defined theological boundaries, and women were expected to exert an influence mostly within the confines of the household.

It was a different situation among the more plebian groups that sprang up on the margins of polite society (Methodists) or that were dramatically energized by the currents of revival (Baptists). For New England Baptists, among whom congregational autonomy was an important principle, a powerful new sense of community encouraged converted women to speak, allowed for the participation of women in cases of church discipline and featured a new concern for humble egalitarianism on the part of many men. Converted women found the power to act that had hitherto been reserved for men; converted men found depth of caring relationships that had previously been the preserve of women.[4]

Although the Methodists were led by the Tory Anglicans, John and Charles Wesley, these leaders were also unusually attuned to the spiritual potential of ordinary people.[5] Especially the Methodist class meeting opened up unusual new spiritual opportunities for women, and also for lower-class men. Since these cell-groups were lay-led, they encouraged all who attended to give verbal spiritual testimonies, and they also asked each to sit in spiritual judgment on the rest (though, of course, with as much humility as the sanctified saints could muster). These encouragements led naturally to women speaking up in the larger public meetings of Methodists. Usually that public speaking took the form of exhortation rather than formal sermons. But the early Methodist movement and also the outworking of revival among

---

[3] See Katherine M. Faull, *Moravian Women's Memoirs: Their Related Lives, 1750–1820* (Syracuse, NY: Syracuse University Press, 1997).

[4] This summary is taken from Juster, *Disorderly Women*.

[5] As a counterpart to the scholarship on early Methodism in England from Henry Rack, Richard Heitzenrater, David Hempton, John Walsh, W. R. Ward and others, cited in earlier chapters, a solid study for America that features concerns of gender and domesticity is A. Gregory Schneider, *The Way of the Cross Leads Home: The Domestication of American Methodism* (Bloomington: Indiana University Press, 1993).

Baptists and other anti-establishmentarian localists also opened at least some opportunities for women to expound the Scriptures more formally.[6] One of the Methodist exhorters was Sarah Mallett (c.1764–after 1843) who, after joining the Wesleyans and experiencing several trances as a young adult, began in 1786 to exhort in public.[7] John Wesley took note of her situation and urged her to follow the guidance of his assistant in her East Anglian region. At the same time, Wesley also went out of his way to encourage her as a public speaker: 'It gives me great pleasure to hear that prejudice dies away and our preachers behave in a friendly manner', he wrote in December 1789. 'Never continue the service above an hour at once, singing, *preaching*, prayer, and all. You are not to judge by your own *feelings*, but by the word of God. Never scream. Never speak above the natural pitch of your voice; it is disgustful to hearers. It gives them pain, not pleasure. And it is destroying yourself.'[8] From one angle, Sarah Mallett was unusual in assuming public responsibilities as a female, but from another she was only following out what seemed to her the imperatives of the evangelical message.

Traditional gender roles tended to reassert themselves as the heat of the early revivals cooled. In America, the War for Independence opened an opportunity for Baptist and other hitherto marginalized evangelical men to take part in the era's momentous political struggle. The result within the churches was to push women, along with men, back towards sex-segregated roles. For men to play a public political part meant to back away from the intense church communities that had bound the converted, both male and female, into intense spiritual fellowship.[9] In Britain, widespread reaction to the disruption of the French Revolution had a similar effect in reinforcing stronger distinctions between the roles of evangelical men and evangelical women.[10] The Wesleyan Conference, for example, decided in 1803 to prohibit female preaching.

The democratization of American society that occurred from the Revolution onwards allowed some room for evangelical women of all sorts to expand the scope of their spiritual activity. Among anti-formal, anti-establishmentarian

---

[6]   See the early sections of Valenze, *Prophetic Sons and Daughters*; and of Brekus, *Strangers and Pilgrims*.

[7]   *BDEB*, 737 (E. Dorothy Graham, 'Sarah Mallett').

[8]   Wesley to Sarah Mallet (as 'My Dear Sally'), 15 December 1789, in Wesley, *Letters*, 8:190.

[9]   Juster, *Disorderly Women*, 112–113 and *passim*.

[10] For the general situation, without specific reference to evangelicals, see Linda Colley, *Britons: Forging the Nation, 1707–1837* (New Haven: Yale University Press, 1992), 250–272.

evangelicals there arose a surprising number of active women preachers. As described recently in rich detail by Catherine Brekus, during the first four decades of the new century more than a hundred Methodists, Free-Will Baptists, Disciples of Christ and Cumberland Presbyterian women – white and black – left solid documentary record of their service as itinerating preachers or pastors.[11] This activity, however, soon faded away, sometimes helped along by increasingly formal attitudes from male leaders in the once radical denominations. But where this female preaching existed, it was a remarkable testimony to the ability of at least some evangelical groups to bend the boundaries of inherited expectations. Even among those where traditions prevailed, the rise of evangelicalism had begun a trajectory of female activity that would have only multiplying effects in the centuries to come.

Theology

The character of early evangelicalism as both a new movement of personal Christian experience and an ongoing expression of ancient Christian faith is seen most clearly in its theology.[12] For the most part, evangelicals stood with the great Christian traditions by taking for granted the authority of the Bible. Yet biblical authority came to mean more in the eighteenth century, since the weight of other ancient Christian authorities declined so rapidly for so many. When Francis Asbury died, he was eulogized with words that could have been spoken about most leaders of the new evangelical movements: 'The bible, to him, was the book of books, and his grand confession of faith. He was careful to regulate, all his religious tenets and doctrines, by the book of God, and to discard everything that was incompatible with the divine law and testimony.'[13] Soon in nineteenth-century evangelical history, questions of scriptural authority would receive more specific attention, as when

---

[11] Brekus, *Strangers and Pilgrims*.

[12] While there are many excellent studies on the theology of individual eighteenth-century evangelicals, especially Jonathan Edwards and John Wesley, the movement as a whole has not received sufficient attention for its contributions to the history of theology. For noteworthy exceptions, see Bebbington, *Evangelicalism*, 27–34; Alan P. F. Sell, *The Great Debate: Calvinism, Arminianism, and Salvation* (Grand Rapids: Baker, 1983), 59–98; and Allan Coppedge, *John Wesley in Theological Debate* (Wilmore: Wesley Heritage, 1987).

[13] Ezekiel Cooper, *The Substance of a Funeral Discourse ... on the Death of the Rev. Francis Asbury* (Philadelphia: Jonathan Pounder, 1819), 40.

evangelical strands differed in North America over whether it was necessary to affirm 'no creed but the Bible', in Britain over whether the Bible's truthfulness extended to each of its details, and in both regions over when and whether it was necessary to interpret the Bible literally.[14] Many early evangelicals were not at all reluctant to rely on dreams, visions and special words of counsel from the Holy Spirit, but these sources of divine knowledge were usually subordinated to broader understandings of the Bible. In the context of the eighteenth century, evangelicals stood with Arians, proto-liberals and anti-confessionalists in championing the Bible against tradition, but they stood with Christian traditionalists in affirming the Bible against reduced views of God, Christ and the Trinity.[15]

As it was with the Bible, so it was also with other doctrines of classical Christianity. Evangelicalism coloured and often invigorated doctrines like the divinity of Christ, the Trinity, the sinfulness of humanity and the human need for divine salvation. Very occasionally a strict scripturalist like the New Connexion Baptist Dan Taylor might complain about the absence of the word 'Trinity' in the Bible, but such complaints were rare.[16] In theology, as in their hymnody, evangelicals set themselves apart from Christian traditionalists by not emphasizing formal teachings concerning the church itself, earthly human hierarchy or the sacraments, each of which had galvanized great theological discussion since the time of the Reformation. What evangelicals did stress theologically – and so came to argue about as well – were the possibility of living a genuinely holy life and, supremely, the realities of divine grace in personal experience.

A fair bit of polemical theological debate did occur between evangelicals and proponents of other forms of Christianity, whether Jonathan Edwards against the New England critics of the Great Awakening, John Wesley against critics of many sorts who labelled Methodism 'enthusiasm', itinerating Anglicans and Nonconformists against establishmentarian critics who charged them with undermining social order, and several evangelicals in the era of the American Revolution against critics who described them as dangerous political radicals. But evangelicals reserved much of their most intense theological

[14] See Nathan O. Hatch, *The Democratization of American Christianity* (New Haven: Yale University Press, 1989), 41–42, 179–183; and Bebbington, *Evangelicalism*, 86–91.

[15] On the great weight given to the Bible by orthodox, non-Anglican traditionalists, see Gerard Reedy, SJ, *The Bible and Reason: Anglicans and Scripture in Late Seventeenth-Century England* (Philadelphia: University of Pennsylvania Press, 1985).

[16] Adam Taylor, *The History of the English General Baptists*, 2 vols (London: for the author, 1818), 2:471–472. My thanks to David Bebbington for this reference.

partisanship for intramural discussions with other evangelicals. That debate was often complicated by the fact that evangelicals took different approaches to doctrine itself, as noted in Chapter 4: systematic precision (often Calvinists), a narrower focus on soteriology (often Wesleyans and Arminians), an intentional neglect of doctrine in order to promote piety (often following the Moravians), or a willing acceptance of inherited doctrinal formulas (usually Anglicans or Presbyterians). The many intra-evangelical doctrinal disputes recorded in the pages above almost all involved differences in how best to do theology, as well as what theological principles needed to be defended.

Of self-conscious theological issues, questions of church order and baptism did not loom as large as questions of personal salvation, though the former were not trivial concerns. In America the sting of debate over establishment was drawn as evangelicals of all sorts eventually came to accept the separation of church and state. In Britain, by contrast, social crisis in response to the French Revolution kept alive a degree of intra-evangelical antagonism over whether to support, oppose or ignore the historic establishment of religion. Interest in that question would bulk large in England and Scotland throughout the nineteenth century and continue to be echoed in Ireland, Canada, Australia and South Africa as well. Evangelical differences also included debate about baptism – especially what it signified and who should receive it. In the eighteenth century, differences between paedobaptists (the overwhelmingly majority position) and proponents of baptism upon profession of faith were not nearly as important as they became when, in subsequent years, the number of Baptists and others holding to believers' baptism grew to make up a much larger proportion of evangelicalism.

For doctrinal controversy nothing in the eighteenth century was as important, or has survived over the centuries since with more force, than the questions about personal salvation that are usually described as pitting Calvinists against Arminians. Without playing down the importance of such differences, however, it is important from a perspective in the early twenty-first century to recognize the substantial degree of theological agreement among all but a few of the first evangelicals. Almost all, that is, believed in original sin (humans by nature were lost in a rebellion against God that was both generally inherited and personally affirmed). They believed as well in justification by faith (humans were redeemed by an act of faith when they relied upon what God accomplished for needy sinners in the person and work of Jesus Christ). They believed in the substitutionary atonement (Christ on the cross paid the penalty for sinners). And they affirmed sanctification in and through the power of the Holy Spirit (the same divine grace that brought initial salvation in Christ sustained, encouraged and enabled believers to grow in grace). Only a few evangelicals in only a few specific eighteenth-century locations would have disagreed: perhaps some of New England's Free-Will Baptists on the fact of original sin, perhaps a few Presbyterian seceders in Scotland on the liveliness of personal faith required for justification, perhaps Andrew Fuller and a few New England theologians by the end of the century on the character of Christ's substitution. Sometimes, to be sure, it took the passage of time for the broad commonality of theological affirmation to be noticed. But as one of many possible examples, it is possible to cite the *Biblical Repertory and Princeton Review* from the middle of the next century. Although this American journal gave way to no-one in its thorough Calvinism, it could also offer a positive view of eighteenth-century Wesleyans, who, in the author's strongly Reformed opinion, had properly affirmed

> Man's ruin by the fall; his native depravity and alienation from God; his absolute need of a Saviour, and utter inability to save himself; the necessity of regeneration by the Holy Spirit; justification, not by works, but by faith alone in the blood and righteousness of Jesus; the free offer of salvation to every human being, without money and without price; the necessity of holiness, not to merit heaven, but to become meet for it – these articles constituted the very burden of their preaching.[17]

Even with commonalities duly noted, it remains the case that Calvinist–Arminian discord provided flash-points for the period's most intense theological arguments. Jonathan Edwards' landmark writings can be described as focusing on the beautiful harmony of God's glory, but in writing aimed at promoting that end his articulate defence of traditionally Calvinist views was always prominent. Similarly, John Wesley's defence of Arminian notions was intended to promote the practice of a lively faith, yet defend them he did. On such issues, evangelicals in the eighteenth century aligned themselves more or less with Edwards' positions, more or less with Wesley's, or – by a deliberate act of theological moderation – more or less in between.

Although the divisive issues were not new, concentration during times of revival and awakening on the vitality of divine grace gave these issues a distinctive eighteenth-century colouring. With Wesleyans in the lead, the era's Arminians affirmed

- that God's grace in Christ opened a path to salvation for all;
- that God's prevenient grace (an enabling grace that came before justifying grace) mercifully restored 'free will' to every human being;

---

17 Anonymous, 'Annals of the American Pulpit', *Biblical Repertory and Princeton Review* 33 (July 1861): 507.

- that the same 'free will' by which humans could choose God allowed them as believers to fall from salvation;[18] and
- that fellowship in the Holy Spirit could lead on to Christian perfection in this life.

The Arminianism of these assertions differed from the views of Jacob Arminius (1560–1609) and the Remonstrants who, with him, protested against the Dutch Calvinists of their day, because its driving force was not so much intellectual problems with Calvinist doctrine as what the Wesleys and other non-Calvinists of the eighteenth century took to be the actual experiences of the Christian life.

Calvinists offered learned defences of the positions Arminians denied, and writers on all sides tried to show how their interpretations squared with the most consistent interpretations of Scripture. During one of the early episodes of theological disagreement, George Whitefield described his Calvinistic opinions in a letter to John Wesley with a succinctness more characteristic of Wesley than of himself: 'Though I hold to particular election, yet I offer Jesus freely to every individual soul. You may carry sanctification to what degrees you will, only I cannot agree with you that the in-being of sin is to be destroyed in this life.'[19] Calvinist objections to Christian perfection were probably more extensive than to any other aspect of distinctively Wesleyan teaching.

From the middle decades of the century, Calvinist–Arminian debates flared up regularly. Whitefield and Wesley had established the terms of debate in 1740–1741 for much that followed. In 1755 the evangelical Anglican clergyman, James Hervey (1714–1758), published *Theron and Aspasio*, a series of dialogues that defended a Calvinist view of imputation (God first 'reckoned' all sinners as spiritually dead in Adam and then 'reckoned' the elect as spiritually alive in Christ). In response, Wesley fired back with *A Preservative Against Unsettled Notions in Religion* (1758), in which he suggested that strong notions of imputation turned Calvinists into passive antinomians who neglected the disciplines of active Christian life.

The next major clash took place in 1770, when, at their annual conference, Wesleyans revisited earlier decisions and this time came out sounding much more polemical; for example: 'We have received it as a maxim, that "a man is to do nothing in order to justification" [*sic*]. Nothing can be more false.

---

[18] Quotation marks around 'free will' are used to indicate that Calvinists like Jonathan Edwards also affirmed 'free will', but took the phrase to mean an ability to act in accordance with one's own choices, rather than the power to choose in an unprejudiced way between multiple options.

[19] Whitefield to Wesley, 10 October 1741; in Tyerman, *Wesley*, 1:349.

Whoever desires to find favour with God should "cease from evil, and learn to do well" … [Salvation is] not by the *merit* of works, but by works as a *condition*.[20] This apparent affirmation of salvation by works led to consternation among Calvinists, even after Wesley admitted that the minutes were extreme. The Countess of Huntingdon had the offending document burned, an act of intemperance matched in 1776 when that year's Wesleyan Conference asserted that the greatest hindrance to God's work in Britain was the Calvinist expression of Christian faith.[21] Literary fallout from the 1770 incident included fervently anti-Arminian works from Augustus M. Toplady as well as a thoughtful defence of a more moderate Wesleyanism from John Fletcher of Madeley. Fletcher's serially published *Checks to Antinomianism* (1770ff.) provided a thorough defence, but also a clarification of Wesley's teachings; for example,

> what he calls perfection is nothing but the rich cluster of all the spiritual blessings promised to believers in the Gospel; and, among the rest, a continual sense of the virtue of Christ's atoning and purifying blood, preventing both old guilt from returning and new guilt from fastening upon the conscience; together with the deepest consciousness of our helplessness and nothingness in our best estate, the most endearing discoveries of the Redeemer's love, and the most humbling and yet ravishing views of his glorious fullness.[22]

Fletcher's *Checks* provided several generations of Wesleyans, as well as a number of irenic Calvinists, with an unusually attractive statement of Methodist theology.

After the fireworks of the early 1770s, division between Calvinists and Arminians quieted. In America, as we have seen, the students of Jonathan Edwards were moderating his Calvinist views in the direction of the republican and Enlightenment values of the American Revolution, and Presbyterians were distracted from theology by the imperatives of political and ecclesiastical crises. Baptists were probably the ablest American Calvinists in the last decades in the eighteenth century, but many of them were more taken up with the struggle for religious freedom than for doctrinal purity. In both America and Britain, the most visible evangelical leaders by the end of the century deliberately sought to moderate earlier extremes. Thus, Isaac Backus among Baptists in America, Francis Asbury with American Methodists, moderately

---

[20] Wesleyan Conference minutes, quoted in Sell, *The Great Debate*, 68.

[21] Tyerman, *Wesley*, 3:228.

[22] Fletcher, 'The First Check to Antinomianism' (1770), in Thomas A. Langford (ed.), *Wesleyan Theology: A Sourcebook* (Durham, NC: Labyrinth, 1984), 28.

Calvinistic Anglicans like John Newton and Charles Simeon, English lay leaders like Hannah More and William Wilberforce, and Scottish evangelicals like John Erskine were more concerned about promoting active Christian faith than with vanquishing other evangelicals who differed with them on fine points of theology. In later periods of evangelical history, Calvinist–Wesleyan polemics would flare again, but the attitude of the late-century moderates would be more characteristic.

The most important theological monuments of eighteenth-century evangelicalism were the works of Edwards, the works of John Wesley and the central hymnody of the movement, to which Arminians like Charles Wesley, stiff Calvinists like Toplady and moderates like William Williams and John Newton all contributed. The hymns, as we see below, focused on the work of Christ as understood through the main narratives of the Bible. Edwards, in works like *Freedom of Will* (1754) and *The End for Which God Created the World* (posthumously, 1765), excelled at the meticulous articulation of the metaphysics and the psychology of human life transformed by the grace of God. Wesley, especially in his *Standard Sermons* (many from the 1730s and 1740s), excelled in pithy and direct exposition of the biblical themes of salvation. They and the broader theological traditions they represented have never been fully reconciled within evangelical history. In one of his few references to English Methodism, Edwards wondered if 'the followers of the Wesleys', were not lost in 'follies' that included 'false religion, counterfeit conversions, and the want of a genuine renovation of the spirit of their minds'.[23] For his part, Wesley took care to edit out as much Calvinism as he possibly could when he reprinted Edwards' works for his *Christian Library*.

Yet the trajectories marked out by the landmark works of these two pastor-theologians sustained a significant degree of confluence. Nothing, for example, in Wesley contradicted Edwards' climactic statement from his *Treatise Concerning Religious Affections* (1746) about what it meant to live as a Christian: 'Gracious and holy affections have their exercise and fruit in Christian practice. I mean, they have that influence and power upon him who is the subject of 'em, that they cause that a practice, which is universally conformed to, and directed by Christian rules, should be the practice and business of his life.'[24] Similarly, nothing in Edwards contradicted the peroration of Wesley's early signature sermon, 'The Almost Christian': 'May we all thus experience what it

---

[23] Edwards to John Erskine, 5 July, 1750, in Edwards, *Works*, vol. 16: *Letters and Personal Writings*, ed. George S. Claghorn (1998), 349.

[24] Edwards, *A Treatise Concerning Religious Affections* (1746), in Edwards, *Works*, vol. 2, ed. John E. Smith (1959), 383.

is to be not almost only, but altogether Christians! Being justified freely by his grace, through the redemption that is in Jesus, knowing we have peace with God through Jesus Christ, rejoicing in hope of the glory of God, and having the love of God shed abroad in our hearts by the Holy Ghost given unto us!'[25] Commonality lay, above all, in their shared trust in the active power of the Christian gospel.

Hymns

That shared trust was seen nowhere more clearly than in the hymns that evangelicals wrote and sang. For the early generations, hymn-singing was almost sacramental. It was the most physical activity that all evangelicals shared, just as it was the single experience that bound them most closely to each other. In fact, it is difficult to discover any significant event, person or structure of early evangelicalism that did not involve the singing of hymns. It is likewise difficult to discover any significant experience of singing where the hymns had not been freshly written by the evangelicals themselves (or by their friend and supporter, Isaac Watts). Venue, time, social locale and place hardly made a difference. Whether the early revivals in Northampton, Massachusetts, the Wesleys' ministry in Georgia, the white-hot meetings of pentecostal intensity in London during 1738 and 1739, the itinerant preaching of Whitefield, Wesley and so many others, the society meetings in all forms of Methodism, the gatherings of redeemed ex-slaves in South Carolina or Nova Scotia or Sierra Leone, the Sunday schools from the 1770s, the social gatherings at Clapham, the ships that carried evangelical missionaries overseas – all were marked by the robust singing of mostly new evangelical hymns. These hymns, moreover, constituted for almost all evangelical groups what John Wesley wrote in 1780 about his landmark *Collection of Hymns for the Use of the People Called Methodists* – 'in effect a little book of experimental and practical divinity ... [a] distinct and full ... account of scriptural Christianity'.[26]

The hymns of the early evangelical movement proclaimed a rich understanding of Christian faith, but also a somewhat restricted one.[27] Although most of

---

[25] Wesley, 'The Almost Christian' (first preached 1741), in Wesley, *Works* (new), vol. 1: *Sermons I: 1–33*, ed. Albert C. Outler (1984), 141.

[26] Wesley, *A Collection of Hymns for the Use of the People Called Methodists* (1780), in Wesley, *Works* (new), vol. 7, ed. Franz Hildebrandt and Oliver A. Beckerlegge (1983), 74.

[27] The next paragraphs follow in paths pioneered by Stephen A. Marini, 'Rehearsal for Revival: Sacred Songs and the Great Awakening in America', *Journal of the American*

the major hymnwriters of the eighteenth century composed verses on the nature of the church, the sacraments of baptism and communion, the victory of Christ at the end of time and the particular convictions of their own sub-groups, the hymns that were sung widely, that were reprinted time after time, and that won their way deep into the heart of popular evangelicalism did not concern these divisive subjects. Rather, the enduring hymns featured the need of sinners for Christ the saviour, the love of God in Christ, the redeeming power of Christ, the refuge and healing found in Christ, the joy of redemption in Christ and the hope of eternal life in Christ. All efforts to illustrate the themes of the most popular evangelical hymns must be arbitrary, but Stephen Marini's catalogue of the hymns that were most often reprinted across the evangelical spectrum has made possible a greater degree of specificity. One of Marini's lists drawn from eighty-six Protestant hymnals published in North America from 1737 to 1860 illustrates the strong bonds that religious song constructed across the Atlantic, for the vast majority of these hymns were composed by English authors of the eighteenth century. Even more importantly, the texts of the most often reprinted hymns in this list illustrate forcefully the character of evangelical faith, or at least the depictions of this faith that ordinary evangelicals chose to sing about in many different places and through many decades.[28]

Academy of Religion – Thematic Studies 50 (1983): 71–91; 'Evangelical Hymns and Popular Belief', *Dublin Seminar for New England Folklife: Annual Proceedings* 21 (1996): 117–126; and especially 'Hymnody as History: Early Evangelical Hymns and the Recovery of American Popular Religion', *Church History* 71 (June 2002): 273–306.

[28] The eleven most often reprinted hymns (there was a tie for tenth place) in this Marini catalogue ('Hymnody as History', 280) included four by Isaac Watts ('Come, we that love the Lord' ['Come, we'], 'Am I a soldier of the cross' ['Am I'], 'When I can read my title clear' ['When title'], and 'He dies the friend of sinners' ['He dies']), two by the Methodist-become-Moravian John Cennick ('Jesus, my all, to heaven is gone' ['Jesus'] and 'Children of the heavenly king' ['Children']), one each by the Cambridge Baptist Robert Robinson ('Come, thou fount of every blessing' ['Come, thou fount']), Charles Wesley ('Blow ye the trumpet, blow' ['Blow']), the London Baptist Samuel Stennett ('On Jordan's stormy banks I stand' ['Jordan']), and the maverick Methodist Edward Perronet ('All hail the power of Jesus' name' ['All hail']), and one anonymous hymn from the influential *Collection* by the London Baptist John Rippon from 1787 ('How firm a foundation' ['How firm']). Short titles are for references in the text. Hymns are quoted here from *The Baptist Hymnal for Use in the Church and Home*, ed. W. Howard Doane (Philadelphia: American Baptist Publication Society, 1883); *The Methodist Hymnal* (Baltimore, et al.: Methodist Publishing House, 1939); and *Trinity Hymnal* (Philadelphia: Orthodox Presbyterian Church, 1961).

If the popular hymns shied away from some controversial subjects, they were not in the least timorous about affirming the full sinfulness of humanity and the desperate need for a redeemer.

> My grief a burden long has been,
> Because I was not saved from sin.
> The more I strove against its power,
> I felt its weight and guilt the more;
> Till late I heard my Saviour say,
> 'Come hither soul, I am the way.'
> (Cennick, 'Jesus')

Realism about the sinful state continued after conversion, for even those who believed in Christian perfection did not deny the power of human corruption:

> Nothing but sin have I to give:
> Nothing but love shall I receive.
> (Cennick, 'Jesus')

More generally, the life of faith was regarded as a battle requiring constant divine support:

> Prone to wander, Lord, I feel it,
> Prone to leave the God I love;
> Here's my heart, O take and seal it,
> Seal it for thy courts above.
> (Robinson, 'Come, thou fount')

In almost all evangelical hymns the love of God in Christ for ordinary women and men was central, which is why so many of the hymns of Isaac Watts were so popular for so long.

> He dies! – the Friend of sinners dies;
> Lo! Salem's daughters weep around:
> A solemn darkness veils the skies;
> A sudden trembling shakes the ground.
>
> Here's love and grief beyond degree:
> The Lord of glory dies for men!
> But lo! what sudden joys we see, –
> Jesus, the dead, revives again! ...

> Break off your tears, ye saints, and tell
> How high our great Deliverer reigns;
> Sing how he spoiled the hosts of hell;
> And led the tyrant Death in chains.
> (Watts, 'He dies')

For the work of God on behalf of sinners, the merits of Christ's death were central, whether for the Baptist Robert Robinson:

> Jesus sought me when a stranger,
> Wand'ring from the fold of God:
> He, to rescue me from danger,
> Interposed his precious blood.
> (Robinson, 'Come, thou fount')

or the Methodist Charles Wesley:

> Jesus, our great High Priest,
> Hath full atonement made.
> (Wesley, 'Blow')

Many of the hymns depicted joyful responses to the work of God more than detailed description of it:

> Sinners! whose love can ne'er forget
> The wormwood and the gall,
> Go – spread your trophies at His feet,
> And crown Him Lord of all.
> (Perronet, 'All hail')

> Blow ye the trumpet, blow!
> The gladly solemn sound
> Let all the nations know,
> To earth's remotest bound:
> The year of jubilee is come;
> Return, ye ransomed sinners, home.
> (Wesley, 'Blow')

> The men of grace have found
> Glory begun below;
> Celestial fruits on earthly ground

From faith and hope may grow.
(Watts, 'Come, we')

Come, thou Fount of every blessing,
Tune my heart to sing thy grace;
Streams of mercy, never ceasing,
Call for songs of loudest praise.
(Robinson, 'Come, thou fount')

The hymns also say much about the life of faith, and in realistic terms. In response to the question whether 'I' should 'be carried to the skies/On flowery beds of ease', the answer was unequivocal:

Sure I must fight if I would reign:
Increase my courage, Lord;
I'll bear the toil, endure the pain,
Supported by thy Word.
(Watts, 'Am I')

The standard expectation was that life would be difficult, but also that God-in-Christ would make it possible to endure with hope.

Fear not, brethren; joyful stand
On the borders of your land;
Jesus Christ, your Father's Son,
Bids you undismayed go on.
(Cennick, 'Children')

When through fiery trials thy pathway shall lie,
My grace, all sufficient, shall be thy supply;
The flame shall not hurt thee; I only design
Thy dross to consume and thy gold to refine.
(Rippon, 'How firm')

The end in view, repeated in many hymns, was an eternal life of joy and peace gained through final identification with Jesus Christ:

Jesus, my all, to heaven is gone,
He whom I fix my hopes upon;
His track I see, and I'll pursue
The narrow way, till Him I view.

The way the holy prophets went,
The road that leads from banishment,
The King's highway of holiness,
I'll go, for all His paths are peace.
(Cennick, 'Jesus')

Fixation on heaven was strong in the most popular evangelical hymns, but not so strong as to obscure the path that believers took before the end.

The soul that on Jesus hath leaned for repose,
I will not, I will not desert to his foes;
That soul, though all hell should endeavour to shake,
I'll never, no, never, no, never, forsake.
(Rippon, 'How firm')

On Jordan's stormy banks I stand,
And cast a wistful eye
To Canaan's fair and happy land
Where my possessions lie.
O the transporting, rapturous scene
That rises to my sight!
Sweet fields arrayed in living green,
And rivers of delight.
(Stennett, 'Jordan')

When I can read my title clear
To mansions in the skies,
I bid farewell to every fear,
And wipe my weeping eyes.
(Watts, 'When title')

A few other themes were adumbrated in these hymns; for example, the reliability of Scripture: 'How firm a foundation ... Is laid for your faith in his excellent Word!' (Rippon, 'How firm'). But for the most part, the hymns that were most often reprinted held to their narrow focus on the great acts of redemption that disturbed complacent sinners, turned them with longing to Christ, encouraged them in the life of faith and joined them to Christ eternally.

Hymn-singing was one of the strongest transcultural as well as transatlantic evangelical activities. It also provided one of the most important bridges between the classes and the races. Samuel Davies in America, for example, took a particular pleasure from the fact that converted African Americans and Indians became adept at singing hymns he had written himself as well as other hymns of the evangelical revival. In 1756, he informed a British correspondent that, after the welcome reception of some hymnals sent by the Wesleys from England, 'Sundry of them ["the *poor Slaves*"] have lodged all night in my kitchen; and, sometimes, when I have awaked about two or three o-clock in the morning, a torrent of sacred harmony poured into my chamber, and carried my mind away to Heaven. In this seraphic exercise, some of them spend almost the whole night.'[29]

Hymns were also one of the few means open to women for the public expression of their faith. Although there were not too many women hymnwriters, the English Baptist Ann Steele (1716–1779) and the Welsh Calvinistic Methodist Ann Griffiths (1776–1805) were forerunners of what later became a full ensemble of productive author-composers.

Ann Steele, who was permanently injured by a fall from a horse when she was just a teenager, enjoyed anything but an easy life.[30] Yet she wrote persistently about Christian confidence in God and eventually published three volumes of sacred poetry. Her most poignant verse was occasioned by the tragic drowning of her fiancé only hours before their wedding:

> Father, whate'er of earthly bliss
> Thy sovereign will denies,
> Accepted at thy throne of grace,
> Let this petition rise: –
> Give me a calm, a thankful heart,
> From every murmur free;
> The blessings of thy grace impart,
> And make me live to thee.[31]

Ann Griffiths, whose memory for Scripture and sermons was phenomenal, composed hymns that she recited to her household. After she died giving

---

[29] From *Letters from the Rev. Samuel Davies, etc. Shewing the State of Religion in Virginia, Particularly among the Negroes* (London, 1757), 16, as quoted by George William Pilcher, 'Samuel Davies and the Instruction of Negroes in Virginia', *Virginia Magazine of Biography and History* 74 (July 1966): 298.

[30] For introductions, see Vinita Hampton Wright, 'Anne Steele (Theodosia)', *Christian History* ('The Golden Age of Hymns'), no. 31 (1991): 22; and *BDEB*, 1046 (Karen E. Smith, 'Anne Steele').

[31] *Baptist Hymnal* (1883), no. 374.

birth to her first child, one of her servants repeated those hymns to her husband, who wrote them down and saw them published. They made unusually full use of biblical imagery, as in these verses describing Jesus and his work in terms of the 'tent of meeting' and the 'Presence' of God taken from the history of ancient Israel:

> Sinner is my name and nature,
> Fouler none on earth can be;
> In the Presence here – O wonder! –
> God receive me tranquilly;
> See him there, his law fulfilling,
> For his foes a banquet laid,
> God and man 'Enough!' proclaiming
> Through the offering he has made.
>
> Boldly I will venture forward;
> See the golden sceptre shine;
> Pointing straight towards the sinner;
> All may enter by that sign.
> On I'll press, beseeching pardon,
> On, till at his feet I fall,
> Cry for pardon, cry for washing
> In the blood which cleanses all.[32]

Hymns also possessed an almost magical power to smooth over the often sharp theological differences that emerged within the evangelical movement. No example of this power serves better than the very strained relationship between the Arminian Wesleys and the Anglican Calvinist Augustus M. Toplady (1740–1778). As we have seen, Toplady and the Wesleys were prime antagonists in a fresh bout of Arminian–Calvinist disputation beginning in the late 1760s. During this struggle, Toplady roundly denounced John Wesley and one of his colleagues, Walter Sellon, as perpetrators of the very heresies with which others had earlier befouled the church.[33] For his part, Wesley blasted right back. In a pamphlet pretending to give Toplady's view of the contested issues, Wesley parodied like this: 'One in twenty (suppose) of mankind are elected; nineteen in twenty are reprobated. The elect shall be

---

[32] A. M. Allchin, *Songs to Her God: Spirituality of Ann Griffiths* (Cambridge, MA: Cowley, 1987), 100–101.

[33] Toplady, *Works* (1794 edition), 280, 47, as cited in Sell, *The Great Debate*, 123, n. 36.

saved, do what they will: The reprobate shall be damned, do what they can. Reader, believe this, or be damned. Witness my hand, A—— T——.'[34]

Toplady and Charles Wesley were fully up to the challenge of putting this kind of acerbic theological exchange into verse. One of the hymns Toplady published during this time of theological strife was entitled 'Arminianism Renounced'; it began with what Toplady took to be the typical Arminian effort to make human works the key to salvation:

> How have I proudly scorn'd to stoop,
> And cried the Pow'rs of Nature up,
> And trusted to my legal Deeds![35]

Earlier Charles Wesley had written a hymn about the Calvinist doctrine of the decrees of God, which John Wesley reprinted in the *Arminian Magazine* not long after his own fierce polemic against Toplady. It included much that left no doubt about the Wesleys' opinion on the divine decrees, including this stanza:

> Still shall the *Hellish Doctrine* stand?
> And Thee for its dire Author claim?
> No – let it sink at thy Command
> Down to the Pit from whence it came.[36]

In short, the antagonism between the Wesleys and Toplady was almost as sharp, and as fundamentally theological, as one could imagine. And yet not too many years after Toplady first published the hymn he called 'A Living and Dying Prayer for the Holiest Believer in the World', which he intended as a frontal attack on the Wesleyan doctrine of Christian perfection, Methodist hymnals had joined the hymnals of almost all other evangelicals in reprinting it:

> Rock of Ages, cleft for me,
> Let me hide myself in Thee!
> Let the Water and the Blood,

---

[34] Wesley, *The Doctrine of Absolute Predestination Stated and Asserted. By the Reverend Mr. A—— T——* (1770), in Wesley, *Works* (1872), 14:198.

[35] Augustus M. Toplady, *Hymns and Sacred Poems, on a Variety of Subjects* (London: Daniel Segwick, 1860), 149.

[36] Frank Baker (ed.), *Representative Verse of Charles Wesley* (New York: Abingdon, 1962), 31.

From Thy riven Side which flow'd,
Be of Sin the double Cure,
Cleanse me from its Guilt and Pow'r.[37]

Similarly, hymnals of all evangelical varieties – militantly Calvinist, militantly Arminian, and at all points in between – just as eagerly reprinted the Marseille Hymn of Methodism, which appeared as the first entry in all of the Wesleys' later hymnbooks and described the work of salvation in terms remarkably similar to Toplady's:

O for a thousand tongues to sing
My dear Redeemer's praise!
The glories of my God and King,
The triumphs of his grace! ...

He breaks the power of cancelled sin,
He sets the prisoner free;
His blood can make the foulest clean –
His blood availed for me.[38]

Although much did divide evangelicals from each other, hymnody served as a powerful ecumenical counterforce. It was precisely those themes in the hymns that spoke most directly of the sinner's experience of divine grace ('Let the water and the blood ... Cleanse me from [sin's] guilt and power'; 'His blood can make the foulest clean – His blood availed for me') that exerted the strongest unifying power.

Christian experience

In the last analysis, evangelicalism survived and, in some places, flourished because it provided effective spiritual resolution to the seeking hearts of men and women throughout the English-speaking world. Political, social, intellectual, economic, demographic and even military forces played a role in the rise of the movement, but evangelicals themselves would have uniformly affirmed that at the bottom of their religion was a work of God that genuinely redirected lives, genuinely reoriented perspective, genuinely led on to lives of holiness.

---

[37] Toplady, *Hymns and Sacred Poems*, 163.
[38] Wesley, *A Collection of Hymns*, 79–80.

Evangelicalism was not particularly new as a theological movement or as a political force, or even as a method for coping with personal crises. It was new in what it claimed for the power of God in creating and sustaining authentic religious existence.[39]

Books like this one that try to chart the general course of eighteenth-century evangelicalism inevitably devote much attention to public figures like George Whitefield, the Wesleys, Jonathan Edwards, John Newton and Hannah More. But evangelicalism endured as a potent force in church and society mostly because its themes, emphases, preaching, visions of holiness and characteristic habits of mind informed the lives of ordinary men, women and children. Hearing from a few of them is, thus, a fitting way to conclude a chapter on the ideal of true religion that drove the evangelical movements.

Martha Claggett was an older wife and mother when she first came into contact with Methodist preachers.[40] At the time that she penned a spiritual autobiography around 1740, she had already borne eleven children, with the pains of childbirth becoming more unbearable each time. She had also suffered through intermittent illness, had been depressed to the point of considering suicide, had at least once contemplated an abortion and was regularly overwhelmed with the duties of managing a large household. In the autobiography she related that as a young person she had often read the Bible, but also that this habit fell away in favour of dancing and 'the vanities of the world'. After she had the chance to hear George Whitefield, who 'told me of Original Sin and man's fallen estate [and] … talk'd of a new Birth and Change of Nature', Martha Claggett began to revive. She 'delighted in singing hymns when I was sure no one heard me' and she resolved to break old habits of worldliness. Yet spiritual satisfaction remained elusive until personal counsel with the Wesleys pointed her to the fact that Christ's love extended to her as

---

[39] For solid help with a surprisingly neglected subject, see D. Bruce Hindmarsh, 'The Olney Autobiographers: English Conversion Narrative in the Mid-Eighteenth Century', *Journal of Ecclesiastical History* 49 (January 1998): 61–84; Hindmarsh, '"My chains fell off, my heart was free": Early Methodist Conversion Narrative in England', *Church History* 68 (December 1999): 910–929; Hindmarsh, 'Reshaping Individualism: The Private Christian, Eighteenth-Century Religion and the Enlightenment', in Deryck W. Lovegrove (ed.), *The Rise of the Laity in Evangelical Protestantism* (London: Routledge, 2002), 67–84; and James M. Gordon, *Evangelical Spirituality from the Wesleys to John Stott* (London: SPCK, 1991), 11–110.

[40] This account is from Hindmarsh, 'Reshaping Individualism', 72–73, which draws on a manuscript letter in 'Early Methodist Volume', John Rylands University Library, Manchester.

an individual. After praying, thinking and singing, she began to say, '*My* Lord and *My* God.' And then in the middle of a night early in July 1738, she awoke 'in such joy as I never felt before, my Heart overflow'd with the love of God, the Spirit bearing witness that I was the Child of God, and I could not keep [from] joining the immortal choir in their hallelujahs'. Here the narrative breaks off. Martha Claggett, who went on to significant service with the Moravians, was joining those for whom Christianity had moved from the realm of inherited beliefs to the sphere of experimental faith.

Two of the individuals affected by the events at Cambuslang, Scotland, in 1742 were fifty-year-old Bailie Weir and his twenty-eight-year-old wife (identified only as 'Mrs Weir') from Hamilton, just to the south of Cambuslang. Their accounts of what it meant to experience William McCulloch's preaching and then the communion seasons presided over by George Whitefield take on added interest since they seem to have been recorded at least two years or more after that memorable season.[41] Both Weirs were religious folk, but from a perspective on the other side of Cambuslang they looked back upon their earlier lives as only nominal in belief:

> I attended church mainly from custom. I was at the same time fond of idle company, and given to card-playing and drinking even to excess ... I had the advantage of being brought up religiously, was taught to pray twice a-day, and this I have continued ... and the general consistency of my conduct induced the belief that I was in a good way.

But then in February the couple travelled to Cambuslang to hear McCulloch preach on 2 Corinthians 5:17 ('If any man be in Christ, he is a new creature: old things are passed way; behold, all things are become new'), after which they were in turmoil of soul. For Mr Weir the break came in contemplating Isaiah 45:22 ('Look unto me, and be ye saved, all the ends of the earth; for I am God, and there is none else') and 1 John 1:7 ('The blood of Jesus Christ his Son cleanseth us from all sin'). For Mrs Weir there were more steps forward (including the singing of psalms) and then back, until she took to heart another one of McCulloch's texts from 1 John (this time from 5:10: 'He that believeth on the Son hath the witness in himself: he that believeth not God hath made him a liar; because he believeth not the record that God gave of his Son'). Life was not thereafter a spiritual paradise, but Mr Weir could none the less write that 'ever since that time all things seem new', and Mrs Weir could testify that 'I see a

---

[41] The narratives are from D. Macfarlan (ed.), *The Revivals of the Eighteenth Century, Particularly at Cambuslang* (Edinburgh: Johnston & Hunter, 1847), 173–177.

glory in Christ, and a suitableness to all my wants, and I feel resigned to his will, so that I even sometimes desire to be absent from the body, that I may be for ever with the Lord.' A striking feature of their narratives is how readily a life-time of familiarity with Scripture could be brought to the service of an intense period of evangelical conviction, struggle and reassurance.

Olaudah Equiano's *Interesting Narrative* of 1789 is an especially important document, both for its testimony to the literary abilities of an ex-slave and for its encouragement of anti-slavery and missionary efforts. Like *The Life Experience and Gospel Labors of the Rt. Rev. Richard Allen*, Equiano's *Narrative* is also significant for its window into the spiritual journey of its subject, which, however stylized and however influenced by the increasingly powerful con-ventions of evangelical autobiography, none the less testifies impressively to the broad appeal of the new gospel message. In his employment as a sailor Equiano had already travelled widely as a freed slave and had already sought out spiritual counsel from Quakers, Jews, Roman Catholics and a variety of Protestants before his own religious course was set. Coming under the influence of the new evangelical hymnody, like Robert Robinson's 'Come, thou fount of every blessing', reading Alleine's *Alarm to the Unconverted*, pon-dering biblical passages like Acts 4:12 ('Neither is there salvation in any other: for there is none other name under heaven given among men, whereby we must be saved') and attending the sermons of evangelical Anglicans, Methodists and Dissenters – all led up to the breakthrough on the night of 6 October 1774. As Equiano laboured in what he described as 'deep consterna-tion' over the question of whether he was to earn his salvation or accept it as a gift from God,

> the Lord was pleased to break in upon my soul with his bright beams of heavenly light; and in an instant, as it were, removing the veil, and letting light into a dark place (Isa. xxv.7). I saw clearly, with the eye of faith, the crucified Saviour bleeding on the cross on Mount Calvary: the Scriptures became an unsealed book; I saw myself a condemned criminal under the law, which came with its full force to my conscience ... I saw the Lord Jesus Christ in his humiliation, loaded, and bearing my reproach, sin, and shame.[42]

This vision of the suffering Christ convinced Equiano that he was 'a great debtor ... to sovereign free grace', since (referring to himself) 'the Ethiopian

---

[42] Equiano, *The Interesting Narrative of the Life of Olaudah Equiano, or Gustavus Vassa, the African. Written by Himself* (1789), in Adam Potkay and Sandra Burr (eds.), *Black Atlantic Writers of the 18th Century* (New York: St Martin's, 1995), 244.

was willing to be saved by Jesus Christ'.[43] After this experience Equiano resumed his career as a sailor but also became more active in his advocacy against slavery and his efforts to publicize the evils of African slave-trading. His *Narrative* closed with a defence of its publication based on the habit he had acquired of seeking to discern 'the hand of God in the minutest occurrence, and to learn from it a lesson of morality and religion; and in this light every circumstance I have related was, to me, of importance'. But of importance as defined by an evangelical ethos: 'After all, what makes any event important, unless by its observation we become better and wiser, and learn *to do justly, to love mercy, and to walk humbly before God?*'[44]

Almost as interesting in the annals of early evangelical biography as Equiano were the religious twists and turns of James Lackington (1746–1815).[45] Lackington was converted through Methodist preaching as a sixteen-year-old in 1762, and then underwent a series of vocational false starts. In 1774 a loan of £5 from John Wesley enabled him to start a small bookselling business. When he discovered the tactic of buying up publishers' overstocks and making these remainders available to the great population of London, Lackington struck it rich. Within less than two decades he was recognized as a wealthy man and described, in the words of the advertisement for an American edition of one of his books, as in 'the possession of probably the greatest book-store in the known world'.[46] Yet as Lackington became rich, he also became living proof of the dangers that all Methodists perceived in the tempting snares of worldliness. First it was spending more time reading 'novels, romances and poets' than Scripture or Christian books; then it was following the deist argument that, since 'the whole world was God's temple', it was not necessary always to be in church on Sunday. Finally Lackington abandoned Methodism altogether, promoted works by British free-thinkers and sceptical French *philosophes*, and poured a great deal of ribald scorn on his former religious friends in an autobiography published in 1792, *Memoirs of the First Forty-Five Years of the Life of James Lackington*. Yet soon thereafter, Lackington reconsidered. He was sobered by what seemed to be 'an universal deluge of vice and immorality' brought on by 'French philosophy and philosophes'. He was deeply impressed with a reading of William Paley's *Views of the Evidences of Christianity*. And he was won

---

[43] Ibid., 245.

[44] Ibid., 250–251.

[45] For orientation, see Hindmarsh, 'Reshaping Individualism', 77–78, 81.

[46] *The Confessions of J. Lackington, Late Bookseller, at the Temple of the Muses, in a Series of Letters to a Friend* (orig. 1804; New York: Ezekiel Cooper and John Wilson [general book stewards for the Methodist Connection in the United States], 1806), iii.

most of the way back to the Methodists. When in 1804 he published a second autobiography, the change of his reconverted heart, as well as a note of typical evangelical practicality, was indicated by his renewed affection for the Bible:

> There is the sublime and the beautiful ... the grandest description and the most august ideas of the Deity; the most perfect morality; the greatest motives to virtue, and the most awful denunciations against vice. In a word, in that book we are taught the way of holy living; and by so living we ensure to ourselves an eternal state of felicity in the realms of everlasting light and love.

Quite appropriately for a re-converted Methodist he closed this second auto-biography by quoting a Wesley hymn that, to Lackington, showed clearly 'the temper and spirit by which they are actuated': 'Christ, from whom all blessings flow,/Perfecting the saints below...'[47]

In Newport, Rhode Island, Samuel Hopkins confidently believed that his own congregation included several individuals, mostly women, who embodied all that it meant to be a true Christian.[48] Susanna Anthony (1726–1791) had been converted in 1741 and that same year joined the First Congregational Church of Newport, just as the fervour of the First Great Awakening was rising to its peak. After Hopkins moved to Newport in 1770, Anthony began exchanging letters with her pastor, who arranged to have some of these letters and extensive extracts from her journal published after her death. These writings reveal a precise Christian along historic Puritan lines, who battled throughout a long life against herself, her environment and her sense of sin. Anthony's conversion was noteworthy for the remarkable sense of personal struggle she felt with the devil: 'Satan was permitted to fill my mind with the most horrid blasphemies. He that had, but just before, tried to persuade me I was too young to be religious, now turned his temptation to persuade me it was too late.' Her release came through a sermon on Hebrews 7:25 ('Wherefore, he is able to save them to the uttermost, that come into God by him [Christ]'), which became the occasion for 'the Spirit of God [to] ... powerfully apply the texts to my soul. Thus, thus, infinitely lovely did Christ appear to me.' Yet combat with Satan continued for many years after she professed saving faith and joined the Newport church; to this spiritual struggle

---

[47] Ibid., 10, 15, 24, 35–36, 188. The hymn, on pages 188–189, is found in Wesley, *A Collection of Hymns*, 693–694.

[48] For another one of these parishioners, see Charles E. Hambrick-Stowe, 'The Spiritual Pilgrimage of Sarah Osborn (1714–1796)', *Church History* 61 (December 1992): 408–421; and the forthcoming work on Sarah Osborn by Catherine Brekus.

was joined, as well, significant difficulties with eating, sleep and spiritual temptation. At the age of twenty-eight in 1754, Anthony could write, 'I do now find an habitual disposition of soul to rest, in a measure, satisfied with all his [God's] dispensations to me.' But that contentment soon gave way to bouts of painful introspection, feelings of intense unworthiness, terror at thunder and lightning and many 'bodily disorders'. Anthony was the sixth child in a family of seven daughters; she never married, but cared for her parents until they died, and was noteworthy for many years in attending Newport's sick and dying. In his editorial introduction to her writings, Hopkins wrote that during Susanna Anthony's fifty years a church member, 'She appeared wholly, and in a distinguished degree, devoted to the cause of Christ and pure religion.'[49] The bodily anguish as well as the spiritual transports of Anthony's life were reminiscent of similar experiences from mystical Christian women of the late Middle Ages.[50] But to Hopkins it would have been much more pertinent that Anthony seemed to approach the high ideals of Christian life as outlined theologically by his mentor Jonathan Edwards and as exemplified spiritually in the heroic life of David Brainerd.

After John Wesley, Thomas Taylor (1738–1816) served longer as an active itinerant than any other early English Methodist.[51] Taylor's memoir does follow a convention adopted by many Wesleyan itinerants – succinctly described by Bruce Hindmarsh as 'conversion ... enters itinerancy ... other'.[52] But Taylor's 'other' was more than convention, since his career gave new meaning to the word 'peripatetic'. Taylor, who was born in the rural parish of Rothwell in Yorkshire, was orphaned when he was quite young, although he had a strong religious upbringing that included memorization of the Westminster Shorter Catechism by the age of four. While undergoing several onerous apprenticeships, he reported falling from early religious

---

[49] Quotations from Samuel Hopkins (ed.), *The Life and Character of Miss Susanna Anthony ... Consisting Chiefly in Extracts from Her Writings, With Some Brief Observations on Them* (Hartford: Hudson & Goodwin, 1799), 18, 30–31, 43, 143, 4. I thank Monica Cawvey for her seminar paper in 1997 that drew my attention to Anthony.

[50] See Caroline Walker Bynum, *Holy Feast and Holy Fast: The Religious Significance of Food to Medieval Women* (Berkeley: University of California Press, 1987).

[51] This account is from John Telford (ed.), *Wesley's Veterans: Lives of Early Methodist Preachers Told by Themselves*, vol. 7 (orig. 1837–1865; London: Robert Culley, 1912–1914), 7–126. Taylor lived so long that the account of his life in *Wesley's Veterans* was made up of two separate autobiographies (written c.1781 and c.1804) and extensive eulogies dating from shortly after his death.

[52] Hindmarsh, 'Early Methodist Conversion', 917.

interests: 'my mouth was fraught with oaths, lies, and deceit. I … soon became a dexterous gambler, especially at cards.' From about the age of seventeen he came under renewed spiritual impressions: hearing a sermon from Whitefield, reading Bunyan's *Pilgrim's Progress* and Alleine's *Alarm to the Unconverted*, attending services at an Independent chapel. Close to the age of twenty, during a period of direct combat with Satan that was exacerbated by his increasing efforts to pray and read the Bible, Taylor was transformed: 'While I was calling upon the Lord, He appeared to me in a wonderful manner, as with His vesture dipped in blood. I saw Him by the eye of faith, hanging on the cross; and the sight caused such love to flow into my soul that I believed that moment, and never since gave up my confidence.' Soon he felt called to preach, and began with great hesitancy to do so. His initial preju-dices against the Methodists gave way because of testimonies from Whitefield converts who vouched for the Wesleys' reliability. In 1761 he trav-elled to a Wesleyan annual conference and, without being grilled as he expected on his still mostly Calvinist convictions, Taylor was appointed to a circuit, and his course of ceaseless movement was on; several years in several different parts of Ireland and Scotland interspersed with annual or bi-annual relocations within England. During the course of this extraordinary life, he was attacked by a mob in Shropshire; several times he was delivered by special providence from the threat of death brought on by storms at sea, the collapse of a bridge, the stumbling of his horse; he mastered Latin, Greek and Hebrew as aids to his biblical study; he migrated in his theological beliefs from moderate Calvinistic to Wesleyan Arminian; he persevered in the face of antagonism ('Wales is not the most pleasing part of the world for a stranger to wander in. … [In Scotland] the winter was at hand; I was in a strange land; there was no society; no place of entertainment … I had trav-elled by land and by water near six hundred miles to this place; and behold my congregation [of] … two bakers' boys and two old women'); he published several of his sermons; he married, and endured the lengthy illnesses of his wife and children; he observed that evangelical religion spread best where trade was growing; he suffered from severe rheumatism for more than half of his adult life; after the death of John Wesley he became one of the first lay itinerants to be ordained and to offer the Lord's Supper; and always he tended to the nurture of local societies, and preached, preached, preached. What he preached was classic Methodism: 'I laboured to keep as clear as possible of controversy, dwelling chiefly upon repentance, faith, and the new birth.' Sometimes the seed fell on stony ground, sometimes into rich soil. On the English Birstall circuit in 1778–1779 conversions multiplied and societies flourished: 'Prayer-meetings were singularly useful, and so was the preaching; but thunder and lightning, dreams and visions, singing and praying, were all made use of for the awakening of sinners.'[53] And so it would go for nearly forty years more.

About the true religion that Thomas Taylor found and then gave his long life to proclaim there are many useful things to be said in relation to political uncertainties, economic opportunity, the developing infrastructures of British print and travel, the psychology of aspiration in the middle classes and the crises of traditional ecclesiastical ecology. But to understand Taylor and his situation – as also Martha Claggett, Mr and Mrs Weir, Olaudah Equiano, James Lackington and Susanna Anthony – their own accounts in their own words remain of first importance. Although autobiographies can deceive authors and readers in countless ways, they still offer the best place to ascertain what individuals concluded about the meaning of their own experience. An evangelical historian of evangelical history may be pardoned for his own conclusion that in many particulars they also sound like the truth.

---

[53] Taylor, Memoir, in *Wesley's Veterans*, 12, 30, 37, 39, 62.

AFTERWORD

Half a century after George Whitefield's strained conversation with the Anglican clergy of Boston, the exchange with which this book began, a similar dialogue occurred in Digby, Nova Scotia, but with very different results. Joseph Dimock (1768–1846), who had been touched by 'the New Light Stir' of Henry Alline and also encouraged by the itinerant preaching of the Methodist Freeborn Garrettson, had only shortly before begun to itinerate himself. With a number of other energetic young men, including Harris Harding, Edward Manning and James Manning, Dimock was preparing the way for what soon became a flourishing of Baptist churches in the Canadian Maritimes.[1] In July 1791, Dimock came to Digby, which is located on a sheltered inlet off the Annapolis Basin, where his preaching was welcomed by a group of Scottish immigrants. They invited Dimock to return, but before he could get back, the society at Digby 'heard that I was not a Collegiate, and so had not come into the ministry at the door'. Out of their concern that Dimock had not attended college or been properly ordained, the Scots followed genetic proclivity and appointed a committee to meet with the itinerant. When Dimock did return, he told the committee that what they heard was correct. In response, the committee asked 'by what authority [do] you do

---

[1] On this movement, see Daniel C. Goodwin, ' "The Faith of the Fathers": Evangelical Piety of Regular Baptist Patriarchs and Preachers, 1790–1855' (PhD dissertation, Queen's University, Kingston, Ont., 1997).

these things? … by what authority do you preach?' Dimock's reply was classically evangelical: 'I will gladly tell you. When first I was brought to an experimental knowledge of the truth I felt much concerned for those around me that appeared thoughtless and ignorant of salvation, as I had formerly been myself; and I often made some attempt to warn sinners to flee from the wrath to come, both in private and publicly.' To these words, the head of the committee expressed an equally evangelical approval: 'Sir, the state of the country calls loudly for teachers, which with your exercises on the subject, is a sufficient warrant, in my opinion, for you to preach … And now we shall be glad to hear you again this afternoon.' Then the chairman, since the larger group of Scots was not expecting to convene for another fifteen minutes, went on to request Dimock to tell the committee in greater detail about his own pilgrimage of faith. 'Here I gave a short account of my experience, which was heard with much affection.' In the wake of this exchange, Dimock preached regularly to this society, and 'I know of nothing that ever disturbed my harmony with these good folks afterwards'.[2]

By allowing authentic Christian experience to take precedence over inherited church order, the Baptist Joseph Dimock and the Digby Scots, probably Presbyterian-born, demonstrated that they were evangelical. The changes worked in the English-speaking world during the fifty-one years after Whitefield's Boston interview were no better illustrated than by what occurred when Joseph Dimock came to Digby. But by that time, the changes had affected almost the entire English-speaking world, and they were moving rapidly beyond its boundaries as well.

At its worst, this new evangelicalism neglected, caricatured and distorted the inherited traditions of Reformation Protestantism. Evangelical beliefs and practices could foster a self-centred, egotistic and narcissistic spirituality and also create new arenas for destructive spiritual competition. From in-group clichés, associations and institutions, evangelicals sometimes constructed new barriers to alienate humans from each other. They could turn so obsessively inward as to ignore the structures of social evil. Most importantly, evangelicals could trivialize the Christian gospel by treating it as a ballyhooed commodity to be hawked for its power to soothe a nervous, dislocated people in the opening cultural markets of the expanding British empire.

But at its best evangelicalism provided needed revitalization to English-speaking Protestant Christianity. It breathed vibrant religious life into stagnant or confused religious institutions. It created dynamic communities of self-

---

2 Extracts from the journal of Joseph Dimock, in George A. Rawlyk (ed.), *New Light Letters and Songs* (Hantsport, Nova Scotia: Lancelot, 1983), 284–285.

giving love and international networks of supporting fellowship. It reached out to many at the margins of respectable society. From authentic personal experience it provided a dynamism for addressing corporate evils. Most importantly, it communicated the beauty and the power of the Christian gospel in a wide variety of settings and through that gospel provided a wide range of individuals with purpose before God and meaning for this life, and it did so for the long haul.

Evangelicalism was never static or simply given. Right from the start, the energy that brought the movement into existence pushed on to further innovations, expanded the depth and breadth of its reach, suffered from countless mis-steps, divided into hotly competing fragments and entered into ever-new connections with the broader society. Always at the centre was engagement with the gospel. And the years from 1740 to 1795 were only the beginning.

SELECT BIBLIOGRAPHY

The resources for studying evangelical movements in the eighteenth century are vast beyond number. This bibliography features works that I used in the preparation of this volume, but it is also supplemented by a few other studies of special value for those who wish to pursue related subjects for their own purposes.

One hundred primary sources of the era

This list of primary sources constitutes a beginning point for works by eighteenth-century evangelicals. Publication information, except for date of first printing, is omitted, since these works are found in many different editions, on both sides of the Atlantic, and from the eighteenth century and later. The list also includes works by earlier figures whom evangelicals read with appreciation and a few works as well by their opponents. Out of deference to the titles presented in their extended eighteenth-century style, capitalization is minimized throughout.

Alleine, Joseph (1672), *Alarm to the unconverted.*
Allen, Richard (1833), *The life experience and gospel labors of the Rt. Rev. Richard Allen, To which is annexed the rise and progress of the African Methodist Episcopal Church in the United States of America.*
Allestree, Richard (1657), *The whole duty of man.*
Alline, Henry (1783), *The anti-traditionalist.*
— (1795), *Hymns and spiritual songs.*

Anthony, Susanna (1799), *The life and character of Miss Susanna Anthony ... Consisting chiefly in extracts from her writings, With some brief observations on them* (ed. Samuel Hopkins).

Arndt, Johann (1605–1610), *On true Christianity.*

Asbury, Francis (1792), *An extract of the journal of Francis Asbury ... 1771 to ... 1778.*

Backus, Isaac (1772), *A history of New-England with particular reference to the denominations of Christians called Baptists.*

— (1773), *An appeal to the public for religious liberty.*

Baxter, Richard (1650), *The saints' everlasting rest.*

Bellamy, Joseph (1750), *True religion delineated; or, Experimental religion, as distinguished from formality on the one hand, and enthusiasm on the other.*

Boston, Thomas (1720), *Human nature in its fourfold state.*

Bunyan, John (1666), *Grace abounding to the chief of sinners.*

— (1678, 1684), *Pilgrim's progress.*

Butler, Joseph (1736), *The analogy of religion, natural and revealed, to the constitution and course of nature.*

Carey, William (1792), *An enquiry into the obligations of Christians, to use means for the conversion of the heathens: In which the religious state of the different nations of the world, the success of former undertakings, and the practicability of other undertakings, are considered.*

Cennick, John (1745), *The life of J. Cennick: With an account of the trials and tribulations which he endured till it pleased our Saviour to shew him his love, and send him into his vineyard.*

— (1752), *Sacred hymns, for the use of religious societies.*

Chauncy, Charles (1743), *Seasonable thoughts on the state of religion.*

Clarkson, Thomas (1786), *Essay on the slavery and commerce of the human species.*

Coke, Thomas (1783), *A plan of the society for the establishment of missions among the heathen.*

Coke, Thomas, and Francis Asbury (1792), *The doctrines and discipline of the Methodist Episcopal Church in America.*

Cranz, David (1767), *The history of Greenland: Containing a description of the country, and its inhabitants, a relation of the mission carried on for above thirty years by the Unitas Fratrum,* ET.

Davies, Samuel (1757), *Letters from the Rev. Samuel Davies, etc. Shewing the state of religion in Virginia, particularly among the Negroes.*

— (1766), *Sermons on most useful and important subjects* (reprinted as *Sermons on important subjects*).

Dickinson, Jonathan (1742), *A display of God's special grace.*

— (1755), *Hymns founded on various texts of Scripture.*

Doddridge, Philip (1744), *The rise and progress of religion in the soul.*

Edwards, Jonathan (1737), *A faithful narrative of the surprizing work of God in the conversion of many hundred souls in Northampton, and the neighbouring towns and villages of New-Hampshire* [sic] *in New-England.*

— (1738), *Discourses on various important subjects, nearly concerning the great affair of the soul's eternal salvation ... Delivered at Northampton, chiefly at the time of the late wonderful pouring out of the Spirit of God there.*

— (1743), *Some thoughts concerning the present revival of religion in New England.*

— (1746), *A treatise concerning religious affections.*

— (1747), *An humble attempt to promote explicit agreement and visible union of God's people in extraordinary prayer for the revival of religion and the advancement of Christ's kingdom on earth.*

— (1754), *A careful and strict inquiry into the modern prevailing notion of that freedom of will, which is supposed to be essential to moral agency, vertue and vice, reward and punishment, praise and blame.*

— (1765), *Two Dissertations: I. Concerning the end for which God created the world. II. The nature of true virtue.*

Edwards, Jonathan (ed.) (1749), *The life of David Brainerd.*

Equiano, Olaudah (1789), *The interesting narrative of the life of Olaudah Equiano, or Gustavus Vassa, the African.*

Erskine, John (1743), *Signs of the times considered, Or the high probability that the present appearances in New England, and the West of Scotland, are a prelude of the glorious things promised to the church in the latter ages.*

— (1765), *Dissertation on the nature of Christian faith.*

Fisher, Edward (1645; reprinted 1718), *The marrow of modern divinity.*

Fletcher, John (1770–1775), *Checks to antinomianism.*

Fuller, Andrew (1785), *The gospel of Christ worthy of all acceptation.*

Gibson, Edmund (Bishop of London) (1744), *Observations upon the conduct and behaviour of a certain sect usually described by the name of Methodists.*

Gillies, John (1754), *Historical collections relating to remarkable periods of the success of the gospel, and eminent instruments employed in promoting it.*

Hall, Robert Sr (1781), *Help to Zion's travelers.*

Hervey, James (1755), *Theron and Aspasio.*

Hopkins, Samuel (1776), *A dialogue concerning the slavery of the Africans: Shewing it to be the duty and interest of the American colonies to emancipate all their African slaves: with an address to the owners of such slaves. Dedicated to the Honorable the Continental Congress.*

— (1793), *System of doctrine contained in divine revelation.*

Horne, Melville (1794), *Letters on missions.*

Horneck, Anthony (1681), *The happy ascetick ... Concerning the holy lives of the primitive Christians.*

Jarratt, Devereux (1806), *The life of the Reverend Devereux Jarratt ... written by himself.*

Kilham, Alexander (1795), *The progress of liberty among the people called Methodists.*

Lackington, James (1804), *The confessions of J. Lackington, late bookseller, at the Temple of the Muses, in a series of letters to a friend.*

Lavington, George (1749–1751), *The enthusiasm of Methodists and Papists compared.*

Law, William (1728), *A serious call to a devout and holy life.*

Lewis, John (1740–1748), *The Christian amusement containing letters concerning the progress of the gospel at home and abroad* (later renamed as *The weekly history: Or, an account of the most remarkable particulars relating to the present progress of the gospel. By the encouragement of the Rev.*

Mr. Whitefield; An Account of the most remarkable particulars relating to the present progress of the gospel; and *The Christian history or general account of the progress of the gospel in England, Wales, Scotland and America, as far as the Rev. Mr. Whitefield, his fellow labourers and assistants are concerned*), London.

McCullough, William (1741–1742), *The Glasgow-Weekly history relating to the progress of the gospel at home and abroad*, Glasgow.

Maurice, Matthias (1737), *A modern question modestly answered.*

Milner, Joseph (1800), *The history of the church of Christ.*

More, Hannah (1790), *An estimate of the religion of the fashionable world.*

Newton, John (1764), *An authentic narrative of some remarkable and interesting particulars in the life of ********.*

Newton, John, and William Cowper (1779), *Olney hymns.*

Prince, Thomas (1743–1745), *The Christian history: Containing accounts of the revival and propagation of religion in Great Britain and America*, Boston.

Ramsay, James (1784), *Essay on the treatment and conversion of African slaves in the British sugar colonies.*

Rippon, John (1787), *A selection of hymns from the best authors: Intended to be an appendix to Dr. Watts's psalms and hymns.*

Robe, James (1743–1746), *The Christian monthly history or an account of the revival and progress of religion abroad and at home*, Edinburgh.

Rowland, Daniel (1774), *Eight sermons upon practical subjects.*

Scougal, Henry (1691), *The life of God in the soul of man.*

Spangenberg, A. G. (1785), *Instructions for members of the Unitas Fratrum who minister in the gospel among the heathen.* ET.

— (1788), *An account of the manner in which the Protestant Church of the Unitas Fratrum, or United Brethren, preach the gospel and carry on their missions among the heathen.* ET.

Spener, Philip Jakob (1675), *Pia Desideria.*

Steele, Anne (1780), *Miscellaneous pieces: in verse and prose.*

Tennent, Gilbert (1740), *The danger of an unconverted ministry.*

Toplady, Augustus M. (1790), *Psalms and hymns for public and private worship.*

Venn, Henry (1763), *The complete duty of man: Or, A system of doctrinal and practical Christianity, designed for the use of families.*

Walker, Samuel (1755), *Fifty-two sermons.*

Watts, Isaac (1706, 1709), *Horae Lyricae: Poems chiefly of the lyric kind. In three books sacred.*

— (1707, 1709), *Hymns and spiritual songs.*

— (1719), *The psalms of David imitated in the language of the New Testament, and apply'd to the Christian state and worship.*

Wesley, John (1739–1791), *Journals.*

— (1743), *The nature, design, and general rules of the United Societies.*

— (1745), *An earnest appeal to men of reason and religion.*

— (1746), *Standard sermons.*

— (1754), *Explanatory notes upon the New Testament.*

— (1757), *The doctrine of original sin.*

— (1771), *Sermons on several occasions.*

— (1774), *Thoughts upon slavery.*

— (1775), *A calm address to our American colonies.*

— (1777), *A plain account of Christian perfection.*

Wesley, John, and Charles Wesley (1780), *A collection of hymns for the use of the people called Methodists.*

Wesley, Samuel (1700), *Letters concerning the religious societies.*

Wheatley, Phillis (1773), *Poems on various subjects, religious and moral.*

Whitefield, George (1739), *A sermon on regeneration, Preached to a numerous audience in England.*

— (1768), *A letter to the Reverend Dr. Durrell, Vice-Chancellor of the University of Oxford; Occasioned by a late expulsion of six students from Edmund-Hall.*

— (1772), *A select collection of letters of the late Reverend George Whitefield*, 3 vols.

Wilberforce, William (1797), *A practical view of the prevailing religious system of professed Christians in the higher and middle classes in this country, contrasted with real Christianity.*

Williams, William (1749), *Aleluia; neu, gascliad – hymnau.*

Witherspoon, John (1753), *Ecclesiastical characteristics; Or, The arcane of church policy. Being an humble attempt to open up the mystery of moderatism.*

Woodward, Josiah (1699), *An account of the rise and progress of the religious societies in the City of London.*

Later editions of eighteenth-century works

Contemporary students of eighteenth-century evangelicalism now enjoy the benefit of many later editions of works from this period. Most of these contain extensive editorial and bibliographical material as well.

Alline, Henry. George A. Rawlyk (ed.) (1997), *Henry Alline: Selected Writings*, New York: Paulist.

Asbury, Francis. Elmer T. Clark (ed.) (1958), *The Journals and Letters of Francis Asbury*, Nashville: Abingdon.

Brackney, William H. (ed.) (1998), *Baptist Life and Thought: A Source Book* (rev. ed., 1998), Valley Forge: Judson.

Buchanan, Dugald. Donald Maclean (ed.) (1913), *The Spiritual Songs of Dugald Buchanan*, Edinburgh: J. Grant.

Burr, Esther Edwards. Carol F. Karlsen and Laurie Crumpacker (eds.) (1984), *The Journal of Esther Edwards Burr*, New Haven: Yale University Press.

Bushman, Richard L. (ed.) (1970), *The Great Awakening: Documents on the Revival of Religion, 1740–1745*, New York: Atheneum.

Doddridge, Philip. Geoffrey F. Nuttall (ed.) (1979), *Calendar of the Correspondence of Philip Doddrige DD (1702–1751)*, London: Her Majesty's Stationery Office.

Edwards, Jonathan. Wilson M. Kimnach, Kenneth P. Minkema and Douglas A. Sweeney (eds.) (1999), *The Sermons of Jonathan Edwards*, New Haven: Yale University Press.

— Perry Miller, John E. Smith and Harry S. Stout (eds.) (1957–), *The Works of Jonathan Edwards*, New Haven: Yale University Press.

— John E. Smith, Harry S. Stout and Kenneth P. Minkema (eds.) (1995), *A Jonathan Edwards Reader*, New Haven: Yale University Press.

Erskine, Ebenezer. Samuel McMillan (ed.) (2001), *The Beauties of Holiness, Selected from His Complete Works*, Grand Rapids: Reformation Heritage.

Heimert, Alan, and Perry Miller (eds.) (1967), *The Great Awakening*, Indianapolis: Bobbs-Merrill.

Jeffrey, David Lyle (ed.) (1987), *A Burning and Shining Light: English Spirituality in the Age of Wesley*. Grand Rapids: Eerdmans.

Langford, Thomas A. (1984), *Wesleyan Theology: A Sourcebook*, Durham, NC: Labyrinth.

More, Hannah. Robert Hole (ed.) (1996), *Selected Writings of Hannah More*, London: William Pickering.

Potkay, Adam, and Sandra Burr (eds.) (1995), *Black Atlantic Writers of the 18th Century*, New York: St Martin's.

Rawlyk, George A. (ed.) (1983), *New Light Letters and Songs: Baptist Heritage in Atlantic Canada*, Hantsport, Nova Scotia: Lancelot.

Romaine, William. Peter Toon (ed.) (1970), *The Life, Walk and Triumph of Faith*, Cambridge: James Clarke.

Sandoz, Ellis (ed.) (1991), *Political Sermons of the American Founding Era, 1730–1805*, Indianapolis: Liberty Press.

Spener, Philip Jacob. Theodore Tappert (ed.) (1964), *Pia Desideria*, Philadelphia: Fortress.

Wesley, Charles. Frank Baker (ed.) (1962), *Representative Verse of Charles Wesley*, New York: Abingdon.

— Kenneth G. C. Newport (ed.) (2001), *The Sermons of Charles Wesley*, New York: Oxford University Press.

— John R. Tyson (ed.) (1989), *Charles Wesley: A Reader*, New York: Oxford University Press.

Wesley, John. Nehemiah Curnock (ed.) (1938 [orig. 1911–1912]), *The Journal of the Rev. John Wesley*, London: Epworth.

— Richard P. Heitzenrater and Frank Baker (eds.) (1975–), *The Works of John Wesley*, Bicentennial Edition, Oxford: Oxford University Press, and Nashville: Abingdon.

— Thomas Jackson (ed.) (1872), *The Works of John Wesley*, London: Wesleyan Conference Office.

— Albert C. Outler (ed.), *John Wesley* [selections] (1964), New York: Oxford University Press.

— John Telford (ed.) (1938), *The Letters of the Rev. John Wesley*, London: Epworth.

Wesley, Susanna. Charles Wallace, Jr (ed.) (1997), *Susanna Wesley: The Complete Writings*, New York: Oxford University Press.

Wheatley, Phillis. Julian D. Mason, Jr (ed.) (1966), *The Poems of Phillis Wheatley*, Chapel Hill: University of North Carolina Press.

Whitefield George. (1960), *George Whitefield's Journals*. London: Banner of Truth.

— J. C. Ryle and R. Elliot (eds.) (1958), *Select Sermons of George Whitefield*, London: Banner of Truth.

Wilberforce, William. Kevin Charles Belmonte (ed.) (1996), *A Practical View of Christianity*, Peabody: Hendrickson.

Secondary sources

Most of the works listed here treat evangelicals or evangelical groups directly, but several provide more general background for the eighteenth century. This list includes a few titles kindly supplied by David Bebbington and Bruce Hindmarsh that augment the volumes I consulted. If the books in which essays appear are listed separately, the entry with the essay will be abbreviated.

It is crucial to stress again how important the recent *Blackwell Dictionary of Evangelical Biography, 1730–1860*, has already become for any endeavour at historical synthesis like that attempted in this book.

Reference works

Barrett, David B., et al. (2001), *World Christian Encyclopedia*, 2nd ed., New York: Oxford University Press.

Cameron, Nigel M. de S., et al. (eds.) (1993), *Dictionary of Scottish Church History and Theology*, Edinburgh: T. & T. Clark; Downers Grove: InterVarsity Press.

Cross, F. L., and E. A. Livingstone (eds.) (1997), *The Oxford Dictionary of the Christian Church*, 3rd ed., New York: Oxford University Press.

Garraty, John Arthur, and Mark C. Carnes (eds.) (1999), *American National Biography*, New York: Oxford University Press.

Gaustad, Edwin Scott, and Philip L. Barlow (2001), *New Historical Atlas of Religion in America*, Oxford and New York: Oxford University Press.

Hart, D. G. (ed.) (1999), *Dictionary of the Presbyterian and Reformed Tradition in America*, Downers Grove: InterVarsity Press.

Larsen, Timothy (ed.) (2003), *Biographical Dictionary of Evangelicals*, Leicester: Inter-Varsity Press.

Lewis, Donald M. (ed.) (1995), *The Blackwell Dictionary of Evangelical Biography, 1730–1860*, 2 vols, Oxford: Blackwell.

Matthew, Colin, and Brian Harrison (eds.) (2004), *Oxford Dictionary of National Biography*, Oxford: Oxford University Press.

Reid, Daniel G., et al. (eds.) (1990), *Dictionary of Christianity in America*, Downers Grove: InterVarsity Press.

Rogal, Samuel J. (1997), *A Biographical Dictionary of Eighteenth-Century Methodism*, Lewiston: Edwin Mellen.

Sprague, William B. (1857–1869), *Annals of the American Pulpit*, 9 vols, New York: Robert Carter.

Stephen, Leslie (ed.) (1885–1901), *Dictionary of National Biography*, 22 vols, London: Oxford University Press.

Secondary sources

Abelove, Henry (1987), 'The Sexual Politics of Wesleyan Methodism', in Jim Obelkevich, Lyndal Roper and Raphael Samuel (eds.), *Disciplines of Faith: Studies in Religion, Politics and Patriarchy*, London: Routledge & Kegan Paul.

Allchin, A. M. (1987), *Songs to Her God: Spirituality of Ann Griffiths*, Cambridge, MA: Cowley.

Andrews, Dee E. (2000), *The Methodists and Revolutionary America, 1760–1800: The Shaping of an Evangelical Culture*, Princeton: Princeton University Press.

Armstrong, Maurice (1946), 'Neutrality and Religion in Revolutionary Nova Scotia', *New England Quarterly* 9: 50–62.

— (1948), *The Great Awakening in Nova Scotia, 1776–1809*, Hartford: American Society of Church History.

Baker, Frank (1963), *William Grimshaw, 1708–63*, London: Epworth.

Bebbington, D. W. (1982), 'Religion and National Feeling in Nineteenth-Century Wales and Scotland', in Stuart Mews (ed.), *Religion and National Identity*, Oxford: Blackwell.

— (1989), *Evangelicalism in Modern Britain: A History from the 1730s to the 1980s*, London: Unwin Hyman.

— (1999), 'Science and Theology in Britain from Wesley to Orr', in Livingstone et al. (eds.), *Evangelicals and Science in Historical Perspective*.

Bennett, Richard (1962), *The Early Life of Howell Harris*, trans. G. M. Roberts, London: Banner of Truth (Welsh orig. 1909).

Berens, John F. (1978), *Providence and Patriotism in Early America, 1640–1815*, Charlottesville: University Press of Virginia.

Berg, Johannes van den (1956), *Constrained by Jesus' Love: An Enquiry into the Motives of the Missionary Awakening in Great Britain in the period between 1698 and 1815*, Kampen: J. H. Kok.

Berg, Johannes van den, and Martin Brecht (eds.) (1995), *Geschichte des Pietismus*, vol. 2: *Der Pietismus im 18. Jahrhundert*, Göttingen: Vandenhoeck & Ruprecht.

Bergman, Marvin (1990), 'Public Religion in Revolutionary America: Ezra Stiles, Devereux Jarratt, and John Witherspoon', PhD dissertation, University of Chicago.

Bloch, Ruth H. (1985), *Visionary Republic: Millennial Themes in American Thought, 1756–1800*, New York: Cambridge University Press.

Bowden, Henry Warner (1981), *American Indians and Christian Missions*, Chicago: University of Chicago Press.

Brackney, William H. (1997), *Christian Voluntarism: Theology and Praxis*, Grand Rapids: Eerdmans.

Bradley, James E. (1990), *Religion, Revolution and English Radicalism: Non-conformity in Eighteenth-Century Politics and Society*, New York: Cambridge University Press.

Brecht, Martin (ed.) (1993), *Geschichte des Pietismus*, vol. 1: *Der Pietismus vom Siebzehnten bis zum frühen achtzehnten Jahrhundert*, Göttingen: Vandenhoeck & Ruprecht.

Breen, T. H. (1986), 'An Empire of Goods: The Anglicization of Colonial America, 1690–1776', *Journal of British Studies* 25: 487–499.

Brekus, Catherine A. (1998), *Strangers and Pilgrims, 1740–1845: Female Preaching in America*, Chapel Hill: University of North Carolina Press.

Bridenbaugh, Carl (1962), *Mitre and Scepter: Transatlantic Faiths, Ideas, Personalities, and Politics, 1689–1775*, New York: Oxford University Press.

Brooke, Peter (1987), *Ulster Presbyterianism: The Historical Perspective, 1610–1970*, New York: St Martin's.

Bruce, Steve (1983), 'Social Change and Collective Behaviour: The Revival in Eighteenth-Century Ross-shire', *British Journal of Sociology* 34: 554–572.

Brunner, Daniel L. (1993), *Halle Pietists in England: Anthony William Boehm and the Society for Promoting Christian Knowledge*, Göttingen: Vandenhoeck & Ruprecht.

Bumsted, J. M., and John E. Van de Wetering (1976), *What Must I Do To Be Saved? The Great Awakening in Colonial America*, Hinsdale: Dryden.

Bushman, Richard L. (1970), *From Puritan to Yankee: Character and the Social Order in Connecticut, 1690–1765*, New York: W. W. Norton.

Butler, Diana Hochstedt (1995), *Standing Against the Whirlwind: Evangelical Episcopalians in Nineteenth-Century America*, New York: Oxford University Press.

Campbell, Ted A. (1991), *The Religion of the Heart: A Study of European Religious Life in the Seventeenth and Eighteenth Centuries*, Columbia: University Press of South Carolina.

Canny, Nicholas (ed.) (1998), *The Oxford History of the British Empire*, vol. 1: *The Origins of Empire*, New York: Oxford University Press.

Cashin, Edward J. (2001), *Beloved Bethesda: A History of George Whitefield's Home for Boys, 1740–2000*, Macon: Mercer University Press.

Chamberlain, Ava (2000), 'The Immaculate Ovum: Jonathan Edwards and the Construction of the Female Body', *William and Mary Quarterly* 57: 289–322.

Champion, J. A. I. (1992), *The Pillars of Priestcraft Shaken: The Church of England and Its Enemies, 1660–1730*, Cambridge: Cambridge University Press.

Christie, Nancy (1990), '"In These Times of Democratic Rage and Delusion": Popular Religion and the Challenge to the Established Order, 1760–1815', in George A. Rawlyk (ed.), *The Canadian Protestant Experience*, Burlington, Ont.: Welch.

Clark, J. C. D. (2000), *English Society, 1660–1832*, 2nd ed., Cambridge: Cambridge University Press.

Claydon, Tony, and Ian McBride (eds.) (1998), *Protestantism and National Identity: Britain and Ireland, c.1650–c.1850*, Cambridge: Cambridge University Press.

Clifford, Alan C. (1990), *Atonement and Justification: English Evangelical Theology, 1640–1700: An Evaluation*, Oxford: Clarendon.

Coalter, Milton J., Jr (1986), *Gilbert Tennent, Son of Thunder: A Case Study of Continental Pietism's Impact on the First Great Awakening in the Middle Colonies*, Westport: Greenwood.

Colley, Linda (1992), *Britons: Forging the Nation, 1707–1837*, New Haven: Yale University Press.

Collins, Kenneth J. (1997), *The Scripture Way of Salvation: The Heart of Wesley's Theology*, Nashville: Abingdon.

Condon, Ann Gormon (1994), '1783–1800: Loyalist Arrival, Acadian Return, Imperial Reform', in Phillip A. Buckner and John G. Reid (eds.), *The Atlantic Region to Confederation: A History*, Toronto: University of Toronto Press.

Conforti, Joseph A. (1981), *Samuel Hopkins and the New Divinity Movement*, Grand Rapids: Eerdmans.

Connolly, S. J. (1992), *Religion, Law, and Power: The Making of Protestant Ireland, 1600–1760*, Oxford: Clarendon.

Cook, Faith (1997), *William Grimshaw of Haworth*, Edinburgh: Banner of Truth.

— (2001), *Selina, Countess of Huntingdon: Her Pivotal Role in the Eighteenth-Century Evangelical Awakening*, Edinburgh: Banner of Truth.

Coppedge, Allan (1987), *John Wesley in Theological Debate*, Wilmore: Wesley Heritage.

Cornman, Thomas H. L. (1998), 'Securing a Faithful Ministry: Struggles of Ethnicity and Religious Epistemology in Colonial American Presbyterianism', PhD dissertation, University of Illinois at Chicago.

Cowing, Cedric B. (1971), *The Great Awakening and the American Revolution: Colonial Thought in the Eighteenth Century*, Chicago: Rand McNally.

Crawford, Michael J. (1976), 'The Spiritual Travels of Nathan Cole', *William and Mary Quarterly* 33 (Jan. 1976): 89–126.

— (1991) *Seasons of Grace: Colonial New England's Revival Tradition in Its British Context*, New York: Oxford University Press.

Currie, David Alan (1990), 'The Growth of Evangelicalism in the Church of Scotland, 1793–1843', PhD dissertation, University of St Andrews.

Currie, Robert, Alan Gilbert and Lee Horsley (1977), *Churches and Churchgoers: Patterns of Church Growth in the British Isles since 1700*, Oxford: Clarendon.

Curry, Thomas J. (1986), *The First Freedoms: Church and State in America to the Passage of the First Amendment*, New York: Oxford University Press.

Dallimore, Arnold A. (1970, 1979), *George Whitefield: The Life and Times of the Great Evangelist of the Eighteenth-Century Revival*, 2 vols, Westchester, IL: Cornerstone.

Davie, Donald (1993), *The Eighteenth-Century Hymn in England*, New York: Cambridge University Press.

Davies, Horton (1961), *Worship and Theology in England: From Watts and Wesley to Maurice, 1690–1850*, Princeton: Princeton University Press.

Davis, David Brion (1975), *The Problem of Slavery in the Age of Revolution, 1770–1823*, Ithaca: Cornell University Press.

Davis, Derek (2000), *Religion and the Continental Congress, 1774–1789: Contributions to Original Intent*, New York: Oxford University Press.

Demers, Patricia (1996), *The World of Hannah More*, Lexington: University Press of Kentucky.

Dreyer, Frederick (1996), *The Genesis of Methodism*, Bethlehem, PA: Lehigh University Press.

Duffy, Eamon (1977), 'Primitive Christianity Revived: Religious Renewal in Augustan England', in Derek Baker (ed.), *Renaissance and Renewal in Christian History*, Oxford: Blackwell.

Elliott-Binns, L. E. (1953), *The Early Evangelicals*, London: Lutterworth.

Embree, Ainslie T. (1962), *Charles Grant and British Rule in India*, New York: Columbia University Press.

Essig, James D. (1982), *The Bonds of Wickedness: American Evangelicals Against Slavery, 1770–1808*, Philadelphia: Temple University Press.

Evans, Eifion (1985), *Daniel Rowland and the Great Awakening in Wales*, Edinburgh: Banner of Truth.

Faull, Katherine M. (1997), *Moravian Women's Memoirs: Their Related Lives, 1750–1820*, Syracuse, NY: Syracuse University Press.

Fawcett, Arthur (1971), *The Cambuslang Revival: The Scottish Evangelical Revival of the Eighteenth Century*, London: Banner of Truth.

Ferm, Robert L. (1976), *Jonathan Edwards the Younger, 1745–1801: A Colonial Pastor*, Grand Rapids: Eerdmans.

Fiering, Norman (1981), *Jonathan Edwards's Moral Thought and Its British Context*, Chapel Hill: University of North Carolina Press.

Fitzmier, John R. (1998), *New England's Moral Legislator: Timothy Dwight, 1752–1817*, Bloomington: Indiana University Press.

Foster, R. F. (1989), *Modern Ireland, 1600–1972*, London: Penguin.

Foster, Stephen (1991), *The Long Argument: English Puritanism and the Shaping of New England Culture, 1570–1700*, Chapel Hill: University of North Carolina Press.

Frey, Sylvia R. (1991), *Water from the Rock: Black Resistance in a Revolutionary Age*, Princeton: Princeton University Press.

Frey, Sylvia R., and Betty Wood (1998), *Come Shouting to Zion: African American Protestantism in the American South and British Caribbean to 1830*, Chapel Hill: University of North Carolina Press.

Gaustad, E. S. (1957), *The Great Awakening in New England*, New York: Harper & Bros.

George, Carol V. R. (1973), *Segregated Sabbaths: Richard Allen and the Emergence of Independent Black Churches, 1760–1840*. New York: Oxford University Press.

George, Timothy (1998), *Faithful Witness: The Life and Mission of William Carey*. Worcester, PA: Christian History Institute.

Gewehr, Wesley M. (1930), *The Great Awakening in Virginia*, Durham, NC: Duke University Press.

Goen, C. C. (1969), *Revivalism and Separatism in New England, 1740–1800*, 2nd ed., Hamden: Archon.

'Golden Age of Hymns' (1991), *Christian History*, no. 31.

Goodwin, Daniel C. (1997), '"The Faith of the Fathers": Evangelical Piety of Regular Baptist Patriarchs and Preachers, 1790–1855', PhD dissertation, Queen's University.

Gordon, Grant (1992), *From Slavery to Freedom: The Life of David George, Pioneer Black Baptist Minister* (Baptist Heritage in Atlantic Canada), Hantsport, Nova Scotia: Lancelot.

Gordon, James A. (1991), *Evangelical Spirituality from the Wesleys to John Stott*, London: SPCK.

Greenall, R. L. (ed.) (1981), *Philip Doddridge, Nonconformity and Northampton*, Leicester: University of Leicester Press.

Greene, Jack P. (1988), *Pursuits of Happiness: The Social Development of Early Modern British Colonies and the Formation of American Culture*, Chapel Hill: University of North Carolina Press.

Haas, John W., Jr (1994), 'Eighteenth-Century Evangelical Responses to Science: John Wesley's Enduring Legacy', *Science and Christian Belief* 6: 83–100.

Habermas, Jürgen (1989), *The Structural Transformation of the Public Sphere: An Inquiry into a Category of Bourgeois Society*, trans. Thomas Berger, Cambridge, MA: MIT Press.

Halévy, Elie (1971), *The Birth of Methodism in England*, ed. and trans. Bernard Semmel, Chicago: University of Chicago Press.

Hall, Timothy D. (1994), *Contested Boundaries: Itinerancy and the Reshaping of the Colonial American Religious World*, Durham, NC: Duke University Press.

Hambrick-Stowe, Charles E. (1982), *The Practice of Piety: Puritan Devotional Disciplines in Seventeenth-Century New England*, Chapel Hill: University of North Carolina Press.

— (1992), 'The Spiritual Pilgrimage of Sarah Osborn (1714–1796)', *Church History* 61 (December 1992): 408–421.

— (1993), 'The Spirit of the Old Writers: The Great Awakening and the Persistence of Puritan Piety', in Francis J. Bremer (ed.), *Puritanism: Transatlantic Perspectives on a Seventeenth-Century Anglo-American Faith*, Boston: Massachusetts Historical Society.

Hatch, Nathan O. (1977), *The Sacred Cause of Liberty: Republican Thought and the Millennium in Revolutionary New England*, New Haven: Yale University Press.

— (1989), *The Democratization of American Christianity*, New Haven: Yale University Press.

— (2001), 'The Puzzle of American Methodism', in Hatch and Wigger (eds.), *Methodism and the Shaping of American Culture*.

Hatch, Nathan O., and Harry S. Stout (eds.) (1988), *Jonathan Edwards and the American Experience*, New York: Oxford University Press.

Hatch, Nathan O., and John H. Wigger (eds.) (2001), *Methodism and the Shaping of American Culture*, Nashville: Kingswood.

Heitzenrater, Richard P. (1989), *Mirror and Memory: Reflections on Early Methodism*, Nashville: Abingdon.

— (1995), *Wesley and the People Called Methodists*, Nashville: Abingdon.

Hempton, David (1987), *Methodism and Politics in British Society, 1750–1850*, 2nd ed., London: Hutchinson.

— (1990), 'Religion in British Society, 1740–1790', in Jeremy Black (ed.), *British Politics and Society from Pitt to Walpole*, London: Macmillan.

— (1994), 'Noisy Methodists and Pious Protestants: Evangelical Revival and Religious Minorities in Eighteenth-Century Ireland', in George A. Rawlyk and Mark A. Noll (eds), *Amazing Grace: Evangelicalism in Australia, Britain, Canada, and the United States*, Grand Rapids: Baker, and Kingston and Montreal: McGill-Queen's University Press.

— (1996), *The Religion of the People: Methodism and Popular Religion, c.1750–1900*, London: Routledge.

— (2002), 'Enlightenment and Faith', in Paul Langford (ed.), *Short Oxford History of the British Isles: The Eighteenth Century*, Oxford: Oxford University Press.

Hempton, David, and Myrtle Hill (1992), *Evangelical Protestantism in Ulster Society, 1740–1890*, London: Routledge.

Hempton, David, and John Walsh (2002), 'E. P. Thompson and Methodism', in Mark A. Noll (ed.), *God and Mammon: Protestants, Money, and the Market, 1790–1860*, New York: Oxford University Press.

Heyrman, Christine Leigh (1997), *Southern Cross: The Beginnings of the Bible Belt*, New York: Knopf.

Higman, B. W. (1996), 'Economic and Social Development of the British West Indies, from Settlement to ca. 1850', in Stanley L. Engerman and Robert E. Gallman (eds.), *The Cambridge Economic History of the United States*, vol. 1: *The Colonial Era*, New York: Cambridge University Press.

Hindmarsh, D. Bruce (1996), *John Newton and the English Evangelical Tradition Between the Conversions of Wesley and Wilberforce*, Oxford: Clarendon.

— (1998), 'The Olney Autobiographers: English Conversion Narratives in the Mid-Eighteenth Century', *Journal of Ecclesiastical History* 49: 61–84.

— (1999), '"My chains fell off, my heart was free": Early Methodist Conversion Narratives in England', *Church History* 68: 910–929.

— (2002), 'Reshaping Individualism: The Private Christian, Eighteenth-Century Religion and the Enlightenment', in Lovegrove (ed.), *The Rise of the Laity*.

Hodges, Graham Russell (ed.) (1993), *Black Itinerants of the Gospel: The Narratives of John Jea and George White*, Madison: Madison House.

Hofstadter, Richard (1971), *America at 1750: A Social Portrait*, New York: Knopf.

Hole, Robert (1989), *Pulpits, Politics and Public Order in England, 1760–1832*, Cambridge: Cambridge University Press.

Hoppit, Julian (2000), *A Land of Liberty? England, 1689–1727*, New York: Oxford University Press.

Hutson, James H. (1998), *Religion and the Founding of the American Republic*, Washington: Library of Congress.

Hylson-Smith, Kenneth (1988), *Evangelicals in the Church of England, 1734–1984*, Edinburgh: T. & T. Clark.

Isaac, Rhys (1982), *The Transformation of Virginia, 1740–1790*, Chapel Hill: University of North Carolina Press.

Johnson, Curtis D. (1993), *Redeeming America: Evangelicals and the Road to the Civil War*, Chicago: Ivan Dee.

Johnson, Thomas H. (1940), *The Printed Works of Jonathan Edwards, 1703–1758: A Bibliography*. Princeton: Princeton University Press.

Jones, Owain W. (1976), 'The Welsh Church in the Eighteenth Century', in David Walker (ed.), *A History of the Church in Wales*, Penarth: Church in Wales Publications.

Jones, R. Tudur (1962), *Congregationalism in England, 1662–1962*, London: Independent.

Juster, Susan (1994), *Disorderly Women: Sexual Politics and Evangelicalism in Revolutionary New England*, Ithaca: Cornell University Press.

Kenny, Michael G. (1994), *The Perfect Law of Liberty: Elias Smith and the Providential History of America*, Washington: Smithsonian Institution Press.

Kent, John (2002), *Wesley and the Wesleyans: Religion in Eighteenth-Century Britain*. New York: Cambridge University Press.

King, James (1986), *William Cowper: A Life*, Durham, NC: Duke University Press.

Kling, David W. (1993), *A Field of Divine Wonders: The New Divinity and Village Revivals in Northwestern Connecticut, 1792–1822*, University Park: Penn State University Press.

Krueger, Christine L. (1992), *The Reader's Repentance: Women Preachers, Women Writers, and Nineteenth-Century Social Discourse*, Chicago: University of Chicago Press.

Kuklick, Bruce (2001), 'An Edwards for the Millennium', *Religion and American Culture* 11: 109–117.

Lachman, David C. (1988), *The Marrow Controversy*, Edinburgh: Rutherford House.

Lambert, Frank (1994), *'Pedlar in Divinity': George Whitefield and the Transatlantic Revivals*. Princeton: Princeton University Press.

— (1999), *Inventing the 'Great Awakening'*, Princeton: Princeton University Press.

Landsman, Ned (1989), 'Evangelicals and Their Hearers: Popular Interpretations of Revivalist Preaching in Eighteenth-Century Scotland', *Journal of British Studies* 28: 120–149.

Langford, Paul (1989), *A Polite and Commercial People: England, 1727–1783*, New York: Oxford University Press.

LeBeau, Bryan F. (1997), *Jonathan Dickinson and the Formative Years of American Presbyterianism*, Lexington: University of Kentucky Press.

Lewis, H. Elvet (1900) *Sweet Singers of Wales*, London: Religious Tract Society.

Lindman, Janet Moore (2000), 'Acting the Manly Christian: White Evangelical Masculinity in Revolutionary Virginia', *William and Mary Quarterly* 57: 393–416.

Livingstone, David N., D. G. Hart and Mark A. Noll (eds.) (1999), *Evangelicals and Science in Historical Perspective*, New York: Oxford University Press.

Lovegrove, Deryck W. (1988), *Established Church, Sectarian People: Itinerancy and the Transformation of English Dissent, 1780–1830*, Cambridge: Cambridge University Press.

Lovegrove, Deryck W. (ed.) (2002), *The Rise of the Laity in Evangelical Protestantism*, London: Routledge.

Lovelace, Richard F. (1979), *The American Pietism of Cotton Mather: Origins of American Evangelicalism*, Grand Rapids: Eerdmans.

Lyerly, Cynthia Lynn (1998), *Methodism and the Southern Mind, 1770–1810*, New York: Oxford University Press.

Macbean, Lachlan (1919), *Buchanan, the Sacred Bard of the Scottish Highlands: His Confessions and His Spiritual Songs Rendered into English Verse*, London: Simkin, Marshall, Hamilton Kent.

McBride, I. R. (1998), *Scripture Politics: Ulster Presbyterianism and Irish Radicalism in the Late Eighteenth Century*, Oxford: Clarendon.

McClymond, Michael J. (1998), 'The Protean Puritan: *The Works of Jonathan Edwards*, Volumes 8 to 16', *Religious Studies Review* 24: 361–367.

Macfarlan, D. (ed.) (1847), *The Revivals of the Eighteenth Century, Particularly at Cambuslang*, Edinburgh: Johnston & Hunter.

McFarland, E. W. (1994), *Ireland and Scotland in the Age of Revolution*, Edinburgh: Edinburgh University Press.

McGonigle, Herbert Boyd (2001), *Sufficient Saving Grace: John Wesley's Evangelical Arminianism*. Carlisle: Paternoster.

MacInnes, John (1951), *The Evangelical Movement in the Highlands of Scotland, 1688 to 1800*. Aberdeen: Aberdeen University Press.

McIntosh, John R. (1998), *Church and Theology in Enlightenment Scotland: The Popular Party, 1740–1800*, East Linton: Tuckwell.

McLoughlin, William G. (1967), *Isaac Backus and the American Pietist Tradition*, Boston: Little, Brown.

— (1971), *New England Dissent, 1630–1833: The Baptists and the Separation of Church and State*, 2 vols, Cambridge, MA: Harvard University Press.

McLoughlin William G. (ed.) (1968), *Isaac Backus on Church, State, and Calvinism: Pamphlets, 1754–1789*, Cambridge, MA: Harvard University Press.

Maddox, Randy L. (ed.) (1990), *Aldersgate Reconsidered*, Nashville: Kingswood/Abingdon.

Marini, Stephen A. (1982), *Radical Sects of Revolutionary New England*, Cambridge, MA: Harvard University Press.

— (1983), 'Rehearsal for Revival: Sacred Songs and the Great Awakening in America', *Journal of the American Academy of Religion – Thematic Studies* 50: 71–91.

— (1996), 'Evangelical Hymns and Popular Belief', *Dublin Seminar for New England Folklife: Annual Proceedings* 21: 117–126.

— (2002), 'Hymnody as History: Early Evangelical Hymns and the Recovery of American Popular Religion', *Church History* 71: 273–306.

— (n.d.), 'The Government of God: Religion and Revolution in America, 1764–1792', unpublished manuscript.

Marsden, George M. (2003), *Jonathan Edwards: A Life*, New Haven: Yale University Press.

Marshall, P. J. (ed.) (1998), *The Oxford History of the British Empire*, vol. 2: *The Eighteenth Century*, New York: Oxford.

Mason, J. C. S. (2001), *The Moravian Church and the Missionary Awakening in England, 1760–1800*, Woodbridge: Boydell.

Mathews, Donald G. (1965), *Slavery and Methodism: A Chapter in American Morality, 1780–1845*, Princeton: Princeton University Press.

Maxson, Charles Hartshorn (1920), *The Great Awakening in the Middle Colonies*, Chicago: University of Chicago Press.

May, Henry F. (1976), *The Enlightenment in America*, New York: Oxford University Press.

Meek, Donald E. (1997), 'Protestant Missions and the Evangelization of the Scottish Highlands, 1700–1850', *International Bulletin of Missionary Research* 21: 67–72.

Minutes of the Annual Conference of the Methodist Episcopal Church for the Years 1773–1828 (1840), New York: T. Mason and G. Lane.

Morgan, Derec Llwyd (1988), *The Great Awakening in Wales*, trans. Dynfnallt Morgan, London: Epworth.

Murray, Iain H. (1987), *Jonathan Edwards*, Edinburgh: Banner of Truth.

Noll, Mark A. (1976), *Christians in the American Revolution*, Grand Rapids: Eerdmans.

— (1976), 'Observations on the Reconciliation of Politics and Religion in Revolutionary New Jersey: The Case of Jacob Green', *Journal of Presbyterian History* 44: 217–237.

— (1979), 'The Founding of Princeton Seminary', *Westminster Theological Journal* 42: 72–110.

— (1989), *Princeton and the Republic, 1768–1822*, Princeton: Princeton University Press.

— (1999), 'Science, Theology, and Society: From Cotton Mather to William Jennings Bryan', in Livingstone et al. (eds.), *Evangelicals and Science in Historical Perspective*.

— (2002), *America's God, from Jonathan Edwards to Abraham Lincoln*, New York: Oxford University Press.

Noll, Mark A., David W. Bebbington and George A. Rawlyk (eds.) (1994), *Evangelicalism: Comparative Studies of Popular Protestantism in North America, the British Isles, and Beyond, 1700–1990*, New York: Oxford University Press.

Nuttall, Geoffrey F. (1951), *Richard Baxter and Philip Doddridge: A Study in a Tradition*, Friends of Dr Williams's Library Lecture, London: Oxford University Press.

— (1965), *Howel Harris, 1714–1773: The Last Enthusiast*, Cardiff: University of Wales Press.

— (1981), 'Methodism and the Older Dissent: Some Perspectives', *United Reformed Church Historical Society Journal* 2: 259–274.

O'Brien, Susan Durden (1976), 'A Study of the First Evangelical Magazines', *Journal of Ecclesiastical History* 27: 255–275.

— (1986), 'A Transatlantic Community of Saints: The Great Awakening and the First Evangelical Network, 1735–1755', *American Historical Review* 91: 811–832.

— (1994), 'Eighteenth-Century Publishing Networks in the First Years of Transatlantic Evangelicalism', in Noll, et al. (eds.), *Evangelicalism*, 38–57.

Pailin, David A. (1994), 'Rational Religion in England from Herbert of Cherbury to

William Paley', in Sheridan Gilley and W. J. Shiels (eds.), *A History of Religion in Britain*, Oxford: Blackwell.

Parry, R. (ed. and trans) (n.d.), *Hymns of the Welsh Revival*, Wrexham: Hughes & Son.

Phipps, William E. (2001), *Amazing Grace in John Newton: Slave-Ship Captain, Hymnwriter, and Abolitionist*, Macon: Mercer University Press.

Pilcher, George William (1966), 'Samuel Davies and the Instruction of Negroes in Virginia', *Virginia Magazine of Biography and History* 74: 293–300.

— (1971), *Samuel Davies: Apostle of Dissent in Colonial Virginia*, Knoxville: University of Tennessee Press.

Piper, John (2001), *The Hidden Smile of God: The Fruit of Affliction in the Lives of John Bunyan, William Cowper and David Brainerd*, Wheaton: Crossway; UK edition: *Tested by Fire: The Fruit of Suffering in the Lives of John Bunyan, William Cowper and David Brainerd*, Leicester: IVP, 2001.

Podmore, Colin (1998), *The Moravian Church in England, 1728–1760*, Oxford: Clarendon.

Pointer, Richard W. (1988), *Protestant Pluralism and the New York Experience: A Study of Eighteenth-Century Religious Diversity*. Bloomington: Indiana University Press.

Pollock, John (1977), *Wilberforce*, London: Constable.

Porter, Roy (2000), *The Creation of the Modern World: The Untold Story of the British Enlightenment*, New York: Norton.

Rack, Henry D. (1987), 'Religious Societies and the Origins of Methodism', *Journal of Ecclesiastical History* 38: 582–595.

— (1989), *Reasonable Enthusiast: John Wesley and the Rise of Methodism*, Philadelphia: Trinity.

— (1990), 'Survival and Revival: John Bennet, Methodism, and the Old Dissent', in Robbins (ed.), *Protestant Evangelicalism*.

Rawlyk, G. A. (1988), *'Wrapped Up in God': A Study of Several Canadian Revivals and Revivalists*, Burlington, Ont.: Welch.

— (1994), *The Canada Fire: Radical Evangelicalism in British North America, 1775–1812*, Kingston and Montreal: McGill-Queen's University Press.

Rawlyk, G. A. (ed.) (1997), *Aspects of the Canadian Evangelical Experience*, Kingston and Montreal: McGill-Queen's University Press.

Reed, Ralph E., Jr (1988), 'From Riots to Revivalism: The Gordon Riots of 1780, Methodist Hymnody, and the Hálevy Thesis Revisited', *Methodist History* 26: 172–187.

Richey, Russell E. (1991), *Early American Methodism*, Bloomington: Indiana University Press.

— (1996), *The Methodist Conference in America: A History*, Nashville: Kingswood.

Rivers, Isabel (1991, 2000), *Reason, Grace, and Sentiment: A Study of the Language of Religion and Ethics in England, 1660–1780*, 2 vols. New York: Cambridge University Press.

Robb, George (1990), 'Popular Religion and the Christianization of the Scottish Highlands in the Eighteenth and Nineteenth Centuries', *Journal of Religious History* 16: 18–34.

Robbins, Keith (ed.) (1990), *Protestant Evangelicalism: Britain, Ireland, Germany and America, c. 1750–c.1950, Essays in Honour of W. R. Ward*, Oxford: Blackwell.

Roberts, Phil (2001), 'Andrew Fuller', in Timothy George and David S. Dockery (eds.), *Theologians of the Baptist Tradition*, Nashville: Broadman & Holman.

Rogal, Samuel J. (1978), 'John Wesley on War and Peace', in Roseann Runte (ed.), *Studies in Eighteenth-Century Culture*, vol. 7, Madison: University of Wisconsin Press.

Rohrer, James R (1995), *Keepers of the Covenant: Frontier Missions and the Decline of Congregationalism, 1774–1818*, New York: Oxford University Press.

Rosman, Doreen (1984), *Evangelicals and Culture*, London: Croon Helm.

Roxburgh, Kenneth B. E. (1999), *Thomas Gillespie and the Origins of the Relief Church in 18th Century Scotland*, Bern: Peter Lang.

Rupp, Ernest Gordon (1986), *Religion in England, 1688–1791*, New York: Oxford University Press.

Ruth, Lester (2000), *A Little Heaven Below: Worship at Early Methodist Quarterly Meetings*. Nashville: Kingswood.

Ryken, Philip Graham (1999), *Thomas Boston as Preacher of the Fourfold State*, Carlisle: Paternoster.

Saillant, John (2003), *Black Puritan, Black Republican: The Life and Thought of Lemuel Haynes, 1655–1833*, New York: Oxford University Press.

Sanneh, Lamin (1999), *Abolitionists Abroad: American Blacks and the Making of Modern West Africa*, Cambridge, MA: Harvard University Press.

Scheuermann, Mona (2002), *In Praise of Poverty: Hannah More Counters Thomas Paine and the Radical Threat*, Lexington: University Press of Kentucky.

Schlenther, Boyd Stanley (1997), *Queen of the Methodists: The Countess of Huntingdon and the Eighteenth-Century Crisis of Faith and Society*, Durham: Durham Academic Press.

— (1998), 'Religious Faith and Commercial Empire', in Marshall (ed.), *Oxford History of the British Empire*, 2:129–139.

Schmidt, Leigh Eric (2001), 'The Edwards Revival: Or, the Public Consequences of Exceedingly Careful Scholarship', *William and Mary Quarterly* 58: 580–586.

— (2001), *Holy Fairs: Scottish Communions and American Revivals in the Early Modern Period*, 2nd ed., Grand Rapids: Eerdmans.

Schneider, A. Gregory (1993), *The Way of the Cross Leads Home: The Domestication of American Methodism*, Bloomington: Indiana University Press.

Sell, Alan P. F. (1982), *The Great Debate: Calvinism, Arminianism, and Salvation*, Grand Rapids: Baker.

Semple, Neil (1996), *The Lord's Dominion: The History of Canadian Methodism*, Kingston and Montreal: McGill-Queen's University Press.

Shiels, Richard D. (2001), 'The Methodist Invasion of Congregational New England', in Hatch and Wigger (eds.), *Methodism and the Shaping of American Culture*.

Simonson, Harold (1974), *Jonathan Edwards: Theologian of the Heart*, Grand Rapids: Eerdmans.

Skoczylas, Anne (2001), *Mr. Simson's Knotty Case: Divinity, Politics, and Due Process in Early 18th-Century Scotland*, Kingston and Montreal: McGill-Queen's University Press.

Smaby, Beverly Prior (1988), *The Transformation of Moravian Bethlehem: From Communal Mission to Family Economy*, Philadelphia: University of Pennsylvania Press.

Smylie, James H. (1974), 'Charles Nisbet: Second Thoughts on a Revolutionary Generation', *Pennsylvania Magazine of History and Biography* 98: 189–205.

Sommerville, C. John (1992), *The Secularization of Early Modern England: From Religious Culture to Religious Faith*, New York: Oxford University Press.

Stanley, Brian (1992), *The History of the Baptist Missionary Society, 1792–1992*, Edinburgh: T. & T. Clark.

Stewart, Gordon, and George Rawlyk (1972), *A People Highly Favored of God: The Nova Scotia Yankees and the American Revolution*, Toronto: Macmillan.

Stout, Harry S. (1977), 'Religion, Communications, and the Revolution', *William and Mary Quarterly* 34: 519–541.

— (1986), *The New England Soul: Preaching and Religious Culture in Colonial New England*, New York: Oxford University Press.

— (1991), *The Divine Dramatist: George Whitefield and the Rise of Modern Evangelicalism*, Grand Rapids: Eerdmans.

— (1994), 'George Whitefield in Three Countries', in Noll, et al. (eds.), *Evangelicalism*.

Stout, Harry S., and Kenneth P. Minkema (forthcoming), 'The Edwardsian Tradition and Ante-Bellum Anti-Slavery'.

Stout, Harry S., and Peter Onuf (1983), 'James Davenport and the Great Awakening in New London', *Journal of American History* 70: 556–578.

Sykes, Norman (1934), *Church and State in England in the Eighteenth Century*, Cambridge: Cambridge University Press.

Tait, L. Gordon (2001), *The Piety of John Witherspoon: Pew, Pulpit, and Public Forum*, Louisville: Geneva.

Taylor, Adam (1818), *The History of the English General Baptists*, 2 vols, London: published privately.

Telford, John (ed.) (1912–1914), *Wesley's Veterans: Lives of Early Methodist Preachers Told by Themselves*, 7 vols, London: Robert Culley (orig. 1837–1865).

Thomas, George M. (1989), *Revivalism and Cultural Change: Christianity, Nation Building, and the Market in the Nineteenth-Century United States*, Chicago: University of Chicago Press.

Thompson, E. P. (1963), *The Making of the English Working Class*, New York: Pantheon.

Thompson, R. W. (1958), *Benjamin Ingham and the Inghamites*, Kendell: published privately.

Tolley, Christopher (1997), *Domestic Biography: The Legacy of Evangelicalism in Four Nineteenth-Century Families*, Oxford: Clarendon.

Tracy, Joseph (1845), *The Great Awakening: A History of the Revival of Religion in the Time of Edwards and Whitefield*, Boston: Charles Tappan.

Tracy, Patricia J. (1979), *Jonathan Edwards, Pastor: Religion and Society in Eighteenth-Century Northampton*, New York: Hill & Wang.

Trinterud, Leonard J. (1949), *The Forming of an American Tradition: A Re-examination of Colonial Presbyterianism*, Philadelphia: Westminster.

Turley, Briane K. (1991), 'John Wesley and War', *Methodist History* 29: 96–111.

Turner, Steve (2002), *Amazing Grace: The Story of America's Most Beloved Song*, New York: HarperCollins.

Tyerman, Luke (1876), *The Life and Times of the Rev. John Wesley*, 3 vols, 3rd ed., London: Hodder & Stoughton.

— (1876), *The Life of the Rev. George Whitefield*, 2 vols, London: Hodder & Stoughton.

Tyson, John R. (2000), 'Lady Huntingdon and the Church of England', *Evangelical Quarterly* 72: 23–34.

Valentine, Simon Ross (1997), *John Bennet and the Origins of Methodism and the Evangelical Revival in England*, Lanham: Scarecrow.

Valenze, Deborah M. (1985), *Prophetic Sons and Daughters: Female Preaching and Popular Religion in Industrial England*, Princeton: Princeton University Press.

Valeri, Mark (1984), 'Francis Hutcheson', in Emory Elliott (ed.), *American Colonial Writers, 1735–1781*, Detroit: Gale.

— (1991), 'The Economic Thought of Jonathan Edwards', *Church History* 60: 37–54.

— (1994), *Law and Providence in Joseph Bellamy's New England: The Origins of the New Divinity in Revolutionary America*, New York: Oxford University Press.

Virgin, Peter (1989), *The Church in an Age of Negligence: Ecclesiastical Structure and Problems of Church Reform, 1700–1840*, Cambridge: James Clark.

Walls, Andrew F. (1970), 'A Christian Experiment: The Early Sierra Leone Colony', in G. J. Cuming (ed.), *The Mission of the Church and the Propagation of Faith*, Cambridge: Cambridge University Press.

— (1994), 'The Evangelical Revival, The Missionary Movement, and Africa', in Noll, et al. (eds.), *Evangelicalism*.

— (1996), 'Missionary Societies and the Fortunate Subversion of the Church', in Walls, *The Missionary Movement in Christian History: Studies in the Transmission of Faith*, Maryknoll: Orbis.

— (2002), 'The Protestant Missionary Awakening in Its European Context', in Walls, *The Cross-Cultural Process in Christian History*, Maryknoll: Orbis.

Walsh, John (1959), 'Joseph Milner's Evangelical Church History', *Journal of Ecclesiastical History* 10: 174–187.

— (1965), 'Methodism at the End of the Eighteenth Century', in Rupert Davies and Gordon Rupp (eds.), *A History of the Methodist Church in Great Britain*, vol. 1, London: Epworth.

— (1966), 'Origins of the Evangelical Revival', in G. V. Bennett and Walsh (eds.), *Essays in Modern Church History in Memory of Norman Sykes*, New York: Oxford University Press.

— (1972), 'Methodism and the Mob in the Eighteenth Century', in G. J. Cuming and Derek Baker (eds.), *Popular Belief and Practice*, Cambridge: Cambridge University Press.

— (1974), 'The Anglican Evangelicals in the Eighteenth Century', in *Aspects de l'Anglicanisme*, Paris: Presses Universitaires de France.

— (1975), 'The Cambridge Methodists', in Peter Brooks (ed.), *Christian Spirituality: Essays in Honour of Gordon Rupp*, London: SCM.

— (1975), 'Elie Halévy and the Birth of Methodism', *Transactions of the Royal Historical Society* 25: 1–20.

— (1986), 'Religious Societies: Methodist and Evangelical, 1738–1800', in W. J. Shiels and Diana Wood (eds.), *Voluntary Religion*, Oxford: Blackwell.

— (1990), 'John Wesley and the Community of Goods', in Robbins (ed.), *Protestant Evangelicalism*.

— (1993), *John Wesley, 1703–1791: A Bicentennial Tribute*, Friends of Dr Williams's Library Lecture, London: Dr Williams's Trust.

— (1994), '"Methodism" and the Origins of English-Speaking Evangelicalism', in Noll, et al. (eds.), *Evangelicalism*.

Walsh, John, Colin Haydon and Stephen Taylor (eds.) (1993), *The Church of England, c.1689–c.1833*, Cambridge: Cambridge University Press.

Ward, W. R. (1972), 'The Religion of the People and the Problem of Control, 1790–1830', in G. J. Cuming and Derek Baker (eds.), *Popular Belief and Practice*, Cambridge: Cambridge University Press.

— (1973), *Religion and Society in England, 1790–1850*, New York: Schocken.

— (1980), 'Power and Piety: The Origins of Religious Revival in the Early Eighteenth Century', *Bulletin of the John Rylands University Library* 63: 231–252.

— (1992), *The Protestant Evangelical Awakening*, New York: Cambridge University Press.

— (1998), 'Missions in their Global Context in the Eighteenth Century', in Mark Hutchinson and Ogbu Kalu (eds.), *A Global Faith: Essays on Evangelicalism and Globalization*, Sydney: Centre for the Study of Australian Christianity.

— (1999), *Christianity Under the Ancient Régime, 1648–1789*, New York: Cambridge University Press.

— (2000), *Kirchengeschichte Großbritanniens vom 17. bis zum 20. Jahrhundert*, Leipzig: Evangelische Verlagsanstalt.

— (2000), 'Methodist History', *Epworth Review* 27: 48–51.

Watson, J. R. (1997), *The English Hymn: A Cultural and Historical Study*, Oxford: Clarendon.

Watts, Michael (1978, 1995), *The Dissenters*, vol. 1: *From the Reformation to the French Revolution*; vol. 2: *The Expansion of Evangelical Nonconformity, 1791–1859*, Oxford: Clarendon.

Welch, Edwin (1995), *Spiritual Pilgrim: A Reassessment of the Life of the Countess of Huntingdon*, Cardiff: University of Wales Press.

Westerkamp, Marilyn J. (1988), *Triumph of the Laity: Scots-Irish Piety and the Great Awakening, 1625–1760*, New York: Oxford University Press.

Wheeler, Rachel (2003), 'Women and Christian Practice in a Mahican Village', *Religion and American Culture* 13: 27–68.

Wigger, John H. (1998), *Taking Heaven by Storm: Methodism and the Rise of Popular Christianity in America*, New York: Oxford University Press.

Williams, Eric (1944), *Capitalism and Slavery*, Chapel Hill: University of North Carolina Press.

Wolffe, John (2004), 'William Wilberforce', in *Dictionary of National Biography*, Oxford: Oxford University Press.

Wood, A. Skevington (1960), *The Inextinguishable Blaze: Spiritual Renewal and Advance in the 18th Century*, Grand Rapids: Eerdmans.

Yarwood, A. T. (1977), *Samuel Marsden: The Great Survivor*, Melbourne: Melbourne University Press.

Young, B. W. (1998), *Religion and Enlightenment in Eighteenth-Century England: Theological Debate from Locke to Burke*, Oxford: Clarendon.

INDEX